THE HUMAN WEB

THE HUMAN WEB

A BIRD'S-EYE VIEW OF

WORLD HISTORY

J. R. McNeill and William H. McNeill

W · W · Norton & Company   New York   London

For information about permission to reproduce selections from this book, write to
Permissions, W. W. Norton & Company, Inc., 500 Fifth Avenue, New York, NY 10110

Manufacturing by Maple-Vail Book Manufacturing Group

Book design and web illustration by Margaret M. Wagner

Production manager: Julia Druskin

Maps by maps.com

LIBRARY OF CONGRESS CATALOGING-IN-PUBLICATION DATA

McNeill, John Robert.

The human web : a bird's-eye view of world history / J.R. McNeill and William H. McNeill.

p. cm.

Includes bibliographical references and index.

ISBN 0-393-05179-X (hardcover)

ISBN 0-393-92568-4 (softcover)

1. World history. I. McNeill, William Hardy, 1917– II. Title.

D20 .M484 2003

930—dc21

2002013329

W. W. Norton & Company, Inc., 500 Fifth Avenue, New York, N.Y. 10110

www.wwnorton.com

W. W. Norton & Company Ltd., Castle House, 75/76 Wells Street, London W1T 3QT

6 7 8 9 0

For E. D. M.

CONTENTS

CONTENTS

LIST OF MAPS

LIST OF TABLES

PREFACE

This book is written for people who would like to know how the world got to be the way it is but don't have time to read a shelf or two of history books. It is written by a father and son who wanted to know as well, and who had the chance to read several shelves of books. The project began when the son had the erroneous idea that if Stephen Hawking could compress the history of the universe into 198 pages,[1] then he ought to be able to squeeze the history of humankind into 200 pages. He soon realized he couldn't, but recruited his father, who had already written a history of humankind (at 829 pages), as coauthor.[2] Thus began a collaboration between two stubborn historians. Our discussion sputtered and flickered on and off over several years, through visits, telephone calls, and old-fashioned letters. The result you hold in your hands.

Many colleagues and friends helped us along the way, chiefly by reading parts of the manuscript and showing us the errors of our ways. For that service we thank Tommaso Astarita, Harley Balzer, Tim Beach, Jim Collins, JoAnn Moran Cruz, Peter Dunkley, Catherine Evtuhov, David Goldfrank, Chris Henderson, David Painter, Scott Redford, Adam Rothman, Howard Spendelow, and John Witek, S.J., all of Georgetown University. For the same helpful service we also thank Ian Campbell and Nicola di Cosmo of Canterbury University, David Christian of San Diego State University, Nick Creary of Marquette University, Dennis

[1] Stephen Hawking, A Brief History of Time: From the Big Bang to Black Holes (New York, 1988).

[2] William H. McNeill, The Rise of the West: A History of the Human Community (Chicago, 1963).

Flynn and Arturo Giraldez of the University of the Pacific, Johan Gouds-blom and Fred Spier of the University of Amsterdam, Alan Karras of the University of California at Berkeley, John Richards of Duke University, Carl Trocki of the Queensland Institute of Technology. We thank Andrew Sherratt of the Ashmolean Museum for his help correcting dates, data, and interpretations concerning prehistory. Aviel Roshwald and John Voll, both of Georgetown, and John Donnelly read the manuscript in its entirety, for which they deserve special thanks. Lastly we thank our extended family, for providing a human web in which we both could thrive, and for cheerfully putting up with our lengthy conversations that on occasion threatened to commandeer the normal routines and agendas of family life.

J. R. McNeill   William H. McNeill
Washington, DC   *Colebrook, Connecticut*

THE HUMAN WEB

INTRODUCTION:
WEBS AND HISTORY

HARDLY ANYTHING COULD BE MORE ISOLATED OR MORE SELF-CONTAINED
THAN THE LIVES OF THESE TWO WALKING HERE IN THE LONELY HOUR BEFORE
DAY. . . . AND YET THEIR LONELY COURSES FORMED NO DETACHED DESIGN AT ALL,
BUT WERE PART OF THE PATTERN IN THE GREAT WEB OF HUMAN DOINGS THEN
WEAVING IN BOTH HEMISPHERES FROM THE WHITE SEA TO CAPE HORN.

— THOMAS HARDY, *The Woodlanders* (1887)

This book mixes old and new wine, and pours the blend into a new bottle. Some of the ideas and perspectives offered here are distilled versions of ones first proposed half a century ago. Others are set forth here for the first time. The new bottle, giving shape to the book, is the notion of the centrality of webs of interaction in human history.

A web, as we see it, is a set of connections that link people to one another. These connections may take many forms: chance encounters, kinship, friendship, common worship, rivalry, enmity, economic exchange, ecological exchange, political cooperation, even military competition. In all such relationships, people communicate information and use that information to guide their future behavior. They also communicate, or transfer, useful technologies, goods, crops, ideas, and much else. Furthermore, they inadvertently exchange diseases and weeds, items they cannot use but which affect their lives (and deaths) nonetheless.

The exchange and spread of such information, items, and inconveniences, and human responses to them, is what shapes history.

What drives history is the human ambition to alter one's condition to match one's hopes. But just what people hoped for, both in the material and spiritual realms, and how they pursued their hopes, depended on the information, ideas, and examples available to them. Thus, webs channeled and coordinated everyday human ambition and action—and still do.

Although always present, over time the human web changed its nature and meaning so much that we will speak of webs in the plural. At its most basic level, the human web dates at least to the development of human speech. Our distant ancestors created social solidarity within small bands by talking together, and exchanging information and goods. Furthermore, bands interacted and communicated with one another, if only sporadically. Despite migrations that took our forebears to every continent except Antarctica, we remain a single species today, testament to the exchange of genes and mates among bands through the ages. Moreover, the spread of bows and arrows throughout most of the world (not Australia) in remote times shows how widely a useful technology could pass from group to group. These exchanges are evidence of a very loose, very far-flung, very old web of communication and interaction: the *first worldwide web*. But people were few and the earth was large, so the web remained loose until about 12,000 years ago.

With the denser populations that came with agriculture, starting some 12,000 years ago, new and tighter networks arose within the loose, original web. The first worldwide web never disappeared, but segments within it became so much more interactive that they formed smaller webs of their own. These arose in select environments where agriculture or an unusual abundance of fish made a more settled life feasible, allowing regular, sustained interactions among larger numbers of people. These tighter, denser webs were local or regional in scope.

Eventually, about 6,000 years ago, some of these local and regional webs grew tighter still, thanks to the development of cities that served as crossroads and storehouses for information, goods, and infections. They became *metropolitan webs*, based on interactions connecting cities to agricultural and pastoral hinterlands, and to one another. Metropolitan webs did not link everyone. Some people (until recent times) remained outside, economically self-sufficient, culturally distinct, and politically independent. The first metropolitan web formed around the cities of ancient Sumer beginning nearly 6,000 years ago. Some metropolitan webs spread, and absorbed or merged with others. Others prospered for a time but eventually frayed and fell apart: the process of web building had many reversals. The largest, the *Old World Web,* spanning most of Eurasia and North Africa, formed about 2,000 years ago by a gradual amalgamation of many smaller webs. In the last 500 years, oceanic navigation united the world's metropolitan webs (and its few remaining local webs) into a single *cosmopolitan web.* And in the last 160 years, beginning with the telegraph, the cosmopolitan web became increasingly electrified, allowing more and far faster exchanges. Today, although people experience it in vastly different ways, everyone lives inside a single global web, a unitary maelstrom of cooperation and competition. The career of these webs of communication and interaction constitutes the overarching structure of human history.

Before we begin our brief account of that history, a few further observations about webs are in order, concerning their cooperative and competitive character; their tendency to expand; their growing importance in history; and their impact on the earth's history.

(1) All webs combined cooperation and competition. The ultimate basis of social power is communication that sustains cooperation among people. This allows many people to strive toward the same goals, and it allows people to specialize in what they do best. Within a cooperative framework, specialization and division of labor can make a society far richer and more powerful than it would otherwise be. It also makes that society more stratified, more unequal. If a cooperative framework can be maintained, the larger the web gets, the more wealth, power, and inequality its participating populations exhibit.

But, paradoxically, hostile competition also fostered a parallel process. Rivals shared information too, mainly in the shape of threats. Threats, when believed, provoked responses. Effective responses usually involved some closer form of cooperation. If, for example, one kingdom threatens another, the threatened king will seek ways to organize his subjects more effectively in defense of the realm. He may also seek closer alliance with other kingdoms. Competition at one level, then, promoted cooperation at other levels.

(2) Over time, those groups—families, clans, tribes, chiefdoms, states, armies, monasteries, banking houses, multinational corporations— that achieved more efficient communication and cooperation within their own ranks improved their competitive position and survival chances. They

acquired resources, property, followers, at the expense of other groups with less effective internal communication and cooperation. So the general direction of history has been toward greater and greater social cooperation—both voluntary and compelled—driven by the realities of social competition. Over time, cooperating groups of every sort tended to grow in size to the point where their internal cohesion, their ability to communicate and conform, weakened and broke down.

Larger metropolitan webs of interaction, linking all sorts of groups, also tended to grow, for three reasons. First, they conferred advantages on their participants. Through their communication and cooperation, societies inside metropolitan webs became far more formidable than societies outside. Participation in such a web brought economic advantages via specialization of labor and exchange. Military advantages came in the form of larger numbers of well-equipped warriors, often full-time specialists in the arts of violence, aware of (and usually choosing to use) the cutting edge of military technology. Epidemiological advantages also accrued to people born inside metropolitan webs, because they were more likely to acquire immunities to a wider array of diseases than could other people.

All these advantages to life inside a metropolitan web came at a cost. Economic specialization and exchange created poverty as well as wealth. Skilled warriors sometimes turned their weapons against people who looked to them for protection. And populations acquired disease immunities only by repeated exposure to lethal epidemics. Nonetheless, the survivors of these risks enjoyed a marked formidability in relation to peoples living outside such webs.

But there was more to the expansion of metropolitan webs than this. Webs were unconscious and unrecognized features of social life. Nonetheless, they contained within them quite conscious organizations—lineages, tribes, churches, companies, armies, bandit gangs, empires—all of which had leaders who exercised unusual power. These leaders caused metropolitan webs to expand by pursuing their own interests. Leaders of any hierarchy enjoyed an upward flow of goods, services, deference, and prestige. They normally sought to expand the scope of their operations so as to increase this upward flow. Their followers helped, to avoid punishment and to earn a share (however paltry in comparison to the leaders') of the anticipated rewards. In the past, this urge to expand often came at the expense of people outside of metropolitan webs, who were poorly organized to defend their own persons, property, resources, or religion. Survivors found themselves enmeshed in new economic, political, and cultural linkages, in a word, in a web. Thus, leaders of organizations, seeking to enhance their own power and status, persistently (if unconsciously) expanded the webs in which they operated.

Finally, metropolitan webs tended to expand because communications and transport technology improved. Writing, printing, and the Internet, for example, were major advances in the transmission of information. Each reduced information costs, and made it easier to build and sustain larger networks of cooperation and competition. Sailing vessels, wheels, and railroads similarly cut transport costs and promoted exchanges of goods and information over broader spaces and among larger populations.

(3) So webs involved both cooperation and competition, and over time their scale tended to grow. So too did their influence upon history. The original worldwide web lacked writing, wheels, and pack animals. The volume and velocity of messages and things that circulated within it was always small and slow by later standards. Its power to influence daily life was weak, although it could occasionally transmit major changes. But the more tightly woven metropolitan webs that evolved beginning about 6,000 years ago transmitted more information and more things more quickly, and thus played a larger role in history. As these webs grew and fused, fewer and fewer societies existed in isolation, evolving in parallel with others, and more and more existed and evolved in communication with others. Between 12,000 and 5,000 years ago, at least seven societies around the world invented agriculture, in most cases quite independently: parallel pressures led to parallel solutions. But the steam engine did not have to be invented seven times to spread around the world: by the eighteenth century, once was enough.

(4) The power of human communication, cooperation, and competition shaped the earth's history as well as human history. Concerted human action upset prevailing ecological relationships, first through the deliberate use of fire, coordinated hunting of big game, and the domestication of animals and plants. Gradually, humankind learned to divert ever larger shares of the earth's energy and material flows for our own purposes, vastly expanding our niche and our numbers. This, in turn, made the infrastructure of the cosmopolitan web, the ships, roads, rails, and Internet, easier to build and sustain. The process of web building and the process of enlarging the human niche supported one another. We would not be 6 billion strong without the myriad of interconnections, the flows and exchanges of food, energy, technology, money, that comprise the modern worldwide web. We have inaugurated a new era of

earth history—the *Anthropocene*—in which our actions are the most important factor in biological evolution, and in several of the planet's biogeochemical flows and geological processes.

How people created the webs of interaction, how those webs grew, what shapes they took in different parts of the world, how they combined in recent times into a single cosmopolitan web, and how this altered the human role on earth is the subject of our book. With luck, this perspective on the past will shed a ray of light on the dilemmas of the present—and future.

I
THE HUMAN APPRENTICESHIP

Shattered bones, chipped stones, and bits of charcoal are all the evidence we have of how our remote ancestors actually lived. By now, archeologists have studied thousands of sites and retrieved millions of fragments from them; but interpreting how humanity's career on earth got started on the basis of such evidence remains a matter of guesswork. A lively imagination is needed to reconstruct human communities from scattered bones and stones; and the resulting figments of expert imagination immediately become targets for other experts to shoot down. Yet some landmarks seem sure; and recently introduced techniques of chemical analysis date many finds with more and more precision. All the same, almost everything remains tentative. Even a single new discovery may upset currently prevailing notions at any time.

Amidst the resulting uncertainty, what are the most plausible guesses about the human apprenticeship starting from the time when our ancestors came down from the trees?

First of all, this fateful grounding took place in Africa, where our apelike ancestors ventured onto savanna landscapes something like 4 million years ago. Savannas are dry, grassy plains with scattered clumps of drought-resistant trees that presumably offered them more or less secure sleeping places at night. On the savanna, rainy seasons alternate with dry periods when access to water for drinking was essential for grazing animals and for our ancestors as well. Protohumans were unusually versatile. They sustained their bodies and their energy-consuming, enlarged brains with a varied, high-quality diet of nuts, fruits, roots, and leaves as well as the bodies of small animals, insects, and grubs. Almost certainly, they were themselves food for big cats, and probably competed with vultures and hyenas for meat left over from the cats' other kills.

Their concentrated, varied diet made adaptation to climate change relatively easy. Indeed, humanity's subsequent success resulted in no small part from that fact, since repeated episodes of glaciation and melt-back, beginning about 2.5 million years ago, provoked severe climate changes in all parts of the earth and upset ecosystems everywhere. Our ancestors, in effect, specialized in adaptability, becoming a superior weed species, quick to move into disturbed landscapes by finding new kinds of food and inventing new ways of getting it as time went by.

That success, in turn, arose out of other peculiarities of protohuman life on the African savanna. Since they walked on two feet most or all of the time, our ancestors could use their hands to wield sticks and throw stones. Sticks and stones could also be shaped to suit particular pur-poses; and, though wooden tools may well be older, so far as existing evi-dence goes, human toolmaking began something like 1.8 million years ago. That is when deliberately chipped stones, with sharp edges that could cut up animal carcasses or shape wooden digging sticks and spears, begin to appear in the archeological record. Most animals rely on teeth to seize and process their food. Our ancestors, on the contrary, could afford smaller and smaller teeth because they were using big arm and leg muscles to capture and process foods with the help of sticks for digging and stones for cutting. In defending against predators our ances-tors also substituted sticks and stones for teeth, and so were able to put a modest distance between themselves and their attackers, thereby much diminishing the risk of wounds.

Substituting tools for teeth was a good bargain from the start, and over time the advantage grew with improvements in stick and stone technology. But before far-ranging elaboration of tools appears in the archeological record, humankind embarked upon a second fundamental change in its way of life by learning how to use and control fire. Exactly when and how this occurred is uncertain.[1] But just as people could and did improve the tools they used, they also altered their relationships with fire. They eventually learned how to use it for repelling predators and for driving game into traps or ambushes, as well as for warmth, light, cook-ing, and as a focus of social life. By deliberately igniting dry vegetation,

---

[1] Recent finds in East Africa have been interpreted as showing that humanlike creatures man-aged fire as much as 1 million years ago. Whether or not that is correct, about 400,000 years ago human control of fire became both unambiguous and widespread.

our ancestors also remade landscapes to improve hunting. Control of fire, indeed, became so valuable that only those bands that learned the full spectrum of fire's uses survived.

These behavioral peculiarities presumably helped to shape our ancestors' biological evolution. Surviving bone fragments do not permit reliable reconstruction of how apelike ancestors turned into modern humankind. But we do know that brains became larger, and that about 1.6 million years ago *Homo erectus* attained about the same stature as moderns, with feet and legs like ours, specialized for long-distance running and walking.[2]

Then, more than a million years ago, pioneering *Homo erectus* bands left the African savanna behind by moving first into Asia and later into Europe. Bones, discovered in Java and North China to the east and in Hungary to the west, show that they were able to survive under diverse natural conditions, including freezing cold in wintertime. Clothing (perhaps a bearskin on the back), shelter in caves and in artificial huts or tents, and the skill needed to maintain (and perhaps to kindle?) hearth fires were probably necessary to permit a formerly tropical creature like *Homo erectus* to survive freezing temperatures. But archeological evidence is ambiguous, so one cannot be completely sure.

The remarkable adaptability exhibited by *Homo erectus* bands was eventually surpassed by their successors, our direct ancestors, *Homo sapiens*. Further enlargement of the braincase, together with other small changes in skeletal design, distinguish *Homo sapiens* from *Homo erectus*. Subsequently, behavioral and social changes widened the gap enormously. These behavioral differences may not have appeared until long after the time, between about 200,000 and 130,000 years ago, when fragments of *Homo sapiens* bones first show up in Africa. Humanity's modern style of persistent technological changeability seems to have emerged only about 40,000 years ago. It was signaled both by proliferating tool types, varying with place and time, and by the very rapid spread of human beings throughout the habitable earth.[3] First Australia

---

[2] In addition, erect posture, sweat glands, and hairless skin combined to give humankind an exceptionally efficient cooling system. Animals that depend on panting to cool their bodies cannot sustain prolonged muscular effort nearly as well as humans. Australian Aborigines, for example, can bring down speedy kangaroos simply by chasing them for a few hours until the animals faint from overheating.

[3] Recent archeological finds in Central Africa, dated between 90,000 and 75,000 years ago, may establish an earlier horizon for technological changeability associated with *Homo sapiens*. See John Reader, *Africa: A Biography of a Continent* (New York, 1998), 139.

(between 60,000 and 40,000 years ago), then the Americas (about 20,000 years ago) were the largest new areas thus occupied; but *Homo sapiens* populations also displaced or absorbed Neanderthals from Europe and Southwest Asia about 35,000 years ago, as well as penetrating a broad arc of islands off Southeast Asia. By 10,000 years ago, only ice-covered areas and remote islands remained untouched by humans.

No comparably global expansion of a large-bodied life form, leaping across both climatic and water barriers, had ever occurred before. Human adaptability transcended ordinary environmental limits. As a result, human impact on other forms of life began to affect local ecosystems almost everywhere on the earth's land surfaces.

If we try to imagine what made this extraordinary career possible, the most plausible explanation is to suppose that marked improvements in the web of human communication and cooperation were what allowed roving *Homo sapiens* bands to colonize the habitable globe and establish themselves everywhere as a dominant species. The key innovation was probably the full deployment of language to create symbolic meanings. Once human beings became able to construct a world of agreed-upon meanings by talking things over, and assigning conventional names to objects, actions, and situations, they interposed a verbal filter between personal experience and everything outside (including all the other individuals in the immediate community and their possible or likely actions). This, in turn, allowed social behavior to attain increasingly precise coordination. For, as with tools and with fire, agreed-upon meanings could be changed and improved whenever experience disappointed expectation.

Since such disappointments were (and remain) chronic, the stimulus to invention was ever present. Thus, an otherwise inexplicable takeoff in the pace of innovation becomes intelligible. Simply put: ever since language began to shape an intelligible world of agreed-upon meanings among human beings, friction between expectation and experience has never ceased to provoke efforts to adjust those meanings so as to change behavior and compel the world to conform better to human wishes, hopes, and intentions.

A restless, irresistible explosion of new actions and ideas ensued, giving the human weed species a rapidly increasing power to transform its behavior and alter surrounding environments. This meant that symbolic evolution among human communities largely supplanted genetic evolution as the driving force of biological change on earth, and what may properly be called the human era of ecological history began about 40,000 years ago.

So it appears that our species is unique in a very special way. It alone created a world of symbolic meanings, capable both of exceedingly rapid evolution and also of coordinating the behavior of indefinite numbers of individuals—totaling, in our time, billions of persons. That accomplishment is, in fact, what this book is about.

Grammatical and intelligible speech was the critical prerequisite to the symbolic world humans created. Since monkeys and apes are noisy, social creatures, and use voice signals to give alarms and communicate other messages, it is altogether probable that our remoter ancestors did the same. But surviving bones tell nothing about such behavior, so we are left to imagine how gestures, vocalization, enlarged brains, a relocated voice box, prolonged infant dependency, and a perpetual web of social interactions within small bands of humankind permitted and rewarded incremental improvements in the speed, scope, and accuracy of communication.

One important landmark in this evolving process was the invention of song and dance, for when human groups flex their big muscles and keep together in time by moving and giving voice rhythmically, they arouse a warm sense of emotional solidarity that makes cooperation and mutual support in dangerous situations much firmer than before. As a result, song and dance became universal among human communities. This behavior is as distinctive of our species as speech itself. Its great advantage was that larger bands could hold together, resolve quarrels, and defend territory more effectively since joining in dance and song on festive occasions had the effect of dissipating frictions and rivalries among all who took part.

Even the simplest human societies known to anthropologists recognize scores and usually hundreds of individuals as belonging to their own group. Chimpanzee bands, by comparison, are much smaller, and on one closely observed occasion, rivalries among as few as fifteen adult males led to division into two separate, hostile communities. Lethal warfare ensued, and within a few years the smaller band was exterminated. If our ancestors behaved in anything like a similar manner, it is easy to believe that larger numbers, united by fellow feeling aroused by song and dance, had a decisive advantage over smaller bands and more conflict-riven neighbors. That, we may imagine, sufficed to make song and dance as universal as use of fire had become, and established an enlarged, human-scale polity among our ancestors.

Larger communities, in turn, rewarded improvements in vocal communication. Eventually, a critical threshold was passed sometime between 90,000 and 40,000 years ago, inaugurating an enormously fertile interaction between agreed-upon meanings and actual encounters with the external world. Like control of fire and like song and dance, speech capable of creating a world of common meanings had such overwhelming advantages for survival that it too became universal among humans. These three forms of learned behavior thus became and remain distinctive hallmarks of our species.

The extraordinary human expansion around the globe between about 40,000 and 10,000 years ago probably resulted from territorial rivalries among adjacent human bands, like those recently observed among adjacent bands of chimpanzees. Chimpanzees patrol their territorial borders at frequent intervals, and regularly probe adjacent territories, snatching extra food and testing themselves against their neighbors with noisy displays and occasional mortal combat. Every so often, such confrontations lead to border changes, since rising and falling numbers within adjacent bands result in sporadic reapportionment of territory.[4]

If our ancestors acted similarly, and if their superior skills sustained increasing numbers—as seems certain—all that was needed for global expansion was a capacity to find food and shelter in new environments. Humankind was already prepared for that, thanks to its unusually diverse diet, an expanding toolkit, and the accelerated capacity for invention and discovery that language conferred upon different bands in different natural environments.

The result was spectacular. Human bands began their expansion as skilled hunters, and preferred big game since the return from a kill was proportionate to the size of the carcass. Big beasts were probably very

---

[4] Jane Goodall started systematic observation of a band of wild chimpanzees at the Gombe Reserve, Tanzania, in 1960. The secession and subsequent war to the death occurred there in 1970-72. Efforts to observe other bands have added to our understanding of chimpanzee territoriality and some apparent boundary changes have been surmised. But human encroachment on chimpanzee habitat is very rapid in contemporary Africa, so that observations in "the wild" are affected not merely by the presence of the professional observers themselves but also by intensified encounters with other humans. The results are drastic. Chimps at Gombe, for instance, suffered from a serious epidemic of infantile paralysis, presumably transferred to them from humans. Existing chimpanzee populations are clearly at risk and cross-border relations among adjacent bands are under corresponding stress as human encroachment on their "wild" territories continues. For details, see Jane Goodall, *The Chimpanzees of Gombe: Patterns of Behavior* (Cambridge, MA, 1986), and Joseph H. Manson and Richard Wrangham, "Intergroup Aggression in Chimpanzees and Humans," *Current Anthropology* 32 (1991), 369–92.

easy to approach in new environments, being unwary and quite unafraid of physically unimpressive humans. At any rate, in both Australia and the Americas the arrival of human hunters closely coincided with a widespread die-off of large-bodied animals.

In both places, sharp climate change coincided with the appearance of humans, so no one can be sure that hunters were responsible for destroying these animals. But it seems likely that they were a decisive factor, as was certainly the case on islands like New Zealand and Madagascar, where human colonization came much later and resulted in the die-off of large-bodied game within a few hundred years. By contrast, in Africa, where climate changes were as severe as anywhere else, comparable die-offs were few, presumably because human bands and animal populations had coexisted there from the beginning of humankind's career on earth and had plenty of time to get used to one another. It looks therefore as though skilled human hunters colliding with inexperienced big beasts—perhaps already adversely affected by changing climate—constituted a lethal mix for a great many large animals. Species of potential use as domesticates were among those that disappeared from America—horses and camels in particular. This may be the earliest evidence of our destructive impact on other species, although it is very probable that some human communities recklessly exhausted other local resources even prior to the die-offs in America and Australia—just as we continue to do today.

Human expansion around the world both required and promoted proliferation of new technologies to tap the resources of diverse landscapes. And as human bands began to make use of more elaborate shelter, clothing, and new sorts of tools, weapons, means of transport, and decorations, their impact on the surrounding environment intensified. Overall, fire was by far the most potent device at their disposal for changing landscapes. By deliberately starting wildfires in the dry season, hunters could improve forage for the animals they hunted. Among the continents, Australia was most affected, since its dryness made fire especially powerful there. Tropical rainforests were usually too moist for firing, and food resources at ground level were scant, so human occupation of those environments was correspondingly slender. Savanna and temperate forest lands, on the other hand, could be fired easily in dry seasons; and human hunters did so throughout Africa, Eurasia, and the Americas.

Fire breaks down organic material into the chemical nutrients required for new plant growth much faster than bacteria can do the same job. By setting wildfires and producing more ashes than volcanic or lightning fires could do, humans therefore accelerated the circulation of nutrients across successive plant generations, enlarging scope for some species and marginalizing others. Accordingly, propagation of fire-tolerant forms of vegetation was another mark of the human migration around the world. This was quite as important for plants as the die-off of large-bodied game was for animal life.

The development of varied and more complex tools, weapons, and other devices was another, more familiar accompaniment of humanity's worldwide dispersion. The exact use of particular stone tools can only be guessed; and how surviving shaped stones were combined with the other constituents of an expanding toolkit—skins, vegetable fibers, sticks, bones, mineral pigments, even eggshells—remains even more uncertain since surviving fragments of such perishable materials are very few. One trend, nonetheless, shows clearly: a systematic improvement in the effective range of weaponry. For example, hand-held spears were eventually supplemented by lighter javelins, launched with throwing sticks that increased velocity and range.[5] Then bows and arrows appeared somewhere in Eurasia or Africa between 30,000 and 15,000 years ago. These lightened the projectile and greatly increased its velocity and range, thanks to almost instantaneous release of energy stored in the tensions of a drawn bow. Killing at a distance with javelins and arrows was much safer than coming in close, and game animals had to adjust to these enhanced human skills by learning to flee whenever they sensed a human presence.

Hunting, of course, provided only part of the human diet. Finding plant foods was quite as essential as hunting for human success in penetrating so many different environments. Modern hunter-gatherers are very knowledgeable about locations, seasons, and how to gather and process a great many different foods, including a surprising number that are poisonous in the raw. We can be sure that our remote ancestors built up similar expertise, and from time to time discovered or invented new methods of gathering that were just as important for their nutrition as improvements in projectiles were for hunting. Most innovations in gathering left no archeological trace; but pierced stone weights, which facilitated the procurement of roots by driving digging sticks deeper into the soil, attest to one aspect of the process.

[5] The eye-hand-body coordination required for throwing stones and javelins accurately (and aiming arrows as well) was another human physiological peculiarity, as important for ancient hunters as their sweat glands and long-distance-running capabilities. See Alfred W. Crosby, *Throwing Fire* (New York, 2002).

Women and children specialized as gatherers, since infants, who had to be carried, were too burdensome to accompany the hunt, which became men's domain. Under these circumstances, food sharing between male hunters and female gatherers had obvious advantages and eventuated in the formation of family units that systematically apportioned food among parents and children.[6] Families, in turn, established particularly intensive webs of their own, transmitting an ever-growing body of skills and knowledge from parents to children.

Specialization was not confined to food getting. In particular, as language emerged, experts in the spirit world differentiated themselves from ordinary persons, presumably on the strength of ritual roles and an unusual capacity to enter into trance. Siberian shamans, who communicate with the spirits through dance and trance, are commonly supposed to be heirs and exemplars of the earliest form of such expertise, and perhaps they are.

The concept of a spirit world, invisible and parallel to human society, was the first great intellectual system human beings devised, for it readily explained everything that happened. If each human body acquired life, feeling, and will from an invisible spirit that inhabited it when awake, and if such spirits could move about the world as they wished, then such diverse experiences as consciousness, sleep, dreams, death, illness, and trance all made sense, being obviously due to the way particular spirits moved into and out of human bodies. Breath, departing with death, offered a plausible model of the concept of a living, invisible spirit, and the fact that sleepers could meet the dead and even talk with them in dreams provided an experiential basis for the notion of a world inhabited by disembodied spirits. And if other moving objects also embodied spirits resembling ours, the rest of the world assimilated itself to human society, along with the invisible world of (perhaps only temporarily) disembodied spirits.

Accordingly, the spirit world had to be navigated with the same care and delicacy that prevailed in interpersonal and interband relations. That was where experts in the supernatural came in. As intermediaries between the spirits and ordinary people, they could relay important information, dispelling anxiety and defining what needed to be done to mitigate or avert disappointment and disaster. Learning how to enlist the

---

[6] Changes in women's menstrual cycle, allowing human sexual activity to expand beyond the short period of time when a ripe ovum was available to receive sperm, undoubtedly contributed to family formation as well; but when and how this happened is unknown.

aid of good spirits and appease evil or angry ones, in effect, expanded the code of manners that defined interpersonal relations within the band to embrace the whole wide world, including, not least, relations with neighboring bands. It also cushioned collisions with the natural world by making all that happened seem readily intelligible and—within limits— ritually curable as well.

Animism, to give this idea its modern label, was and remains the most emotionally accessible worldview that humankind has ever created. Since it is shared by surviving hunters and gatherers in all parts of the earth, animism was probably part of the cultural baggage that humans carried with them during their global expansion. Religious and philosophical systems that arose later never displaced animism entirely; and neither have modern scientific ideas. No worldview has lasted nearly so long nor explained so much to so many so convincingly. As such it deserves our respect.

Others with special skills—for example, toolmakers—may also have existed in some communities; but throughout the time when human bands were expanding across the face of the earth, groups remained comparatively small. What experts call "fission-fusion" sociality, of the sort that prevails today among chimpanzees, was probably part of the human heritage. This means that one or more families went off independently in search of food for much of the time, but when members of the same band met, they recognized one another at once. Moreover, at the times of year when food abounded, the whole band might assemble, and meet with other bands to enjoy song and dance, arrange marriages, and exchange information and precious objects as well.

Such festival encounters established a slender web of communication extending over long distances, and capable of diffusing useful and portable innovations, like the bow, even across the Bering Strait between Siberia and Alaska. Exogamous marriage was also biologically critical, since early bands were very small and harmful inbreeding could only be avoided by mating with outsiders. Such marriages appear to have been universal, and the resulting diffusion of genes kept humankind a single species despite its worldwide spread and diverse adaptation to different environments. This was the first human worldwide web, for a slender but significant flow of genes and information seeped unceasingly from band to band everywhere that humans went.

Among the earliest human communities, leadership may have rested more on personal skills and experience than on inherited status. No one actually knows. What seems sure is that overall numbers increased as wandering bands learned how to tap new resources in new territories. Many of the tropical parasites that had evolved with humankind in Africa could not survive freezing temperatures, and so were left behind by populations living in temperate climates, or who passed through them en route to the Southeast Asian and American tropics. This undoubtedly reduced lethal and debilitating infections; and since parasites that could survive freezing were slow in discovering how to feed on humans, the resulting ecological imbalance permitted population growth that probably put recurrent strains on local food supplies.

Wherever humans arrived they altered landscapes by their activities, especially by their use of fire. In effect, humans deployed their cumulating knowledge and skill to make more and more of the natural energy flows of their environment serve their hopes and wants, thereby enlarging their own ecological niche along with the niches of other species that fitted into the new regime that human societies began to shape.

Some species were, from a human point of view, welcome sources of food and were deliberately fostered. Others multiplied despite human intentions and were treated as weeds and pests. But we can be sure that a host of compatible plants, animals, insects, and microorganisms—a veritable Noah's ark—expanded its place in the balance of nature as the human tide spread across the surface of the earth. Details varied with climate and landscape. Modern reconstruction of what happened to vegetation depends on pollen samples from sedimentary deposits; animal remains are too scattered to tell a coherent story, while insects and microorganisms usually leave no trace. Yet, armed with fire, even small wandering human bands were capable of radically transforming the natural world around them, and changes in pollen deposits show that they did so to plant life on every continent except Antarctica.

Localized population growth becomes unmistakable about 16,000 years ago when the most recent major glaciation began to melt back and a few human communities learned to preserve food, thus assuring year-round nutrition. Consequences were considerable. First and most obvious: larger human communities became viable when temporary gluts, created by harvesting migratory species like reindeer and salmon or ripe stands of wild-growing grain, could be consumed throughout the year. But food storage on a large scale meant staying in one place for all, or most, of the year. It also invited rapid improvements in bulky and elaborate equipment needed to take full advantage of temporary food gluts— things like weirs, traps, nets, smokehouses, storage spaces, and similar capital investments. Housing, too, became far more commodious when people settled down at one spot. Most distinctive of all: leisure time, arising when a year's supply of food could be acquired in a few weeks or months, invited all sorts of ritual elaboration. Under such circumstances, different communities embarked on radically different cultural paths and the comparative uniformity of life in migratory bands (which may not have been as uniform as their stone tools suggest to us) entered upon an extravagant diversification. By way of example, we therefore conclude this chapter with brief descriptions of three specialized and more or less sedentary hunting-and-gathering societies.

By far the best known (because they survived until the nineteenth century) were located along the Pacific and Arctic coasts of North America where diverse peoples learned how to capture migratory fish (mainly salmon) and whales. In effect, their weirs, nets, and harpoons harvested the wide expanse of the Pacific, allowing them to concentrate large quantities of food at strategic locations along the coast all the way from northern Alaska to California.

Salmon fisheries started to leave archeological traces along the Pacific coast as early as 8,000 years ago, but techniques for capturing large numbers of fish and for preserving them only became capable of supporting large, permanent settlements after about 500 C.E.[7] Or perhaps it was bows and arrows, imported from Asia sometime between 100 and 500 C.E., that compelled salmon fishers to cluster together for defense against threatening neighbors. But when effective fishing weirs and nets were in place, and smokehouses for drying the fish had been built, a few weeks of intensive effort sufficed to provide comparatively large populations with most of the food they needed year round. The resulting spare time allowed an extraordinary elaboration of dwellings, totem poles, and potlatch ceremonies. Potlatches allowed individuals to assert their personal distinction and social prestige by giving away accumulated goods to invited guests in accordance with carefully defined kinship connections and social ranks, thereby obligating the recipients to distribute equivalent gifts at subsequent potlatches. These ceremonies fostered an intricate exchange of precious goods across hundreds of miles. They also defined, and ceremonially validated, complex social

---

[7] The traditional dating system in which B.C. stands for before Christ and A.D. for anno domini is increasingly unpopular because it is anchored in a specific religious tradition. Here we follow a system in which the numbers remain the same, but C.E. (Common Era) replaces A.D. and B.C.E. (before the Common Era) replaces B.C.

rankings in each of the participating communities. Wars were sometimes fought over access rights to advantageous fishing locations along
the rivers and shores, but intercommunity relations were mostly defined
by potlatches to which leading personalities from far and wide were regularly invited.

The severe landscapes of the Arctic coastline make the parallel
achievements of Inuit (Eskimo) whale hunters even more remarkable.
Techniques for successful whaling developed about 800 C.E., when skin
boats large enough to carry a crew of eight men, and harpoons with
detachable heads reliably attached to skin floats, made it possible to pursue and kill even so large a creature as a wounded whale. In summertime, at key places along the Alaska coast both north and south of the
Bering Strait, migratory whales came close inshore to feed. Inuit whale
hunters based themselves at these locations (scores or even hundreds of
miles apart) wherever prevailing winds, currents, and the shape of the
shoreline gave them the best opportunities. In the eighteenth century, a
single Inuit whaling crew expected to capture a dozen or more whales in
a season; and since each whale weighed several tons, their catch sufficed to support hundreds of persons.

Not surprisingly, whale boat captains became social leaders and
their crew members ranked above others whose contribution to the
community's food supply was trivial by comparison. Whale meat was
preserved by freezing, and the frozen meat was stored underground and
in such quantity that sharing it with sled dogs, used for transporting
goods across the snow, became routine. Whale blubber yielded oil for
indoor cooking and for the lamps that made the winter darkness tolerable. All Inuit equipment was ingenious, including tailored fur and skin
clothing, large and small skin boats, bows and arrows, dogsleds, snow
igloos, sophisticated harpoons, and much else.

Its efficiency in exploiting resources of the Arctic shoreline was such
that this style of Inuit technology spread rapidly along the eastern Siberian coastline and across northernmost Canada, even penetrating places
where whales never came and the inhabitants had to subsist on seals
and walruses as before.[8] On the west coast of Greenland, between the
thirteenth and fifteenth centuries C.E., expanding communities of whale
hunters encountered Norse colonists. Armed clashes with the Inuits

---

[8] Settlement of the Arctic coastline of Canada and Greenland was far older, dating back to
about 6,000 years ago, but the earliest Arctic dwellers could not capture whales.

probably hastened the extinction of the Norse Greenlanders; and in later times similar warfare, involving the use of whalebone armor, also occurred among rival Inuit communities in Alaska.

Yet peaceable assemblies, involving as many as a thousand persons, also took place along the Alaskan coast in the eighteenth century and presumably before. Far-ranging trade connections, both with caribou hunters inland and with coastal communities in Asia (whence apparently a few pieces of manufactured iron reached the Inuits before European ships arrived on the scene), added to the whale hunters' resources. By any standard, their achievement in exploiting the bleak Arctic environment ranks as an amazing example of human ingenuity and adaptability.

The famous Magdalenian cave art of southern France and northern Spain, dated between about 16,000 and 13,000 years ago, is an equally amazing product of human cooperation and inventiveness. People who, it is now believed, harvested migratory reindeer, having learned to store the meat (presumably by smoking it, as the Indians of the Pacific coast smoked their salmon), used their spare time to elaborate the mysterious rituals of the caves—whatever they may have been. Almost nothing is known about the so-called Magdalenian society that gave birth to this extraordinary cave art. A great variety of tools, made of bone and wood as well as of stone, and a few ivory carvings, attest to very considerable manufacturing skill; and the precision of line exhibited by the cave paintings leads some art historians to suppose that the draftsmen were full-time professionals.

Archeologists have recently discovered Magdalenian living sites, located close to defiles through which migrating reindeer had to pass as they moved from winter to summer pastures. A 95 percent predominance of reindeer bones among animal remains at these campsites is, indeed, the only basis for supposing that the Magdalenians stayed put and relied on migratory herds for food throughout the year. We may imagine how large numbers of reindeer may have been captured and killed each year by driving them into trap-enclosures constructed ahead of time along the routes of migration; but since no traces of such structures have yet been found, no one knows for sure.

The ideas behind Magdalenian cave art and the ceremonies that most certainly took place deep within the bowels of the earth are equally unknowable. Very likely singing and dancing were central. Some of the galleries adorned by Magdalenian painters resound eerily to the human voice; and it is tempting to suppose that they were once the site of echoing musical conversations with the spirit world. But no one knows; and no one is even sure of what happened to the Magdalenians. Climate change eventually allowed forests to grow on what had been a lush tundra, fed by moisture and warmth from the Atlantic; and as that occurred, reindeer migrated northward. Magdalenian hunters may have gone with them. But, like North American potlatches and totem poles, the cave art they left behind constitutes an extraordinary example of what humans can do with spare time when seasonal harvesting of food suffices year round.

A less spectacular but more important example of how to ride the crest of a seasonal food surplus comes from Southwest Asia. Beginning about 15,000 years ago, a warmer, moister climate allowed wheat to grow wild on hillslopes in such abundance that a few human communities were able to feed themselves most of the year by harvesting the ripe seeds. So-called Natufian sites, scattered from Sinai northward to the southern border of modern Syria, attest to what such populations could do. Sickles to cut the grain stalks and grinding stones to make flour from the seeds constitute a sort of signature for Natufian settlements; but antelope and some other animal bones show that hunting continued even after harvested wheat became their principal source of food. Other remains— marine shells and other imports—attest to trade with outsiders; and luxury grave goods, in some cases associated with child burials, indicate that heritable social rank existed among the Natufians. They also built houses and storage pits, kept domesticated dogs; and to judge by the size and distribution of Natufian sites, overall population increased quite rapidly during the 2,500 years these villages continued to flourish.

Then, about 13,000 years ago, the climate became drier again so that natural stands of wheat shrank back and withered away. Some Natufian populations are believed to have become migratory hunters and gatherers again; but a few continued to depend largely on harvested wheat by learning how to make that plant grow where it did not grow naturally.

To sum up: The ability of early humans to communicate and cooperate strengthened by fits and starts. Language was the most important break-through, but dance, ritual, and art were important too. With these new kinds of communication, early humans formed larger and larger, yet still cohesive and coordinated, groups. This allowed them to spread far and wide across the earth, adapting to a broad range of environments, and altering them to suit at least some of them, at least for a while. The greatest such alteration, centered initially in Southwest Asia, was the development of grain farming. With farming, radically new possibilities for human life opened up and an agrarian era of deliberate, laborious food production dawned. Neither human history nor the earth would ever be the same.

II

SHIFTING TO FOOD PRODUCTION, 11,000–3,000 YEARS AGO

A few hundred domesticated species of plants and animals established a new intimacy with humankind when small groups of people, located in at least seven different parts of the earth, began to produce most (and eventually almost all) of the food they consumed by resorting to agriculture and herding. An enormous increase in the number of people and in the number of domesticated plants and animals followed, because mutual dependence allowed domesticated plants, animals, and humans to capture far more energy from the face of the earth than they had done before. Humans and some, but not all, of their domesticated animals also had to work harder, and by changing the environment more radically than before, created greater risks for themselves from famine, disease, and warfare.

Humans managed all these new relationships. Their acts and choices altered the traits and behavior of the plants and animals that submitted to domestication so radically that archeologists can usually distinguish bones and seeds of domesticated species from those of their wild relatives. Humans also altered their own behavior radically when tending gardens, fields, and herds became a daily routine; and, for all we know, some of our hereditary traits deriving from the long era of hunting and gathering may have been altered through selection for those who best endured laborious routines of farming.

Recent improvements in radiocarbon analysis allow reliable dating of even a single grain of wheat; and statistical analysis of pollen deposited in ancient bogs and lake bottoms can reconstruct ancient plant assemblages with great precision. Such methods, and careful archeological digging, have gone far to clarify the beginnings of agriculture in Southwest Asia,

Central America, and the eastern woodlands of the United States, but comparable precision for China, Southeast Asia, South America, and sub-Saharan Africa is only beginning to emerge. Table 2.1 summarizes recent results:

[handwritten marginalia: When and what was domesticated]

Table 2.1
Domestications of Plants and Animals

DATE	PLACE	MAIN CROPS	MAIN ANIMALS
Uncertain	Southeast Asia	taro, yams, sugar cane, coconut, citrus fruits, rice	pigs, chickens
11,000–4,000 years ago	Southwest Asia	barley, wheat, lentils	goats, sheep, cattle, pigs, donkeys, camels, horses
9,000–6,300 years ago	China	South China: rice North China: millet, soybeans	pigs, chickens, water buffalo
6,000–4,000 years ago	central Mexico	squash, maize, beans	none
5,000–4,000 years ago	South America	lowlands: manioc, sweet potato highlands: potato, quinoa	lowlands: none highlands: llamas, alpacas, guinea pigs
5,000–3,000 years ago	sub-Saharan Africa	sorghum, millet, rice	cattle

Why and how farming started has been much debated ever since studies of contemporary hunters and gatherers in the 1960s showed that they spent only a few hours each day getting food, and enjoyed a far better diet than hardworking peasant farmers who depended on a single staple for nearly all their nourishment. Who, then, would ever wish to become a farmer?

[handwritten marginalia: Reason for farming]

What seems to have happened is that in unusually rich and diversified landscapes, communities of hunters and gatherers found it convenient to settle down for all or most of the year, whereupon already familiar methods for encouraging the growth of useful plants acquired wider scope than before. Hunters and gatherers had long been accustomed to using many different plants for different purposes. Plant fibers supplied clothing, nets, bow strings, and the like. Herbal medicines, poisons, and mood-altering drugs were highly valued; so was the nourishment that some plants

Map 2.1 Multiple Separate Inventions of Agriculture

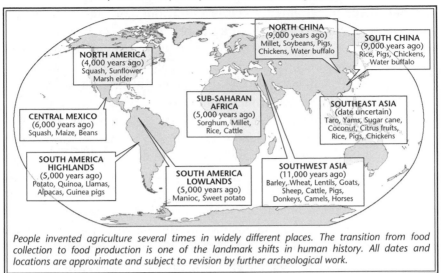

NORTH CHINA
(9,000 years ago)
Millet, Soybeans, Pigs,
Chickens, Water buffalo

SOUTH CHINA
(9,000 years ago)
Rice, Pigs, Chickens,
Water buffalo

NORTH AMERICA
(4,000 years ago)
Squash, Sunflower,
Marsh elder

**SUB-SAHARAN
AFRICA**
(5,000 years ago)
Sorghum, Millet,
Rice, Cattle

SOUTHEAST ASIA
(date uncertain)
Taro, Yams, Sugar cane,
Coconut, Citrus fruits,
Rice, Pigs, Chickens

CENTRAL MEXICO
(6,000 years ago)
Squash, Maize, Beans

**SOUTH AMERICA
HIGHLANDS**
(5,000 years ago)
Potato, Quinoa, Llamas,
Alpacas, Guinea pigs

**SOUTH AMERICA
LOWLANDS**
(5,000 years ago)
Manioc, Sweet potato

SOUTHWEST ASIA
(11,000 years ago)
Barley, Wheat, Lentils, Goats,
Sheep, Cattle, Pigs,
Donkeys, Camels, Horses

People invented agriculture several times in widely different places. The transition from food collection to food production is one of the landmark shifts in human history. All dates and locations are approximate and subject to revision by further archeological work.

provided. Whenever communities settled down, it was convenient to have especially useful plants growing close by. Wherever soil and climate allowed selected seeds and cuttings to flourish in new locations, such gardens could then be expanded until they provided most and eventually almost all of the food and other vegetable products people required.

Understanding how plants reproduced was surely age old. But as long as wandering human bands consumed food as it became available and shared it among all their members, the extra effort needed to cultivate gardens was unattractive and, above all, storing seed for next year's harvest was impractical. Only when familial units became independent consumers of food could farming take off. Very likely, sedentary living brought on this change. It is easy to imagine that whenever individual women began to create gardens of useful plants around their dwellings, they developed a sense of personal and familial ownership on the strength of the sweat they expended and the proximity of the garden to their home. Only when this principle replaced the sharing ethos of wandering bands could gardening and farming develop.

But gardening did not expand solely because of deliberate human choices. Other factors almost surely played a critical role. More particularly, a settled way of life in unusually rich environments allowed families to support more than a single small child, whereas among roving bands of hunters and gatherers population growth was restrained by the fact that mothers could usually carry only one infant when moving from

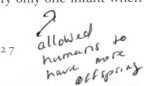
allowed to
humans to
have more
offspring

place to place, and toddlers easily got hungry, thirsty, tired, and lost. Settlement therefore permitted far faster population growth, and a growing population intensified local hunting and gathering, making wild food supplies scarcer and scarcer. This meant that settled groups were likely to find themselves trapped into an increasingly laborious routine of life, working first in small gardens, then in larger fields as returns from old-fashioned hunting and gathering diminished.

At the start, gardening was women's work. Raising plants before harvesting them was only a variation on gathering plants in the wild, as women and small children had always done. Tools for cultivation derived directly from the knives and digging sticks needed to cut wild-growing stems and dig wild-growing roots. But when gardens became fields, and yields from the hunt diminished so that each family's food supply for a whole year came to depend mainly on the harvest, men may have accepted new roles by helping to cut ripe grain and get it safely into storage. In Africa and pre-Columbian North America, cultivation remained mainly women's work. Perhaps it was only when domestic animals, under men's control, started to pull plows through the soil that men began to work in grainfields as a matter of course. No one knows.

In Southwest Asia, wheat and barley were the main crops while goats and sheep were the first herbivorous[1] domesticated animals. As we saw in the previous chapter, wild stands of wheat and barley were dense enough on some hillslopes of that region to invite year-round settlement, beginning about 15,000 years ago. Then drier climates set in and these settlements disappeared; but where soils were unusually moist, or where seasonal flooding occurred, a few communities began to sow wheat on land where grain did not grow naturally. Large springs in the Jordan Valley near Jericho began to sustain this sort or agriculture 9,800 years ago—the earliest well-attested example of settled farming yet discovered.

By then, wheat plants at Jericho had already adjusted to new conditions created by harvesting, storing, and sowing seed for the next year's crop. In particular, the stem attaching each seed to its stalk became tougher so fewer seeds fell to the ground when sickles cut the stalks. After all, when human hands began to sow the seed, only grains that reached storage bins safely could propagate themselves the following

[1] Experts agree that dogs were domesticated among ancient hunters long before agriculture began. They assisted humans in the hunt by transferring wolfpack patterns of dominance and cooperation to a new, trans-species, human-canine society. The resulting range and precision of aural and gestural communication between dogs and humans is unique, as every dog owner knows.

could control size of plants

year. The further fact that plants with tough seed stems brought more food into humans' storage bins made the change mutually beneficial. Later on, several other mutations occurred spontaneously, and farmers deliberately selected mutants they recognized as advantageous. So more and larger seeds per plant, with thinner coats, and husks easier to remove, soon distinguished cultivated from wild varieties of wheat and barley.

Wherever alluvial fans and springs provided the necessary moisture, similar experiments with wheat farming occurred along the inland side of the coastal hills of the Levant as far north as Damascus. Further north in Syria and Iraq, barley was domesticated at about the same time by an exactly parallel process. Simultaneously, the breeding of goats by farmers in the foothills of the Zagros Mountains (western Iran) and of sheep by farmers in the foothills of the Taurus Mountains (southern Turkey) also came under human control.

Penning the herd at night and protecting it against other predators as the animals grazed by day was essential to the new relationship between humans and animals. As with the grains, radical adjustment on both sides ensued. Human herdsmen, safeguarding the animals and leading them to pasture by day and into corrals at night, took over the role of the dominant male in the social structure of domesticated flocks. From the animals' point of view, human weapons were no doubt better protectors than horns. But herdsmen could only make their leadership effective by killing off defiant animals, thus inadvertently breeding selectively for submissive behavior. This altered genetic traits very quickly, as the thinner bones of domesticated flocks and herds plainly show. At the same time hunters had to learn to safeguard the animals they once had preyed upon, killing selected individuals only occasionally.

protected herds

The development of settled farming injected new kinds of information into the human web. Apprentice farmers constantly exchanged skills, knowledge, seed, and breeding stock with neighboring communities. Within a few centuries a core assemblage of improved varieties of wheat, barley, sheep, and goats came together in an ever-growing number of agricultural villages scattered throughout the fertile crescent that extended through the better-watered plains and foothills of Iraq, Syria, and Israel. Many other plants were soon brought under cultivation as well. Lentils supplemented grains from the start. Olives, grapes, figs, and dates also became valued crops in suitable locations beginning about 8,000 years ago. Various green vegetables and spices added variety and vitamins to the diet as well. Flax was raised for its linen fibers.

spread of ideas and crops

From its initial cradleland, the Southwest Asian style of mixed farming and animal domestication proceeded to expand in every direction. With suitably enlarged irrigation works, such farming proved feasible, for example, even in desert lands along the lower reaches of the Tigris and Euphrates rivers. This specialized environment, in fact, became the initial seat of urban living and complex, stratified society—that is, civilization—as we will see in the next chapter.

grain →

Of equal importance, however, was the adaptation of grain farming to higher elevations and more northerly latitudes where sufficient rain fell to sustain forests. Cutting the bark of deciduous trees killed them and allowed sunlight to reach the ground so that grain scattered beneath needed only naturally occurring rainfall to mature successfully. Fertility could be renewed subsequently by spreading ashes produced by burning the dead trees; and when early farmers occupied rich soils, especially windblown loess, permanent settlement was feasible. But when pioneers cleared poorer soils, yields soon declined, so forest farmers often found it best to move to a new location and begin the slash and burn cycle again. By doing so repeatedly in a single lifetime, they therefore created a moving frontier of settlement in suitably forested regions by about 4,000 years ago.

moving frontier →

When agricultural expansion into the forested zone of Eurasia was still in its early stages, however, new domestications and new ways of exploiting flocks and herds greatly enhanced the productivity of this Southwest Asian style of farming. The list of additional animal domestications is long:

Table 2.2
Southwest Asian Domesticated Animals

Animal	Date	Probable Site of First Domestication
sheep	10,000 years ago	Taurus Mountains
goats	10,000 years ago	Zagros Mountains
pigs	8,700 years ago	Southwest Asia and China
cattle	8,000 years ago	unknown
donkeys	7,000 years ago	Egypt
horses	6,000 years ago	Ukraine
two-humped camels	before 4,700 years ago	Central Asia
one-humped camels	before 3,000 years ago	southern Arabia

These domesticated animals provided much of the impetus for the subsequent spread of the Southwest Asian style of agriculture into Europe, across much of the rest of Asia, and into parts of Africa, and, much later, into America and Australia as well. What made that world-girdling expansion so irresistible was an amazing elaboration of human relationships with their domesticated flocks and herds. For example, between 6,000 and 5,000 years ago a mutant wool-bearing variety of sheep appeared somewhere in Southwest Asia and soon spread widely, since wool plucked (later sheared) from sheeps' backs proved to be an extremely useful fiber for making textiles.[2] About the same time, first goats, then sheep were also persuaded to allow human hands to milk them. Herdsmen, in effect, substituted themselves for kids and lambs as consumers of milk—an extraordinary perversion of natural biological relationships. Cattle and even mares and camels were subsequently induced to provide milk for human consumption as well, but only some human populations of Western Asia and Europe evolved the capacity to digest fresh milk. These populations retain an infant trait into adult-hood, enabling them to exploit the possibilities of milking to the full. This is the clearest known case of a genetic modification among humans provoked by agriculture and herding.

From a human point of view, milking had the enormous advantage of increasing caloric yields from the fodder a lactating animal consumed by something like four times over what slaughter for meat could provide. From the animals' point of view, it meant that humans began to maintain far larger herds than before; and on the grasslands of Eurasia and Africa, where full-blown pastoralism came to prevail, domesticated herds eventually far outnumbered their human attendants. This constituted a wry sort of reward for the diversion of food resources from lambs, kids, calves, and foals that made milk, cheese, butter, and yogurt available to humans.

A second, and almost equally important, use of domestic animals was as beasts of burden, and for pulling plows and wagons. Donkeys were the first pack animals; but horses, mules, and camels later super-seded them for most long-distance transport because of their greater carrying capacity. Cattle were the primary traction animals at first, since hitching a plow or wagon to their horns was comparatively easy, and oxen—that is, castrated males—were placid and strong.

In most fertile environments soft ground and watercourses

---

[2] Wild sheep were hairy, with a short woolly undercoat. Wool-bearing sheep exaggerated the undercoat, perhaps due to selection by humans who already knew how to clothe themselves by spinning and weaving flax and other vegetable fibers into cloth.

obstructed transport, so wheeled vehicles[3] could only be used for short hauls at first. And long after imperial governments built roads suitable for carts, plowing remained by far the most important use of animal muscle power since it multiplied the amount of ground that a family could cultivate manyfold. Above all, this meant that in most years, on many different sorts of soil and in various climates, humans and oxen could produce more grain than they needed for their own consumption. This created an ecological opening for the emergence of cities and civilization that soon proved readily adaptable to diverse regions of the world. That fact, together with the priority in time that Southwest Asian civilizations enjoyed over all others, helps to explain why their heirs in Western Asia, India, and Europe became so dominant in subsequent millennia.

The beginning of agriculture in China is less well known. Firm evidence that rice was cultivated in the Yangzi Valley about 8,500 years ago on seasonally flooded banks of lakes and streams was only discovered in the 1980s, and new sites continue to turn up. Exactly how and where such practices began remains unclear. Rice has the enormous advantage of yielding far more abundantly than the grains of Southwest Asia. Modern harvest to seed ratios for rice are as much as 100:1 even when using traditional methods, whereas in medieval Europe a yield of 6:1 for wheat was exceptionally high.

On the other hand, rice cultivation was (or became) more laborious than Southwest Asian grain agriculture. Rice farmers start their plants in special seedbeds and then transplant them one by one and by hand into the standing water of paddy fields.[4] They subsequently weed and harvest by hand as well. Water buffalo sometimes plow the soil to prepare it for planting; but in general animal power played a much lesser role in rice paddy cultivation than in Southwest Asian cereal farming. Human labor was critical, especially after farmers started to grow water-loving rice on higher, uneven ground. They then faced the enormous task of creating artificially leveled fields, diking each one separately, and then diverting streams from their natural course to create shallow ponds, only a few inches deep, in each paddy field. The necessary water engineering had

---

[3] Wheeled vehicles were known in Mesopotamia about 5,500 years ago, as proven by a pictograph from Erech scratched onto a clay tablet. Actual wooden remains have been discovered only from much later times.

[4] Varieties of rice will also grow on dry land, but wet rice cultivation became basic to the East Asian style of farming. Marginal communities in mountain districts of Southeast Asia still raise rice on rain-watered land, but their yields are far below those of paddy fields.

to be perpetually maintained. It also required complex local agreements to regulate access to, and delivery of, the running water needed to keep the growing rice in each paddy field suitably inundated until the time came to drain the field and harvest the ripened crop.

Consequently, when rice farming became basic to Chinese and other East Asian societies, incessant work in the fields shaped family relations and larger social structures along different lines from what prevailed elsewhere. But rice did not become China's main staple until after about 200 C.E. Before then, the core of historic China was situated in the valleys of the Huang He (Yellow River) and some of its tributaries where an entirely different style of agriculture, featuring millet, soybeans, and pigs (with up to two dozen lesser crops) began about 7,500 years ago. In this part of China, early farmers hoed soft, fertile loess (i.e., windblown) soils, and depended on fluctuating monsoon rainfall to assure the harvest.

Beginning about 4,000 years ago villages practicing this sort of agriculture supported the earliest Chinese dynasties, whereas rice farmers of the south lived in simpler societies that proved incapable of resisting Chinese expansion. Why this was the case, even though rice cultivation was (or became) so much more productive and reliable than raising millet, is well worth asking. But an answer must await extensive archeological investigation throughout the vast expanse of Southeast Asia and its offshore islands. Scattered discoveries suggest that settled communities (often living along the shore or beside inland lakes and streams where fish and other aquatic foods were available) may be very ancient in that part of the world, and a tropical style of garden cultivation, featuring starchy roots like taro and yams, and a variety of tree crops together with sugar cane and sometimes also rice, may have arisen at a very early date.

Gardens located in secluded highland valleys of New Guinea, discovered by the outside world as recently as the 1930s, show what human societies could do by cultivating a large number of different kinds of plants in the tropics where year-round growth permitted continual harvesting of just enough for immediate consumption. Though quite populous, these communities remained small, mutually hostile, and isolated from the outer world both by choice and by an unusually hostile lowland environment.[5]

---

[5] The coastal plains of New Guinea are intensely malarial and were thinly populated. Even the most eager imperialists found little to attract them to the mangrove swamps that lined the coast, which is why the upland farmers of New Guinea were able to preserve their isolated, independent ways of life until very recently.

Similar farming and fishing communities in tropical Southeast Asia may well be very old indeed, for many tropical roots can be propagated simply by cutting off the top of the tuber and putting it back in the ground. That simple way of maintaining a valued food source was probably familiar to hunters and gatherers from time immemorial. After all, such plants produced another tuber in a period of a few months ready to greet and reward migratory humans when they returned to the spot. But even when communities settled down and began to depend on food from enlarged gardens, as upland New Guinea peoples did, archeological traces remain very slender. As a result, no one can yet reconstruct the history of this kind of tropical cultivation.

It is nevertheless worth noting that settled communities of fisherfolk may have arisen very early. And the monsoon seas of the Indian Ocean, the Indonesian archipelago, and the South China Sea are especially conducive to long-distance sailing. The prevailing winds blow equally from one direction for half of the year and in an opposite direction for the other half, making return voyages comparatively easy. The dispersal of Austronesian and Polynesian languages, to Madagascar off the African coast and throughout the Pacific, attests to the eventual range of such voyaging. And the initial human occupation of Australia 60,000–40,000 years ago shows how early humans learned to cross open water—at least 170 kilometers or 105 miles—by some sort of flotation.

It therefore seems likely that the use of rafts and boats was very old among inhabitants of the islands and coastlands of Southeast Asia. On the strength of such devices, settled communities of fisherfolk may have supplemented what they gathered from the sea by creating tropical gardens long before agricultural villages arose in Southwest Asia or anywhere else. But rising sea levels due to the most recent retreat of glaciers means that any and all ancient coastal settlements are deep underwater today. Settled fishing communities located inland along lakeshores or riverbanks are therefore the most likely places for finding traces of this sort of early tropical gardening.

Yet even if tropical gardening antedated grainfields by thousands of years, as seems likely, it remained comparatively insignificant for human history as a whole. That is because tropical gardeners leave roots and fruits where they grow until ready for consumption. Grains that ripen all at once must be harvested and stored; and the consequent availability of concentrated supplies of food in farmers' storage bins and jars made the rise of states and cities possible. Priests and soldiers could demand and get part of the grain harvest from those who had raised it as a price for protection from supernatural and human harm. But without storage, massive and regular transfer of food from farmers to city folk was impracticable, inhibiting social and occupational differentiation. Consequently, the specialized skills of urban life could not arise on the basis of tropical gardening, however productive it might be.

It is therefore plausible to believe that when grain farmers of North China started to sustain powerful states and armies about 4,000 years ago, the rulers of these states found that armed expansion southward at the expense of tropical gardeners was comparatively easy. Thereupon, farmers from the north enlarged the material basis of the Chinese state system by moving south and making harvested rice—which must be stored and is easily transported—their principal crop; this in turn compelled tropical subsistence gardeners, among whom rice was only a subordinate crop, to withdraw to marginal, mountainous terrain.

China armies

In sub-Saharan Africa, another center of plant domestication arose about 5,000 years ago. The Sahara Desert began to expand when a drier climate set in about 6,000 years ago. This made human life more difficult in West Africa. But some groups were able to expand their food supply many times over by planting seeds of sorghum and two different kinds of millet on soft, moist soils that were exposed in the dry season when water levels receded in several now-vanished lakes on the southern fringe of the Sahara.

Cattle herding was another successful response to climate change on Africa's wide savanna grasslands. Cattle keeping, perhaps introduced from Southwest Asia, spread further and faster than farming in West Africa, and eventually prevailed throughout most of the continent's many grasslands. But where tsetse flies abounded, lethal sleeping sickness (transmitted to humans by these flies) kept some African grasslands safe for wild animals, where they survive into the twenty-first century. By comparison, the southward spread of agriculture in Africa proceeded more slowly than herding because early farming specialized in exploiting lakeshore environments, and these diminished as lakes dried up.

In the Americas, agriculture began in three distinct places. In Mexico, maize, beans, and squash became the dominant cluster, beginning more than 5,000 years ago. Along riverbanks in the eastern woodlands of the United States a less productive group of plants, of which sunflowers and gourds are familiar to us, came under cultivation about 4,500 years ago. And in South America, root crops, including manioc and sweet

American farming

potato, were domesticated in the tropical lowlands at least 5,000 years ago, while in the Andean altiplano—the high plains in today's Bolivia and Peru—another very productive crop cluster, featuring potatoes and quinoa, came under cultivation between 5,000 and 4,000 years ago. Peoples of the high Andes also domesticated llamas, alpacas, and guinea pigs. Llamas worked as pack animals, but none of the animals were milked or used for plowing or traction. Instead, human muscles performed all the labor of cultivation in the Americas, and except in the high Andes, transport was by human portage, supplemented by watercraft.

Of these agricultural complexes, the Mexican proved the most capable of penetrating new environments. Maize, squash, and beans spread northward into the southwestern United States about 3,200 years ago and began to displace older crops in the eastern woodlands about 1,000 years ago. Similarly, maize, squash, and beans arrived in South America perhaps as much as 5,000 years ago, but did not thrive in the harsh environment of the altiplano, where potatoes and quinoa remained securely dominant.

Even though the caloric yield per acre of both maize and potatoes almost matches paddy rice and far exceeds what wheat and barley can provide, America, like sub-Saharan Africa, lagged behind Eurasia in developing new sources of power over nature and new ways of coordinating human effort. Eurasia had the advantages of greater size, far more numerous domesticable species, and, above all, a more capacious communications web embracing its much larger population.[6] All of these contributed to an accelerating rate of invention and change in that part of the world. As a result, beginning about 5,500 years ago, different styles of village agriculture in Southwest Asia and in China supported different styles of complex, specialized, and socially stratified (i.e., civilized) society and polity that became protagonists of this innovative process. But before pursuing that story, a few general remarks about the rural underpinning that sustained early civilizations in Eurasia, Africa, and the Americas seem in order.

First of all, living in the same place all year round allowed rapid elaboration of useful artifacts that were too heavy to carry about. In temperate climates, weatherproof housing and clothing made from vegetable and animal fibers brought real advances in comfort. New ways of prepar-

---

[6] At least 70 percent of humankind lived in Eurasia for the last several thousand years, making it more crowded, competitive, and interactive than anywhere else.

ing food by boiling, baking, and brewing added both to human welfare and to women's work. Spindles and looms were needed for weaving; grinding stones and ovens were needed for baking; and, eventually, cunningly designed flues and chimneys raised oven heat high enough to allow the manufacture of pottery for use as plates, cups, storage jars, water pots, and other purposes. Stone axes to fell trees, hoes to till the soil, and sickles to cut the grain were additional novelties in the farmer's toolkit, which, together with human—and livestock—population growth, allowed these communities to transform natural environments far more radically than before.

Farmers, after all, displaced variegated natural vegetation with more or less uniform stands of a few chosen plants, along with some weeds that defied human efforts to eliminate them. Domesticated animals also transformed landscapes by their intensified grazing; and both agriculture and grazing accelerated erosion. In addition, human impact on the environment was further enhanced by population growth that resulted from resorting to food production.

In temperate climates, where diseases were less burdensome than in tropical lands, farming village populations clearly grew much faster than hunting bands had previously done. We know this because, in a given locality when suitable soils had all been occupied, or lost their initial fertility, farmers regularly looked around for new places to settle. As a result, the Southwest Asian style of agriculture spread across all of Europe between 8,000 and 6,700 years ago. Intrusive colonists seem to have pioneered the exploitation of windblown loess and other specially favored soils in Eastern and Central Europe. Older inhabitants subsequently borrowed ideas and techniques from the newcomers to develop various combinations of hunting and gathering with pastoral and agricultural ways of life. Eastward expansion of the Southwest Asian style of farming has been much less carefully studied. Yet archeologists know that wheat and barley farmers penetrated to the borders of northwest India about 8,000 years ago, and these same crops reached northern China about 3,500 years later, where they supplemented but did not replace the older staple of millet. Archeology also shows how Mexican corn, squash, and beans spread to North and South America, but the dispersal was slowed by the fact that maize had to adjust genetically to different day lengths in different latitudes before it could ripen with the seasons.

Such population growth and territorial expansion constituted an extraordinary biological success for farmers and their domesticated plants and animals. Indeed, the way domestication altered older ecological niches for wild as well as for domesticated forms of life is as exceptional in biological history as the initial spread of humankind around the entire earth had been. Human adaptability and conscious choices lay behind both. Webs of communication and concerted human behavior once again demonstrated their power to transform earth's ecosystems, and this time more drastically than before.

Yet success generated new risks and dangers. For example, settled communities were more vulnerable to infections, since they remained in close contact with their own wastes and garbage instead of moving on as hunters and gatherers did. As a result, the disease burden that human bands had radically reduced when they left tropical African infections behind and learned to endure freezing temperatures began to rise again. Moreover, humans were liable to contract viral herd diseases from their domesticated animals so that such historically significant diseases as smallpox, measles, and influenza could begin to bedevil them.[7] Stands of grain also became vulnerable to viral and insect attack, as well as to drought, hail, and flood. Crop failure meant famine, and throughout ensuing millennia famine combined with epidemic disease, and with another new scourge—organized warfare—to limit human numbers.

There is no clear archeological evidence of warfare among early farming villagers. Arrowheads do not usually tell whether they were aimed against people or against animals; and, as was the case among the farmers of the New Guinea highlands until very recently, fighting among early village communities in Africa and Eurasia was probably mainly a matter of exchanging missiles with enemies from a suitable distance. Yet we can be sure that herdsmen routinely used weapons to defend their flocks from animal and human predators, and farmers had to protect their stores of grain from human robbers as well as from insects, rats, and mice. A few ancient rock carvings in Spain and North Africa portray battle scenes, and walled and stockaded villages also appear both in Europe and China. Moreover, as we will see in the next chapter, finding ways of coping with organized violence became one of the principal reasons village farmers submitted to the heavy cost of supporting cities and states.

Life in settled communities also seems to have weakened the ties of extended kinship and encouraged solidarity with neighbors instead.

---

[7] DNA analysis suggests that smallpox, perhaps humanity's greatest scourge over the centuries, was derived from camelpox carried by Arabian camels.

Exactly how this happened is obscure. Village populations were usually larger than hunting bands, and fields were probably tended by separate families in most cases. When it became necessary to safeguard stored grain against raiders, farmers gathered together into comparatively large settlements and sometimes erected walls or stockades for defense. In proportion as local defense became vital, neighborhood perhaps took over from kinship as the primary basis of solidarity. Or so one may suppose.

Finally, in temperate climes, knowing when to plant was of critical importance. This focused attention on the seasonal movements of sun, moon, and planets. Calendrical astronomy became the province of experts whose special knowledge established a new kind of social leadership. Professional guides to the world of spirits had certainly existed among hunters and gatherers. Cave art alone is sufficient evidence of that. But accurate measurement of the seasons required a different sort of knowledge and skill, and in due course became another critical ingredient for the rise of cities and civilization.

By about two millennia after their emergence, agricultural villages had spread like a rash across Eurasia, Africa, and the Americas and became the frame within which the majority of humankind lived and died. The overwhelming majority of our predecessors continued to reside in such villages until very recently. Once initial adjustments to local conditions had been worked out, customary rural routines transmitted all necessary knowledge and skills from generation to generation across millennia, with only occasional and usually modest alterations. In short, biological and cultural continuities among our predecessors depended on village custom. Even when compelled to pay rents and taxes to outsiders, village autonomy prevailed in daily affairs; and sporadic disruption by famine, epidemic, and war rarely prevented survivors from resuming familiar routines as soon as local conditions permitted.

In effect, sedentary villages replaced roving bands of hunters and gatherers as the basic cells of human society. Within each village the web of face-to-face communication was intense and assured continuity of custom. But such villages were also embedded in a far-flung web, denser than before, yet still very slender in comparison with what was to follow when cities and civilizations, traders and missionaries, professional fighting men and specially skilled artisans began to operate across wider and wider regions of the earth. Long after cities first arose they remained exceptional and unstable. But of course it was the instability of urban life, together with its tensions and challenges, that provoked city folk to undertake most of the technological, religious, intellectual, political, economic, and institutional changes of subsequent history. We turn to their emergence next.

III

WEBS AND CIVILIZATIONS IN THE OLD WORLD, 3500 B.C.E. – 200 C.E.

The rise of civilizations established connections among scores of thousands, and then among millions of persons, who necessarily remained strangers to one another. For the first time, key relationships and important everyday transactions routinely transcended the primary communities within which human beings had previously lived. With greater and greater frequency, city dwellers, villagers, migratory pastoralists, as well as increasingly marginalized hunters and gatherers, all had to deal with strangers—somehow. For everyone within reach of civilization a variable mix of voluntary exchange of goods and services with involuntary submission to plunder, rent, and taxes became inescapable entanglements of ordinary life.

people now exposed to each other

Moreover, once started, civilizations tended to expand just as agricultural villages continued to spread across fertile landscapes, and as bands of skilled hunters and gatherers had previously occupied almost the entire habitable earth. The reason for expansion was the same. Civilized forms of human society could wring more food and energy from the environment than before, thereby generating superior wealth and power. Nor did the process stop with the rise of separate civilizations and separate metropolitan webs. Instead, evolving skills, habits, and ideas sustained conflict and cooperation among larger and larger numbers of people, until what had begun as separate civilizations came to impinge on one another so as to create an ever-thickening web throughout most of Eurasia and much of Africa by 200 C.E. This we will call the Old World Web.

cities bring more resources

The rise of civilizations altered the shape and expanded the importance of human webs. Until cities arose, face-to-face communication within small communities carried almost all the important messages governing human behavior. Encounters with strangers and neighbors were only occasional and seldom brought anything new to local attention that required or invited changes in existing habits. Novel information carried by the worldwide web, in other words, was weak and intermittent before the rise of civilizations. Gossip, discussion, dance, and ritual lost none of their power over local community life when cities and civilizations arose. So local communities remained fundamental and continued to give meaning and value to the lives of most people. All the same, their autonomy eroded. Messages from outside compelled attention, often imposing compulsory labor or payment of rents and taxes. With such burdens came stories of the wonders of urban living: temples so high they touched the sky and metal tools that shone in the sun and would not shatter, as stone tools sometimes did. But the new skills and knowledge of city folk rarely affected daily village routines at first.

On the other hand, web strands connecting urban centers with one another and with rural elites did spread attractive novelties from the start. As urban skills diversified, city-to-city contacts began to carry more and more useful knowledge, even across long distances. More important still were the connections between local elites and urban centers. This was what drove the expansion of civilization to new ground, because local chieftains often chose to set their followers to work producing some sort of raw material that city folk wanted. In return they got city-made luxuries and used them to exhibit their own power and importance.

The differentiation of skills between cities and surrounding populations established webs of exchange and communication ranging across hundreds and eventually thousands of miles. Each civilization acquired hinterlands, where landowners and other privileged persons did what they could to mimic chosen aspects of urban life. This elite formed its own regional webs, resting, in turn, on top of older, local, village webs; and had the effect of making ordinary villagers—people we can now call peasants—serve their social superiors in many different ways. Cities thus became able to tap resources far and near, enjoying fruits from what was mostly the involuntary labor of millions. That was how early civilizations achieved the wealth and power that made them so attractive to outsiders.

Local differences remained profound, but an encompassing process of trial and error rewarded all those changes in social organization, technique, and communication that enhanced deliberate control both over natural resources and over concerted human effort. We are still caught in this historic process and unlikely to escape it, simply because most people, most of the time, prefer collective and personal wealth and power to poverty and weakness, even at the cost of subordination to rules and commands issued by distant strangers.

The First Civilizations

Nodes of intensive communication generated this civilizing process in four different parts of the world. The earliest civilized cluster arose on irrigated land along the banks of three different river systems: the Tigris-Euphrates in Mesopotamia (modern Iraq); the Nile in Egypt; and the Indus and its tributaries in Pakistan. The dozen or more Sumerian cities that arose near the mouths of the Tigris-Euphrates between about 3500 B.C.E. and 3000 B.C.E. enjoyed modest priority over the Egyptian and Indus civilizations, where comparable social complexity emerged two to five centuries later. Coastal shipping, supplemented by overland caravans, sustained contacts between all three; and it seems best to conceive them as parts of a single interacting whole from the beginning. Let us call it the Nile-Indus corridor, the first big metropolitan web.

A similar interactive region centered on the loess soils of northern China along the middle reaches of the Huang He beginning about 3000 B.C.E. This East Asian center remained separate from the Nile-Indus

Map 3.1 The Earliest Civilizations of Eurasia and Egypt

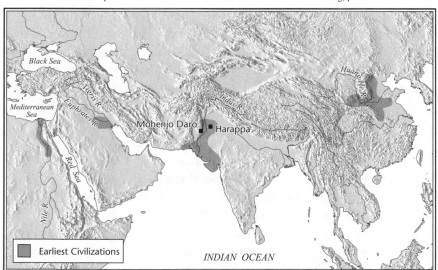

corridor even after unknown, indirect contacts across the intervening steppes and deserts introduced novelties from the west that enlarged local skills and techniques. Some were significant, like wheat and barley, bronze metallurgy, the seven-day week, and, sometime after 1500 B.C.E., chariots and horses. The Chinese example soon inspired regional variants among neighboring peoples, with the result that throughout recorded history an East Asian metropolitan web, centering in China, continued to expand onto new ground down to the present: the second big metropolitan web.

Oddly enough, a comparable duality existed also in the Americas and, as in eastern and western Eurasia, the parallel civilizations of Central and South America were based on quite different forms of agriculture. In Mexico and Guatemala, artificially drained gardens situated in swampy terrain devoted mainly to maize and squash sustained social differentiation comparable to that of Eurasian civilizations, beginning with the Olmecs about 1300 B.C.E. Mayan ritual centers and city-states came later—about 600 B.C.E.—and comparable societies arose in the valley of central Mexico after 400 B.C.E. These Mesoamerican centers never fused like the civilizations of the Nile-Indus corridor, but their growing interaction spun the first metropolitan web in the Americas.

In South America, complex ceremonial centers arose in deserts along the Peruvian coast, perhaps as early as 2500 B.C.E. The teeming waters of the Humboldt current supplied a rich diet of fish; and coastal fishermen learned to supplement their catch by growing roots, beans, and squash on irrigated fields along the banks of the several small rivers that descend from the Andes. Then, about 900 B.C.E., the Chavin civilization arose at a site where a pass over the Andes facilitated exchanges with peoples of the altiplano and the upper reaches of the Amazon basin. On the lofty altiplano, potatoes and quinoa already supported relatively dense populations; hunting and gathering presumably prevailed in the upper Amazon forests. But circulation of portable and valuable goods—bird feathers, seashells, precious metals—as well as exchange of knowledge and skills for dealing with the supernatural and natural worlds knitted diverse peoples of the shore, altiplano, and forest into a South American metropolitan web. Its principal center shifted from time to time, migrating to the altiplano around 100 C.E.

In South America and the Indus Valley, the absence of decipherable written records (there are indecipherable ones from the Indus) prevents us from knowing much about the ideas and institutions that sustained their civilizations. But even where modern scholars can read ancient texts, translation into modern languages remains inexact because assumptions embedded in our words do not conform to those of ancient peoples. Imperfect understanding and speculative reconstruction is all one can hope for.

Fortunately, for the oldest center of civilization, based in the desert lands of modern Iraq along the lower course of the Tigris and Euphrates rivers, information is abundant. Cuneiform writing evolved across hundreds of years in Mesopotamia, as modern scholars, in imitation of ancient Greeks, call the Tigris-Euphrates floodplain. It started with simple tallies recording receipts and disbursements from temple storehouses. Since such records were scratched onto clay tablets which, when baked, became durable, they survive in comparatively vast numbers. A few texts, written much later and for different purposes, even cast a dim light on civilized beginnings, but archeology and inference still remain the principal guides to understanding how the world's oldest civilization got started.

The certain fact is that beginning about 3500 B.C.E. people began to build large clusters of mud brick buildings near the mouths of the Tigris and Euphrates rivers.[1] About a dozen of these protocities, each inhabited by several thousand people, used the Sumerian language, drew their food from irrigated fields along the riverbanks, and traded by land and sea with a wide circle of neighboring peoples. About 3000 B.C.E., massive walls, built of mud brick to protect these settlements from external attack, mark the definitive attainment of a new level of social organization: the Sumerian city.

What made such cities possible was the intersection of a relatively new overland communications web, involving both river transport and donkey caravans, with much older shipping linkages that skirted shorelines of the monsoon seas. Previously, tropical jungles and other terrain obstacles meant that shipping along the coasts of the Indian Ocean had very limited inland contact. A narrow ribbon of coastal settlements was all that could easily enter into whatever exchanges of goods and ideas occurred among the fishermen and gardeners of these coasts. But after the domestication of donkeys in Egypt or perhaps in Southwest Asia (ca. 5000 B.C.E.) overland caravans began to span hundreds of miles, bringing the diverse ecological zones of the Southwest Asian hinterlands into far closer contact with coastal shipping. These two webs of transport and

---

[1] The shoreline of the Persian Gulf altered markedly in historic times. Sumerian cities, now as much as 150 kilometers (100 miles) inland, were once on or near the sea. The Euphrates also shifted its course from time to time, so sites in howling desert now were once on the riverbank.

communication converged at the head of the Persian Gulf, and this was where cities, and the complex society we call civilized, first arose.

Sumerian cities comprised three distinct elements. A group of privileged citizens farmed irrigated land nearby, and headed substantial households comprising relatives, a staff of dependent field workers, and a few imported slaves. Outside the walls, on the riverbank, a harbor community accommodated merchants, caravan personnel, and sailors who came and went, bringing necessary imports to the city like timber, metals, and other precious materials, while exporting woolen textiles, date wine, and other manufactures in exchange. The most distinctive element of Sumerian cities, however, was the presence of one or more divine households, or temples. These households were much larger than private ones, but the distribution of duties and income among members conformed in essentials to the way tasks and rewards were arranged within private households.

Yet scale made a critical difference. Each divine household pastured sheep on the seasonal grasslands of the floodplain and managed broad fields of irrigated grain, cultivated by hundreds of workers. The god's personal servants—that is, the priests—then used the comparatively vast quantities of grain, wool, and other agricultural commodities that arrived in temple warehouses to elaborate a luxurious style of life for the resident god and for themselves as well. They built ever more magnificent houses to shelter the divine image and fed it with ritual meals (twice a day), while providing new clothing, amusement, and other delectations on special occasions. Indeed, a boundless desire to increase ritual splendor may have been the driving force behind the rapid elaboration of skills that raised Sumerian cities above the level of neighboring peoples, for wealthy divine households could afford to support specialized craftsmen to create magnificent consumer goods, pleasing to even the most capricious divinity.

Precious raw materials like sky-blue lapis lazuli had to come from afar, and priestly managers relied on itinerant merchants to bring them. Priests likewise supervised the wool workers who produced textiles to clothe the god and all the human members of his household. Surplus textiles went to merchants to exchange for imported luxuries. And, to sustain the god's magnificence, a rural workforce labored under the priests' direction, tending flocks, maintaining dikes and canals, cultivating the grainfields, and bringing the harvest in each year.

Behind such specialized effort and exchange lay the notion that unless the god was pleased by the splendor of the temple where he or she resided, divine displeasure might have very nasty results—flood, famine, epidemic, or raid. Early efforts to understand their rich yet risky life on the floodplains had led Sumerian priests to adjust older animist ideas by attributing overriding power to a handful of great gods. Temple cult statues were carved to embody one or another of these powerful, invisible divine spirits who came and went at will. Making the statue and its environs attractive was necessary to prevent the god from departing to reside somewhere else. That was important, because only when the divine spirit was actually present in the cult statue could humans hope to keep the god on their side with praise and prayer, and by serving him or her faithfully and well. An angry god was dangerous, so placating divine wrath required daily effort and special skill to interpret the god's state of mind. Omens read from the livers of sacrificed animals and careful recording of the movements of sun, moon, and planets were among the methods Mesopotamian priests used for interpreting divine intentions. They also devised elaborate prayers and rituals to divert divine wrath and win the god's goodwill.

Each city had one or more gods in residence, but every local god had to take account of others and was therefore not all-powerful. Sumerian priests believed that a council of the seven great gods—sun, moon, earth, sky, fresh water, salt water, and storm, the greatest of them all—presided over the cosmos and met each New Year's Day to decide what the year would bring. The priests who developed these ideas presumably modeled their gods' behavior on the way Sumerian citizens managed public affairs by meeting to decide on common action—whether mounting a military expedition, building a new canal, or erecting a wall around the city itself. Captains were chosen to carry out such enterprises. But as warfare became common, temporary captains turned into lifelong rulers or kings, and built up warrior households of a size that rivaled, and eventually exceeded, those of the gods. As a result, by about 2300 B.C.E. military leaders had reduced even the greatest temple households to an uneasy subordination.

To begin with, however, beliefs and rituals elaborated within the divine households of Sumer appear to have been the precipitating factor that shaped the entire urban complex. Cities probably originated when heads of households, working newly irrigated land, gathered around ritual sites to assure supernatural protection, whereupon the expanding wealth and ambitions of priests and citizens combined to attract (or create) specialized craftsmen, merchants, sailors, and caravan personnel to serve their ever-expanding ritual and other material needs.

[margin note: Construct canals]

At first everything was new. Only a scant population of hunters and gatherers had lived in the Mesopotamian floodplain before irrigation works made agriculture rewarding. But hundreds of laborers were needed to construct the necessary dikes and canals, and organizing a large enough workforce for such tasks was no easy matter. Success presupposed a hinterland of crowded villages whence the necessary workers could be recruited by force or persuasion. Strangers arriving by sea may have been the entrepreneurs who seized this possibility, organizing the human effort needed to bring river water to the fields at the right time and in the right amount, thereby becoming the privileged citizens and priestly managers of the early Sumerian cities.[2]

[margin note: Key tools exports]

A short list of Sumerian products will suggest the sorts of innovations these cities fostered. Woolen cloth was the staple export. Copper and bronze weapons and tools, wheel-spun pottery, and cunningly incised cylinder seals were among the improved products of Sumerian workshops. Their most conspicuous creations were temples built from millions of mud bricks. No human construction on such a vast scale had ever been attempted before.

Canals, dikes, plows, wagons, and sailing ships, all of which appear unambiguously in Sumerian records for the first time, were more fundamental to the new form of society. Canals and dikes must have been invented in several places. Ships were certainly much older than Sumer; and wagons and perhaps plows may have been invented elsewhere too. But Sumerian cities gave greater scope to these devices. In particular, the concentrated agricultural surplus that supported specialists of every sort depended on cultivation by ox-drawn plows and on wagons to carry the harvest to urban storehouses. And, as previously pointed out, coastal shipping links along the shores of the monsoon seas together with donkey caravans gave the Sumerian cities a head start on all the rest of the world in creating a civilization.

The enhanced role of military leadership that became apparent after 3000 B.C.E. was, in turn, connected with the rise of pastoral societies, based on the seasonal grasslands that surrounded the comparatively tiny irrigated area of southern Mesopotamia. For during the same centuries when Sumerian cities were rising on irrigated land, herdsmen were

---

[2] The Sumerian language has no known linguistic relatives. The fact that Sumerian texts refer to rural workers as the "black-headed people" suggests some ethnic divide existed within Sumerian cities between social classes. A few religious texts also refer to arrival by sea from the south.

learning how to exploit available pasture by moving flocks of sheep and goats, from north to south and from lowland to highland with the seasons. Further north, an arc of village farmers occupied the regions where farming had started in the valleys and foothills that surround the Mesopotamian floodplain. Beyond them an agricultural frontier of settlement was expanding across Europe and Asia, flanked, in turn, by new, pastoral societies that established themselves on the vast Eurasian steppe. These relied more on cattle and horses than on sheep and goats.

As contrasting pastoral, agricultural, and urban ways of life defined themselves throughout western Eurasia after 3500 B.C.E., trading and raiding connected each with the others. At first, Sumerian accomplishments towered so high that even remote Indo-European–speaking pastoralists, living on steppelands far to the north, incorporated elements of the Sumerian pantheon into their religion. As a result, Aryan, Greek, Roman, Celtic, and Germanic deities of later times bore traces of their ancestors' early encounter with the seven great gods of the Sumerian religion.

Perennial jostling among city, village, and pastoral ways of life became fundamental to subsequent Eurasian and African history and governed political and military affairs for millennia. City dwellers and herdsmen were comparatively few but nonetheless enjoyed systematic military advantages over the village majority. Pastoralists specialized in protecting their flocks and herds. This inculcated military habits, since repelling human raiders was always more difficult than keeping animal predators at bay. In addition, pastoralists' mobility made it possible to assemble substantial raiding forces quickly wherever worthwhile targets beckoned. Farmers' stored grain was a perennial target, though negotiated peaceable exchanges of animal products for grain and luxuries from urban workshops was always an alternative.

The military advantages of urban dwellers arose from their access to superior (initially bronze) weapons, and their capacity to support specialized warriors, trained to fight in formation and obey a single commander. Such professional fighting men were initially few—far fewer than pastoral tribesmen among whom every adult male was a potential fighter. Their relations with other urban dwellers were awkward since professional fighters were liable to use their weapons against citizens and rent-paying villagers as well as against one another. The resulting tensions within urban society occasionally fueled rebellions; and when internal revolt coincided with pastoralists' raids, rulers might be supplanted by either revolutionary reformers or outside conquerors. In either case, the new rulers soon found that they needed military specialists and tax collectors to maintain their power, thereby making themselves vulnerable again to the same political cycle whenever the morale and obedience of soldiers and tax collectors wavered.

Overall, farming villagers bore the brunt of the unstable balance between pastoralist and urban military capability that emerged in Southwest Asia after about 3000 B.C.E. Except where mountains or marshes obstructed external attack, local groups of farmers could not match the organized violence that pastoralists and urban-based professional soldiers routinely exerted. Submission was inevitable and preferable to resistance since more or less predictable rents and taxes were easier to bear than unrestrained plundering. This was true for all concerned, and such arrangements therefore became standard and customary. In effect, herders together with professional soldiers and rulers of agrarian states established an informal but effective market in protection costs, setting rent and tax payments at a level that assured survival for villagers by leaving them a margin in ordinary years to guard against occasional crop failures. After about 2500 B.C.E. this sort of protection market subordinated peasants and sustained urban civilizations across subsequent millennia almost until the present.

More or less voluntary trade exchanges among diverse elite groups supplemented the fundamental transfer of rent and taxes from peasants to landowners and rulers. Sumerian cities engaged in such trade from the beginning. In particular, metals and timber could not be found on the floodplain. One of the roles played by early Sumerian kings may have been to lead armed expeditions to seize needed goods from bordering mountain peoples. The *Epic of Gilgamesh* suggests as much, with its tale of how that heroic leader brought back timber to Uruk after killing the protector of a distant cedar forest.

But when local chieftains undertook to organize their followers to cut trees, dig ore, or prepare some other commodity sought by distant city folk, a more advantageous way of getting needed goods arose. Local chieftains who chose the path of cooperation with itinerant merchants could count on regular access to precious city-made goods and weapons, otherwise unavailable to them. As such chieftains learned to tolerate— and even protect—merchant caravans, contacts between urban centers and outlying communities multiplied, allowing imported urban luxuries to become status symbols for local elites. This marked them off from commoners and, as urban tastes spread, a privileged class emerged and began, in turn, to patronize local artisans. Status differentiation and occupational specialization thus combined to drag local society toward urban levels of complexity. Forcible seizure of merchants' goods was an alternative way to get hold of precious objects; but even successful raiders still required access to markets to convert their jumble of booty into a usable assortment of what they wanted. And forcible seizure brought diminishing returns, because it discouraged merchants from returning. Hence cooperation with merchants usually prevailed, thickening the metropolitan web of the Nile-Indus corridor and expanding it in every direction.

Beginning with the rise of Sumer, then, trade and raid, based primarily in cities and secondarily among pastoralists, combined to spread urban goods, tastes, and complex social structures across a widening area of Southwest Asia, North Africa, and Southeast Europe. Indeed, the same and always painful civilizing process continues today in a few places, such as remoter Amazonia and highland New Guinea, where contacts with outsiders are still in their initial stages.

Indus

Early developments in the Nile and Indus valleys added to the metropolitan web that arose around Sumer. Both of these river valleys probably participated in the Mesopotamian web-building process from the start. But it is hard to say: groundwater inhibits uncovering the earliest strata at Mohenjo Daro, and undue haste and outright errors made long ago in excavating at Harappa prevent archeologists from knowing just how and when the Indus peoples founded their two great cities. But Sumerian seals and other artifacts discovered there attest to trade links with Sumer. Since coastal shipping made travel easy, exchanges of ideas and skills may have stimulated developments on the banks of the Indus from the beginning.

The Indus cities brought water management to a high art, segregating drinking water from waste water with what appears to be the world's first sewage system. It presumably helped reduce some of the disease risks of urban life. But scholars have not deciphered the Indus script, so nothing is reliably known about the religion and government that created the monumental buildings and waterworks of these cities. Archeology does show that the influence of Indus culture spread widely along the coasts of the Arabian Sea, and to some inland sites as well. Images carved on a few Indus seals also suggest that some of the gods of Hinduism originated as Indus deities.

Since Egyptian hieroglyphics have been accurately deciphered, scholars know far more about how civilization arose in the Nile Valley, and archeological traces of initial connections with Sumer are unambiguous. For example, the earliest Egyptian step pyramids show conscious borrowing from Sumerian architecture, even though the Egyptians used stone rather than mud brick, and quickly developed distinctive techniques and art styles of their own. Hieroglyphic writing may also reflect conscious imitation of cuneiform writing, for the Egyptian script appears all at once as a complete system, quite unlike the slow elaboration of Sumerian inscriptions.

Whatever useful hints early Egyptians picked up from contacts with Sumer, geographic and cultural differences soon launched Egypt on a different path from what prevailed in Mesopotamia. Their easy access to stone for buildings and statues was one such difference. But more basic was the Nile, which assured Egypt of cheap, capacious, and reliable internal transport by boat. Northeast trade winds that blow regularly across Egypt made it easy to sail south before the wind, and the gentle Nile current carried boats northward with similar ease and reliability. This meant that after about 3100 B.C.E., when the first Pharaoh united the whole of Egypt, political unification persisted with only sporadic interruption throughout the country's subsequent history. Nowhere on earth was it easier to merge village and local webs into a metropolitan one.

By controlling Nile shipping, Pharaoh could command his servants to concentrate grain and other resources wherever he wished, and use tax income from the whole country to support an enormous workforce for building his personal pyramid-tomb, or in any other way he chose. Egypt's early rulers claimed to be living gods who, in effect, turned the entire country into a single temple community. The resulting concentration of disposable wealth allowed Pharaoh's household to support a generous complement of highly skilled craftsmen and to organize enormous undertakings, of which the great pyramids are the most famous examples.

The initial unification of Egypt took place when irrigation agriculture was only beginning to transform the Nile floodplain. But Pharaoh's commands, combined with population growth and endless toil, soon turned the bottomlands into a narrow strip of fertile fields, and brought the Nile delta under cultivation as well. The Nile's gentle floods made canals unnecessary. Instead, Egyptians relied on basin irrigation, trapping floodwater behind dikes, letting the fertile silt settle on the land,

and then allowing surplus water to run off downstream when it came time to plant. This prevented salt buildup, whereas in Mesopotamia salt accumulated year after year when irrigation water evaporated from the fields, since even fresh water contains a little salt. This process eventually turned the land of Sumer into the desert it is today. Egypt, however, remained fertile.

For millennia, unparalleled ease of internal transport and ecologically sustainable irrigation gave Egyptian society its unusual stability. The distinctive style of Egypt's monumental art emerged under the dynasties of the Old Kingdom (2615–1991 B.C.E.) and remained standard thereafter until Roman times, even though the initial concentration of wealth, power, and specialized skill in Pharaoh's household diminished with time. Locally based landowners and temple priesthoods, serving diverse gods, increasingly made good a claim to part of the harvest and used such incomes for their own purposes.

The lengthy survival of Old Kingdom ideas and ideals was much assisted by Egypt's security from external threats. Formidable deserts made frontier defense much easier than in Mesopotamia, and for most (but not all) of antiquity, Egyptians stayed home. They did not need a costly military establishment like that of their contemporaries in Southwest Asia.

Egypt's unique geography limited but did not prevent encounters with the rest of the world. The coastal delta is readily accessible to seafarers, with the result that Egyptian techniques and ideas spread into Mediterranean lands. In particular, Minoan art in Crete derived part of its inspiration from Egyptian styles of sculpture and painting. Swamps and deserts made access to sub-Saharan Africa more difficult, but Egyptian influence extended well beyond the first cataract where Nile shipping came to a halt. Proof lies in the elaborate archeological remains from Nubia, along the upper Nile in today's Sudan, some of which are as old as Egypt's own beginnings. Scholars debate how much farther into Africa ancient Egyptian influence extended, and what influence Nubia had upon Egypt. Firm evidence is very scant.

Once they had established their own style of civilization, Egyptians generally found little worthwhile beyond their own borders. Such indifference was risky, as they discovered when warlike foreigners from Asia, known as Hyksos, overran their country. Using newly perfected military equipment, chiefly horse-drawn chariots, the Hyksos could traverse the desert barrier of the Sinai Peninsula. As a result, Hyksos rulers

Margin annotations: "fresh water", "surce of", "art", "access by sea", "rest africa tough to ba", "asia conflict"

(1678–1570 B.C.E.) abruptly dragged Egypt into a system of warlike imperial states that had formed around the ancient Mesopotamian center as
successive generations of military rulers, struggling to secure their
power, created larger and larger bureaucratic empires.

Before surveying that history, however, we turn to China, where parallel processes of cooperation and conflict among ever larger groups generated another metropolitan web with features all its own.

China evolved quite differently from Mesopotamia and Egypt. First of
all, the ritual-political-military relationships that created Chinese civilization emerged gradually from much older, well-developed villages.
These lay not in the floodplain but on loess terraces perched above and
on either side of the middle reaches of the Yellow River. By contrast, the
river floodplains of Mesopotamia and Egypt were agricultural frontier
lands, without much in the way of preexisting villages when Sumerian
priests and Pharaoh's household framed their respective civilizations. In
China, however, large, walled villages appeared about 3000 B.C.E., and
are associated with a few richly appointed tombs that attest to growing
differentiation between local elites and commoners. Fine wheel-spun
pottery, and the high-temperature ovens needed for their manufacture,
also suggest the emergence of artisan specialists; and marks on a few
painted pots appear to be ancestral to the Chinese script.

The authority of local leaders probably rested initially on their
monopoly of ritual access to powerful ancestral spirits. Well-disposed
ancestors were needed to intercede with other spirits who controlled the
harvest. The cult of ancestral spirits was built around offerings of alco-
holic beverages presented in ritual vessels of especially fine workman-
ship. Such vessels, cast in bronze, constitute the chief surviving
examples of early Chinese art.

But, as in Mesopotamia, population growth and increasing wealth
soon combined to intensify warfare. Spiritual protection had therefore to
be supplemented by military mobilization, and elite families, accustomed to managing relations with the spirits, organized the labor needed
to erect village walls and directed their defense as well. With spiritual
and political-military leadership in the same hands, the polarity between
priests and kings, characteristic of Mesopotamia, never arose in China.

Large, walled villages did not retain full autonomy for long. Instead,

after walls

local clan leaders formed shifting coalitions across a widening area of North China by agreeing to recognize the primacy of one or another lineage. Later literary tradition held that the Xia lineage (traditional dates 2205–1766 B.C.E.) were the first merely human rulers to gain such primacy among the walled communities of China. A firmer basis for political-military power emerged when the Shang dynasty (traditional dates 1523–1028 B.C.E.) imported an expensive weapons system, featuring compound bows,[3] bronze armor, horses, and chariots. Finds at Anyang, the last Shang capital, show a recognizably Chinese style of civilization firmly in place by 1300 B.C.E. In particular, inscriptions on thousands of so-called oracle bones, recording ritual inquiries addressed to diverse and often unspecified spirits, are so close to China's historic script that scholars could read them immediately.

Since it was local village elites that coalesced to support imperial government in China, ancestral spirits and the lineages descended from them remained far more prominent in Chinese society and politics than in the Nile-Indus corridor. There cities had formed initially by attracting strangers from afar, and in later ages imperial rulers set out to counterbalance local elites by appointing outsiders, usually with a military background, to exercise bureaucratic authority. When military encounters with the outer world compelled it, China accepted the same bureaucratic principle, but did so by appointing officials recruited from the landowning class who were selected in part on the basis of their superior literacy.

lineage

when (right?)

Rise of Bureaucratic Empire

The chariots and horses Shang rulers relied upon derived ultimately from southwestern Asia, signifying China's remote involvement in a political-military maelstrom centered around Mesopotamia. The upshot of the endlessly destructive armed conflicts of Western Asia was the development of imperial, bureaucratic government in civilized land-

---

[3] Compound bows were made of wood, bone, and sinew, glued together to make a short, resilient arc. Such bows shot faster and carried farther than bows made only of wood. Introduced to Mesopotamian warfare about 2350 B.C.E., they reached China some 800 years later with the Shang.

scapes and the countervailing emergence of shifting, far-ranging tribal alliances among pastoralists on the grassland steppes.

The principal empires in Mesopotamia and surrounding regions were as follows:

Table 3.1

Empires of Southwest Asia and Egypt

DATES B.C.E.	RULERS	PREVAILING WEAPONRY	LOGISTICAL BASIS
ca. 2350 (ca. 2250)	Akkadians (Sargon)	compound bow	plunder by small military elite
ca. 2000–1650	Amorites (Hammurabi)	bows and spears	taxes, rents, plunder
ca. 1600–1200	Mitanni, Hittites	horse-drawn chariots, bows, spears	taxes, rents, plunder
ca. 1600–1200	Egypt: New Kingdom	bows, spears, bronze armor, chariots	taxes, rents, plunder
ca. 1200–1000	small, local states (no major empires)	iron armor, swords, spears, bows	plunder
935–612	Assyrians	bows, spears, chariots, cavalry, siege engines	taxes, rents, plunder
550–330	Persians	bows, spears, cavalry, siege engines, warships	taxes, rents, plunder

This table disguises three landmarks. First was the chariot revolution that spread across most of Eurasia, starting from the northern borderlands of Mesopotamia where light, sturdy horse-drawn chariots capable of carrying a driver and an archer into battle were perfected by about 1700 B.C.E. Like tanks in European warfare between 1918 and 1945, chariots proved irresistible when new by combining mobility with firepower (and the terror aroused by facing galloping horses). Consequently, charioteers overran Mesopotamia, conquered Egypt (after 1678 B.C.E.), and penetrated northern India (ca. 1500 B.C.E.). Chariots also arrived in such distant lands as China and Sweden within a few centuries of their first invention.

A second landmark came when common foot soldiers, equipped with comparatively cheap iron armor and weapons, overthrew charioteer elites after 1200 B.C.E. Democratization of warfare ensued and a rash of more egalitarian, local states supplanted large empires for a while. But, rather quickly, armed struggles once again led to bureaucratic consolidation, and cheaper armaments and larger armies soon made the

Map 3.2 Ancient Empires of Southwest Asia and Egypt

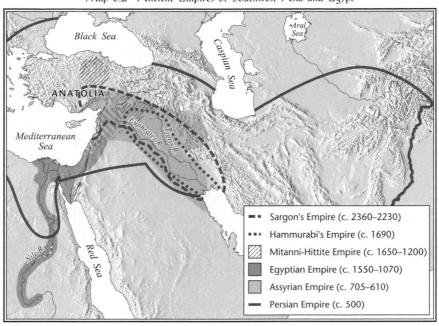

Assyrian and Persian empires far more formidable than their predecessors had been.

Iron metallurgy got started in Cyprus or perhaps eastern Anatolia about 1200 B.C.E. and diffused even farther than chariotry had done, spreading throughout Europe, India, and China, and penetrating sub-Saharan Africa after 600 B.C.E.[4] Abundant ores made the metal cheap enough that many farmers could afford iron plowshares, hoes, and sickles, making cultivation of heavy clay soils much easier than before. For the first time rural majorities had a stake in maintaining urban-based exchanges that kept specialized miners, smelters, and merchants busy supplying blacksmiths with the iron needed to make their tools. Before long, iron proved so abundant and valuable that itinerant blacksmiths began to make tools and weapons for the rural inhabitants of regions such as Northern Europe and sub-Saharan Africa, which helped narrow the gap between remoter hinterlands and the urban cores of the expanding metropolitan webs. In Africa, ironworking may have emerged inde-

---

[4] Iron smelting required higher temperatures than copper and bronze casting. Furnaces designed to produce stronger drafts (often enhanced by mechanical bellows) together with charcoal fuel made such higher temperatures possible.

pendently, because archeological finds suggest that iron smelters were in use in East Africa as early as 900–700 B.C.E., before ironworking had come to Egypt.

A third transformation came in the seventh century B.C.E. when cavalry archers became numerous and skilled enough to alter the military-political balance of Eurasia once more. Horses abounded on the steppes; so when herdsmen learned how to keep their seat while loosing the reins and using both hands to shoot arrows from the back of a galloping horse (no mean feat), the speed and endurance of their mounts allowed them to concentrate superior force wherever they chose. Cavalrymen from urbanized states might hope to catch and match raiding pastoralists, but since grass was scant in cultivated landscapes, and feeding horses with grain was expensive, a small elite of mounted warriors was all that could ever be mobilized by agrarian empires against steppe cavalry raiders.

Consequently, even modest populations of herders became militarily formidable. Among them, every male adult was a potential cavalryman, and a successful captain could readily form alliances and attract followers from far and near. Any weakening of civilized defenses therefore invited raids from the steppe. And if resistance broke down, successful raiders could linger on the spot, learn to substitute rents and taxes for plunder, and swiftly make themselves rulers of civilized populations.

The strategic advantages steppe raiders enjoyed were enough to introduce an irregular political cycle into Eurasian history that lasted from 612 B.C.E., when Scythian cavalrymen from the Ukraine participated in the overthrow of the Assyrian empire, through 1644 C.E., when Manchu bannermen founded a new dynasty in China. Across the intervening centuries, most civilized governments of Eurasia descended from steppe conquerors, directly or indirectly. Island Japan and forested Western Europe were both insulated by geography from pastoralist raiders most (but not all) of the time. Closer to the frontier between grassland and farmland, in China, the Middle East, and India, an irregular alternation between steppe conquest and native resurgence prevailed until 1757, when Chinese armies (with an assist from smallpox) destroyed the last steppe confederation to challenge an agrarian empire in Eurasia (see chapter 6).

This uneasy military balance was almost unparalleled elsewhere. It meant that improvements in civilized defenses continued to spread across Eurasia just as chariots and cavalry had done; while steppe confederations extended their size and improved their equipment and organization to match. The appearance of stirrups soon after 200 C.E. is an example of how a valuable innovation could spread so rapidly that no one now can tell for sure where the initial (seemingly obvious) invention was made. As a result, for century after century, unremitting instability across the pastoralist-civilized steppe frontier made Eurasian military organization and equipment far more formidable than armed forces elsewhere.

The military prowess of pastoralists in Eurasian and North African history meant more than political instability and rapid diffusion of the arts of war: their mobility sustained trade links, as well as exchanges of microbes, religious ideas, and technologies. Pastoralists, in short, bound the agrarian heartlands together from the shores of the Mediterranean to the Yellow Sea, persistently tightening the strands of existing webs, and eventually fusing them together into the Old World Web.

As for civil society, the long agony of military-political upheavals around the Mesopotamian core between 2350 B.C.E. and 331 B.C.E. provoked three fundamental innovations: bureaucratic government; alphabetic writing; and portable, congregational religions.

The bureaucratic principle meant that an individual—any individual in principle—could expect to be obeyed by those around him simply because some distant monarch delegated royal authority to him. When generally accepted, such delegated authority made it easier to collect taxes and enforce public laws across long distances, so long as appointed officials remained obedient to their superiors. Bureaucratic appointment to office was firmly in place by the time of Hammurabi (reigned ca. 1792–1750 B.C.E.); and despite temporary and local disruptions, the idea and practice of bureaucratic government never subsequently disappeared.

When officials and soldiers remained obedient to a distant sovereign, public laws made encounters among strangers more peaceable and predictable. Private contracts and public obligations attained customary and legal definitions allowing specialized occupations to proliferate and entangle more and more persons in webs of exchange. As specialization advanced, skill and wealth increased proportionately, and the civilizing process continued to attract new recruits and expand to new ground, despite the recurrent destruction wrought by warfare and the always precarious obedience of soldiers and bureaucrats to their superiors.

Second, technological improvements in transport and communication extended the range of social interaction. Chief among these was alphabetic writing, which transformed older social relationships by democratizing literacy. Other significant inventions like the hub and spoke design for wheels made chariot warfare feasible and also improved haulage. Specially constructed military roads, which the Assyrians began to build, had a similar dual function. Little is known about changes in shipbuilding, but after 1000 B.C.E. ships increased in number, variety, and carrying capacity, as the rise of Phoenician merchant cities along the Mediterranean coast and the invention of specialized war galleys indicates.

But new ways of writing affected human society much more radically. By Hammurabi's time, royal letters dispatched by special messengers to local officials allowed the king to control distant provinces —more or less. And the famous law code he inscribed on stone for public inspection illustrates another use of writing for the management of public affairs. Moreover, the somewhat simplified cuneiform script that Hammurabi used was later converted into the medium of diplomacy among the linguistically diverse empires of the chariot age, with the result that archeologists in Egypt discovered a cache of diplomatic documents written in the Mesopotamian script.

After about 1300 B.C.E., localized alphabetic scripts democratized literacy, at the same time that iron weapons democratized warfare. Numerous inscribed pottery fragments show that private persons routinely used alphabetic scripts to record business contracts. This facilitated trade, allowing market relations to reach across time and space more easily and securely than before. But a more important effect of alphabetic writing was to make sacred scriptures accessible to laymen, who proceeded to create portable, congregational religions on the basis of holy scriptures.

shaped history
- Gov
 - writing
  - religion

Portable, Congregational Religions

Portable religions were a third innovation that shaped subsequent human history as profoundly as bureaucratic government and alphabetic writing have done. Religions had previously been local. Each people's gods were believed to protect (and punish) those who worshiped them. But amidst strangers with different gods what divine protection was there for exiles like the Jews, carried off to Babylon by Nebuchadnezzar after he captured Jerusalem and destroyed their temple in 586 B.C.E.? The exiles relied on a complex collection of scriptures they already regarded as sacred to construct a radically new sort of religion, centered upon weekly meetings where men and women gathered together to hear authoritative explications of God's will as revealed by the sacred writings. Since the priests of Jerusalem had disappeared with the temple, teachers known as rabbis, whose authority rested on their skill at reconciling apparently discrepant passages of sacred scripture, took their place.

Earnest study and meditation on the scriptures allowed them to create a code of conduct for the exiled community that maintained morale and kept the exiled Jews distinct from those around them. And by affirming that God's power was universal, using mighty kings like Nebuchadnezzar to punish the Jewish people for their sins, and subsequently punishing him with madness for his, the rabbis of Babylon collaborated with a succession of prophets—Isaiah, Nehemiah, Ezra—to turn Judaism into an emphatically monotheistic faith. Its continued viability ever since attests to Judaism's power to guide and support believers wherever they may live and whatever hardships they may encounter.

About the sixth century B.C.E., and probably somewhere in the eastern provinces of the Persian Empire, revelations to a single prophet, named Zoroaster, inaugurated another universal faith that also came to rest on the authority of sacred scriptures. Despite (or perhaps because of) official state patronage in the time of King Darius (reigned 522–486 B.C.E.), Zoroaster's followers did not establish a secure, popular basis, as Judaism did, and so never spread very widely, though Parsees in India today honor him as founder of their faith.

Judaism and Zoroastrianism were universal, portable religions, worshiping a just, stern God whose jurisdiction extended over the whole earth. Both also relied on revealed, sacred scriptures to define a moral code for believers. Mutual support and peaceable behavior toward strangers were other important aspects of the new faiths.

In subsequent centuries, urban dwellers, and particularly poor, marginal persons, found that authoritative religious guidance, shared faith, and mutual support among congregations of believers could substitute for the tight-knit custom of village existence (within which the rural majority continued to live) and give meaning and value to ordinary lives, despite daily contact with uncaring strangers. Such religious congregations, in turn, helped to stabilize urban society by making its inherent inequality and insecurity more tolerable.

Bureaucratic administration, alphabetic writing, and portable, congregational religions have never been surpassed as instruments for sustaining civilized societies, and stand as the most important innovations generated among ancient Southwest Asian peoples between 2350 B.C.E. and 331 B.C.E. All three innovations sustained and intensified the metropolitan web that made civilization so formidable, and simultaneously helped smooth relations among the diverse peoples caught up in it.

not egypt

Three other population centers—in India, China, and around the shores of the Mediterranean—each had important contacts with the principal seat of civilized society in and around Mesopotamia. By 200 C.E., all three had succumbed to bureaucratic imperial government like that pioneered in the Mesopotamian area. But local differences remained profound and deserve notice.

Indian Civilization

cheriot invade india

Mohenjo Daro, Harappa, and other Indus cities were abandoned about 1500 B.C.E. At about the same time Aryan charioteers, expanding across the steppe, invaded Iran and may have reached northern India. What actually happened is unknown. Military attack, if it occurred, left no clear trace. Peasant flight from burdensome taxation, the onset of malaria, floods, drought, and climate change, or some unrecorded withdrawal of faith in the religious authority of Indus rulers may explain the urban collapse. Assuredly, Aryan warriors did arrive from the north bringing a new language and new religious ideas and practices with them, while literacy and the specialized artisan skills of Indus civilization disappeared. The Aryans' encounter with darker-skinned indigenous peoples probably led to the emergence of hereditary castes, but how that happened, not being recorded,[5] remains mysterious. It is possible that castes already existed among the Indus peoples and that the Aryans, as dominating newcomers, simply fitted themselves into an older social system, as subsequent conquerors of India were to do.

caste

One thing is sure. The caste system became a distinctive feature of Indian society, organizing people into distinct groups based on birth and occupation. Caste identities eventually came to be seen as necessary and

distinct groups

[5] Orally transmitted religious texts, though bulky, cast little light on social and political aspects of Indian society. Faithful memorization of increasingly unintelligible words became an end in itself for Brahmins and their pupils. Sanskrit thus preserved old linguistic forms, to the delight of nineteenth-century philologists, who sought to reconstruct the Indo-European family of languages. But by deliberately freezing the forms of their sacred words the bearers of this oral tradition hid historical changes going on in the society around them.

just, because everyone expected to be reborn up or down the scale of existence, depending on one's *karma*, that is, on how well each reembodied
human soul had previously conformed to the roles befitting its caste. Belief
in reincarnation became a way to explain the injustices and inequities of civilized society. By conforming to caste rules, a soul born into a low caste
assured rebirth in a higher caste. Conversely, flouting caste rules led to
rebirth lower in the caste hierarchy. Thus everyone got what he or she
deserved.

Contact with other castes was restricted by notions of ritual contam-
ination; and since marriage was strictly confined to fellow caste members, the system was self-perpetuating. Newcomers became another
caste automatically, simply because older inhabitants treated them as
such. Today, India has about 25,000 subcastes loosely grouped into some
3,000 castes, all classified into four distinct ranks, called *varnas*. In theory, these four varnas corresponded to priests, warriors, merchants, and
commoners or laborers. But in practice actual occupations often do not
match inherited caste.

Cities and states reappeared in India after about 700 B.C.E., centered
this time in the wetter Ganges Valley and depending more on rice than
on the wheat and barley familiar to Indus farmers. Iron metallurgy,
spreading from Iran, perhaps helped to stimulate the new growth since
iron tools surely made it easier to clear the jungle. So too, probably, did
sorghum and millet, African crops adapted to dry conditions, both of
which arrived in India around 1000 B.C.E. With new tools and new crops
from afar, northern Indians could now efficiently exploit terrains both
moist and dry.

But the resurgent Indian civilization shaped its own path from the
beginning. Structuring society around inherited caste identities may not
have become definitive until Hinduism achieved a modicum of doctrinal
definition after 200 C.E. But the core idea of reincarnation perhaps harks
back to the Indus civilization; and when the reemergence of cities and
states on Indian soil sharpened social stratification anew, that ancient
notion was available to justify and reinforce the caste principle.

A second distinctive trait of the emergent civilization of India was
the deference accorded to ascetics, whose ecstatic experiences gave
them access to a transcendant spiritual realm. Ordinary encounters with
the material world were judged trivial and tawdry by comparison, and
techniques for attaining mystic ecstasy, as elaborated among Indian holy
men, eventually affected religious practices in most of the rest of the
world. The ascetic lifestyle achieved a lasting institutional definition

among the followers of Gautama Buddha (died ca. 483 B.C.E.), whose monastic communities subsequently propagated themselves across South and East Asia. Buddhist monks specialized in holiness, and soon attracted widespread reverence among laymen. Monks and laymen developed rituals and routines of piety appropriate for their distinctive roles, and, like the new, universal religions of Southwest Asia, the resulting doctrines and practices of Buddhism were valid everywhere and available to anyone who chose to accept them.

Buddhists sought to free themselves from the suffering inherent in bodily existence by annihilating self and so attaining Nirvana. But on an everyday basis monks constructed communities of fellow believers even more all-embracing than the congregations Jews had invented in Babylon. At the same time, obligations for Buddhist laymen were fewer than those Jews observed. The combination of greater rigor for self-selected religious athletes and less demanding rules for ordinary believers turned Buddhism into the most successful missionary religion of the ensuing millennium. Christian monks replicated the Buddhist pattern, beginning soon after 200 C.E.; and later on, when Islam supplanted Buddhism as the most successful missionary religion (after about 1000 C.E.), Muslim success depended on the acceptance into Islam of a similar division of roles between religious devotees—the dervishes—and an admiring laity, among whom less rigorous piety was the norm. Buddhist-style monasteries surrounded by supportive laymen therefore turned out to be as important an institutional invention as the portable, congregational religions of the Judaic-Christian-Muslim tradition. Like those religions, Buddhism made the trials and hardships of entry into the Old World Web more tolerable for millions of ordinary people.

In other respects, the way Indian cities and rulers struggled among themselves and modeled emergent imperial government along bureaucratic lines appears to recapitulate what had already happened in and around Mesopotamia. The Maurya dynasty (ca. 321–184 B.C.E.) was the first to control the whole of northern India, but Indian rulers found it difficult to resist raiders from Central Asia, largely because, as one caste among many, they did not command much loyalty from the rest of the population. In addition, since horses did not thrive in India, invading cavalrymen easily concentrated superior force against ill-mounted defenders. As a result, successful raiders from the north repeatedly transformed themselves into rulers over parts or all of India in subsequent centuries.

Thanks largely to the spread of Buddhist monasticism, Indian influence among the other peoples of Eurasia was primarily religious and secondarily commercial. Some Indian products, especially cotton cloth and pepper, achieved wide distribution overseas and overland, and merchants based in India did much to provoke the rise of local states and civilizations in Southeast Asia, beginning soon after the Common Era. The court cultures of Java, Cambodia, and their neighbors derived largely from India, though local ideas and practices made each state and people different in detail. Buddhist practices also played a critical part in commercializing Chinese society after about 700 C.E., as we shall see in the next chapter.

Chinese Civilization

Like India, China also elaborated its own style of civilization between 1500 B.C.E. and 200 C.E. while continuing to receive important stimuli from Western Asia and the steppes. Links westward became firmer in the first millennium B.C.E. when the Chinese appetite for jade from Khotan and adjacent regions of Central Asia merged with the Mesopotamian demand for lapis lazuli from Iran and Afghanistan. This created a slender transmission belt extending across the Eurasian continent. As steppe and oasis dwellers learned to produce such luxuries for distant urban markets, the metropolitan webs of East Asia and the Nile-Indus corridor forged a common link. As before, changes in military technology were especially significant, for when cavalry warfare began to intrude on the Chinese frontier, about 350 B.C.E., it soon brought a militarized and far more centralizing dynasty to power in China, as chariot warfare had done a millennium before.

Chinese literary texts provide a detailed political record with none of the chronological mistiness that pervades early Indian history. These records make clear that under the Zhou dynasty (ca. 1122–256 B.C.E.) enterprising landowners and princes presided over the extensive diking and drainage needed to bring the vast floodplain of the Yellow River under cultivation for the first time. By the end of the Zhou era, a carpet of fertile fields had spread across that floodplain, and throughout its lower reaches the Yellow River started to flow above ground level, confined between artificial levees. On elevated loess terraces, millet and wheat were still raised on rain-watered fields just as before, but they became less important than crops produced in the rich new bottomlands.

This enormous engineering project transformed Chinese society and politics profoundly, even though the notion of (largely ritual) subordina-

Map 3.3 Han Empire as of ca. 1 C.E.

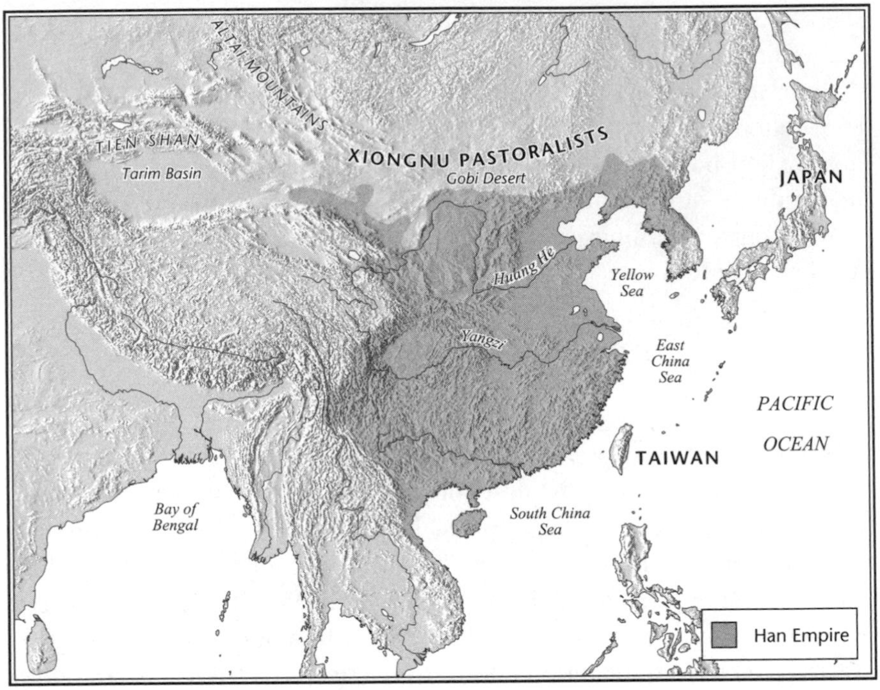

tion to the Zhou emperor was not easily repudiated. Enterprising local landowners may have started to reclaim the floodplain, but really large-scale water engineering had to be arranged by territorial princes, who became sovereign over the reclaimed lands in all but name. Thereafter, armed conflict among them mounted in intensity until, in 221 B.C.E., a single prince from a border region conquered all the warring states of China. But his ruthlessness roused so much resistance that the new dynasty did not last. Instead, shortly after his death another bout of warfare intervened before China attained a more stable political and social order under the Han dynasty (202 B.C.E.–221 C.E.).

As in India, this political record resembled the military upheavals around Mesopotamia and had a similar upshot: the establishment of imperial, bureaucratic government. But Chinese society and bureaucracy rested on different and more secure foundations. The dikes and canals constructed for flood control formed a network of navigable waterways that extended throughout the most productive farmland of the entire country. This allowed the state to use canal boats to concentrate tax income (initially collected in kind) at the imperial court.

An intellectual achievement also had an important role in stabilizing

Confucius during rough time

imperial government. Living in a time of political turmoil, Confucius[6] (551–479 B.C.E.) invoked the example of a more stable past in his teachings about the proper way to live. Gentlemen, he said, ought to maintain good relations with the spirits by acting with proper decorum both in private life and as imperial officials. His disciples quickly codified his teachings, combining revered ancient writings with a collection of sayings attributed to Confucius himself. Under the Han, meticulous study of these classics became the mark of an educated man and a qualification for holding office. In time, shared book learning and moral expectation shaped in a predominantly Confucian mold united China's landowning class in obedience to the emperor just as effectually as canal boats united the imperial economy.

China could not cope with steppe riders

On the other hand, China found no lasting solution to the problem of how to cope with steppe raiders. As noted already, cavalry warfare appeared on the northwest frontier of China about 350 B.C.E. The border state of Xian bore the initial brunt of organizing resistance by equipping infantry with crossbows (then a new Chinese invention) and developing (or hiring) a cavalry force of its own. But maintaining large cavalry forces in China was hideously expensive since, in the absence of grass, a horse ate about as much grain as a dozen persons. The best the first emperor of China could do to keep steppe horsemen away was to start constructing defensive walls on the northern frontier. This did not work very well. A vast garrison of crossbowmen, stationed along the wall, could hope to prevent mounted raiders from crossing it, but maintaining such a force and getting enough archers to a threatened location quickly enough was always difficult. Hiring nearby steppe cavalrymen to guard the approaches to China was a far cheaper alternative. But that, too, could fail whenever such guards decided to join in raiding the Chinese countryside instead.

archer expense

On other frontiers, China's state power, supported by continuing population growth and persistent agricultural pioneering (especially in the south), made expansion comparatively easy. Although the Yangzi Valley remained thinly occupied in Han times, perhaps because its warmer and wetter climate exposed immigrants from the north to lethal infections, nonetheless, Han rulers established control over most of the Yangzi Valley and much of southern China. They even extended a more tenuous military occupation to the oases of the Tarim basin. But this

---

[6] In Chinese, Kong Fuzi, or master Kong. His personal name was Kong Qia.

heightened the empire's vulnerability to steppe raiders. When Emperor Wudi (140–87 B.C.E.) learned that far off in the west a special breed of "blood-sweating" horses carried men whose heavy armor made them proof against arrows, he dispatched an expedition to bring back this promising new instrument of war. In 101 B.C.E., his emissaries returned from the Ferghana Valley (in today's Uzbekistan) with a few such horses, and the alfalfa on which they fed. But it turned out that feeding the big horses in Chinese landscapes was so expensive that China never maintained large forces of armored cavalry.

But after Emperor Wudi's expedition had shown the way, organized caravan trade and direct communication between China and Western Asia was never broken off for long. What had previously been only indirect and intermittent contact between the separate centers of Eurasia's growing web became continuous. Ideas, techniques, diseases, crops, and other novelties began to flow unceasingly across the grasslands and deserts of Central Asia as well as through the monsoon waters off Asia's southern coasts. This consolidated the Old World Web, and inaugurated a new era in world history. But before exploring it, we must glance at what happened around the shores of the Mediterranean Sea in the centuries when Indian and Chinese civilizations were assuming their classic forms.

Greek and Roman Civilization

Even before 3500 B.C.E., when sailing vessels began to traverse the eastern Mediterranean, peoples living near the coastline had easy contact with one another by boat. This meant that when civilized societies appeared in Egypt and Syria, other Mediterranean communities were soon affected. Minoan society, with its palace-temples at Knossos and Phaistos in Crete (ca. 2100–1400 B.C.E.), was a country cousin of Pharaonic Egypt: different in art style, in religion, and in its reliance on overseas trade, Crete nonetheless resembled Egypt in the concentration of resources in the hands of a sacred ruler who probably controlled overseas shipping just as Pharaoh controlled the boats on the Nile that undergirded his power.

Similarly, the Bronze Age warriors of Mycenae in mainland Greece who flourished after about 1400 B.C.E. closely resembled contemporary chariot aristocracies of the Hittite and Mitanni empires. For the Mycenaeans, however, ships, like those that carried Agamemnon's warriors to

Maritime civilization

ships were more important than horses for chariots / trading

Troy, were more important than chariots for their raiding and trading. And when invading Dorians, equipped with iron weapons and tools, flooded into Greece about 1100 B.C.E., the migrations and political fragmentation that followed closely resembled contemporary political changes in Southwest Asia.

Then Greek public life took a distinctive turn when cities and civilization revived around the Aegean after about 800 B.C.E. Population, wealth, and trade grew, and Greek society started to divide between rich and poor. The familiar Southwest Asian polarity between a governing elite of rent and tax receivers and poverty-stricken tax and rent payers seemed about to emerge. But instead the Greeks invented a new master institution for themselves—the *polis*—by combining old ideas about justice with new ways of defending themselves from outside attack.

Greek society changing

The polis was an association of citizens, led by magistrates who derived their authority from a legal process of selection or election. They held office for a limited period of time, usually one year. This implied unceasing negotiation between citizens and their leaders as to what actions were just and right since magistrates who came to office only through the support of their fellow citizens could not easily exercise power to benefit only a few rich and powerful families. Their task instead was to initiate public actions acceptable to all citizens, to enforce agreed-upon laws, and to sustain an effective common defense against outsiders.

elections

Citizenship was always a privilege open only to adult males. Women, slaves, and foreigners were excluded since citizenship required fighting for the polis, actively and in person. Collective valor supplanted individual actions on the field of battle when, after about 650 B.C.E., phalanx warfare proved its effectiveness against more random, individualized combat of the sort Homer had celebrated in the *Iliad*. Thereafter, military success came to depend on how bravely and skillfully each citizen kept his place in line, wielding his spear against the foe while helping to protect the man next to him with his shield. Phalanx fighting had the effect of checking individual rivalries by transferring heroic pursuit of fame and glory from individual warriors to the polis as a whole.

citizen ship

Transformed into a collective hero, the polis, at least in Sparta and Athens, attracted overriding loyalties among the citizens. Kin groups, religious groups, economic activities—all were subordinated to it. Temporary magistrates instead of hereditary priesthoods took charge of most religious rituals, and displaced or diminished the power of hereditary kings. When too many citizens fell into debt and became unable to equip themselves for the phalanx, radical reformers like (the perhaps mythical)

polis vero popular

When armies failed

Lycourgos of Sparta (ca. 610 B.C.E.) and the entirely historical Solon of Athens (594 B.C.E.) canceled debts and rearranged property and voting rights. They thereby deliberately diminished the gap between rich and poor and increased the number of citizens properly equipped for phalanx fighting.

Because so many citizens learned to cooperate freely and effectively in pursuit of common purposes, the polis proved extremely successful. In response to local land shortages, beginning about 750 B.C.E., the Greeks established hundreds of new and independent Greek cities at selected locations in southern Italy and Sicily and along other parts of the Mediterranean and Black Sea coasts. Armed conflicts with Phoenicians, Carthaginians, and Etruscans eventually checked this expansion, but not before Greek trade had come to dominate most of the Mediterranean and Black Sea shores.

Coinage

The introduction of coinage, initially issued by King Croesus (reigned ca. 560–546 B.C.E.) of Lydia in today's western Turkey, encouraged such trade by establishing readily recognizable tokens of value. Gold coins came first, and may have been merely a simpler way of using gold for paying off Greek and other mercenary soldiers serving the Lydian king.[7] But Greek cities soon began to mint base metal coins of lesser value to use in everyday market transactions. The effect was to liberate citizens from the awkwardness of barter, which required sellers and buyers to find someone willing to part with the right amount of the particular commodity each party wanted. Standards of value had been used from Sumerian times, or before: rare kinds of seashells, ox-hide-shaped tokens of bronze, and the like. But coins, bearing the distinctive imprint of an official mint, were small and portable, quickly recognizable, yet easy to hide and difficult to debase without changing their appearance. By making it easy to assign an exact monetary value to everything offered for sale, coins simplified, sped up, and extended retail and wholesale trade. Artisan and agricultural specialization intensified, and Greek cities became locations for wholesale and retail market exchanges among ordinary citizens, resident foreigners, and sometimes slaves as well.

Specialized production, eased by the monetization of everyday economic transactions, rapidly increased Greek skills, wealth, and knowl-

---

[7] Persian monarchs also minted gold coins, but hoarded so many of them in the royal treasury that coinage played a far more limited role in the economic life of the Persian Empire than it did among the Greeks and Romans.

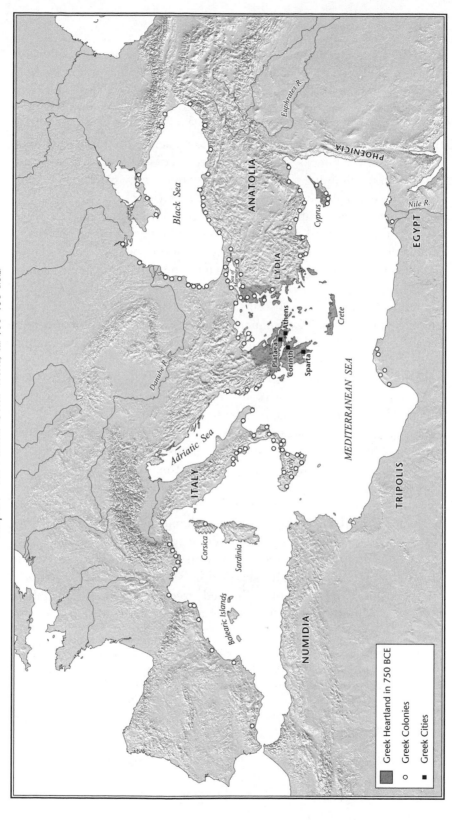

MAP 3.4 The Ancient Greek World, CA. 750–450 B.C.E.

Greek Heartland in 750 BCE
○ Greek Colonies
■ Greek Cities

Black Sea

Euphrates R.

ANATOLIA

PHOENICIA

Cyprus

Nile R.

EGYPT

LYDIA

Sea of Marmara

Crete

Athens
Plataea
Corinth
Sparta

MEDITERRANEAN SEA

Danube R.

Adriatic Sea

ITALY

Sicily

TRIPOLIS

Corsica

Sardinia

Balearic Islands

NUMIDIA

edge. Yet for about three centuries citizens preserved an unusually large measure of the social solidarity and individual freedom inherited from their ancestors. The Phoenicians, Etruscans, and Assyrians built their cities and states on similar heritages from tribal Iron Age invaders. The Old Testament prophets who demanded righteousness and justice from the kings of Israel—mostly in vain—harked back to the same egalitarian heritage. But the Greeks were much more successful than their contemporaries in maintaining a lively sense of commonality within each polis, despite increasingly diverse occupations and styles of life.

[margin note: Greeks much friendly with their leaders]

In effect, they combined the advantages of tribal and village solidarity with the skills and wealth of urban civilization. That achievement only endured for two or three centuries before upper and lower classes parted company among the Greeks as had happened long before among other civilized peoples. But while shared outlook and action endured, Greek civilization achieved forms of expression which outsiders found immensely impressive. Consequently, for a few centuries (primarily after the Greek polis world had lost its autonomy to Macedonian conquerors in 338 B.C.E.), a modified upper-class Greek style of life became very enticing to the diverse elites of Europe, Western Asia, and North Africa.

Throughout the classical age (510–338 B.C.E.), phalanx warfare remained the primary school of citizenship. When a few cities also organized navies to protect their overseas trade, a military role opened for poorer citizens who could not equip themselves with the full panoply of land war. A strong back and a sense of rhythm were the only requisites for rowing in a war galley.[8] Consequently, when landowning farmer-citizens, who manned the phalanx, began to share defense of the polis with landless urban dwellers, Athenian democracy of the classical age became more practicable, just, and even necessary.

[margin note: Persian invasion]

A crucial test of polis society came in 480 B.C.E. when the Persian imperial army, supported and supplied by ships and crews conscripted from Phoenicia and Asia Minor, invaded Greece. Against all expectation, a ragged coalition of about twenty Greek cities inflicted defeat on the

---

[8] Galleys attacked by ramming hostile ships, so speed through the water and nimble maneuver were critical. Precisely coordinated rowing achieved that result, and the necessary keeping together in time mimicked dance and probably aroused sentiments of solidarity just as dancing did. Charging phalanxes likewise maintained a solid shield front by keeping time to a paean—that is, to musical shouts—so Greek warfare both on land and sea tapped emotional linkages like those aroused by dance. The extraordinary intensity of individual commitment to the polis perhaps depended largely on the shared emotion such exercises generated. See William H. McNeill, *Keeping Together in Time* (Cambridge, MA, 1995), 112–20.

Persians in the battle of Salamis, followed the next year by Persian defeat on land at Plataea. In their enthusiastic exploitation of that surprising success, the people of democratic Athens gave Greek civilization a lasting expression, partly in political acts and visual art but primarily through works of literature that became classical in subsequent centuries.

Soon after alphabetic writing had reached Greece from Phoenicia in about 700 B.C.E., the Homeric epics were written down. Homer's example inspired the subsequent flowering of Greek literature, for even though the pursuit of justice was always the foundation of the polis, an equally conscious pursuit of fame, truth, and beauty was not far behind. Those aspirations, in turn, inspired an extraordinary outpouring of poetry, drama, history, and philosophy that defined the good life for later generations of Greek and Roman citizens.

Medical and physical science simultaneously took off in new directions when a few bold thinkers supposed that just as citizens of the polis ordered their lives by obeying laws expressed in words, physical nature too perhaps obeyed laws that might also be set forth in words. This stab in the dark generated a multiplicity of ideas such as the atomic theory of matter that were destined to a great future. Scientists and philosophers simply disregarded all the confused and conflicting tales about the gods set forth in the poetry of Homer, Hesiod, and others, and trusted instead to their own powers of verbal reasoning.

The absence of authoritative priesthoods to make sense of the jumble of inherited ideas about the gods made this possible. The polis magistrates who became responsible for conducting religious rituals cared more for splendor and spectacle than for coherent doctrine. The effect was to unleash speculative thought, checked only by acute observation of celestial and earthly phenomena and of human behavior as well. For a few centuries a handful of philosophers were therefore free to apply verbal and mathematical reasoning to human affairs and natural phenomena, and did so with such success that subsequent philosophers continued to study their surviving writings, down to the present.[9] Rival schools eventually codified Greek philosophical and scientific ideas into convenient guides for upper-class living. The initial tumult of intel-

---

[9] At about the same time, Chinese thought exhibited a similar efflorescence when rival warring states (traditional date 403-221 B.C.E.) discredited older moral and religious ideas. And, as in Greece, initial efforts to understand everything soon hardened into rival schools that still continue to command the attention of Chinese scholars.

lectual exploration began to subside when heartfelt questions raised by Plato (died 347 B.C.E.) gave way to Aristotle's (died 322 B.C.E.) logical and plausible answers to almost everything his predecessors had discussed.

Aristotle's achievement coincided with Macedonian conquest of Greece that ended the political and military autonomy of Greek cities in 338 B.C.E. After that, the nexus within which Greek art, literature, and thought had flourished dwindled away, although royal patronage, especially of science, continued to produce new and important medical, astronomical, and geographical ideas.

Long before the eclipse of polis sovereignty ended the classical age, profound contradictions inherent in the polis ideal had become painfully evident. Energetic pursuit of collective glory by one polis quickly turned into attack on the autonomy of others. This collided with deep-seated notions of justice, so empire building, first by Athenians, then by Spartans, led only to failure, as rival coalitions formed to defeat them. Then a Theban drive for dominance was cut short by Macedonian conquerors, first by King Philip in 338 B.C.E., and then by his son, Alexander (reigned 336–323 B.C.E.). The resulting loss of political autonomy hobbled polis life profoundly, but did not eclipse Greek civilization. Instead, when Alexander of Macedon conquered the Persian Empire between 334 and 331 B.C.E., the old heartlands of Southwest Asia and Egypt suddenly came under strong Greek influence, because the Macedonian generals, who divided up Alexander's empire among them, relied on thousands of Greeks to help manage their kingdoms.

The empire of Alexander the Great spread superficial aspects of Greek culture—athletic games, theater performances, and wine drinking—as far as India, along with Greek styles of monumental art and some scientific and philosophical ideas. More important was the way in which Greek-style urban markets took root across Southwest Asia and in Egypt, thanks in large part to a sudden infusion of coinage minted by Alexander's successors from the royal treasure Persian kings had accumulated.

A monetized economy began to emerge when private lenders made loans to state officials and in return acquired the right to collect money taxes from ordinary folk. These tax farmers often used extortionate methods to get their money back, as the evil reputation of "publicans" in the New Testament shows; but the effect was to impose a money economy on a large proportion of the population in the anciently civilized lands of Western Asia and Egypt for the first time.

Bankers' loans to merchants also allowed long-distance trade to assume far larger scale, and had the effect of extending the reach of market prices across political and cultural boundaries more powerfully than ever before. As a result, much of Eurasia and North Africa became tangled in a far-ranging commercial network, centered primarily on Mediterranean coastlands, but supplemented by overland commerce, reaching eastward to China by caravan and northward into Europe and Asia along navigable rivers. Moreover, the ancient sea trade along the shores of the Indian Ocean and across the waters of Southeast Asia linked up with this intensified Mediterranean trade system when Greek seamen from Egypt learned how to sail to and from southern India before the monsoon winds, beginning about 120 B.C.E. Sea links between China and India also became routine after about 140 B.C.E., though portage across the Kra isthmus in Malaya raised the costs of transport substantially. The Old World Web thus began to operate far more intensively than before, disseminating attractive techniques and ideas as well as goods and services across wider and wider regions.

Within Southwest Asia and Egypt, a novel form of urban self-government also established itself among hundreds of Greek colonies founded by Hellenistic rulers. Such cities were not free in the classical sense, since they dared not challenge royal military power. Instead, they confined public life to maintaining order locally, adjudicating legal disputes, managing festivals, and constructing temples, theaters, and other outward trappings of polis living.

Implanting such semiautonomous cities in Southwest Asian and Egyptian society provided a new basis for subsequent compromises between imperial bureaucracy and local urban elites. But in the rural landscape, which always predominated, social arrangements remained as before. In Greece itself society tended to lose its old cohesion, dividing sharply between rich and poor, and coming to resemble the West Asian pattern. So, when Roman armies conquered Greece and extinguished the last vestiges of polis autonomy (215–146 B.C.E.), the Greeks finally succumbed to imperial, bureaucratic governance at the same time that the Roman elite was succumbing to the charms of what had by then become an exclusively upper-class style of Greek urban culture.

The rise of the Roman Republic (ca. 509–30 B.C.E.) recapitulated Greek polis history, with some notable variations. Patricians, deliberating in the Senate, countervailed the power of ordinary Roman citizens more effectively than Greek aristocracies had done. But the military basis of Roman citizenship closely resembled the Greek, even after tactical and equipment changes made Roman legions far more flexible, and able to operate on uneven terrain where Greek-style phalanxes could not.[10] Then, during the Second Punic War against Carthage (218–201 B.C.E.), when Roman armies remained in the field for years on end and started to operate overseas, citizen-farmers recruited into the ranks ceased to be farmers and instead assimilated themselves to the professional soldiery that had long supported imperial bureaucratic government in the civilized lands of Asia and Egypt. Not surprisingly, therefore, Roman victories fastened bureaucratic imperial government on the city-states of Greece after 146 B.C.E. and on all the rest of the Mediterranean world by 30 B.C.E.

With the inauguration of the Roman Empire by Augustus in 30 B.C.E., the reality of active citizenship disappeared. But city life persisted and spread to new ground (especially in the western provinces), and nostalgia for the glorious civic past remained alive until long after 180 C.E., when undisguised military autocracy triumphed in the Mediterranean world. Long before then, however, narrow oligarchies had supplanted the wider franchises of Greek classical and Roman republican times. Commoners became mere spectators at public ceremonies, and dependent rural populations did not even enjoy spectator status. Instead, they paid the rents and taxes that supported a handful of urban landlords in hundreds of Roman provincial towns who did their best to remember and mimic ancient freedom and glories.

Thus, Greek and Roman republican patterns of state and society were eccentric and lasted only a few centuries. But the literature they produced preserved ideals of freedom and citizenship even after the last traces of the Roman Empire disappeared. Later generations retained limited familiarity with this literature until, beginning about 1300 C.E., competing city-states emerged in parts of Italy, whereupon the similarity of their public life with that of antiquity suddenly gave new relevance to the study of ancient texts. Ideals of freedom and citizenship took on fresh life. They were later adapted and applied north of the Alps in the much larger states of Western Europe. Then, beginning in the eighteenth century and continuing to our own day, further adaptation and adjustment spread ideals of free and democratic government around the world.

Quite a career for such small and exceptional states, but under-

---

[10] After difficult hill fighting in southern Italy, sometime around 370 B.C.E. the Romans subdivided their legions into smaller units called maniples that could still maintain an unbroken shield front on rough ground. In addition, javelins and swords replaced the heavy spears Greek and Macedonian phalanxes had relied upon.

Map 3.5 The Roman Republic as of 50 B.C.E.

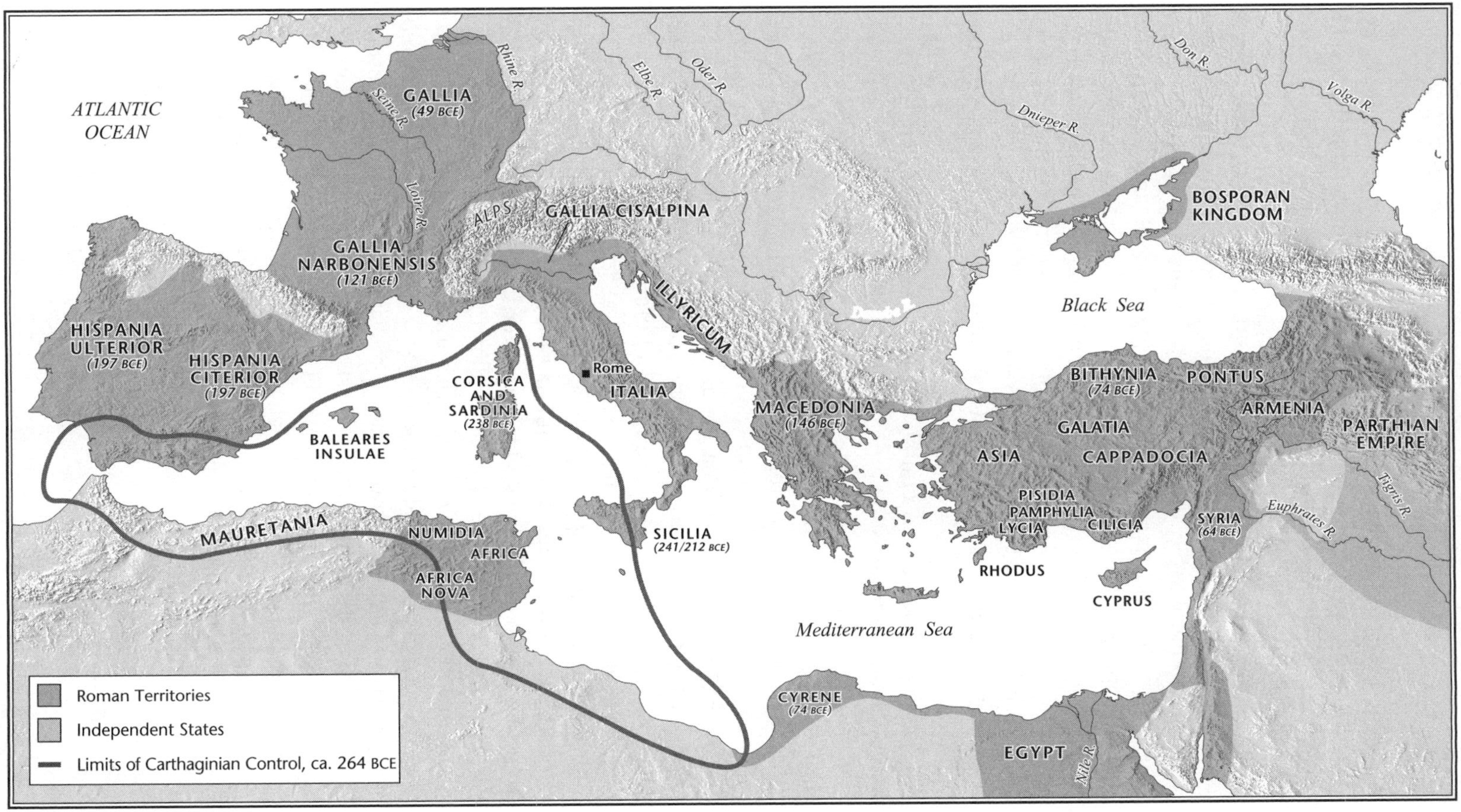

ATLANTIC
OCEAN

Rhine R.

Seine R.

Loire R.

Elbe R.

Oder R.

Danube R.

Volga R.

Don R.

Dnieper R.

Tigris R.

Euphrates R.

Nile R.

GALLIA
(49 BCE)

GALLIA
NARBONENSIS
(121 BCE)

HISPANIA
ULTERIOR
(197 BCE)

HISPANIA
CITERIOR
(197 BCE)

BALEARES
INSULAE

ALPS

GALLIA CISALPINA

ILLYRICUM

Rome
ITALIA

CORSICA
AND
SARDINIA
(238 BCE)

SICILIA
(241/212 BCE)

MACEDONIA
(146 BCE)

Black Sea

Mediterranean Sea

BOSPORAN
KINGDOM

BITHYNIA
(74 BCE)

PONTUS

GALATIA

ASIA

PISIDIA
PAMPHYLIA
LYCIA

CILICIA

CAPPADOCIA

ARMENIA

PARTHIAN
EMPIRE

SYRIA
(64 BCE)

CYPRUS

RHODUS

CYRENE
(74 BCE)

EGYPT

MAURETANIA

NUMIDIA

AFRICA

AFRICA
NOVA

Roman Territories

Independent States

Limits of Carthaginian Control, ca. 264 BCE

standable if one remembers how polis and republican government reconciled two apparently incompatible advantages, combining the wealth and power of urban, civilized states with the freedom, equality, and cohesion of tribal society.

After the crucifixion of Jesus (ca. 30 C.E.), when Christianity began to spread through the Roman Empire, a new kind of community became accessible to humble city dwellers, and eventually filtered into the countryside as well. Christianity began as a Jewish sect, and inherited the Jewish scriptures and tradition, along with the New Testament,[11] which recorded and interpreted Jesus' life and teachings. Converts from pagan society brought their own ideas with them; and when Christians rejected the Jewish law, as elaborated by generations of rabbis, the church went its own way, developing ideas, rituals, and a way of life for believers that blended Greek and Jewish heritages.

Active participation in church affairs—attending religious services, aiding the sick, and resisting pressures to conform to pagan practices—was a real substitute for the vanished polis community; and the hope of Heaven made earthly hardship more bearable. In short, Christian churches created a new identity and community for the poor and oppressed of the Roman world, and soon began to flourish beyond Roman borders in Mesopotamia and as far away as India.

At first, Christians had to compete with several other new "mystery religions" in Mediterranean cities, and churches remained few, small, and inconspicuous. This changed after 165–180 C.E. when the Roman Empire suffered catastrophic epidemics that probably reduced the population by about a quarter. The Chinese Empire also experienced serious epidemics at almost the same time. The ever-tightening Old World Web was responsible for these disasters, allowing travelers and armies to extend infections across older boundaries and introduce lethal diseases to inexperienced populations at the western and eastern margins of the web. By contrast, so far as very imperfect records show, new disease exposures had far smaller effect on African, West Asian, and Indian populations.

Lethal epidemics did not cease in 180 C.E. and, by reducing the wealth and population of the Roman and Chinese empires, contributed to their collapse. Moreover, since Christians coped with lethal epidemic much more successfully than any other element in Roman society, the

---

[11] An agreed canon including twenty-seven books in the New Testament eventually emerged on the authority of St. Athanasius of Egypt (died 373 C.E.).

church began to flourish as never before. Thereafter, within the Roman Empire, pagan society retreated before the advancing Christian tide, signifying a new era in Mediterranean and world history.

Before exploring that era, a brief summary of what had happened around the globe between 3000 B.C.E. and 200 C.E. may help to put the experiences of the diverse Eurasian and North African civilizations into perspective.

Population, Environment, and Disease

Substantial growth of human numbers was basic. By the beginning of the Common Era, the Han and Roman empires had populations of about 60 million apiece. Elsewhere no worthwhile estimates are possible, but substantial population growth in most parts of the earth is certain, for food producers continued to expand at the expense of hunters and gatherers wherever suitably fertile soils could be found. Hunters and gatherers still occupied Australia as well as a good deal of Africa, Southeast Asia, and most of the Americas in 200 C.E., and some Pacific islands had not yet been colonized at all. But a massive global shift toward village life was an accomplished fact.

By 200 C.E. the vast majority of human beings lived in such communities, and a growing proportion of them were paying taxes and rents to urban-based rulers and landowners. The rise and spread of civilized imperial states attests to this transformation. In addition, the four principal civilizations of Eurasia were matched by emergent civilizations in North and South America. We describe them in the next chapter, since their classic form was still in the making in 200 C.E.

Growing numbers, reinforced by the large-scale coordination of human effort characteristic of civilization, had a strong environmental impact. Deforestation was the most conspicuous result, promoted by the spread of farming, the pasturage of sheep and especially of goats, and the use of charcoal to feed metallurgical furnaces and pottery kilns.

In Mediterranean coastlands and through much of Southwest Asia, deforestation and resultant erosion had begun to damage farmland by 200 B.C.E. The Greek countryside emptied out after 323, for example, partly because alternative careers opened for so many Greeks in Southwest Asia and Egypt, and partly because so many Greek hillsides had lost their topsoil. Something similar happened in southern Italy. In

China, too, expanding cultivation of soft, loess soils invited rapid erosion. As a result, the Huang He (Yellow River) began to carry even more silt than before, and became a periodic menace. As the flow of the river slowed across the flat floodplain, silt sank to the bottom and raised the riverbed. As a result, the Huang He earned its nickname—China's Sorrow—by repeatedly breaking through restraining dikes and flooding far and wide before new dikes could be built and the cycle begin anew.

Salinization of the plains of Sumer made them completely barren. Other forms of soil damage also occurred, especially along the frontiers of agricultural expansion where slash and burn cultivation in former forestlands often mined the fertility of shallow soils. But in most agricultural landscapes, once fallowing, manuring, crop rotation, and other customary practices became standard, land degraded much more slowly, so that contemporaries normally did not notice it. Egyptian agriculture, thanks to the Nile flood, was indefinitely sustainable. But farmers everywhere still had to worry about bad weather, insect plagues, and infections that brought occasional crop failure and famine.

Human health was also precarious. The rise of cities intensified the circulation of germs that attack the intestinal tract. Most Eurasian and North African cities had become so unhealthy by 200 C.E. that they had to depend on migrants from the countryside to maintain their numbers. On top of that, urban demographic vulnerability was dramatically enhanced by the advent of new kinds[12] of viral herd diseases. The disease disasters that afflicted the Roman and Han empires in the second century C.E. were provoked by such viral herd infections, spreading among dense, intercommunicating populations with no inherited or acquired immunities to blunt their lethal effect.

Such diseases—recently familiar as childhood afflictions like smallpox, measles, mumps, and a few others—were onetime risks, since they either killed their hosts or provoked lifelong immunities. Large numbers—up to 300,000 persons in frequent contact with one another—were required to assure the constant availability of susceptible hosts. As the fate of the Roman and Han empires showed, getting used to them by building up the necessary antibodies was a slow and demographically costly process.

---

[12] New to humans, that is, for they were transfers from animals, occurring only when human populations achieved sufficient size and density to sustain them, and after domestication made close contacts between living animals and humans normal. Consequently, they were and remain distinctive diseases of civilization.

Conclusion

By 200 C.E., epidemiological adjustment to higher population densities was far from complete in Eurasia, and had not begun in other parts of the earth. The same can be said of the social and psychological adjustments dictated by urban life and the encounters among strangers it generated. Nonetheless, two opposite and enduring reactions had emerged clearly. This was due to the profound ambivalence created among peoples outside, or on the fringes of, the metropolitan webs, who, recognizing their own vulnerability, either sought to remedy the situation by borrowing and adapting whatever made others so powerful—or, alternatively, deliberately tried to reject outside corruption by defending, strengthening, and reaffirming what made them different.

Consequently, as skills, goods, and attitudes spread from the heartland of each civilization, a cultural slope defined itself, and social and environmental strains multiplied everywhere along it. Whenever local elites chose to imitate civilized ways by striving to acquire urban habits and luxuries, they had to betray local rites, rights, and custom. They often had also to intensify and commercialize agriculture to support their new tastes. When local leaders instead repudiated civilized seduction, that too introduced strains since it meant strengthening older ways—somehow. Within agrarian empires, similar social tensions opened between capital city and provinces, and, most conspicuously of all, between rulers and subjects, and among all the diverse ethnic and occupational groups that gathered into cities.

Yet these very real costs did not stop the spread of civilized society. The wealth and power generated by its high levels of exchange and cooperation were too attractive, outweighing inherent social tensions. Moreover, as we saw, a powerful antidote for personal distress was already at hand in the form of portable religions: Judaism, Buddhism, and Christianity chief among them, soon to be followed by Islam. The sustaining power of such faiths became evident in succeeding centuries, constituting a powerful psychological compensation for the distresses and uncertainties of civilized life. Accordingly, the central theme of the next chapter will be the continued process of expanding, intensifying, and mingling the metropolitan webs, both in the Old World and in America.

IV

THE GROWTH OF WEBS IN THE OLD WORLD AND AMERICA, 200–1000 C.E.

Overland and seaborne transport links, inaugurated shortly before the Common Era, kept the civilizations of the Old World persistently in contact with each other across the eight centuries with which this chapter is concerned. Resulting interactions wrought three principal changes: (1) shifts in relative wealth and power raised India and Southwest Asia to new levels of prosperity and influence; (2) the Old World Web spread civilized forms of society to new ground, incorporating vast new areas of Asia, Africa, and Europe; and (3) universal religions offering hope of eventual compensation for the pains and disappointments of everyday life spread widely among the peoples of Eurasia and Africa. The net effect was to increase human numbers, wealth, and power and to make the injustices and inequality inherent in civilized society more bearable. During these same centuries, peoples of the Americas created a parallel web embracing the civilizations of Mexico and Peru together with a circle of interacting societies surrounding and connecting these two primary centers. But a later start and weaker communications meant that technical skills and mobilization of human effort for common purposes in the Americas lagged far behind what Eurasians and North Africans within the Old World Web could do.

Shifts in Relative Wealth and Power

The breakup of the Roman and Han empires, together with epidemics and violence accompanying subsequent invasions, severely damaged urban and agricultural populations both in the far east and in the far

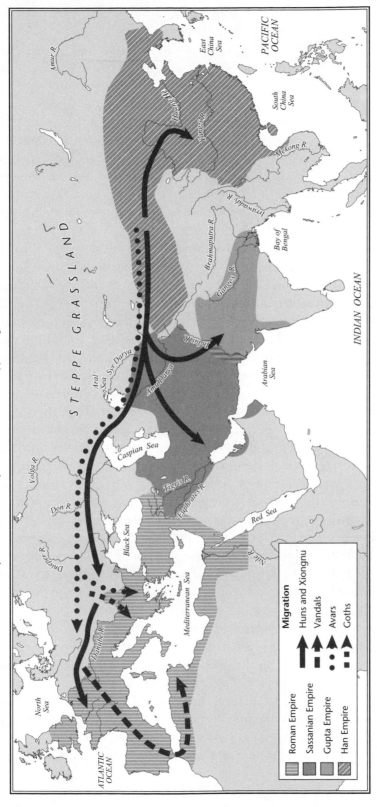

Map 4.1 Eurasian Imperial Frontiers and Steppe Migrations, ca. 200–600 C.E.

Migration

Huns and Xiongnu

Vandals

Avars

Goths

Roman Empire

Sassanian Empire

Gupta Empire

Han Empire

Eurasia. Mediterranean Europe suffered most. Population
urban centers withered, and, with the decay of literacy, a dark
that lasted until almost the end of the millennium. North
China underwent similar experiences, but recovered sooner, thanks
largely to resources derived from population growth in the Yangzi Valley
and regions further south. But what happened in North China and
Mediterranean Europe was exceptional. Nearer the center of the Old
World Web, in India and Southwest Asia, this was a time of economic
and cultural efflorescence; consequently, these regions influenced others (including China and backward Europe) by exporting manufactures,
skills, and knowledge just as civilized centers had always done.

Shifting military balances between steppe raiders and civilized
defenders go far to explain why the Mediterranean and China underwent similar setbacks while the center of the Old World Web continued
to flourish. The critical change was this: the Parthians in Iran invented
effective local defenses against steppe attacks, thereby diverting steppe
raiders toward less well defended frontiers to the east and to the west.

The Parthian kingdom dominated northern Iran (247 B.C.E.–224
C.E.), profiting from its position along Eurasian trade routes. Its military
achievement was simple but also costly. A Parthian warrior class arose
whose members were able and eager to resist raiders from the steppes
because their own well-being required them to protect the plowing peasants who paid them rents. These warriors equipped themselves and their
heavy horses with enough armor to make hostile arrows ineffective. With
bowshots of their own they could therefore repel attackers quickly and
routinely. But dispersed armored cavalrymen were unruly subjects, and
the Parthian kings eventually saw their power disintegrate. Their successors, the Sassanians (226–651 C.E.), presided over a tumultuous array of
formidable fighting men who sometimes followed royal commands but
often defied them, or engaged in local struggles among themselves.

Parthian-style armored cavalry required big, strong horses—the
"blood-sweating" steeds that had provoked the Chinese emperor Wudi in
101 B.C.E. to send an expedition to the west and thus inaugurate regular
caravan connections across all of Asia. Such horses required better forage than grew naturally on the open steppe. This established a military
standoff, for steppe peoples could not prevail against armored cavalry
nor easily support such expensive horses themselves, and, conversely,
heavy cavalrymen could not pursue steppe raiders very far onto the open
grasslands where their horses could not find sufficient forage.

Hay made from cultivated alfalfa was what allowed the Iranians to support the new breed of big horses. Since alfalfa could be sown on grainfields in lieu of fallowing, its cultivation did not diminish supplies of human food. On the contrary, bacteria growing on alfalfa roots (and on the roots of other legumes) concentrated nitrogen from the air in nodules underground, thus fertilizing the soil and improving subsequent grain harvests. Moreover, alfalfa grew rapidly enough in spring to crowd out most weeds, accomplishing the main purpose of fallowing. On the other hand, alfalfa required more water than rainfall in the Iranian lands usually supplied. But wherever water could be brought to the fields in summer from melting mountain snows (often by constructing under-ground tunnels, called *qanats*, to tap seeping groundwater), the dry Iran-ian countryside became capable of sustaining areas of very productive agriculture. These, in turn, supported a host of armored warriors who radically transformed Eurasian military-political balances between 200 and 651 C.E. by defending local cultivators so effectively and defying royal authority so frequently.

Recurrent political upheavals in Iran itself and indecisive wars with East Roman (Byzantine) imperial forces absorbed most of the resources Parthian and Sassanian kings could mobilize. Mud brick ruins of a few palaces and fragmentary, often enigmatic texts attesting royal patronage of a revived form of Zoroastrianism and of the new-sprung faith of Manichaeism[1] are all that survive from the high culture of the age. So much has disappeared that accurate appreciation of Iranian achieve-ments is impossible; but their mud brick buildings may have pioneered the domes and mosaic wall decoration characteristic of Byzantine archi-tecture; and from the time of Diocletian (ruled 284–305 C.E.) Roman emperors imitated Sassanian court ritual and symbolism. The Romans also imitated Iranian armored cavalry, hiring mobile corps of cataphracts (to give them their Greek name). But the expense of maintaining such troops severely limited their numbers, since imperial policy did not allow them to escape from central control by living on local rents as their Iran-ian counterparts were doing.

The cities of Mesopotamia prospered under Parthian and Sassanian rule. Their wealth rested partly on the strength of participation via the

---

[1] Mani (ca. 216–276 C.E.) was a self-conscious prophet who claimed to correct the errors of Zoroastrian, Buddhist, and Christian doctrines through his own revelations. He lived in Mesopotamia and the religion he founded spread westward to the Roman Empire and east-ward toward China. Manichaeism resurfaced in medieval Europe among heretics known as Cathars in the thirteenth century, and survived in Bosnia until after the Ottoman conquest in the fifteenth century.

Persian Gulf in intensified trade networks linking the coasts of the Indian Ocean,[2] but mainly on agriculture, thanks to qanat and canal building that extended irrigation further than ever before. Sassanian water engineering, in fact, was not equaled again in the Tigris-Euphrates valleys until quite recently. In addition, sugar cane, cotton, and some other new crops imported from India and Southeast Asia enriched the agriculture of Mesopotamia and the Mediterranean lowlands. Despite serious gaps in surviving evidence, therefore, it seems safe to say that Southwest Asian lands enjoyed considerable prosperity and exhibited impressive cultural creativity in the centuries when Western Europe and North China were reaching their nadir.

India under the Gupta dynasty (ca. 320–535 C.E.) entered upon a classical age, featuring economic expansion, cultural creativity, and religious transformation. Like Sassanian Iran, India's efflorescence rested on intensified agriculture—principally the spread of rice paddy cultivation in the better-watered parts of India—supplemented by wide-ranging trade. The Ganges plain remained the core area, but coastlands of southern India also became seats of vigorous commercial agriculture, exporting spices like pepper and cinnamon to the rest of Eurasia. Cotton textiles constituted an even more important staple of Indian trade and manufacture. Cotton may be native to the subcontinent; and Indians excelled in all aspects of its preparation—especially dyeing the cloth—from Gupta times (and before) until the Industrial Revolution of the eighteenth century disrupted handicraft production of textiles in India and everywhere else. Consequently, Gupta prosperity and Indian exports intensified traffic within the maritime web along the coasts of the Indian Ocean.

Yet India's major influence on its neighbors was religious. Wandering Buddhist and Hindu holy men traveled along the trade routes, bringing a hope of salvation from worldly sufferings to millions across most of Asia. Hindus attracted followers mainly in Southeast Asia; Buddhists ranged more widely, establishing monasteries in Southeast and Central Asia, China, Korea, and Japan. Buddhist art, sacred texts, and a way of life that reconciled holiness with buying and selling in a market economy allowed Buddhist monks to affect the high culture and society of much of Asia

---

[2] Gold, silver, and copper coins began to lubricate Indian Ocean trade and permitted private bankers through loans and letters of credit to expand its scale substantially after the Greek kingdom of Bactria (ca. 190 B.C.E.–40 C.E.) overran part of northwest India and showed other Indian rulers the tax and commercial advantages to be derived from coinage.

Map 4.2 China, ca. 900 C.E.

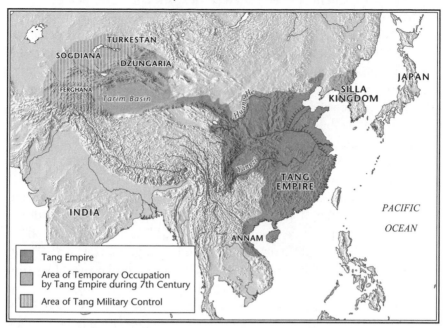

between 200 and 1000 C.E. Even in China, where nativist reaction drove Buddhism underground after 845, Confucians prevailed only by incorporating many Buddhist themes and ideas into their own practices.

The balance among Eurasian civilizations altered again with the reunification of China under the Sui dynasty in 589, and with the explosive emergence of the realm of Islam between 622 and 751. China's political-military unification endured, at least in name, under the Sui (581–618), Tang (618–907), and Song (960–1279) dynasties. This reflected a greatly expanded potential for the exercise of central, imperial power, thanks to the completion of the Grand Canal in 611. Formerly the politically dominant north and the economically vibrant south had been precariously linked by seagoing vessels that were much at risk to storms and pirates. But the opening of the Grand Canal inaugurated safe, cheap water transport between the lower Yangzi and the Huang He valleys. This allowed imperial administrators to expand their resources enormously by using canal boats to bring taxes in kind from the burgeoning south to support armies stationed along the northern frontier. The canal also brought the imperial court a flood of precious goods from near and far.

Reaffirmation of Confucian traditions among the Chinese landowning class also strengthened the intellectual and moral acceptance of imperial government by educated officials. The Confucian revival involved ingenious reinterpretations of classical texts to answer questions raised by Buddhist teachings and rituals. China's Confucianism therefore began to resemble other religions more closely as it acquired a stronger emphasis on the supernatural. And when Confucians persuaded the government to persecute Buddhism and other foreign faiths after 845, they confirmed a mounting xenophobia nurtured by China's persistent vulnerability to armed incursions from the steppe.

Since steppe horsemen could always move faster than infantry, however numerous they might be, China's defenses to the north and west remained problematic. China's enlarged material resources could indeed support vast armies, and the Sui emperors used such armies to invade Korea, while the first Tang rulers pushed their armed forces (including numerous cavalrymen) deep into Central Asia. But armies stationed on distant frontiers were difficult to supply and hard to control, as the Tang emperors discovered in 755 when massive revolt broke out along the northwest frontier. The Tang dynasty was rescued only by the armed intervention of Uighur Turks from Central Asia, who subsequently extracted heavy subsidies from an impoverished court. Imperial resources gradually shrank as provincial Chinese military commanders found it possible and even necessary to support forces under their command by intercepting tax income before it reached the capital. After 960, the Song dynasty restored more effective central control over Chinese armies, but the emperors remained unable to expel steppe invaders from China's northernmost provinces.

The heavy tributes paid to steppe peoples had the effect of spreading Chinese goods and ways across the eastern steppelands and deep into Central Asia. There was a lot to spread, for massive growth of Chinese numbers, especially in the south, sustained economic expansion and an impressive elaboration of artisan skills and of high culture, establishing norms for subsequent Chinese painting and poetry, and much else. Consequently, long-distance caravan trade into Central Asia and India, and overseas commerce with adjacent coasts and islands from Korea and Japan to Java, spread a Chinese sphere of influence through Central and Eastern Asia that remained robust despite Muslim challenges.

Muslims took over the central role as custodians and builders of the Old World Web after 634. They introduced a new civilization of their own based on God's revelations to the Prophet Muhammad (ca. 570–632 C.E.), combined with heritages from pagan Arabia and selected borrowings from the Jewish, Sassanian, Greco-Roman, and Indian traditions. The rapid emergence of Islamic civilization is the preeminent example in human history of how ideas proclaimed by a single person can change the lives of millions and hundreds of millions within a generation and across subsequent centuries. The Old World Web that made this possible already existed. What Muhammad did was to inject a powerfully attractive new message into the web, one that resonated far and wide.

As a result, religion became inextricably mingled with war and politics when Muhammad fled from his native Mecca in 622 to become ruler of the nearby oasis of Medina. Oral revelations believed to come from God, and later gathered into the Qur'an, shaped the conduct of the Community of the Faithful that gathered around him. The conviction that God was with them in every encounter with unbelievers allowed the Muslims to return victoriously to Mecca in 630 and unite all the tribes of Arabia before Muhammad died in 632. That conviction was powerfully reinforced by a spate of decisive victories over Roman (Byzantine) and Sassanian (Persian) armies between 634 and 651. Christendom survived due to the failure of Muslim arms before the walls of Constantinople in 673–78 and again in 717–18, but renewed victories on far-flung frontiers of the realm of Islam—in Spain and northwest India after 711, and against the Chinese in Central Asia in 751—seemed to prove that the Islamic faith did indeed have God on its side.

Camels provided the only material basis for Islam's initial victories. The Arabs, having mastered the arts of camel management, had larger numbers of these animals at their disposal than anyone else, and so could supply their armies across desert landscapes more effectively than their rivals. This advantage goes far to explain the geographic range of the initial conquests, extending from North Africa and Spain in the west to Iran and its outliers in the east. Yet religious conviction among the Arabs, and the bonds of solidarity that went with it, contributed more to the extraordinary early Muslim victories than camels did.

Intensive religious faith swiftly defined a new style of civilization throughout the realm of Islam. Despite local divergences, Muslim society acquired a distinctive stamp from daily religious prayers and other observances, supplemented by the Sacred Law, painstakingly constructed on the basis of the Qur'an and traditions about how Muhammad and his associates had conducted themselves in daily life. Moreover, the religious requirement of learning Arabic in order to memorize and recite the Qur'an, together with the duty of pilgrimage to Mecca by all who could afford it, kept elites from all parts of the expanding Muslim world at least loosely in touch.

But political and military leadership after Muhammad's death in 632 presented an awkward problem. The first three caliphs, successors to the Prophet, were chosen by informal consultation among an inner circle of leading Muslims. Then in 656 the caliph Uthman, a member of the Umayyad family, was murdered and Muhammad's son-in-law, Ali, emerged as victor from the civil war that followed. In a second bout of warfare, his son Hussein was killed (680) and the Umayyad family, from its base in Damascus, made good what became a hereditary claim to the caliphate. The Umayyad caliphate lasted until a rival Meccan family, the Abbasid, overthrew them in 750 and moved the capital to Baghdad.

Many pious Muslims found the resort to armed violence for choosing the caliph appalling. Some, known as Shi'a, chose to remain faithful to the memory of Ali and Hussein, and refused to accept the legitimacy of either Umayyad or Abbasid rule. They became an enduring opposition to the military and political leaders of the Community of the Faithful. The Sunni majority recognized the victorious Umayyad and Abbasid successors to the Prophet as chosen by God to manage military affairs; but they relied on private experts in the Sacred Law to settle religious matters and most other questions of conduct. The resulting split between Sunni and Shi'a, and the gap between religious-social and political-military leadership, created fault lines within the Community of the Faithful that still endure.

Another enduring trait of Muslim society was inherited from the Meccan alliance of townsfolk with nomads. Close cooperation between urban merchants and the nomadic tribes of camel herders who staffed and protected their caravans had sustained Mecca's trade for centuries. Muhammad himself had traveled to Byzantine Syria as a merchant before becoming a prophet. As a result, Muslims respected merchants and the habits of the marketplace far more than rulers of earlier empires had done. Camels also became more numerous and important than before, and informal urban-nomad alliances became characteristic of the new Muslim society. Conversely, farming peasants and rural landowners found themselves subordinated to rulers and policies favoring merchants and herdsmen. Not surprisingly, agriculture suffered setbacks in Mesopotamia and surrounding regions. In Spain, however, it reached new heights, thanks to new South Asian crops and irrigation techniques that the Muslim conquerors brought with them from drier regions.

Map 4.3 Muslim Expansion to 900 C.E.

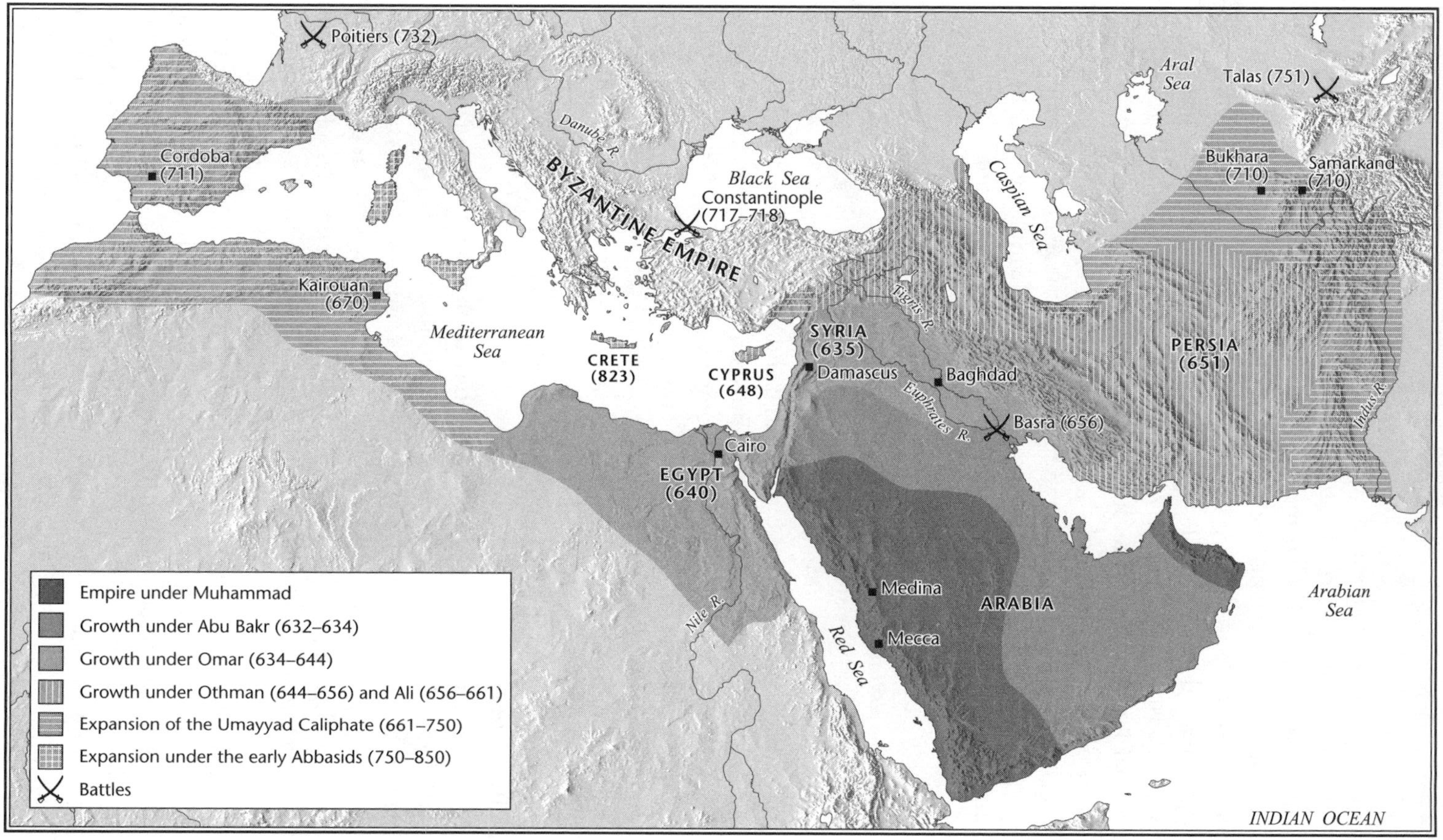

INDIAN OCEAN

Arabian
Sea

Samarkand
(710)

Talas (751)

Bukhara
(710)

Aral
Sea

PERSIA
(651)

Caspian Sea

ARABIA

Basra (656)

Baghdad

Medina

Mecca

Tigris R.

Euphrates R.

Red Sea

SYRIA
(635)

Damascus

Black Sea

Constantinople
(717–718)

CYPRUS
(648)

Cairo

Nile R.

EGYPT
(640)

BYZANTINE EMPIRE

CRETE
(823)

Danube R.

Mediterranean
Sea

Poitiers (732)

Kairouan
(670)

Cordoba
(711)

Indus R.

Empire under Muhammad

Growth under Abu Bakr (632–634)

Growth under Omar (634–644)

Growth under Othman (644–656) and Ali (656–661)

Expansion of the Umayyad Caliphate (661–750)

Expansion under the early Abbasids (750–850)

Battles

The Muslim faith was slow to spread into the countryside. The Qur'an required the faithful to tolerate Christians and Jews as long as they submitted to a head tax. That made Muslim rulers reluctant to diminish tax income by encouraging conversions. Accordingly, Muslims, Christians, and Jews lived side by side for centuries, and each religious community was expected to manage its own affairs, subject only to taxes and a few other constraints imposed by Muslim rulers. A complex process of mutual accommodation set in. Muslims found much to appropriate from the urban sophistication of their new subjects. Conversely, the victorious Muslim faith attracted large numbers of converts, especially among Iranians, who allowed the Zoroastrian religion to dwindle away until only a small remnant survived in northwest India—the Parsees of today.

The umbrella of early Islam brought far-ranging economic exchanges together under one roof as merchants constructed a far-flung economic web. They could operate from Morocco to Iran and (by 700) find Muslim law and a consistent notion of contract wherever they went. Camel caravans linked the river valleys and oases more closely together, mobilizing new productive capacities. The frontier land of southern Spain, for example, became conspicuously prosperous under Muslim caliphs, thanks to new irrigation works and crops such as sugar and citrus fruits, introduced from further east. The enhanced web of trade also utilized shipping on the Mediterranean, Red, and Arabian seas, underwriting the magnificence of Cordoba, Fez, Cairo, and other trading cities. Muslims, Christians, and Jews all took part in this commercial activity, but prosperity required unity and peace within the realm of Islam, a condition difficult to maintain.

The major challenge to Muslim unity came from the Iranian frontier with Central Asia. The collapse of the Sassanian state in 651 was accompanied by a mysterious decay of the rural Iranian warriors who had previously guarded the countryside so effectively against steppe raiders. Perhaps their agricultural income diminished as centuries of irrigation allowed salt to accumulate in the fields, or underground water supplies may have shrunk from overuse or from climate change. Or perhaps Iranian landowners, once converted to Islam, preferred the comforts of town living where the prescriptions of their new faith could be properly observed. No one knows. But the practical effect was an increasing intimacy between Turkic tribesmen from the steppes and the urban centers of Southwest Asia. In particular, the Abbasid caliphs came to rely on bodyguards of Turkic slaves for their personal protection; whereupon, as early as 861, slave soldiers began to intervene in Abbasid court intrigues and eventually made the caliphs into their puppets. Provinces broke away completely, and by 1000 Turkic adventurers and conquerors, converts to Sunni Islam, wielded political power over most of the Southwest Asian heartland. Islam's always precarious political unity thus became a mere pretense.

A second challenge to Muslim unity and Abbasid leadership arose in North Africa when, in 909, a man who claimed to be descended from Muhammad's daughter, Fatima, proclaimed himself to be the Mahdi, destined to restore true Islam by assuming his rightful role as caliph of the Community of the Faithful. His movement, an extreme form of the Shi'a version of Islam, attracted enthusiastic support from Berber tribesmen living in the mountains of North Africa who, under the Fatimid banner, quickly won control of coastal cities in Morocco, Algeria, and Tunisia. One of the Mahdi's successors conquered Egypt and made Cairo into his capital; but by then the initial religious enthusiasm had waned, and the Fatimid caliphs of Egypt (968–1171), like their Abbasid rivals, found it safer to rely on slave soldiers. Nevertheless, a Shi'a underground, more or less sympathetic to Fatimid claims, enjoyed considerable support in many parts of the Abbasid domain, making Sunni Muslims and their rulers insecure at a time when their claim to divine favor was weakening as victories over Christian and Hindu unbelievers ceased.

Muhammad's revelation from God claimed to correct errors that had crept into Jewish and Christian scriptures, and as long as Muslim armies remained victorious, that claim seemed persuasive to all concerned. But the situation changed when, in 718, for a second time, Muslim besiegers failed to capture Constantinople. Until then it seemed as though the Byzantine Empire might go the way of the Sassanian state, bringing almost all Christians under Muslim sway, as had happened to Zoroastrians. After 718, however, Christians could again believe that God still favored them. Subsequent fluctuations of the military-political balance between Christendom and Islam, though substantial, never shook each side's commitment to their respective versions of the one True Faith. Consequently, Crusade and jihad—raid and counter-raid—came to prevail in Christian-Muslim borderlands, even though trade and intellectual contacts were never broken off.

Western Eurasia thus divided into antagonistic religious blocs. Almost the same thing happened in eastern Eurasia, where after 845 the attachment of China's ruling elite to their own, predominantly Confucian traditions began to set them against foreign religious and other cultural influences, despite innumerable encounters with Manichaean

Uighurs, Buddhist Tibetans, and Muslim traders who established themselves in urban ghettos along China's coastal and steppe frontiers. Yet stiffened resistance to the Muslim faith among Confucians and Christians did not prevent the rapid spread of new skills, crops, and ideas among the civilized peoples of Eurasia and into surrounding regions as well.

Expanding and Thickening the Old World Web

Improved transportation extended the web almost throughout Eurasia and North Africa—and beyond. Seafaring on the stormy waters off Northern Europe assumed a new significance and technical capability when Viking raiders, traders, and settlers from Scandinavia began to traverse the Baltic and North seas and then ventured into the Atlantic, settling Iceland (875), Greenland (982), and Newfoundland (only briefly) soon after 1000. Seafaring in the Indian and Pacific oceans underwent an even more significant geographical expansion and technical improvement, but we have nothing like the Icelandic sagas to tell us exactly what happened or when.

Nonetheless, it seems safe to surmise that the invention of outriggers to stabilize dugout canoes even in turbulent seas made possible the lengthy Polynesian voyages that led to settlement of such distant places as Easter Island and Hawaii (both settled around 400 C.E.), and New Zealand (about 1300). But Polynesian settlers on these remote islands did not maintain contact with the rest of the world. In contrast, ships traversing the Indian Ocean and western Pacific created an increasingly capacious trade network that embraced all the coastlands of the Asian mainland and extended to the Indonesian islands to the south and the Japanese archipelago to the north.

Little is known about how these ships were constructed, manned, or financed. But we can be sure that navigational skills and naval architecture improved across time, allowing ships to sail long distances out of sight of land. As a result, by about 400 C.E. the western Pacific and Indian oceans became a single sea room. Previously ships had hugged the coast and unloaded cargoes for portage across the Kra isthmus of Malaya. This exposed merchants to frequent levies by local authorities all the way from India to China and back again. But when ships began to sail straight across the Bay of Bengal and rounded the Malay Peninsula into the South China Sea, they reduced protection costs radically by putting in to fewer ports. As protection costs shrank, and as coinage and banking became everywhere familiar, long-distance trade markedly expanded in scale. Commodities like cloves and nutmeg from Indonesia, gold and ivory from Africa, porcelain and silk from China, pepper and cotton from India, and much else began to circulate far more widely and in greater quantities than before.

Caravans also connected previously isolated people and places more cheaply and regularly when camels became the standard beasts of burden. Domesticated camels had been known as curiosities in Southwest Asia from about 2000 B.C.E., but they were difficult to manage and to ride, and almost impossible to load until, by or before 200 C.E., the invention of a high-built saddle circumvented the fatty hump by resting the weight of rider and/or load firmly on the animal's rib cage.[3]

This invention made camels far superior to horses or mules as pack animals in desert landscapes, for they carried heavier loads and could feed on thorny vegetation. Arabia and adjacent parts of Northeast Africa were the first places to exploit saddled camels' capabilities and, as we saw, the art of camel management spread far and wide with the victorious Muslim armies. Consequently, the steppes and deserts of Central Asia and the African Sahara became far more permeable than before, allowing new commodities—African gold and Turkic slaves, for example—to flood into Muslim cities. The use of camels also had the effect of banishing wheeled transport (and the costs of road maintenance) from the Muslim heartlands since camels carried loads cheaply and could traverse swampy, rough, and rock-strewn landscapes, not to mention narrow alleys in cities and villages, where carts could not pass.

The enhanced range and carrying capacity of ships and caravans between 200 and 1000 extended and strengthened the Old World Web especially along the oceanic coasts and through the dry belts of Southwest Asia and North Africa. Civilization ceased to be exceptional as the exchange of crops, manufactures, ideas, diseases, and other aspects of civilized life altered human experiences almost everywhere. Before 200 C.E., civilized societies had extended only spottily within the Old World Web. By 1000, further southward expansion brought much of Africa and the whole of Southeast Asia and offshore islands into the circle of Old World civilization. Northward expansion involved fewer people but a wider area, affecting Korea, Japan, and Northern Europe, and folding all

---

[3] The saddling of horses to anchor stirrups, introduced about 200 C.E., may have stimulated nomads of the northern Arabian desert to design the more complicated saddles required to fit camel anatomy. See Richard W. Bulliet, *The Camel and the Wheel* (Cambridge, MA, 1975).

the peoples of the steppes and northern forests into an ever closer symbiosis with civilized agrarian populations. As a result, by 1000 the Old
World Web had attained unexampled size, embracing nearly all of Eurasia and much of Africa, and entangling perhaps 200 million people.

Among the many changes involved in this process of expansion, the
spread of rice paddies in southern Asia affected more persons than any
other single transformation of the age. Paddy fields increased food production enormously, but only at the cost of exposing the harvest to
seizure by outsiders—whether raiders or tax and rent collectors. Garden-
style cultivators of southern Asia presumably resisted the spread of rice
paddies, as the survival of numerous "forest peoples" until our own time
in India, Southeast Asia, and Indonesia suggests. But rice meant more
food as well as more work, even when rulers and landowners took a large
share of the harvest; and more food, in turn, meant more people. As a
result, between 200 and 1000, pioneering Indian and Chinese rice farmers steadily encroached on all the various forest peoples living between
their respective heartlands, and put vast new contiguous territories and
much enlarged resources at the disposal of their respective ruling
classes. India's prosperity under the Gupta and China's recovery under
the Sui after 589 depended on this laborious transformation of forest,
swamp, and floodplain into artificially diked and leveled paddy fields.
One of the world's great blocks of tropical forest slowly retreated to
make room for rice.

Wherever rice cultivation established itself at greater remove from
the Indian and Chinese core areas, newly consolidated independent
states took root with the rice plants. Korea, for example, had acquired
rice from China before 1000 B.C.E., but only after about 100 C.E. did the
enormously productive combination of irrigated rice, iron tools, and oxen
for plowing take hold. It undergirded the southernmost of the three
kingdoms that dominated Korea for seven centuries before the Silla
dynasty unified the peninsula (618–76 C.E.). Buddhism became the state
religion in these same centuries, while Confucian learning and Chinese
script also took root and became the main ingredients of Korean aristocratic culture. To enhance its revenues and power, the Silla (618–935)
spread irrigated rice cultivation to every suitable valley in Korea,
although in the north barley and sorghum remained important crops.

Japan recapitulated the same process a little later. Wet rice reached
the Japanese islands about 300 B.C.E., but only after 250 C.E. did it
become sufficiently widespread to sustain the Yamoto state from which
Japan's imperial line descends. The arrival of Buddhist monks from Korea

in 552 brought literacy to Japan and established much more intimate contact with the mainland. And when in 593 the Japanese court decided to patronize the imported faith, the Buddhist connection permitted systematic importation of Chinese ideas and practices, even though, away from the court, Japanese rural society remained defiantly itself.

Similarly, in all of the principal river valleys of the Southeast Asian mainland, as well as on the islands of Java and Sumatra, new states arose as rice paddies spread to geographically favorable locations, and trade contacts with India and China multiplied. Nearly all of the new-sprung monarchs of the region elaborated on diverse local traditions by importing court ritual and religion from India. They presided over farming populations who, in proportion as they began to rely mainly on rice, found themselves trapped into sharing the harvest with tax and rent collectors, since the ditching and diking needed to create paddy fields was too much of an investment to abandon. But age-old styles of shifting cultivation, supplemented by fishing, hunting, and gathering, survived in many locations, quite beyond the reach of tax collectors. Such forest peoples occupied far more of Southeast Asia than they did of India itself. As a result, the court circles of Southeast Asia, and the palace-temple cities they inhabited, remained semiexotic enclaves amid surrounding tropical gardeners.

The extension of the web to remoter islands, like the Moluccas (in today's Indonesia), brought different results. There the local way of life remained close to the sort of tropical gardening traditional among the forest peoples of Southeast Asia even after the islanders began to produce cloves, nutmeg, mace, and other condiments for export. Exactly what induced or compelled the commercial production of these spices is unknown. But to judge by the organization of the trade in the sixteenth century, family-scale cultivators did the work, turning the spices over as a kind of tribute to local chieftains, while feeding themselves from their own gardens as before. Yet the power and wealth of local rulers remained modest since they sold spices to foreign merchants who kept most of the profits for themselves. As a result, the outward trappings of civilization did not much disturb local society on the Moluccas, even after these small islands began to sustain a very profitable export of cloves and nutmeg.

In Africa, expanding sea and caravan trade networks affected fewer people across a larger geographical area between 200 and 1000. Slender links by sea were already ancient. Egyptian pharaohs had sent ships to southern Arabia and down the African coast in search of gold and myrrh, for example, and in Greco-Roman times sea trade intensified when

Mediterranean sailors learned about the monsoons and started to travel regularly between the Red Sea and southern India. The kingdom of Aksum, based in the Ethiopian highlands near the mouth of the Red Sea, prospered by contributing gold, ivory, and other precious goods from the African interior to this trade. About 350, connections with Egyptian Christians persuaded the king of Aksum to make Christianity the official religion of state. Christian kingdoms survived in Ethiopia and Nubia even after Muslims cut them off from the coast; but once Egypt and North Africa came under Muslim control between 636 and 711, African contacts with the rest of the world were chiefly with Muslims.

Camels spread into Africa from Arabia, starting about the beginning of the Common Era and reaching as far as Lake Chad by 300 C.E. when caravan travel across the Sahara began. Urban merchants had operated within the Niger River valley for at least 500 years before the opening of trans-Saharan routes began to stimulate placer gold collection and salt mining in the desert. This encouraged state formation in West Africa along the boundary between desert and savanna land, wherever seasonal river floods sustained millet and root-crop agriculture. Rulers acquired prestige goods such as woven cloth from across the Sahara, and organized the collection and export of gold and desert salt in return. African merchants began to favor Islam before 800, and the first (known) African king to become a convert did so in 985. Before then, West African rulers refrained from accepting the faith, with all the advantages of literacy and participation in the wider world that Islam brought with it, since conversion required repudiation of claims to sacred power derived from local religious traditions. Nonetheless, as regular caravans began to connect the pastoral and settled populations of West Africa with the Mediterranean coastlands, the North African version of Islamic civilization seeped southward across the desert, preparing the way for West Africans to participate more fully in the world of Islam shortly after 1000.

The centuries between 200 and 1000 also brought sharp changes to East Africa. The Old World Web affected societies along the East African coast through two distinct contacts. The first issued from the eastern shores of the Indian Ocean. By or before 500 C.E., mariners from what is now Indonesia had ventured as far as Madagascar, bringing Southeast Asian food crops with them. Indonesian bananas, yams, and taro thrived in moist conditions, whereas African millets and sorghum did not. Consequently, when these Asian crops reached East and Central Africa, they allowed more rapid settlement of forest zones, especially around the Great Lakes. Bantu speakers, descendants of migrants originating in today's Cameroon (West Africa), took them up and used them to colonize well-watered parts of the East African interior.

East Africans subsequently intensified their contacts with Southwest Asia. Iranian pottery from the fifth to seventh centuries C.E. has been found as far south as Mozambique, and Chinese pottery from the eighth or ninth century, relayed via the Persian Gulf, was familiar in coastal towns of modern-day Kenya. When Red Sea and Persian Gulf mariners adopted Islam in the seventh and eighth centuries, they brought their faith to the East African coast. The first mosque in the region, large enough for only nine worshipers, dates from the eighth century. Islam soon spread up and down the coast, until the growing cities became predominantly Muslim and developed a local language, Swahili, strongly influenced by Arabic. But Islam scarcely penetrated beyond the coastlands, since trade links to the interior were controlled by Bantu-speaking Africans who remained content with their own religions for centuries to come.

The extreme south, and areas of the African interior where agriculture and herding were unrewarding, remained the domain of hunters and gatherers. But human settlement of most of the continent had been transformed by new crops, iron technology, and the expanded range of camel caravans and of cattle herding before the turn of the millennium. Africa, in short, had become a frontier region of the Old World Web.

The African interior remained a frontier for a long time, because of ecological and geographic constraints. The fact that humans had evolved in tropical Africa amid a complex array of parasites kept human population growth in check. In many parts of Africa, malaria, yellow fever, sleeping sickness, river blindness, and other lethal and debilitating diseases restrained not only settlement and population growth but communication, specialization, and urbanization as well, despite ingenious efforts at environmental management. Moreover, in much of tropical Africa, cattle, horses, and camels suffered from a fly-borne disease (trypanosomiasis) that made it impractical to use these beasts for transport. African diseases proved even more dangerous to outsiders, which helped keep them out, and delayed the interior of Africa's full inclusion into the Old World Web until the nineteenth and twentieth centuries. Africa's geography exercised a parallel effect. Its great rivers—the Niger and the Congo, for example—are admirably suited to shipping, but they are all cut off from the sea by rapids or waterfalls near their mouths, making linkups between maritime and riverine trade more difficult in Africa than elsewhere.

To the north, the entire length of the Eurasian steppe also joined the web more fully during these same centuries. Steppe nomads retained distinctive ways of life, riding on horseback and guarding their herds when they were not hunting wild animals or raiding agricultural settlements. But raiding was never an efficient way of getting what they wanted. Randomly assorted booty always had to be exchanged for what they needed and really valued. This, in turn, required steppe raiders to tolerate merchants and protect the goods merchants carried across the steppe.

An obvious way to make circulation of goods between nomads and settled populations more efficient was to negotiate protection costs directly. Steppe chieftains who could deliver protection from raids in return for desired products from distant artisan workshops could also expect to confirm their power locally by distributing prestige goods among their followers. Civilized rulers, in turn, could hope by such an arrangement to assure themselves of uninterrupted tax income from their rural subjects who were spared destructive raids. Mutual advantages were obvious, yet difficult to sustain since the leaders both of civilized governments and of steppe confederations were perpetually liable to challenges from discontented subordinates who preferred to pursue the riskier, but more immediate, rewards of raid and rebellion.

All the same, the violence that so often disrupted trade-tribute arrangements between pastoralist confederacies and civilized governments only made interaction between herdsmen and farmers more intimate, especially when it led to nomad conquest of civilized populations. That was what happened when the Toba confederation (probably headed by Turkic-speaking nomads, but comprising other language groups as well) ruled northern China between 368 and 534, for example. Similarly, when the Huns appeared in Europe and began to raid far and wide from headquarters in the Hungarian plain (374–453), they triggered Germanic migrations that erased the Roman border along the Rhine and Danube and eventually made Northern Europe part of a new, Christian society, uniting Mediterranean and Baltic coasts and all the lands between.

Within the steppelands themselves, the repeated emergence and disruption of far-ranging confederacies between 200 and 1000 had two general consequences. First of all, these recurrent political-military upheavals provoked a long series of migrations across the steppe, for defeated peoples regularly fled toward choicer grasslands, seeking pastures either to the southeast in Manchuria and North China, or westward in the direction of the Ukraine and Hungary. This explains the long succession of newcomers to Eastern Europe between 200 and 1000, for Europe's raiding and conquering Huns, Avars, Bulgars, Khazars, Pechenegs, and Magyars were, in fact, refugees, fleeing from other nomad groups further east.

A second, more significant change provoked by political-military turmoil among the steppe peoples was that they all became accustomed to allowing caravans to pass safely in return for protection payments that were low enough to allow long-distance trade to continue. Records do not reveal exactly how appropriate attitudes and understandings were propagated; but the spread of Buddhism, Manichaeism, the Nestorian form of Christianity, and Islam among the oases of Central Asia and then across the open steppes registered and promoted the change.

Pastoral peoples, possessing an abundance of suitable animals, had taken part in caravan trade from the inception of their distinctive way of life. But caravans on the steppes expanded their scale when barges and sleighs began to carry goods up and down the rivers of Russia and Siberia, bringing the northern forestlands into regular contact with the grassland and, by caravan, with settled agricultural landscapes further south. The result was to weave steppe nomads into a long-distance trade net, allowing them to supplement what they produced for their own consumption with furs from the north and with grain and manufactures, like silk or metal goods, from the south. With these imports, exposure to new religious and other ideas and techniques reached everywhere across the steppes and began to seep into the northern forests as well. But nomadism, requiring frequent movement to new pastures, severely limited what steppe peoples could incorporate into daily routines, while the combination of hunting and gathering with slash and burn cultivation, which prevailed among the forest peoples of Siberia, kept them even more marginal.

In the far west, ever since Neolithic times, the mild, moist European climate created by westerly winds blowing across the Gulf Stream had allowed a modified Southwest Asian style of grain agriculture to flourish on unusually well drained soils. Cattle grazing and shifting, slash and burn cultivation prevailed in less favorable locations. The heavy clay soils of the North European plain were too waterlogged for grain to prosper until, near the beginning of the Common Era, a new sort of heavy plow improved drainage. Early experiments met with enough success to support increasing numbers of German farmers in the Rhinelands. As a result, their reliance on cattle diminished and grainfields multiplied, so that when Roman frontier defenses collapsed in the fifth century, German settlers surged across the Rhine and displaced Latin-speaking populations from its west bank. Others crossed the North Sea and turned Celtic Britain into Anglo-Saxon England by bringing that island's clay soils under cultivation for the first time.

Heavy plows, equipped with a moldboard that turned a furrow over to one side, were the instruments that eventually allowed the previously waterlogged clay soils of Western Europe to become permanently productive grainfields. They did so by piling the soil into "lands," with lower "baulks" between each land, thus creating an effective system of artificial drainage. But for several centuries after such plows had been invented, their cost, and the difficulties in assembling plow teams of six to eight oxen needed to drag them through the soil, hindered their use. Nevertheless, the heavy moldboard plow and associated methods of cooperative cultivation did spread, so that, by 1000, between the Loire and the Elbe rivers, a carpet of grainfields began to stretch across the landscape, replacing ancient forests and swampy meadows, and changing what had previously been a backward, thinly inhabited part of the world into a productive, growing node within the Old World Web.

The spread of moldboard plow agriculture across the plains of Northern Europe invites comparison with the earlier, and more extensive, spread of rice paddies in monsoon Asia. Both added to the extent and complexity of the Old World Web and, in time, altered the balance of wealth and power within it.

Yet for a long time local disorder and renewed invasions held Western Europe back. Three successive waves may be distinguished amidst the turmoil: initial Germanic invasions of France, Britain, Spain, and North Africa between 378 and 489, precipitated by flight from the Huns; a second wave between 568 and 650, precipitated by the arrival of the Avars in Hungary, that drove Lombards to Italy and Slavs into the Balkans; and a third wave between about 800 and 1000, when repeated assaults by Viking seafarers from Scandinavia, Magyar horsemen from Hungary, and Spanish and North African Muslims subjected Western Europe to even more severe raids than before.

This triple attack provoked what proved to be a very effective local defense in the form of a swarm of European knights, dedicated, like their Parthian and Sassanian predecessors, to the defense of villages from which they drew the rents that supported them. Unlike Iranian heavy cavalrymen and Byzantine cataphracts, European knights disdained archery, preferring to concentrate the momentum of a galloping horse at their spearpoints by charging headlong against the foe. Protected by suits of chain mail, and equipped with swords and battleaxes for close-in combat, such warriors proved formidable indeed. Instead of suffering invasions, as had been the case for centuries, European knights spread rapidly from their initial home in northern France and the Low Countries, and started to prevail on every front—expanding their domain west into Great Britain and Ireland, south into Spain and Sicily, east across the Elbe, and, with the First Crusade (1099), as far afield as Jerusalem.

The Byzantine Empire survived a long series of formidable assaults in these same centuries, thanks to the elaborate fortifications and defensible location of its capital at Constantinople (now Istanbul). Since ships could provision the city from the shores of the Aegean and/or the Black Sea whenever an invading army interrupted access to the city's immediate hinterland, attackers needed superiority both by land and by sea. Until 1204, none of Constantinople's numerous besiegers—Persians, Arabs, Avars, Bulgars, Rus—possessed that capability. This, in turn, allowed the survival of a Christian version of urban life and culture in the Aegean, Adriatic, and Black sea coastlands while a Western European version of Christian civilization was slowly taking form. In the centuries before 1000, both versions of Christian civilization, Western and Eastern, Latin and Greek, attracted Celtic, Germanic, and Slavic peoples. This was part of the general religious reconfiguration of Eurasia and Africa.

New Roles for Religion

Portable, universal religions, whose emergence we discussed in chapter 3, took new forms and attained far greater prominence throughout the Old World Web shortly after 200 C.E. Daily experience took on a new character when hope of a blessed afterlife began to loom large in private consciousness; and the new faiths quickly elaborated new rituals, new styles of art, and new bodies of learning that blended elements from Indian, Iranian, Jewish, and Hellenistic traditions into distinctive and enduring forms. Disasters and injustice became more bearable when sufferers could anticipate future blessedness. The new religions also made alms giving a religious duty for relief of the poor, the sick, orphans, and other sufferers in this world. In addition, joining a successful religious community often brought economic advantages, as merchants who became Muslim readily discovered.

An ambiguous alliance between rulers and religion was a leading feature of the new age. Official patronage of religious institutions—monasteries, temples, churches, mosques, and madrassas—benefitted donor and recipient alike, yet also limited arbitrary royal or imperial power by subordinating rulers to the same moral and religious rules as everyone else. This style of alliance between throne and altar originated in Iran, when the first Sassanian monarch rose to power in 226 C.E., by championing a revived and revised form of Zoroastrianism. But since Zoroastrianism withered after 651 when Iranians went over to Islam en masse, Sassanian religious policy made less impress on the world's subsequent history than did the Roman emperor Constantine's conversion to Christianity in 312. He favored Christianity conspicuously, but did not prohibit traditional paganism or other faiths. Under his successors, however, Christianity became in 395 the only legal religion in the Roman Empire. Christianity also spread eastward as far as China along the caravan routes, and traveled by sea to India and Ethiopia. But, except in Ethiopia, in these parts Christianity remained a slender, alien implant.

Buddhism had far wider reach. From India it traveled by sea to Southeast Asia, beginning soon after Buddha's death (ca. 483 B.C.E.), and helped to shape the official faiths of local kingdoms there. Beyond the Himalayas, Buddhist monks outnumbered Christians along the caravan routes of Central Asia and soon penetrated China, Korea, and Japan. Large-scale conversions, followed by handsome endowment of Buddhist monasteries, dated from 317 C.E. when a ruler of North China embraced Buddhism, and, like his contemporary Constantine, devoted state resources to advancing the new religion. In ensuing centuries official patronage and private conversion turned China into a Buddhist land to all outward appearances, even though Confucian and Daoist[4] learning persisted among conservative scholars and landowners who disliked foreign ideas and practices. From China, the Buddhist path reached Korea, where three rival kingdoms became officially Buddhist between 372 and 528. As we have seen, Buddhist missionaries in Japan also attracted imperial patronage, beginning in 593.

Yet while Buddhism was winning millions of new adherents in East

---

[4] Daoism combines age-old popular rituals built around reverence for powerful local spirits with a tradition of literary learning that stressed spontaneity and an intuitive response to *Dao*—inadequately translated as "The Way" (of all things). Daoist observances borrowed much from Buddhism between 400 and 800, allowing Daoism to rival and complement Confucianism throughout China's subsequent history.

Asia, a newly consolidated Hindu religion displaced it from its Indian homeland. The shift became apparent when the Gupta dynasty (ca. 320–535 C.E.) preferred Hinduism to the Buddhism favored by their Maurya (ca. 321–184 B.C.E.) predecessors. Although wealthy Buddhist monasteries continued to flourish in India during the Gupta era, Buddhism was losing its hold. After invaders from Central Asia plundered Buddhist shrines and monasteries between 490 and 549, devastated monastic communities were not reconstituted, presumably because the Hindu path to salvation through personal identification with either Siva or Vishnu had by then become more attractive for most Indians than the path to Nirvana pursued by wealthy and privileged communities of Buddhist monks.

Buddhism also met with a serious setback in China when, in 845, resentful Confucians persuaded the Tang emperor to close thousands of Buddhist monasteries and confiscate their extensive landholdings. Chinese Buddhism survived underground in popular, sectarian forms that occasionally flared into open rebellion in subsequent centuries, whereas in India Buddhism imperceptibly disappeared, having become, in Indian eyes, only one of many paths for escaping the illusions and sufferings of everyday life, and a needlessly austere, emotionally inaccessible path at that.

Yet Hinduism was not a missionary faith. The emotional vivacity of Hindu ceremonies, and the personal identification that ecstatic worshipers attained with one or another avatar (embodiment) of Siva or Vishnu, never spread much beyond the subcontinent and enclaves of migrant Indians overseas. On the other hand, mystical techniques elaborated among Indian holy men infiltrated Christian monasticism from its inception, and transformed Islam after 1000; while Buddhism brought more obvious Indian influences to all the different religions of East Asia. But the revalidation of innumerable local cults and forms of worship that Hinduism sanctioned, treating any and every local divinity as another embodiment of ultimate spiritual reality, was not exportable. Hinduism's toleration of radically diverse customs and beliefs lacked the doctrinal cohesion of religions based on a limited canon of sacred texts. In short, endorsement of radically diverse and logically incompatible paths to salvation fitted well within the caste system of Indian society, but not elsewhere.

When the abrupt emergence of Islam sharpened religious differences throughout Eurasia, Hinduism came to be more closely confined to the subcontinent. Muslims initially treated Hindu forms of worship as abominable idolatry. Moreover, Islam *was* a missionary religion. When

Muslim military conquests ceased, its expansion took more peaceable forms, since wherever Muslim merchants went they carried their faith with them. No doubt the emotional resonance of Judaism, Hinduism, Christianity, and Buddhism hindered the wholesale acceptance of Muhammad's revelation. But where Muslims encountered pagan peoples, mass conversions soon followed. Turks of the western steppe proved to be especially receptive to merchant-missionaries, nearly all of them becoming Sunni Muslims by 1000. And, as we saw, a parallel process began in Africa as well.

Christians met with similar success across Roman borders in Northern Europe, where monks and other clerics (rather than merchants) preached the saving truths of Christianity to the Celtic, Germanic, and Slavic peoples. Conversion was much assisted by the fact that Christian concepts of government confirmed and expanded the power of local rulers. A Christian clergy, by introducing literacy, could also strengthen state administration and make it more uniform. Accordingly, by the year 1000 missionaries brought all of Europe within Christendom, save for a pocket of paganism along the south shore of the Baltic. Lithuanians, the last to convert, did so definitively only in 1387.

The religions of salvation that spread so widely differed in innumerable respects, yet some commonalities are worth noting. First of all, Buddhism, Christianity, Hinduism, and Islam fundamentally redirected older expectations. Instead of promising divine help in assuring worldly prosperity and protection, as nearly all religions had previously done, they redirected human aspiration toward an eternal, transcendental world—Heaven, Nirvana, reunion with Siva and Krishna, or Paradise, as the case might be. Moral rules for everyday behavior were not relaxed; instead, they were reinforced by fear of eternal punishment in Hell, or, for Hindus and Buddhists, miserable, unending reincarnations.

Such a shift fitted the distressing facts of civilized urban life far better than before. After all, the interdependence among occupational specialists that made cities wealthy and powerful were also persistently unstable, blatantly inequitable in good times and liable to painful breakdown in bad. Hope of redress in a future life made unfairness and disaster on earth easier to bear, since for survivors, despite all hardships, human life still held promise of a better future after death. Peasants, too, welcomed the prospect of future redress for all they endured. Such hopes probably reduced the frequency of peasant rebellion. In short, sustaining hope in time of trouble was the greatest single gift the new faiths gave to individual human beings. Consequently, the spread of these faiths made the social differentiation of civilized society easier to maintain, restore, and extend to new ground. This congruence explains the intimate connection between conversion to one or another of the religions of salvation and the rapid propagation of civilized states and societies across Eurasia and Africa that was such a prominent feature of the centuries between 200 and 1000.

A second distinctive trait, shared by all the religions in question, was that each human soul qualified individually for salvation or damnation. A sort of accountancy between benevolent savior and repentant sinner determined the outcome. Moreover, women had souls as much as men, and took on some important new roles. In particular, they transmitted their faith to children, making conversion hereditary and rooting the new religions firmly in everyday family observances. Women also did charitable work, and sometimes acquired new rights, such as those of inheritance. At the least, new religious rules and rituals defined gender relations more clearly than before, consoled widows and orphans, and sometimes helped to relieve their needs with alms.

Thirdly, religions of salvation connected rulers and ruled through shared subjection to God's will, or, in the Indian religions, subjection to karma that defined each soul's future state. Rituals provided an even stronger link. Buddhist, Christian, Hindu, and Muslim ceremonies varied enormously, but each religion developed emotionally powerful forms of public worship, shared in by rulers and subjects alike. Gifts of landed property to religious institutions made them wealthy, allowing rapid elaboration of the splendor and aesthetic appeal of the ceremonies they conducted. Priests and monks who benefited directly from such gifts reciprocated by preaching obedience to the royal gift givers. The long-standing alliance between throne and altar thus acquired enhanced emotional vibrancy—usually and normally, but not always.

That was because profound ambiguities lurked in the political patronage these faiths attracted. Was a ruler obligated to be just, pious, and doctrinally correct? If he fell short, did rebellion become a religious duty? Rigorous sects frequently came to that conclusion, thus endowing rebels with a sacred cause to propagate, often in secret, and occasionally by force. Consequently, Christendom and Islam spawned a spate of sectarian challenges to constituted governments; and, not infrequently, heretical versions of the faith came to define and defend social groups chronically at odds with dominant neighbors or rivals. In China, too, Buddhist sects were associated with most of the rebellions that broke out after 845. But as a rule the two Indian faiths were less militant than

Christianity and Islam, accepting the validity of alternative paths to salvation as a matter of course, and not really expecting rulers—caught up, as they were, in the illusions of this world—to be holy, or even just.

Finally, the new religions reworked older traditions of art and thought, propagated literacy wherever they took root, and allowed millions of persons to share a common world of meanings. Different civilizations came to be defined primarily by familiarity with, and reverence for, rules and rituals based on sacred texts. To be sure, authoritative pronouncements by Christian theologians and councils of bishops supplemented the words of the Bible, and decisions by Muslim experts in the Sacred Law amplified the Qur'an, while sacred texts for the Indian religions remained far more abundant and multifaceted. Hinduism treated a pair of epics, the *Mahabharata* and *Ramayana,* together with some devotional hymns, as storehouses of sacred lore, while Buddhist sects foraged through an enormous body of religious writing, sometimes choosing particular texts as guides for their distinctive devotions. But everywhere, literacy, the hope of salvation, and participation in a particular civilization came to be linked closely together, creating religiously defined cultural blocs whose heirs still divide most of the earth.

The religious restructuring between 200 and 1000 spread four main faiths. All four had features that made them especially compatible with the spread of civilization and its discontents. Religions that failed to soothe the faithful in the face of inevitable injustice fared poorly. Dozens were absorbed or obliterated as Buddhism, Hinduism, Christianity, and Islam seeped into the backwaters of Eurasia and Africa, gradually converting remote forest and mountain peoples. They also spread across new frontiers in Southeast Asia, in Africa, and in northern Eurasia from Scandinavia to Korea. In so doing they helped extend the Eurasian web so that it became a genuinely Old World Web, stretching from the Atlantic Ocean to the Pacific, and from Siberian forests to the shores of the Indian Ocean.

Emergence of an American Web

The other big change between 200 and 1000 was the emergence of other metropolitan webs in the Americas, as Mexican and Peruvian centers of civilization spread their influence ever wider, and interacted—at least tenuously—with one another. Connections within the American webs remained weaker than in Eurasia, since transportation lagged far behind.

Llamas, the only available pack animals, carried only about a quarter of the load a camel could bear, and were confined to the Andean regions of South America. Rafts and canoes, however, were universally familiar to Amerindian peoples. Contact by sea between the Mexican and Peruvian centers was obviously far easier than travel on foot over rough terrain. But since wooden rafts and boats leave only the faintest of archeological traces, it is impossible to say exactly when sea voyages began along the Pacific coasts of Mexico and Peru, or when dugout canoes began to paddle among the Caribbean Islands, or up and down the Mississippi and Amazon rivers.

It is possible that immigrants from Asia reached America by sea. The early dates of some archeological finds as far south as Chile at least seem to suggest maritime migration. Moreover, Polynesian voyagers, who reached Easter Island about 400 C.E., may have touched on American shores, bringing sweet potatoes back with them to Pacific islands. No archeological trace of such voyaging is known to exist, but the distribution of sweet potatoes among Pacific islands and the pre-Columbian cultivation of cotton in Peru are standing mysteries. Human portage seems the best answer, but when? how? and why not other things as well?[5]

Before cities or conspicuous ceremonial centers arose anywhere in America it is likely that an American style of tropical gardening took root on the northwest shoulder of South America, just south of the isthmus of Panama. This is where the earliest known pottery fragments have been found, and pottery almost requires a sedentary lifestyle. Archeologists also found grains of cultivated manioc, yams, arrowroot, and maize at a site in Panama, dating from 5,000 to 7,000 years ago. In subsequent times, sweet potatoes and manioc were important crops in American tropical lowlands and, combined with fishing, they probably supported the earliest sedentary settlements in the Americas, just as other root crops seem to have done in Southeast Asia.[6]

Tropical gardens, in the Americas as in the Old World, could not support the elaborations of civilization. That required storable grain.

---

[5] The possibility of early trans-Pacific contacts has impressed a good many Asia experts, but few Americanists take the idea seriously. For a review, see Joseph Needham and Lu Gwei-djen, *Trans-Pacific Echoes and Resonances: Listening Once Again* (Singapore, 1984).

[6] We owe this suggestion to Andrew Sherratt. See Warwick Bray, "Ancient Food for Thought," *Nature*, 408, November 9, 2000, pp. 145–46. There is some evidence for cultivation of arrowroot in Colombia from 9,000–10,000 years ago.

Recent and careful work shows that a long process of genetic selection produced domesticated maize from a very different wild ancestor in Mexico, beginning about 4000 B.C.E. The new crop eventually spread widely in every direction even though its diffusion was hindered by the fact that corn plants had to adjust genetically to different day lengths at different latitudes in order to flourish. And maize, supplemented by beans and squash, in due course supported the Amerindian civilizations of North America, though in South America maize remained secondary to potatoes and quinoa.

The Olmecs began building large mounds along the Caribbean coast of Mexico about 1300 B.C.E. The elites who mobilized the labor necessary for erecting such structures participated in a far-ranging exchange network supplying them with precious goods like obsidian, jade, and cacao beans. Conversely, monumental Olmec stone sculpture and religious-political rituals impressed others so much that subsequent Mayan (ca. 600 B.C.E.–840 C.E.) and inland Mexican (ca. 400 B.C.E.–1521 C.E.) civilizations inherited a rich array of motifs and practices from the Olmecs just as Babylonians and Assyrians did from the Sumerians. But when Mayans learned to write they had no occasion to record relationships with ancient Olmec predecessors, so details are unknowable.

Subsequent connections between the diverse Mexican centers of civilization and those of South America also remain almost invisible. But, in addition to the presence of maize, which appeared in Peru and several other scattered sites in South America after 2000 B.C.E., reliance on raised field gardening in the altiplano around Lake Titicaca may (or may not) attest to the spread from Mexico of a distinctive technique for intensifying agricultural output. Suffice it to say that civilizations of the Maya, of central Mexico, and of the Peruvian altiplano all relied on raised fields to produce the agricultural surpluses that sustained their managerial elites and artisan specialists.[7]

Raised fields were created in swampland and along shallow lakeshores by building up artificial, elongated island-fields, leaving narrow access canals of standing water between them. Ample moisture and fertile alluvium, refreshed from time to time by digging more soil from beneath the water, assured rich harvests from such fields, even in the harsh climate of

---

[7] The Olmecs may well have pioneered the technique since their ritual centers were located in swampy coastal areas; but no archeological evidence has yet been detected. This is not surprising, since no one looked for such traces until very recently, when raised fields were first detected at Mayan and then at central Mexican sites.

the Andean altiplano, where mist from the standing water in and around Lake Titicaca had the additional effect of extending the growing season by protecting potatoes and other crops from frost. In the deserts of the Peruvian coast, irrigation canals, like those of ancient Mesopotamia, sustained a different style of intensive cultivation, but it is plausible to suppose that the spread of Mexican maize and of the technique of raised-field gardening may have gone together. Still, no one can say for sure.

The Mayan cities required elaborate water engineering to keep their raised fields wet during months of drought. They did so by storing water in large, artificial reservoirs (very like those used in South India and Southeast Asia) as well as elaborate sluiceways to deliver the stored water to the fields. During the classic era of Mayan history (ca. 250–840 C.E.), governing elites used the wealth created by raised-field farming to build palaces, temples, and plazas out of stone, decorated with abundant sculpture. They also devised a system of writing (fully deciphered only since 1960); and a calendrical system that used mathematical notation (including the concept of zero) to record dates so precisely that they can now be translated into days and years of our own calendar. Mayan rulers, presiding over rival city-states, derived their legitimacy from a mix of family lineage, ritual access to divine favor, and strong-arm resort to military force. Maize, beans, and squash were the staple foods, supplemented by a variety of roots, tomatoes, peppers, and other plants. A landscape almost totally transformed by elaborate water storage and delivery systems sustained the raised-field gardening and terraced fields that supported dense populations.

The raised fields associated with the principal population centers of the Americas resembled the rice paddies of monsoon Asia. Both altered natural contours of the land; both rerouted surface waters; both produced abundant crops; and both put cultivators at the mercy of managerial elites, allowing elaborate palace-temple structures and other trappings of civilization to develop rapidly in suitably moist locations both in the Americas and Asia.

Yet the Mayan system remained precarious, vulnerable to any unusual drought. Political disorders, accompanying the sudden diminution of resources created by drought, were presumably what led to the abandonment of the Mayan lowlands in the two centuries after about 900. The temples along with literacy and much else disappeared beneath the rising canopy of second-growth tropical forests. In subsequent centuries, Maya speakers lived as slash and burn farmers, without cities or elaborate social hierarchy.

Map 4.4 Amerindian Urban Centers, ca. 1000 C.E.

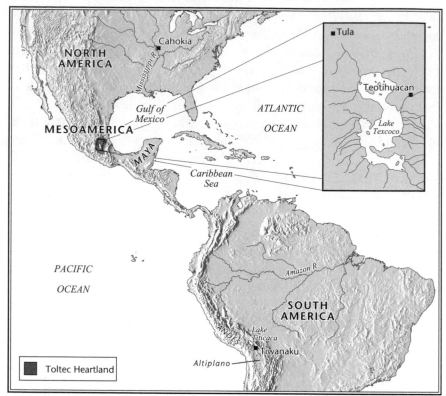

Similar ceremonial centers and political regimes, clustering around the shallow lake that once existed in the valley of central Mexico, were also vulnerable to sporadic disruption. For a while the city of Teotihuacán exerted some sort of imperial sway (ca. 100–700 C.E.) over much of the Mexican interior, including the Mayan cities. But it was plundered about 650, and then, after an interval of disorder, the Toltecs, based at Tula, took over the imperial role, ruling a somewhat less extensive territory from about 800 to 1050. No written records illuminate these events.

In North America in the Mississippi Valley and adjacent watersheds, relatively modest ceremonial centers also arose in suitably rich river bottomlands. The earliest such center, located in Louisiana, dates from about 1000 B.C.E. Further north, massive and abundant Hopewell sites, featuring elaborate earthen mounds, spread along the banks of the Ohio River between about 500 B.C.E. and 500 C.E. The relatively dense populations required to build such mounds depended on fishing, hunting, gathering, and cultivating a variety of crops. Maize was known to

Hopewell peoples, but had only limited, ritual use, presumably in the form of inebriating beer. The presence of copper from Lake Superior, obsidian from Wyoming, and galena from Missouri and Illinois attest to a widespread exchange along the river network. The use of maize indicates some sort of connection with Mexico, and pipes, probably used for smoking tobacco, also suggest links with Mesoamerica.

Hopewell sites were abandoned about 500. Raiders from the north may have disrupted and dispersed ill-protected riverbottom populations by using bows that had come to North America with the Inuit three or four centuries before. At any rate, the Toltecs and their Chichimec allies introduced bows into central Mexico about 800. The professional warriors of Mexico, however, rejected the bow since the capture of prisoners for sacrifice to the sun god was the principal object of their warfare. Arrows that wounded and killed at a distance were useless for such purposes, so, like the Japanese after 1600 who suppressed newly introduced handguns to preserve the way of life appropriate to samurai swordsmen, the Toltecs and their Aztec heirs preserved hand-to-hand combat and disdained missile warfare. The use of the bow for hunting and warfare was routine among Amerindian peoples of the north, as attested by the elaborate earthworks and palisades defending the vast Mississippian ceremonial centers at Cahokia (Illinois) and related sites after about 800. Unlike their Hopewell predecessors, the Mississippians made an improved variety of maize, with larger kernels and cobs, their staple food. As before, they sustained an exchange network for precious goods ranging throughout and beyond the Mississippi basin.

In South America, broad patterns paralleled these developments in Mexico and the North American heartland. Beginning about 2000 B.C.E. irrigation canals, tapping one or another of the short rivers that tumble down from the high Andes, allowed dense populations and ritual centers to arise in the deserts of the Peruvian coast. From the beginning they exploited aquatic riches from the Humboldt current offshore and maintained connections with the Andean altiplano, and with the tropical forestlands of the upper Amazon. Local resources were correspondingly different from Mexico's, for each altitude had its own climate, water regime, and array of plants and animals. As a result, domesticated llamas, alpacas, and guinea pigs complemented potatoes and quinoa that flourished on the altiplano where maize could not ripen; while in the Amazon forests, manioc and other root crops competed with maize. Cultivated cotton, too, supplied fiber that, with hair from alpacas and llamas, allowed Peruvians to turn the weaving of elaborately patterned textiles into a high art. The Mexican triad of maize, beans, and squash, so fundamental in North America, was therefore blended in South America into a much more variegated agricultural (and pastoral) system. Yet the overall pattern of South American development resembled that of Mexico since diverse ritual centers along the coast experienced some sort of subordination first to Chavin (ca. 900 B.C.E.), and then between about 100 and 1000 C.E. to the state of Tiwanaku, located near Lake Titicaca in the altiplano. Teotihuacán and its successor, Tula, did much the same in Mexico.

From the Andean altiplano to the upper Mississippi, an American web was forming by 1000, held together by waterborne transport supplemented mainly by human portage. Its precise character, shape, and extent remain unclear because of long gaps in the archeological record and the absence of written texts (except among the Maya). Although the American web took shape in effective isolation from events elsewhere, resemblances to Mesopotamian and early Chinese history are striking.

Conclusion: Common Patterns

The civilizations of North and South America, Mesopotamia, and China all began when local elites, enjoying special access to the supernatural, organized large-scale agricultural and artisanal effort to ward off divine displeasure. Priestly management was subsequently supplemented and eventually subordinated to much more conspicuously militarized leaders, who extended (often precarious) imperial lordship over wider and wider territories. Simultaneously, long-distance exchange networks circulated luxury and prestige goods across longer and longer distances, propagating familiarity with aspects of civilized capabilities further and further from the principal centers of civilized life.

Close parallels in the development of the Americas, Eurasia, and Africa are apparent. Despite enormous cultural and geographic differences across the continents, it is tempting to suppose that these parallels arose because farming peoples needed the services first of priests and then of warriors to thrive. Farmers had to learn when to plant and how to save enough seed for the next planting. Two kinds of religious rituals, managed by experts, made this possible. Careful observation of heavenly bodies—sun, moon, planets, and stars—allowed priests to determine the proper planting seasons. Other rituals—fasts, sacrifices, and harvest festivals—effectively rationed consumption throughout the year. In addition, when ordinary people, hoping for divine favor, gave gifts of food to the gods, a reserve came under priestly control, which sustained ever more elaborate worship and might also relieve famine in case of need. Thus, farming communities led by priests and regulated by religious rituals were better able to withstand disasters arising from weather, weeds, and pests. Hence the power of priests in early agrarian societies throughout the world.

Priests eventually ceded primacy to warriors, for straightforward reasons. For when priestly management succeeded in creating substantial surpluses, organized robbery became a feasible way of life. This opened a niche for professional fighting men to protect communities from plunderers by monopolizing organized violence in return for negotiated protection payments. Specialized weaponry, discipline, and training gave such warriors combat superiority over most raiders and robbers, allowing both farmers and warriors to benefit from predictable rents and taxes as opposed to the ruinous costs of plunder. Accordingly, professional warriors could and did compel established priestly elites to accept subordination or some form of alliance.[8]

These broad resemblances show that human history evolved along parallel paths even in the absence of direct contact. No one supposes that the development of priest- and then warrior-led states in the Americas owed anything (except the bow) to Eurasian and African precedents. Rather, the dense webs of interaction that grew up in favored locations produced the same kinds of pressures to regulate and defend agricultural societies, producing broadly similar outcomes. There was, nonetheless, a telling difference between the Americas and the Old World. The Americas offered a paltry collection of domesticable animals, making both plowing and pastoralism impossible. This goes far to explain why the wealth and power generated within the American web never approached that created within the Old World Web.

[8] These patterns are persuasively set forth in Johan Goudsblom, Eric Jones, and Stephen Mennell, *The Course of Human History: Economic Growth, Social Process and Civilization* (Armonk, NY, 1996), 31–62.

V

THICKENING WEBS, 1000–1500

Both agriculture and civilization continued to expand to new ground between 1000 and 1500, but more slowly than before because so many of the most favorable regions had already been claimed. Instead, the most significant development was intensified interaction within Eurasia and most of Africa, due largely to improved water transport and to the spread of practices and understandings that facilitated trade and promoted specialization of labor. This was an age of consolidation more than extension of the Old World Web. The same held true in the Americas, where the Andes and Mesoamerica remained the main centers of civilization. They strengthened their links with surrounding regions, a process which generated centralized empires by the 1400s.

Overview

In the Old World Web, the result of this consolidation was greater productivity, the invention and diffusion of new techniques, and a growing ability to mobilize human effort for conscious purposes—religious and intellectual as well as economic and political. As usual, wealth and power concentrated where specialization and mobilization of human effort went furthest and fastest; but, as before, relatively small elites exercised old and new forms of power and controlled new and old kinds of wealth. Populations increased, but haltingly, since lethal infections, most notably bubonic plague, spread along the trade routes of Eurasia. Most ordinary persons were not noticeably better off than before, despite rapid advances in collective manifestations of wealth and power.

Moreover, there was a price to pay. Village solidarities were disrupted wherever peasant farmers began to introduce urban practices into the countryside by learning to buy and sell goods and services on a regular basis. Occupational and property differences had always divided urban dwellers into distinct and sometimes hostile classes. Buying and selling routinely had the effect of dividing villages along similar lines. Commonality weakened as some families prospered by selling surpluses in town instead of consuming them within the village on festive occasions as subsistence farmers had usually done. Other families lost out and had either to work for wages in someone else's fields or supplement what they could grow for themselves by working as part-time artisans, making cloth or something else for sale.

All principal religions of Eurasia deplored unbridled greed, and sought to restrain rulers, merchants, and bankers in their restless pursuit of gain. But religious scruples were incapable of halting the spread of market relations. The Old World Web left the smaller American web and innumerable more isolated human societies further and further behind as its capacity to mobilize common effort for deliberate purposes continued to expand between 1000 and 1500.

Improvements in water transportation sustained and intensified the long-distance exchanges that allowed this process to go forward. With its extensive network of canals and rivers, China was the principal seat of resulting social and economic transformations between 1000 and 1500. Western Europeans expanded the capacity of their communications and transport networks too. They made only minor improvements in the navigable rivers that flowed across the North European plain, but paralleled the Chinese in developing stout, seaworthy vessels for salt-water sailing. Western Europeans also expanded their use of carts, and invested heavily in bridges.

No comparable improvements affected overland transport. Political and economic undertakings in the Muslim heartlands, in Central Asia, and in the African interior (as well as the two core areas in America) therefore continued to operate within limits set by caravan and human portage. But in the interior of India it appears that overland trade and warfare both reached new levels of intensity thanks to the multiplication of bullock carts driven by professional teamsters who hired their services to the highest bidders and lived in specialized quasi-nomadic communities.

On a very different plane, numerical calculation achieved greater range and precision with the spread of place value numeration—what we call Arabic numerals. Large quantities, whether of money or goods, suddenly became almost as easy to keep track of as small ones. The idea of using a symbol for zero consistently was invented in India as early as the third century C.E., but remained unfamiliar (even in India) until the mathematician and astronomer Al-Khwarizmi (ca. 780–850) introduced the idea to the Muslim world.[1] Thereafter, place value decimal numeration spread throughout Eurasia, reaching Europe as an intellectual curiosity shortly after 1000, though most merchants did not abandon clumsy Roman numerals until the fourteenth century.

Every part of the Old World Web participated in the intensified interaction and expanded specialization that cheaper water transport and easier numerical calculation promoted. The ancient spice and cotton trade of Indian Ocean coastlands and offshore islands remained central, and it was mightily reinforced by an infusion of Chinese manufactures—silk and porcelain and much else—beginning about 1000. Sailors of South China and offshore islands in effect joined their commerce with the long-standing sea trade of the Indian Ocean. Regions peripheral to this expanded commercial core linked up with it in varying degrees, depending on transport costs and capabilities.

To the northeast, the Japanese islands developed fishing and commercial fleets, exporting silver and other metals and importing silks and other luxury goods, mostly from China. To the southwest, East Africa expanded the export of gold, ivory, and slaves, and frequent finds of broken porcelain on African beaches show that Chinese goods reached Africa in exchange. To the northwest, during these same centuries, overland portages through Muslim lands brought Indian Ocean spices to Mediterranean coastlands where Italian merchants distributed them.

Italian sailors soon opened direct voyaging to ports ringing the European peninsula, penetrating first to the shores of the Black Sea by conquering Constantinople (1204), and then mastering Atlantic storms and tides to reach ports as far north as the Rhine mouth and the Thames, beginning in 1291. There they encountered an already flourishing sea commerce based in North Sea and Baltic ports. This expanded sea room, connecting to all the lengthy navigable rivers of Northern Europe,

---

[1] Babylonian mathematicians of Hammurabi's age used a symbol for zero in mediate positions, but not at the end of a number, so 202 could be recorded unambiguously, but not 220. Mayans also used a sign for zero, but varying bases for their number systems complicated their arithmetic procedures, and Mayan mathematics disappeared with the collapse of Mayan centers. George Ifrah, *From One to Zero: A Universal History of Numbers* (New York, 1985).

constituted a subordinate theater of rapid commercial growth. Common goods like salt, timber, fish, wool, and grain played a principal role in European sea and river trade; but Asian textiles, spices, and other luxuries, together with European manufactures like woolen cloth and wine, also played important parts. During the fifteenth century, European sailors rapidly expanded the range of their Atlantic navigation, presaging the opening of the world's oceans after 1492. As the Chinese had done before them, European seamen were swiftly transforming even stormy seas into tolerably secure pathways for trade and contact of every kind. As a result, the Old World Web was poised in 1500 to ensnare the rest of the world with catastrophic force and suddenness.

Even in the landlocked interior of Eurasia, boats and sleighs, traversing the rivers of Russia and Siberia, brought the forested zone and much of the steppe into expanded commercial contact with urban centers to the south. The northern forests exported timber, furs, and slaves in much the same way that the landlocked interior of Africa exported gold, ivory, and slaves to Muslim cities of North and East Africa. Simultaneously, in sub-Saharan West Africa, many African kingdoms and cities became Muslim and conducted far-ranging internal trade, in which salt from the Sahara and kola nuts from the rainforests near the coast played a leading part. Slavic and Turkic princes did much the same in the northern Eurasian forests, raiding and trading up and down the navigable rivers of Russia and Siberia, and embracing either Orthodox Christianity or Sunni Islam.

There are no worthwhile statistics of the quantity of goods entering these trade nets, nor of the number of persons whose livelihood came to depend on buying and selling goods and services. But the direction of change is clear. More and more human beings were affected by intensified long-distance exchanges in great or small degree, since the circulation of ideas and skills inevitably accompanied the circulation of people and goods. As a result, buying and selling within the Old World Web exercised increasing influence on the everyday lives of more and more persons. The advantages that groups and individuals everywhere saw in gaining access to otherwise unattainable products drove the process and explains why local disruptions were always temporary.

Nonetheless, these gains were counterbalanced by an increasing inequality, dividing rich from poor, which provoked sporadic, heartfelt, and often violent protest within local communities. Moreover, these gains brought an added element of instability, owing to occasional interruptions of supply. Specialists whose living depended on making goods for sale inevitably incurred serious risks, since they had to rely on complementary and coordinated activities among strangers who sometimes lived very far away.

Yet the five centuries between 1000 and 1500 in Eurasia and Africa were not nearly so unidirectional as these remarks imply. Instead, confusion and cross-purposes everywhere prevailed, with a few nasty surprises along the way. In the thirteenth century, Mongol horsemen under Genghis Khan (ca. 1162–1227) erupted from their sparse grasslands to construct the largest empire of all time, eventually uniting China, Russia, most of Southwest Asia, and almost all the Eurasian steppe under a single sovereignty. Initial destruction was followed by an unprecedented ease of communication. For a few decades, a vast and united Mongol state allowed rapid exchanges of ideas and techniques, as well as the spread of a lethal bubonic infection that ravaged most of the Eurasian continent in the fourteenth century.

The Black Death, as it was called in Europe, brought widespread disaster, just as epidemics of the second century had done. In Europe and Southwest Asia, where the evidence is best, it apparently killed a quarter or a third of the population within six years. It struck (1346–52) when the onset of cooler climate, sometimes called the Little Ice Age (1300–1850), was also inflicting serious crop failures on the northern fringes of the Eurasian agricultural zone. But the "Dark Ages" that steppe raiding and epidemics had previously helped to provoke in China and Europe did not recur. Instead, these were precisely the parts of the world that recovered most successfully from the disease disasters and climatic stresses of the fourteenth century, though China's consolidation of its earlier gains under an imperial bureaucracy inspired by Confucian principles stood in stark contrast to the disorderly merger of commerce with warfare that prevailed in Europe.

The Americas also experienced dramatic upheavals and disasters in these same centuries. In particular, the Cahokia (Illinois) and the Chaco Canyon (New Mexico) ritual centers declined after about 1250, perhaps for climatic reasons; and in Mexico and Peru, older ritual and imperial centers gave way to new as the once marginal Aztecs and Incas created their respective empires. But no transformative enlargement of older capabilities or skills appears in archeological or literary records, and it is probable that ecological difficulties, arising from widespread deforestation and limitations on water supplies for intensive raised-bed cultivation, were already afflicting Mexico and Peru when Spanish conquistadors broke in upon them.

How China Became the First Market Society

A long apprenticeship lay behind China's surge toward modernity after the year 1000. From very early times, China had imported useful things from Western Asia—the seven-day week, wheat, chariots, and cavalry tactics, for example. Local skills and ideas always predominated, but after Buddhism attracted official patronage in the fourth century, a far more pervasive exposure to imported ideas and practices got underway. Richly endowed Buddhist monasteries became centers for diffusing new forms of art, religion, and, not least, market behavior. Monasteries were, after all, economic as well as religious enterprises. Just as in ancient Sumer, suitably splendid worship required a supply of rare and precious goods that gave new scope to long-distance traders.

In the early years of the Tang dynasty (618–907), China's connections with the rest of Asia became especially intense. As long as Tang military power was in the ascendant, lively curiosity about the rest of the world prevailed in China. For example, Chinese monks imported hundreds of authoritative Buddhist texts from India, and then, by systematically translating them, adjusted Chinese minds to Buddhist learning, and vice versa. West Asian religions—most notably Manichaeism, Nestorian Christianity, and Islam—also made modest lodgments in China, and swarms of foreign merchants, arriving mostly from Central Asia, showed the Chinese all there was to know about bazaar trading.

Yet as we saw in chapter 4, once China's military power weakened, a reaction set in. Printing, which first became widespread under the Tang, made Confucian and Daoist as well as Buddhist learning far more accessible than before. After 845, Confucian advisers persuaded the emperor to prohibit foreign faiths and refresh imperial finances by confiscating the land that pious donors had given to Buddhist monasteries. But by then new ideas, new skills, and new outlooks were firmly implanted in Chinese society. Even Confucian scholars found accommodation to new, mostly Buddhist, ideas necessary, elaborating what is known as Neo-Confucianism by asking new questions and discovering ingenious answers by reinterpreting the classic texts.

Acceptance of market behavior had even more significant effects. Buying and selling became more commonplace when Chinese coinage (soon supplemented by skillfully managed paper currency) began to lubricate commerce. Imperial officials modified the ancient Confucian suspicion of merchants so as to allow them greater scope than before. As a result, under the Song dynasty (960–1279), the Chinese economy became increasingly commercialized. Imperial administrators found it convenient to collect taxes in cash rather than in kind, and by the late eleventh century more than half of the government's income took monetary form. This of course required ordinary people to sell something—part or all of the harvest, for the majority—in order to pay their taxes. The government used its cash income to purchase goods and services, often in large quantities, thus sustaining and intensifying market relationships. Cities burgeoned, artisan skills improved, and wealthy landlords and merchants elaborated elegant lifestyles that dazzled outsiders for centuries to come.

Intensified agriculture undergirded this expansion of urban life. Early-ripening rice, introduced from Southeast Asia and first mentioned in Chinese records in the year 1012, allowed farmers in well-watered parts of southern China to produce two crops a year, nearly doubling their harvest at the cost of prolonged hard work in the fields. A single crop of early-ripening rice could also mature on hillslopes where water was only available for a couple of months in the year. Chinese peasants therefore began to construct terraced fields in the hilly landscapes of southern China, vastly expanding the total area of cultivation.

New crops, most notably tea and cotton, also spread widely in China. The practice of drinking tea, steeped in boiling water, undoubtedly reduced intestinal infections by killing off most of the microorganisms that lurk in drinking water. This helped Chinese populations in Tang and Song times to flourish in the warmer and wetter south, an area notoriously unhealthful and only thinly inhabited in Han times. Washable cotton clothing may also have had positive implications for health. It certainly improved comfort for ordinary people, who could not afford silk and had previously worn coarse hempen clothes. All in all, intensified agriculture appears to have kept pace with China's intensified urban manufacturing, assuring the continued preponderance of village life and of an increasingly urbanized landlord class.

Cheap and safe transport along China's rivers and canals was what made the market so effective in concentrating material resources wherever government officials and wealthy private persons wanted them. Canal barges carried tons at a time, and since they relied on wind and current, and used tow ropes only when necessary, they permitted far lower transport costs than overland carriage. Consequently, even small differences in price made it worthwhile to carry local products long distances up and down the waterways. The Grand Canal, connecting the fertile plains of the Yangzi and Huang He valleys after 611, became the main artery of Chinese commerce so that the daily efforts of some 100 million persons came to be linked, far more closely than ever before, by buying and selling in a vast, reliable, well-articulated market.

Cheap transportation allowed goods of common consumption to circulate widely. In favorable locations, a peasant family could concentrate on raising silk worms, or some other commercial crop, and rely on the market for food and other necessities. All the benefits of specialization that Adam Smith was later to analyze so persuasively thus emerged in Song China. Output increased, population grew, skills multiplied, and a burst of inventiveness made Song China far wealthier than ever before—or than any of its contemporaries.

Government officials, who qualified for office by passing written exams based on Confucian texts, presided over this transformation with a wary eye. They still considered wealthy merchants as well as military commanders threats to social justice and good government. Yet in a dangerous, commercialized world, prudent officials could not do without their services. The mandarins attempted to restrain the power of merchants and generals by fixing prices, taxing excessive gains, and occasionally resorting to outright confiscation of their wealth. They sought to weaken generals by subdividing their commands and keeping the delivery of necessary supplies under civilian control.

Such policies limited the mobilization of China's resources. In particular, it made large-scale industrial enterprises evanescent, despite a cluster of high-tech furnaces in North China that, according to surviving tax records, produced no less than 125,000 tons of iron in the year 1078. But China did not launch itself on a self-sustaining industrial transformation like that which came to Great Britain some 700 years later, even though the technological basis for such a takeoff seems, in retrospect, to have existed under the Song. No one knows for sure when or why the coke-fired furnaces that made such great quantities of iron closed down.

In matters military, Song officials wrestled with the perennial problem of supporting a large army to guard against steppe nomads, and met with less than usual success. Nomad confederations had become more formidable than before, thanks to their increasing familiarity with the weapons and administrative methods which Chinese and Central Asian rulers had painstakingly devised to resist them. In particular, tribal and personal rivalries waned when nomad warriors submitted to bureaucratic command and began to fight in arbitrary decimal units—tens, hundreds, and thousands—under commanders chosen and promoted largely on the basis of merit and seniority. Moreover, bureaucratized nomad armies soon learned how to capture walled cities by using catapults, ladders, and other siege engines. Accordingly, the balance between Chinese defenders and nomad raiders tipped markedly in favor of nomad (and ex-nomad) attackers.

This meant that the Song dynasty was never able to control China's northern- and westernmost provinces, where Mongol and Tibetan rulers were busy trying to strengthen their military forces. The shifting balance became clear in 1126, when Jurchen horsemen from Manchuria defeated the Mongols and employed state-of-the-art siege machinery to capture the Song capital, Kaifeng. The Song dynasty survived in the south, thanks to mobile warships that made river crossings dangerous or impossible for the Jurchen horsemen. Rapid development of ship design and projectile weaponry ensued, featuring heavy catapults and novel gunpowder weapons.

Despite such efforts, the river defense line crumbled when the Mongol Kublai Khan, grandson of Genghis Khan, used Chinese labor to build an up-to-date navy with which he conquered all of China by 1279. Kublai also launched a naval attack on Japan in 1274 and again, with greater force, in 1281, but gave up after a typhoon—the kamikaze wind that the Japanese invoked in vain during World War II—destroyed the Mongol fleet while it was anchored offshore. Kublai's death in 1295 also nullified the initial successes of a naval assault on Java, launched in 1293.

Though these overseas ventures had no lasting success, Kublai Khan's empire united China with the rest of Eurasia more closely than ever before. Thousands of people moved back and forth along the caravan routes that ran across the northern grasslands as well as along the ancient Silk Road to the south. And just as China had imported skills and ideas from southwestern Asia in earlier times, in the thirteenth and fourteenth centuries when so many Chinese technologies had become superior, the flow of influence was reversed. Chinese ideas, encased as they were in an ideographic script, were hard to export; but Chinese techniques of painting, printing, compass navigation, gunpowder weaponry, high-temperature furnaces and ovens, and perhaps also shipbuilding found various lodgments among Muslims, Hindus, and Christians. Diverse responses to these new techniques did much to define the subsequent development of each of these peoples. But before sketching China's westward impact, a few remarks are in order about how the Mongol Empire collapsed and the Ming dynasty (1368–1644) consolidated control over a thoroughly commercialized China.

The Mongol conquest, begun by Genghis Khan in 1211 and com-

Map 5.1 Empire of Kublai Khan and Mongol Khanates, ca. 1280

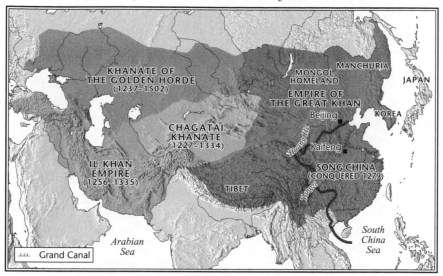

pleted by his grandson, Kublai, in 1279, brought a swarm of foreigners—
Muslims, Buddhists, and even (at least according to his own account)
such an exotic as the Venetian Marco Polo—to high office in China.
Mutual distrust and disdain divided Mongols from their Chinese subjects; yet like other steppe conquerors, the Mongols found it necessary
to rely on Chinese officials for routine, low-level administration.

The Mongol hold on China weakened early in the fourteenth century as a result of factionalism, epidemics, reckless inflation of the paper
currency, and natural disasters—especially a catastrophic flood that
broke the dikes of the Huang He. Chinese rebels gradually prevailed,
and after decades of destructive conflict, a ruthless conqueror named
Yuanzhang (ruled 1368–98)—born a peasant, orphaned in childhood, and
a mendicant Buddhist novice before he took to arms—established the
Ming dynasty. It ruled China until 1644.

With native Chinese back in control, distaste for everything foreign
became a ruling principle among Ming officials. They vigorously reaf-
firmed Confucian ideas and affirmed imperial China's centrality to the
celestial and terrestrial order by treating peaceful encounters with foreigners as "tribute missions." But from the start, the Ming government
always maintained an enormous army to guard against steppe cavalrymen. The government also took pains to repopulate the north, where
Mongols had preferred pasture to farmland, and set up a new capital at
Beijing (Peking) closer to the frontier. An aggressive policy prevailed at

first. The third Ming emperor, Zhu Di (reigned 1402–24), set out to conquer his steppe neighbors, and simultaneously sent a series of formidable naval expeditions into the Indian Ocean (described in chapter 6).

Yet China's imperial overseas ventures stopped as abruptly as they had begun. In 1415, the Grand Canal was deepened, eliminating the need to use sealanes to supply the capital with southern rice. In 1449, the reigning emperor was captured while campaigning against the Mongols. He was released the next year, but the Ming government decided to concentrate available resources on safeguarding the steppe frontier. Efforts at expansion beyond China's southern limits came suddenly to a halt. After years of fighting, an invading Chinese army withdrew from Annam (modern Vietnam), the fleet was allowed to decay, and private overseas trade was prohibited. A few Chinese persisted in defying the law by continuing to sail the high seas, but they did so as pirates, operating from islands offshore.

The Ming government thus deliberately repudiated commercial-imperial expansion of the sort that brought the Portuguese into the Indian Ocean at the very end of the fifteenth century. Consequently, no Chinese explorer ever rounded Africa to reach Europe or discovered America by crossing the Pacific, even though Chinese ships and navigational skills were fully capable of such feats. This, perhaps the greatest might-have-been of modern history, was perfectly sensible from the point of view of China's imperial government. Why waste resources bringing tributes from overseas that China did not need when defense of the land frontier required such strenuous effort?

At home, Ming rulers relied on traditional Confucian statecraft to keep military men and merchants appropriately submissive. They met with very considerable success. The threat posed by steppe raiders diminished, probably through their chronic exposure to bubonic infection that for the first time had become endemic among burrowing rodents of the steppe.[2] Whatever the cause, Ming armies were far more successful than the Song had been in safeguarding the northern frontier.

Improved frontier guard assured peace, and peace allowed recovery

[2] This is uncertain. But the expansiveness of steppe peoples suffered some kind of check after 1350. Some of the best pastures of Eurasia were abandoned, most conspicuously in the Ukraine. For a reconstruction of how that may have happened, see William H. McNeill, *Plagues and Peoples* (New York, 1976), ch. 4. Others disagree, most notably Jean-Noel Biraben, *Les hommes et la peste dans la France et dans les pays européens et méditerranéens* (Paris, 1975), 1, 48ff.

from the severe population losses of the late Mongol era. Moreover, the commercialization of society that had come to the fore under the Tang and Song dynasties remained firmly in place. Officially supervised production of silk, porcelain, and a few other commodities for export increased. Large-scale enterprises were few and official, like the salt administration that combined elaborate engineering, to extract salt from underground deposits, with sophisticated indirect taxation through arbitrary pricing. Private commerce and artisan manufacture throve as before, mostly on a family scale; and successful merchants often invested in land and sent their sons to school, hoping that by passing the imperial examinations they might become officials and join the governing class.

After abandoning initial aggression, the ruling elites of Ming society sought stability. Truth and beauty were securely enshrined in the Confucian classics, and in the achievements of Chinese poets, painters, and writers, especially those of the Tang and Song eras. Foreigners, who did not share that heritage, were a dangerous nuisance, best kept at arm's length. Porcelain, silk, lacquerwork, and the like continued to find ready markets among outsiders, but the Chinese saw little to admire in foreign-made goods, welcoming only silver, copper, and a few other raw materials in return for the various manufactures they produced for export.

Altogether, therefore, the Ming achieved a very successful recovery from the devastations China had suffered under the Mongols, even though after about 1440 the government tried hard to limit Chinese participation in the Old World Web. China's conservative policy of withdrawal of course became Western Europe's opportunity. But a vast population, sustained civil peace, and superior artisan skills meant that China's prestige and primacy faded away far more slowly than brash Europeans, dazzled by their own successes, readily recognized.

The Transformation of Islam, 1000–1500

The Chinese efflorescence rested upon using methods of artisan production and bazaar trading, indigenous to the Muslim heartlands of Southwest Asia, in a different landscape where safe and cheap water transport permitted the Chinese to magnify their effect by transforming millions of peasants into shrewd and diligent commercial farmers. Nothing comparable was possible in Muslim lands, even in Egypt where cheap and reliable water transport on the Nile had supported commercial estate agriculture ever since Roman times. Though rural estates in Egypt produced grain (later also cotton) for export, only a landowning elite reaped any direct benefit. In China, by contrast, peasant families entered the market on their own account to get money to pay taxes and rents and purchase whatever they needed for themselves. This extended incentives for intensifying output to the producers, whereas in Egypt and other plantation-type economies the people who did the work had no reason to depart from established routines. In such circumstances, even innovative managers (where they existed) had serious difficulty in overcoming laborers' resistance to working harder.

The bottleneck for economic advance in Southwest Asia was the absence of navigable inland waterways comparable to those of China and Europe. Camel caravans could only carry comparatively tiny quantities overland, inhibiting long-distance transport of bulk goods of common consumption that became the staples first of Chinese and then of European commerce. This constraint meant that Muslim ships and merchants, even though they shared improvements in seagoing navigation, and continued to introduce Islam to new areas of Africa and Southeast Asia, could not transform rural society in Southwest Asia as the Chinese had done. In addition, climate change (probably) and pastoral expansion (certainly) hurt agriculture throughout the semiarid heartlands of Southwest Asia; and the Black Death of the fourteenth century was very costly as well.

On the other hand, Muslim governments did invent ingenious ways to subsidize caravan trade. Private donors, as acts of religious merit, were permitted to endow caravanserais by assigning rents in kind from agricultural estates to feed itinerant merchants and their camels, usually for a maximum stopover of three days. Such endowments were exempt from taxation and allowed camels to traverse agricultural landscapes without damaging crops by foraging at night. In grasslands and deserts, of course, camels fueled their muscles for the next day's march by grazing on wild vegetation. Endowed caravanserais, in effect, assured free food for camels in settled landscapes as well. The direct cost to merchants of caravan portage therefore shrank considerably wherever a chain of suitably endowed caravanserais existed.

But this did not enable camels to carry heavier loads. High-cost luxuries therefore remained the staples of interregional caravan commerce in Southwest Asia. Peasants, oppressed by rents and taxes in kind, and

Map 5.2 Islamic Heartlands, 1000–1500

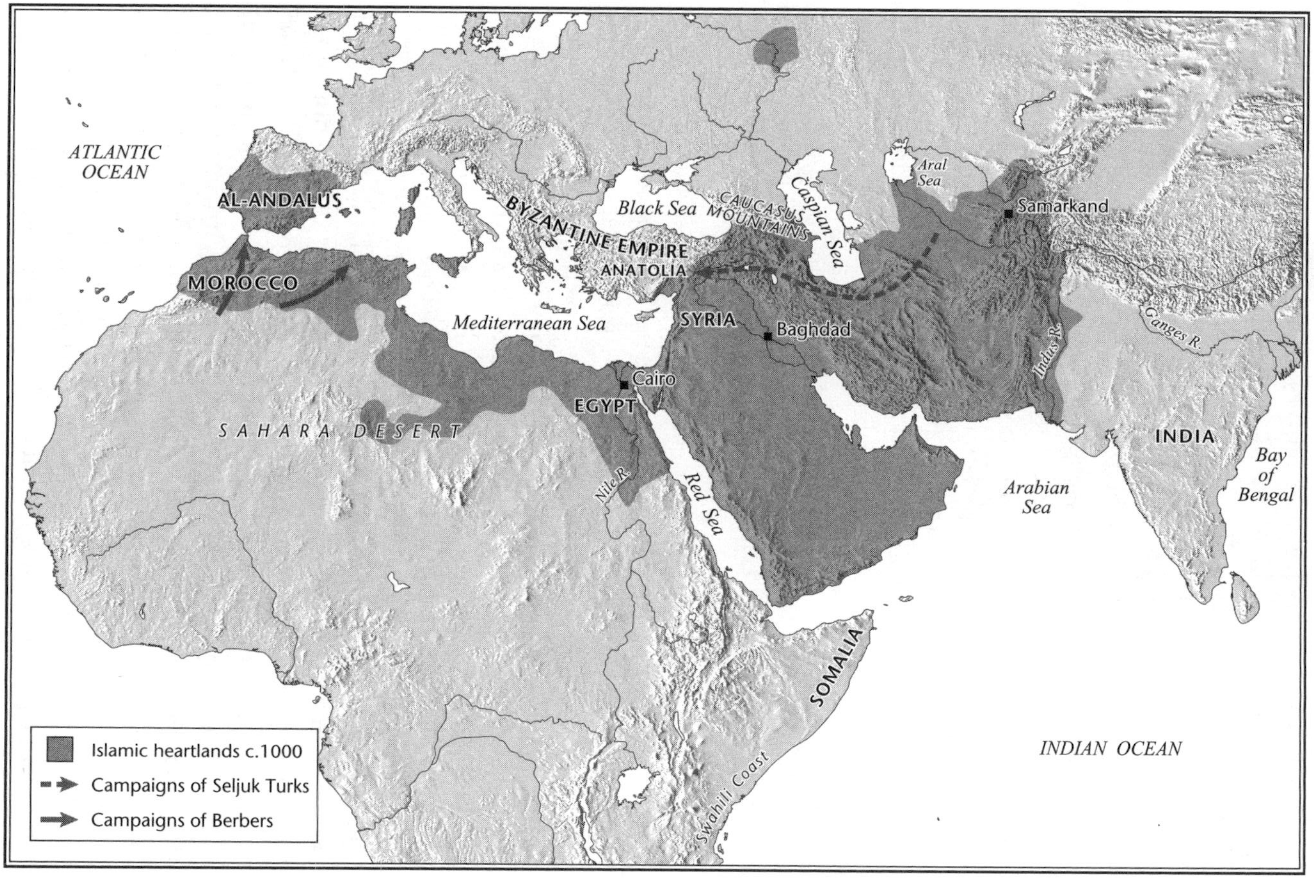

ATLANTIC
OCEAN

AL-ANDALUS

MOROCCO

SAHARA DESERT

Mediterranean Sea

BYZANTINE EMPIRE

ANATOLIA

SYRIA

Black Sea

CAUCASUS MOUNTAINS

Caspian Sea

Aral Sea

Samarkand

Ganges R.

INDIA

Bay
of
Bengal

Indus R.

Arabian
Sea

INDIAN OCEAN

SOMALIA

Swahili Coast

Red Sea

Niger R.

Cairo

EGYPT

Baghdad

Islamic heartlands c.1000

Campaigns of Seljuk Turks

Campaigns of Berbers

often harassed by nomads as well, could only enter marginally into nearby urban markets. Except for the Nile, rivers in Muslim lands were of little use for navigation. In sum, the limited capacity of overland caravans inhibited commercialization of the rural majority in Muslim lands on anything like the scale that China and parts of Europe witnessed after the year 1000, thanks to their interior waterways.

Muslim maritime trade along the shores of the Indian Ocean escaped this limitation. In some shoreline localities, thoroughly commercial agriculture and artisan production for distant markets continued to intensify. But commercial penetration of the Indian and African interiors remained slender, inhibited as always by high transport and protection costs. Nothing to match the transformation of peasant life in the great Chinese river valleys seems to have taken place even along such a promising waterway as the Ganges.

War and politics had much to do with that situation, both in India and in the Muslim world at large. Intensified exposure to nomad and ex-nomad raiding damaged agriculture and held back the Muslim rural economy almost everywhere between 1000 and 1350. Dryland irrigation systems were particularly vulnerable to destruction, since nomads often preferred to see land under grass rather than irrigated crops. New religious currents also diverted attention from material things as congregational exercises, aimed at inducing mystical encounter with God, spread throughout the Muslim world. This made Islam more emotionally vibrant than before, but mystics, living familiarly with God and disdaining worldly things, also reinforced routine conservatism in daily life.

The principal political phenomenon of the centuries between 1000 and 1500 was the accelerated Turkic infiltration of the Muslim heartlands. The revival of Persian cultural consciousness and identity was a parallel change, and the two combined to create a courtly style of Turko-Persian culture, government, and warfare that Muslim conquerors eventually imposed upon almost all of India. In North Africa, Berbers from the desert interior paralleled the Turkic expansion, providing the fighting men who brought successive religious reform movements to power in the Mediterranean coastlands and southern Spain. But unlike the Turks and Persians, Berber conquerors did not develop a literary culture of their own, preferring to use the sacred Arabic language instead.

Turkic expansion depended on mastery of cavalry warfare. In mature form, Turkic armies combined old-style steppe archers with heavy cavalry of the sort the Parthians had invented. A throng of unarmored archers, who could shoot from the back of a galloping horse with considerable accuracy, and a few armored cavalrymen on big horses, who could charge infantry formations with devastating effect, made a formidable combination.[3]

The Turkic advance occurred in two waves, punctuated by the devastating Mongol conquest of most of Southwest Asia between 1245 and 1258. Seljuk Turkish tribesmen rode into the Muslim heartlands after 1037, bringing their flocks and herds with them from the steppes. On marginal, unirrigated land (and there was a great deal of such land in Iran, Syria, Mesopotamia, and Anatolia), settled farming tended to retreat before their advance, perhaps in part because climatic change was making pasturage a more dependable way of life than farming. The Seljuks were Sunni Muslims, and as such were welcomed by the Abbasid caliphs at Baghdad and by urban elites who were facing serious challenges from Shi'a Muslims, among whom the Fatimids of Egypt were the most threatening, and the so-called Order of Assassins based in eastern Iran (1090–1256) the most extreme.

In a sense, the Seljuk influx restored the alliance between nomadic warriors and townsfolk that had first brought martial glory to Islam, with the difference that urban elites from Mecca ruled in the early days of Islam, whereas in the eleventh century political power rested firmly in Seljuk warriors' hands. Nonetheless, long before they left the steppes the Seljuks had learned to respect and benefit from the ways of merchants. They were therefore prepared to allow urban elites to manage their own affairs within rather wide limits. In return they sought political legitimation from Sunni experts in the Sacred Law, duly endorsed by the Abbasid caliph in Baghdad.

A wing of the Seljuk advance broke through the Byzantine frontier in 1071 and swiftly occupied most of Anatolia. Rapid conversion of Greek-speaking Christian villagers to Islam ensued, and the peninsula became predominantly Turkish-speaking. But the territorial sweep of the Seljuk conquests, extending from the shores of the Aegean to the Aral Sea, made it impossible to maintain anything resembling a central

---

[3] The Mongols carried gunpowder with them westward and their Turko-Mongol successors took to guns readily. In southern India, the first recorded use of guns in battle dates from 1358, just twelve years after the battle of Crécy introduced them to European battlefields. But Muslim gunfounders failed to keep up with their European counterparts because, among Muslims, private mineral rights were never secure in law or in practice. This, combined with limitations of overland transport, meant that mining and metallurgy failed to develop on anything like the European scale.

administration. Accordingly, after 1091, when the last great Seljuk captain died, local fighting among rival military adventurers became endemic.[4]

A similar nomad-urban alliance arose in North Africa with the rise of the Almoravids (ruled ca. 1056–1147). They were Berber tribesmen who had recently learned the art of camel herding and proceeded to conquer far and wide on the strength of their enhanced mobility. Unlike their Fatimid predecessors, they championed Sunni Islam, and accordingly found it easy to ally with urban elites when subduing the coastlands of northwestern Africa. From that base they then proceeded (in 1076) to overrun the kingdom of Ghana, lying south of the Sahara near the Niger bend, thus accelerating the spread of Islam in West Africa. They also pushed back the Christians in Spain. When Christian victories in Spain resumed, the Almoravids were superseded by another Berber association of rather more mystical religious reformers, the Almohads (1130–1269). They, like their predecessors, drove back the Spanish Christians for a while, only to suffer a serious defeat in 1212 that confined Muslim rule in Spain to the small kingdom of Granada until it too was overrun in 1492.

While pastoralists thus achieved greater prominence in Islamic lands, an opposite shift was underway in China and Europe, where peasant farmers were extending and intensifying their hold on the landscape. Climate change probably forwarded both processes. There is good evidence that between about 950 and 1250 unusually warm and dry summers favored grain farming and wine-growing in Western Europe. If similar conditions prevailed in Muslim lands (this is uncertain), summer drought must have favored pastoralism. And quite apart from climate, the military-political successes of Turkic and Berber fighting men after 1037 clearly strengthened the pastoral element in Muslim (and Indian) society at the expense of settled farmers.

Muslim politics shifted once again in the middle of the thirteenth century when pagan Mongols, riding westward from their base in China and the eastern steppe, sacked Baghdad in 1258, battered the irrigation systems of Mesopotamia, and killed the last Abbasid caliph. With the

---

[4] This allowed the First Crusade to fight its way overland to Jerusalem in 1099. But when Saladin (1137–1193) overthrew the Fatimids in Egypt and consolidated his hold on the Syrian hinterland, the recapture of Jerusalem in 1187 became easy. Thereafter, only coastal toeholds remained securely in Christian hands, the last of which surrendered in 1291. In general, the Crusades affected Christendom far more than Islam. Muslims found little or nothing to admire in the Crusaders' way of life, whereas Christians had much to learn from Muslims about elegant urban living.

destruction of the caliphate, even the pretense of Muslim political unity evaporated. In due course the Mongol Il-Khans, ruling Persia, Mesopotamia, and part of Syria, became Muslim (1295); but this did not give them religious legitimacy. Pious Muslims, in effect, despaired of politics. Increasingly, their pursuit of holiness took mystical paths. Associations of dervishes, each with its own ways of achieving personal encounter with God, attracted widespread popular support. The dervishes were alienated from, and sometimes in opposition to, an unending series of upstart military adventurers who, though they spoke Turkish and Persian, almost always based their claim to rule on real or fictitious descent from Genghis Khan.

The Mongol khanate fractured after 1353. Thereafter, Turkic, Afghan, and Mongol fighting men created unstable regimes around successful military captains, of whom Timur the Lame (or Tamerlane, ruled ca. 1369–1405) was the most successful. Some of these rulers, including Tamerlane, patronized elegant court cultures, combining Persian, Turkish, and Chinese influences to produce lovely public buildings, brilliantly illustrated manuscripts, and in one instance, a magnificent astronomical observatory. But these captains did not translate the fortunes of war into politico-religious legitimacy or enduring states. Their khanates resembled desert flowers, quick to bloom and quick to wither.

Like their Italian and Byzantine contemporaries, among whom admiration for pagan antiquity gathered headway in the fourteenth and fifteenth centuries, courtiers and urban elites of Southwest Asia also began to flirt with their own style of secularism. This stemmed partly from revival of enthusiasm for pre-Islamic Persian chivalry, as expressed in the epic poetry of Firdawsi (died ca. 1020), and partly from their increasing exposure to foreign cultures. Muslim mystics for example owed a good deal to the practices of Indian holy men, and influential dervishes, like Rumi (died 1273), resorted to Persian poetry to explore the soul's path to God. Later, another famous Persian poet, Hafez (died 1389), toyed with sacrilege by using ambiguous sensuous metaphors confusing divine with human love. Many Muslim princes from Uzbekistan to Spain also patronized science, propelling advances in astronomy, navigation, mathematics, and geography. Ecstatic religion and innovative science fitted awkwardly with the older Muslim emphasis on meticulous obedience to the Sacred Law. But this logical discrepancy was more than counterbalanced by the emotional attraction of the new mysticism and sensual secularism.

Persianized Turkic-Mongol court cultures did not extend to Egypt.

After the death of Saladin in 1193, Egypt was ruled by Mamluk military slaves, most of whom were recruited from the northeastern shores of the Black Sea. A Mamluk army repelled a Mongol attack in 1260; largely on the strength of prestige they thus acquired, Mamluks continued to rule Egypt until 1517. Like the Fatimids before them, the Mamluks fostered Cairo's trade and patronized an Arabic literary tradition in contrast to the Persianized court cultures prevailing further east. Berber rulers and urban elites in the west also sustained an elegant Arab-influenced way of life that endured in Spain until 1492, when Granada fell to Christians.

But the Muslim retreat from Spain was exceptional. Elsewhere, dervish piety and merchant-missionary enthusiasm combined with military enterprise to expand the frontiers of Islam very rapidly. India, Eastern Europe, Africa, and Southeast Asia were the principal theaters of this expansion. Altogether, the realm of Islam almost doubled between 1000 and 1500. No wonder, then, that despite temporary defeat at the hands of Mongol unbelievers and local military failure in Spain, Muslims remained confident that God was with them.

In India, Mahmud of Ghazna (ruled 997–1030) initiated plundering raids from Afghanistan, and in ensuing centuries Muslim rulers extended their power across all of northern India and penetrated far southward as well. Muslim rulers of India relied on an irregular flow of fighting men arriving from the north, eager to carve out careers for themselves by warring against Hindu idolaters. They brought their religion and cavalry skills with them, and at first tried to uproot idolatry by destroying Hindu temples. But family and caste observances preserved Hinduism even when temples disappeared, and Hindu fighting men soon began to match the chivalry of their Muslim rivals. Consequently, Muslim rulers soon found it politic to tolerate public outdoor festivals celebrating one or another avatar of Vishnu or Siva. Hindu converts to Islam, coming mainly from the humbler castes, also added a new strand to Indian society that remained almost wholly apart from the ruling Muslim elite.

Just as in Southwest Asia, the arrival of Turko-Persian warriors increased the prominence of pastoral elements in India. In semiarid landscapes of the interior, Muslim and Hindu pastoralists probably encroached on farmers; but any setback to agricultural output that this may have caused was countered by a growing scale of inland commerce, dependent on bullock carts rather than on camel caravans. Still, as in Southwest Asia, overland transport remained too expensive to permit goods of common consumption to circulate very widely inland.

The Ottoman Empire, emerging about 1290 on the frontier with Christendom in northwest Anatolia, became a more powerful instrument of Muslim expansion than any principality along the Indian frontier. As in India, war against unbelievers at first sanctified raid and rapine; and, as also in India, successful raids allowed the early Ottoman sultans to assign estates to their followers, supporting them for subsequent campaigns. From modest beginnings, therefore, Ottoman armies snowballed quickly, and by 1389 they had conquered northwest Anatolia and most of the Balkan peninsula. They probably got some help from the Black Death, which inflicted fewer losses on the Ottomans' rural manpower than on their more urbanized, maritime enemies.

Keeping a large state together over generations required impersonal institutions that attracted loyalty or commanded obedience. The Ottoman sultans met the age-old problem of making sure that dispersed rural landholders would obey the summons for yet another campaign by creating a personal household of military slaves that was strong enough to overawe, and if necessary to overcome, any local resistance. Slave soldiers had been a feature of Muslim society since the ninth century, and by usurping power had sometimes established enduring regimes, most notably in Mamluk Egypt. But the Ottoman slave household never took power overtly. Instead, it provided the backbone of an unusually powerful state by coordinating the prowess of landed Turkish cavalrymen with its own, specialized military skills. The early sultans systematically trained most of their slaves as infantrymen who served in the formidable Janissary corps, but they also chose the most promising recruits for higher education and appointed them to govern the empire in time of peace and to command levies of Turkish cavalrymen in time of war. Most of the sultan's slave household came from subsistence villages in the western Balkans, where periodic levies of young men and boys became a form of tax. The chief administrators of the Ottoman Empire therefore came to be recruited as adolescents from among the Christian peasantry. They used a Slavic language among themselves, employed Turkish for official purposes, and, as converts to Islam, worshiped in Arabic. Their village origins probably made them more sensitive to peasant interests than were other rulers, making the empire somewhat more secure.

Along other frontiers of Islam, merchant princes and merchant missionaries encouraged conversion to the religion of Muhammad. In West Africa, for example, after the Almoravids conquered the kingdom of Ghana (1076), some West African rulers readily accepted Islam. As a result, successive empires based on the savanna grasslands and along the trade corridor of the Niger River—first Mali (ca. 1235–1430), then Songhai (ca. 1464–1591)—acquired familiarity with Arabic learning and a full array of Muslim institutions. Thriving export trades in slaves, gold, and salt made their monarchs rich. When Mansa Musa, ruler of Mali, went on pilgrimage to Mecca in 1324, he brought so much gold with him that it depressed the price of that metal in Cairo for several years afterward.

Islamic ports along the East African coast also throve on inland trade; but no imposing Muslim state arose in that part of the continent. On the other side of the Indian Ocean, however, local conversions to Islam brought the Malay Peninsula and the principal Indonesian islands under Muslim rule during the fourteenth and fifteenth centuries. After a Hindu kingdom in central Java collapsed in 1526, only remote Bali resisted absorption into the expanding world of Islam.

Missionary successes between 1000 and 1500 registered both the emotional power of dervish forms of Muslim piety and the fact that urban civil society flourished despite the unending upheavals of war and politics. The ready circulation of religious experts sustained a close-knit cultural community across political and ethnic boundaries.[5] A common sacred language, the Sacred Law and public rituals, reinforced by the pilgrimage to Mecca that brought elites from the entire Islamic world together each year, sufficed to maintain effective commonality among Muslims despite political fragmentation and continued, sometimes bitter sectarian disputes.

The renewed Muslim expansion between 1000 and 1500, its central location in the Old World Web, the attractiveness of mystic forms of religion, and the new sensibilities woven into the various elite cultures patronized by local rulers, all demonstrated that Islam was as vigorous as ever. Yet, however spectacular, Muslim innovations were primarily cultural, commercial, and military, and did not much affect the vast majority of the population, peasants at the plow. Indeed, agricultural decline in the heartlands augured ill. Handicapped by the limits of caravan transport, Muslim society lagged behind Chinese and West Europeans in harnessing rural labor to market production. Consequently, for Muslims the Old World Web, with all its new information promoting special-

---

[5] The extraordinary career of Ibn Battuta (1304–1368) illustrates the close cultural linkages Muslims maintained all the way from his native Morocco to China. See Ross Dunn, *The Adventures of Ibn Battuta, a Muslim Traveller of the Fourteenth Century* (Berkeley, 1986).

ization and efficiency for every kind of activity, remained almost wholly confined to an urban and military minority. The brilliance of Turko-Mongol court cultures, the raptures of mystic religion, and Ottoman military success could not compensate for this deficiency.

Christendom's Thickening Web

In the year 1000, most of Western Europe was overwhelmingly rural—no more than a thinly populated backwoods. Christian civilization centered in the east, where a Greek-speaking Roman emperor, in collaboration with the Orthodox Church, ruled the mighty Byzantine Empire from Constantinople. Five hundred years later, that empire had been supplanted by an even mightier and still expanding Ottoman state. But the Turkish triumph did not cause Christendom to crumple. Quite the contrary. Western European skill, knowledge, wealth, and power were increasing rapidly, despite (or perhaps because of) perpetual quarreling that even the Ottoman threat failed to quiet.

Unruly, reckless, often crude, and always curious, the Franks (as Muslims called them) were, like the Japanese at the other end of Eurasia, aware of the innumerable ways in which civilized neighbors excelled their own attainments. For that reason, both were ready to experiment with promising novelties from whatever source. By 1500, therefore, Western Europeans had acquired an impressive array of learning from their Byzantine and Muslim neighbors, and had imported an equally impressive array of technologies from distant China. In short, Western Europeans profited greatly in terms of wealth and power from their uninhibited sampling of ideas, goods, and practices circulating within the Old World Web. This held fateful consequences for American and world history after 1500.

Western Europe's surge passed through two distinct phases, interrupted by a serious setback in the fourteenth century, when bad harvests due to wetter and cooler weather, the catastrophe of the Black Death (1346–52), and sporadic ravages of the Hundred Years' War (1337–1453) dictated a fresh start.

By 1000, in the lands between the Loire and Elbe rivers, mounted knights and moldboard plow teams capable of cultivating flat, waterlogged clay soils protected and supported one another very efficiently. From this core area, knights of Latin Christendom expanded their domain in every direction. Moldboard agriculture followed behind, but never caught up with the military frontier because climatic differences made the heavy plows impracticable in dry Mediterranean lands like Spain and Sicily, as well as in Irish bogs and in the freezing winters of northeast Europe.

But within limits set by the mild winters and year-round rainfall that the Gulf Stream and prevailing westerly winds brought to the plains of Western Europe, agricultural production swelled as peasant villagers established a sustainable style of farming that employed labor almost uniformly throughout the year. By dividing arable land into three fields— one sown in autumn for harvest in late spring, one sown in spring for autumn harvest, and one left fallow to be plowed (for weed control) in summertime—plow teams could work almost year round. They interrupted the task only for the twelve days of Christmas and during the weeks when planting and harvesting required everyone's urgent effort. This regime allowed a single plowman's share of cultivated land to amount to about thirty acres—far more than was needed to feed his domestic animals, himself, and his family.[6]

Cooperative cultivation of open fields in northwestern Europe therefore permitted peasants to sustain formidable fighting men who had a clear self-interest in guarding them against destructive raiders, together with priests and monks who attended to relations with God. Usually they still had something left over in ordinary years to exchange for items they needed or wanted and could not make for themselves. This extended the demand for artisans' wares into peasant homes, furthering urban skills and tightening local trade and transport links. And when noble and clerical rent and tax receivers developed a taste for superior artisan products and rare commodities from afar, urban dwellers, recruited from the fringes of society and often led by pirate traders from the Viking era, began to supply them with what they wanted. They did so partly by specializing as artisans, and partly by importing luxury items from Mediterranean Europe. There towns and trade had not decayed as much as in the north, and rapid revival set in after 1000 when Italian merchants joined the network of long-distance commerce centered in the Indian Ocean and bolstered by China's radical commercialization.

By tightening their links with the rest of the Old World Web in this

---

[6] By comparison, in Mediterranean lands a single family could only keep about ten acres under cultivation, because grapes and olives had to be hoed by hand, and grainfields could only be plowed during a few weeks of the year after the first autumn rains had softened sun-baked soils and before it was time to plant for harvest in the spring.

Map 5.3 Expansion of Christian Control, 1000–1500

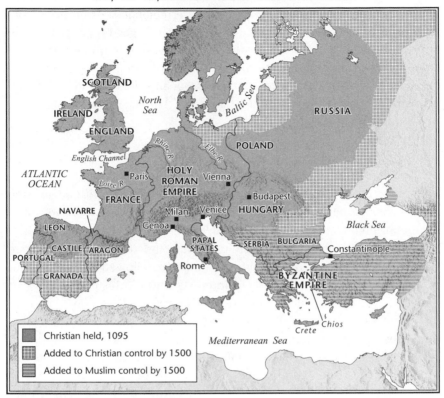

fashion, Western Europeans encountered far more sophisticated and more highly skilled peoples than themselves. But as long as local agricultural and artisanal production expanded as rapidly as they did between 1000 and 1270, and as long as Christian knights continued to be generally successful in battle against foreign foes, crude Westerners could feel confident that God and their Christian faith would safeguard them while they plumbed foreigners' knowledge and skills for purposes of their own.

Then, after three centuries of rapid population growth and intensive colonization of land reclaimed from forest, swamp, and sea, catastrophes devastated Europe in the fourteenth century. Colder temperatures provoked crop failures and widespread famine, peaking between 1315 and 1322. The Black Death followed a generation later. Together, they reduced the population of Western Europe by about one-third. With bad harvests and plague recurring decade after decade, recovery was slow.

By 1500, Europe's population was little if at all larger than in 1300, even though by that time transport and industry were far more efficient than they had been 200 years earlier. Stout, seaworthy ships now connected all the coasts of Europe, and interregional specialization and exchange had gathered momentum as an ever larger proportion of the entire population began to enter the market. Western Europe thus replicated China's commercialization with a delay of three to four centuries; but unlike what happened in China, European rulers and clerics failed to maintain control over the merchants and bankers who managed the new interregional economy.

European merchants and bankers attended to their own defense by gaining political control of a number of sovereign city-states. They could then deal more or less as equals with other local rulers, who found it impossible to do without loans or to repay their debts without making concessions to bankers' and merchants' interests. Since moneyed men were continually on the lookout for anything that might turn a profit, a self-sustaining process of economic, social, and technological change gathered headway wherever political conditions allowed it the freedom to operate. Time and again, local interests and old-fashioned ways of doing things were displaced by politically protected economic innovators, who saw a chance of monetary profit by introducing something new. This situation still persists today, having first transformed European society, and then infected the whole wide world, thus marking modern times off from earlier, more stable forms of human society.

Europe's urban self-government contrasted with the firm subordination of China's far larger urban populations to official control. The freedom of Muslim urban elites stood in between. Their merchants and bankers, many of whom were Jews or Christians, were more constrained and vulnerable than their European contemporaries, even though Muslim artisan guilds and dervish orders were substantially autonomous and sometimes defiant of their political masters. But artisan guilds and dervishes were stalwart defenders of the status quo. Lacking their support, merchants and bankers in Muslim cities were easily reduced to subservience by military upstarts, who often employed them as tax collectors, and occasionally confiscated their ill-gotten gains, just as mandarins did to merchants in China.

Urban self-government in Europe had another distinctive dimension. In Muslim and Chinese society, members of a single, sometimes extended family managed most economic enterprises. The strength of family ties made it difficult or impossible to trust outsiders, thus limiting the scale of most undertakings. Although Europeans adopted the same legal methods for setting up partnerships and settling debts that Muslims and Chinese used, they found it easier to trust fellow citizens, regardless of whether they were blood relatives or not. Perhaps they found it necessary to do so, because extended family ties were unusually weak in most of Western Europe.

As early as 1346, for example, Genoese investors created a limited stock company to organize a fleet for raiding and trading in the eastern Mediterranean. When the fleet conquered the Aegean island of Chios, the investors converted their company into a permanent corporation that governed Chios and managed its profitable export trade until the Ottoman Turks conquered the island in 1566. As a result, for more than 200 years, the Maona, as the corporation was called, distributed dividends among its stockholders from time to time, regardless of who they were or how they might be related (or unrelated, since shares were bought and sold freely) to the original investors.

Self-government, in short, could be applied to common enterprises far afield as well as at home, so that large-scale private undertakings, far beyond the scope of any single family, became routine and familiar. Shipbuilding and mining attained special vigor, thanks to this sort of risk sharing among multiple private investors. As a result, by 1500 the supply of base metals—especially iron—available to Europeans far surpassed what other peoples had at their command.

It is plausible to believe that transfamilial commercial enterprise in the towns of medieval Europe derived from the practices of rural plow teams. Towns were unhealthful places and had to maintain themselves by attracting manpower from the countryside. In the heartlands of Western Europe, such rural recruits brought with them the habit of working in plow teams whose members came from different families. If a plowman failed to do his share of work, or did not deal honestly with his fellows, penalties were dire indeed. Aggrieved neighbors could easily exclude him from their plow teams the next year, making it impossible for the scapegrace to plant his fields or bring in a harvest. Such discipline, requiring mutual trust and cooperation beyond the limits of blood relationship, surely prepared European townsmen to trust one another, rendering conformity to agreed-upon rules for distributing work and gains among all concerned far more reliable.

Overall, European urban society acquired unusual flexibility thanks to moral habits that sustained effective participation in an indefinite number of voluntary, ad hoc corporations, formed not only for making money but also for other purposes—religious, charitable, intellectual, or merely convivial. Europeans, in other words, seem to have sustained a more luxuriant growth of autonomous private groups than other societies did. The plow team was probably the cell from which this capability grew. Travelers may notice that people in those parts of Europe where cooperative moldboard plowing once prevailed still obey rules, form queues, and in general trust one another more than do the inhabitants of lands where separate families cultivated their fields independently and often distrusted their neighbors because of boundary disputes or the like.

Every society, every region has its peculiarities, but few were as consequential as this. In the land of the moldboard plow, the prevailing pattern of nuclear families made the bonds of extended family weak, and created opportunity and incentive for other forms of civic and business organization to flourish. Simultaneously, local rivalries made rulers unable to regulate merchants and bankers effectively, allowing moneyed interests to acquire unusual autonomy. Hence European societies, at least those between the Elbe and the Loire rivers and across the Channel in England, developed an especially active, constantly changing, often disruptive civil society that stood between the overarching subordination to church and state and private family obligations. This made for flexibility in social relations, especially in urban settings, and in turn made adjustment to rapid technological and political change somewhat easier than elsewhere. But flexibility came at the cost of the security and human warmth that extended families can provide, and the peace that imperial states can impose.

Instead, endless violence and rivalry prevailed. Until 1300, the emperor of Germany and the popes of Rome both laid claim to universal jurisdiction over Latin Christendom, while kings, nobles, bishops, and towns contested actual control over the rents, taxes, and legal fees that sustained warfare, church, and state. This was not very different from the political fragmentation besetting Islam in the same centuries, and the failure first of the German emperor (1250) and then of the Roman pope (1303) to consolidate their claims to universal authority resembled the collapse of the caliphate after 1258.

But the array of sovereign city-states that arose in Italy, the Low Countries, and western Germany after the breakdown of imperial and papal power had no analogue elsewhere within the Old World Web. The subsequent consolidation of national kingdoms in France and England also rested in large part on continual bargaining between kings and townsmen whereby, in return for money taxes, the royal administration agreed to protect towns from knightly harassment and allow townsfolk to conduct their internal affairs as they pleased. Merchants, bankers, and poorer urban dwellers, in other words, played a far more prominent role in politics and war than was common elsewhere.

They did so largely because European warfare became more and more commercialized from 1300 onward. By 1282, when a company of crossbowmen destroyed a host of French knights in a battle nicknamed the "Sicilian Vespers," the military primacy that European knights had enjoyed since about 900 was coming to an end. Pikemen and archers, in suitably disciplined array, became capable of repelling charging knights. Soon thereafter, in 1346, field artillery made its noisy, at first inefficient, debut on European battlefields.

Rather suddenly, the military art became more complex. Managing a headlong charge by armored knights had required minimal generalship, even if assembling a host and then supplying it for more than a few days was always difficult. But in the course of the fourteenth century, successful military commanders had to learn to coordinate movements of cavalry, infantry, and artillery in the field. Someone had to recruit, equip, and train appropriate numbers of fighting men for each arm, and find means of supplying them with food, weapons, and other necessities, both in garrison and on campaign.

These tasks presented European governments with difficult logistical, administrative, and financial challenges. A handful of Italian city-states, with Milan and Venice in the lead, showed how to meet them by subcontracting organized violence. They invented bureaucratic ways of making sure that hired fighting men were properly trained and equipped and had effective inducements to obey municipal magistrates instead of seizing power for themselves. Civilian control sometimes faltered, most notably in Milan, but Venice always managed to keep its hired soldiers obedient to elected magistrates.

Regular pay, purchase of arms and other supplies from the lowest bidder, and regular inspections to make sure that men and equipment actually matched what the government had paid for connected the maintenance of a professional armed force to precise financial calculations of what was needed and what could be afforded. This made for flexibility in deployment of men and weapons. Any innovation in weapons or tactics that really worked was sure to spread quickly, since rival cities and territorial rulers were all trying to field the most effective force at the cheapest possible price.

That was also why, by 1450, European gun manufacturers were able to capitalize on local mining and metallurgical capabilities and outstrip the world's other armament makers. By 1480, mobile siege guns abruptly upset the military balance of Christendom by making it possible to breach even the strongest castle walls in a matter of a few hours. And when installed on ships, such guns could launch a devastating broadside against anything afloat and attack shore fortifications with shattering effect—as we shall see in chapter 6.

Gunmaking, like mining and shipbuilding, fell into the hands of private entrepreneurs. Rulers who wanted new or improved weapons had to pay market prices for them, since multiple suppliers and multiple purchasers were in perpetual competition. Trying to decree a lower price, as Chinese administrators were wont to do, simply induced manufacturers to sell to someone else. Government arsenals offered an alternative; but when guns were new and the art of guncasting was changing quickly, no government could keep up with the market. That had to be left to businessmen who kept their furnaces in constant operation, hired full-time professionals to run them, and sought out favorable locations where supplies of fuel and metal were optimal and local rulers were willing, for a share of the profits, to allow them to sell freely to all comers.

As a result, European governments found themselves inextricably entangled in commerce and finance, relying on private businesses to equip their hired fighting men. Finding money to pay for this was always difficult. Rulers could borrow from bankers for a given campaign, but that short-term solution only increased future financial embarrassments. Bankers insisted on grants of mining rights and other revenue-producing privileges as security for such loans. Government indebtedness, by expanding the scope and scale of commercial enterprise, thus compelled even the most reluctant states to protect and forward the commercialization of European society as a whole. This was the exact opposite of what happened in China. It assured the continued dynamism of European technology in general, and of military technology in particular.

Western European technology initially depended heavily on borrowing from Byzantine, Muslim, and Chinese contemporaries. But borrowing always involved adaptation, as we have already seen with respect to artillery. The same was true with other borrowings. Arabic numerals, for example, found an important new application in double-entry bookkeeping, introduced in Italy by the middle of the fourteenth century. It made exact calculation of profit and loss simple for the first time. In that same century, Europeans also made significant inventions of their own, including such everyday conveniences as buttons for clothes and eye-glasses for reading.

More generally, diverse innovations like double-entry bookkeeping, alphabetic printing, musical notation for recording pitch and time, precise geometrical perspective in painting, and mechanical clocks for dividing the day into even-length hours were symptoms of a new way of approaching the endless surprises of the natural world. What happened may be described as creeping digitalization, as Europeans imposed an arithmetical filter upon ordinary sense experience. These innovations had the remarkable effect of increasing the accuracy of communication—expressing time, place, pitch, profit, and other meanings more exactly than before. Greater precision, in turn, made it possible to coordinate human activity more efficiently, just as the recent digitalization of electromagnetic communication is doing today. (Just think of how clocks, by arbitrarily dividing time into hours and minutes, allow us to save time by keeping our appointments!)

Mathematically recorded astronomic observations and advances in shipbuilding also allowed more accurate navigation. This in turn sustained the expansion of West European economic enterprise into the Baltic lands, which became important suppliers of grain, timber, fish, and furs in the fourteenth century. Landowners and city folk in those parts of Europe collaborated to develop a quasiplantation economy, mobilizing compulsory rural labor to produce goods for export while reserving imported luxuries for themselves. Full-blown plantation economies developed in another European frontier region, comprising the Madeiras, Canary, and Cape Verde islands, located off the Atlantic coast of Northwest Africa. In the fifteenth century, Spaniards and Portuguese turned suitable sites on some of these islands into sugar plantations, using techniques—including exploitation of West African slaves—already employed on Mediterranean islands and in Morocco.

Europe's commercialization therefore had opposing effects. In thinly populated peripheral regions, ambitious entrepreneurs needed compulsory labor to bring goods profitably to market, whereas near the principal urban centers, where population abounded, market prices for wage labor prevailed. Compulsory labor on the fringes of commercialized regions was as old as Sumer. What was new was the geographic range and scale of differentiation between core and periphery that politically protected European merchants and bankers could now impose on surrounding peoples, thanks to the more capacious shipping at their command.

Sustained by the commercial matrix of town life, European high culture also exhibited unusual dynamism. Many pious souls, like St. Francis of Assisi (1181–1226) and his followers, abhorred the cash nexus and tried, valiantly but vainly, to repudiate the greed and corruption they saw everywhere around them. In matters of faith, towns bred heresy together with energetic efforts to repress and refute it. Towns also became the seats of what we call Gothic cathedrals—finely crafted stone monuments to prosperity as well as to faith that rank among the most impressive ever erected.

The invention of universities also counts as one of medieval Europe's most significant achievements. Higher education in other civilizations passed on truth and knowledge to the rising generation by reverent study and heroic memorization of authoritative texts, together with whatever commentary was needed to clarify obscure meanings. But because written texts were rare and expensive in eleventh-century Europe, higher instruction in law, theology, and medicine took the form of lectures. Rival teachers soon began to compete with one another by finding new things to say. In particular, Abelard (1079–1142), a famous teacher at Paris, having shown how often the most authoritative Christian writers disagreed, boldly attempted, like innumerable university professors after him, to puzzle out truth for himself by logical argument and reasoning. He did so by lecturing to crowds of admiring students in and around Paris.

From this start, the University of Paris quickly emerged as a self-governing association of teachers. Similar self-governing universities sprang up in several other European towns. Abelard's successors, both at Paris and elsewhere, found that Aristotle's *Logic*, already available in Latin translation, offered an inviting guide for their ongoing debates about truth. The systematic translation of Aristotle's other works, together with Arabic commentaries on them, brought an encyclopedic array of learning to European attention, providing university teachers with a vastly expanded array of questions to argue about. But efforts to arrive at definitive answers by logical reasoning always fell short. Even the judicious and subtle distinctions that St. Thomas Aquinas (1225–1274) brought to the task failed to satisfy everyone.

Europeans therefore continued to disagree about religious, philosophical, and scientific questions, and university lecture halls continued to generate competition among teachers. The use of Latin meant the community of university teachers and students extended across all of

Latin Christendom. Accumulating detail sometimes trivialized academic debate after the fourteenth century (a situation not without parallel today). But that only made way for a second wave of scholarly endeavor based in Italian cities, where privileged upper classes came to feel that learning to live well in civil society was more important than arguing endlessly about abstract questions of theology. Pagan classical authors—Cicero first and foremost—spoke to that need. Self-styled humanists therefore set out to discover, peruse, and correct all available manuscripts of ancient Latin and Greek authors, thereby reinvigorating a discrepant, pagan strand to Christian learning.

Simultaneously, expanding communication brought a flood of geographical and other information about distant peoples and places to European attention. The enthusiasm with which Europeans resorted to printing presses after 1455 to spread all sorts of knowledge and opinion (see chapter 6) was as consequential as their reckless and simultaneous embrace of gunpowder weaponry. Both transformations reflected the fact that these technologies, derived ultimately from China, were managed by private persons, eager for profit, who often escaped priestly or political control. The ability of Europeans to pursue power and knowledge by buying innumerable guns and books meant that religious and political authorities could not possibly maintain a stable status quo.

In Europe, moreover, no public authority could halt the continuing commercialization of society. Wealth increased, but so did poverty, since many people failed to adjust to the dictates of market behavior. Old people, for example, were often cast aside in ways unthinkable in China or Africa. Distress and uncertainty were pervasive counterparts of reckless venturing and incessant innovation. In short, every sort of change was out of control in Europe. This distinguished Latin Christendom from other, better-governed Eurasian societies, where concerted efforts to defend traditional ways of thought and conduct continued, for the most part, to prevail.

The Old World Web's Pacific Flank

As shipping improved and commercial fishing prospered, thanks to cheap supplies of salt needed for preservation, Western European peoples became the Atlantic flank of an expanding Old World Web. A similar and simultaneous expansion took place into the Pacific. Japanese fishermen and pirates played a leading role, and massive Chinese flotillas joined after about 1000, only to withdraw suddenly by government decree after 1435. Further south, Malay sailors and merchants extended the reach of the web into remoter islands of the southwest Pacific—the Moluccas, Borneo, and Mindanao chief among them. State building went hand in hand with intensified raid and trade, as did literacy and the propagation of newly defined, local styles of Buddhism and Islam.

Parallels between the Atlantic and Pacific flanks are striking. On both, multiple ethnic groups participated, and the advance of literacy in local languages strengthened local states and reinforced ethnic and cultural autonomy. Japanese "feudalism" resembled the feudalism of medieval Europe and the ready resort to violence that prevailed among Pacific seafarers resembled the Vikings' behavior. Nothing to match the riches of herring and cod fisheries in Atlantic waters arose in the Pacific, perhaps because cheap salt was not available to preserve the catch long enough for shipment to distant markets. (China monopolized technologically sophisticated methods of salt extraction, and the government kept salt prices high as a form of taxation.) But the variety of goods aboard Pacific ships—spices, porcelains, as well as cheaper ceramics, metals, cotton and cotton cloth, rice, timber, and other articles of common consumption—matched or exceeded what European ships were then carrying.

Along this Pacific flank, Korea, Japan, and Annam resisted Chinese expansion and developed their own distinct cultural and political systems. Both Korea and Annam had land frontiers with China, yet the process whereby Chinese settlers infiltrated and then overwhelmed local peoples by carving out rice paddies on suitable soils did not get far, in contrast to the experience of what is now southern China. Instead, rice paddy cultivation took root among native peoples in Korea and Annam soon enough to sustain native rulers. They sometimes submitted to Chinese suzerainty while retaining effective autonomy, as Koreans did after 996, and sometimes rebuffed the Chinese, as Annam did in 1431 after long struggles against Chinese expeditionary armies.

Japan, too, had to repel expeditionary forces launched from China by the Mongol emperor Kublai Khan in 1274, and again in 1291. But most of the time the Japanese islands were secure from risk of armed invasion, so Japanese elites could pick and choose for themselves what skills and knowledge to import from China or elsewhere, and what to reject or modify. A peculiarity of East Asia was that the ideographs of Chinese writing can also be read in other languages of the region with some help from diacritical marks to indicate grammatical relationships between separate signs (just as 2 signifies *zwei, deux, dos, duo,* etc., as well as two). Learning to read and write Chinese ideographs therefore did not mean abandoning local languages. The Koreans even introduced an alphabetic script of their own in the fourteenth century.

Official patronage of Buddhism became a second shield of cultural independence in Korea, Japan, and Annam. China had suppressed Buddhist monasteries in 845, transforming Chinese Buddhism into an oppositional underground. In Japan, attachments to flourishing, rival, and even armed sectarian forms of Buddhism allowed the Japanese to blend Confucian and Daoist learning into older local cults. The gradual popularization of Shinto observance, elaborated around what began as private rituals of the imperial family, made Japan's cultural identity finally secure, so that Japanese art, literature, and music could freely borrow and depart from Chinese models much as Latin Christians were borrowing and departing from Byzantine and Muslim models in these same centuries. Lady Murasaki's (978–1026) diaries and her novel of court life in Japan, *Tale of Genji*, offer accessible evidence of the emergence of a distinctive Japanese high culture. Further expressions of distinctive Japanese culture soon arose, including the *bushido* code of honor for warriors, No drama, geisha entertainment, and Pure Land, Zen, and Nichiren sects of Buddhism. Japanese painting and architecture also followed their own distinctive paths.

Koreans remained more closely under Chinese domination, culturally as well as politically. Annamese cultural autonomy developed mainly after they attained definitive independence in 1431. Neither escaped the Chinese shadow to the extent the Japanese did.

But all three countries engaged in and were exposed to intensifying seaborne trading and raiding. Even after the imperial government prohibited Chinese sailors from overseas trade, the imposing mass of China always dominated the seaways; and along the Pacific flank of the Old World Web, Chinese culture was as weighty as the Chinese market economy. But since the controlling counterweight of the Chinese imperial bureaucracy did not extend to the peoples of the Pacific flank, free, more competitive, and at least sometimes also more innovative forms of society, economy, and culture prevailed among them—just as they did among the rival states and peoples of the Atlantic flank of Western Europe. It therefore appears that comparable geopolitical, cultural, and technological marginality on the Atlantic and Pacific flanks of the Old

World Web provoked parallel responses. In particular, between 1000 and 1500 both flanks were rapidly expanding their reach across the high seas, preparing the way for the full globalization of the web.

Southern and Northern Frontiers of the Old World Web

South and east of the Pacific flank, the vast arc of Philippine, Indonesian, and Melanesian islands remained a zone of frontier expansion. Muslim sailors, based in Malaya and elsewhere along the Indian Ocean coast, mingled with ships and sailors from the Pacific coasts. Muslims were remarkably successful in propagating their faith in Malaya, Java, Sumatra, and as far afield as Mindanao in the Philippines. Rice paddy agriculture in Java and Sumatra had long sustained local states and far-flung trading networks. Conversion to Islam facilitated their participation in Indian Ocean commerce.

Further to the southeast, the web thinned out. The regular monsoon winds weakened as one got further from the Asian mainland, inhibiting long-distance sea traffic. The interior of Borneo and the whole of New Guinea, for example, remained apart. The hunters and gatherers and tropical gardeners living there were very effectively defended against intruders by dense and malarial mangrove swamps that clogged much of the islands' shorelines. The uninviting shores of northern Australia had the same isolating effect.

More isolated still from the Asian mainland, Polynesian voyagers from the central Pacific colonized New Zealand about 1300. They entered a cooler climate where the tropical food plants they brought with them did not prosper. So Maori, as the first New Zealanders are called, relied on gathering and fishing until they learned to exploit their alien surroundings efficiently. On tropical islands more favorable to Polynesian agriculture, growing population began to press against resources, and militarized chiefdoms emerged in places like Tonga and Hawaii. And on tiny, isolated Easter Island, the inhabitants met with irretrievable ecological and political disaster when they felled all the trees, so supplies of wood—essential for fuel and for making boats and tools—disappeared.

These far-flung Polynesian populations had severed connections with the Old World Web, but the emergence of militarized chiefdoms in the larger island clusters closely resembles the emergence of states elsewhere. This suggests that political responses to population growth and local shortages were uniform, and perhaps even necessary, since states and chiefdoms redistribute goods by circulating gifts and taxes, and do something to restrain disruptive violence (like that which broke out on Easter Island) by monopolizing it.

Sub-Saharan Africa and the forests of northern Eurasia were frontier zones that became more tightly entangled in the Old World Web between 1000 and 1500. In both regions, populations remained thin. Arctic cold limited farming in the north; in Africa, lethal disease regimes and recurrent drought and famine had a parallel effect. Nonetheless, connections with the Old World Web multiplied, and in favored locations powerful states arose and prospered partly on the strength of long-distance trade.

In the sudanic region of West Africa—the grasslands from Senegal to Lake Chad—Islam helped to forge ties to the Old World Web as we noted above. So too did commercial connections sustained by camel caravan across the Sahara. The Niger River had for centuries hosted agricultural societies united by networks of trade along the river. Once they had large horses (introduced from Morocco), saddles, and stirrups, soldiers soon mastered the arts of cavalry warfare and employed them to cow their neighbors, amass booty, and build states, indeed great territorial empires.[7] Mali at its height, around 1330, extended from the Atlantic almost to Lake Chad, and imposed a broad peace that allowed trade and interaction to flourish along the desert edge and savanna grasslands. Its rulers controlled the export (to the Arab world) of what was in the early fourteenth century about two-thirds of the world's gold production, the politically crucial importation of horses, and the southward flow of salt from the Sahara to the salt-deprived forest zone. When trans-Saharan caravan trade flourished, the merchants and rulers of Mali and its successor state Songhai did too. Songhai's fortunes crested around 1470 to 1515. But political unity proved fragile. In the upper and middle Niger region, strong and ancient traditions of civil society and weak ones of central authority helped make the empires of the savanna short-lived, and soon struggles among rival rulers restrained trade by raising protec-

---

[7] This empire building took place in the context of demographic decline, according to Roderick McIntosh, *The Peoples of the Middle Niger* (Oxford, 1998), ch. 10, which runs contrary to previous inferences. It may be that the retrenchment of settlement that McIntosh and other archeologists detect in the Niger basin resulted from trans-Saharan contacts that brought new diseases, perhaps including bubonic plague, to the region.

tion costs. Further, this competition promoted the use of slave raiding as a source of state revenue, constraining agricultural production and population growth, as tens of thousands (there are no reliable numbers) of West Africans were packed off to the slave markets of Marrakesh, Tripoli, and Cairo, and, later on, to Lisbon or the Americas. Climate change, always important on desert edges, may also have constrained agriculture and weakened large states in the savanna zone in the fifteenth and sixteenth centuries. The last gasp of centralized imperial power came in 1591, when a weakened Songhai succumbed to a Moroccan army. The West African sudan now was securely within the Old World Web.

In the Great Lakes region of East-Central Africa, irrigated rice and bananas sustained dense local populations allowing powerful chiefdoms to become full-blown agrarian states, enjoying slender but growing trade connections with the Swahili coast. Further south, at Great Zimbabwe, fourteenth-century ruins attest to the power of a kingdom based on grazing, agriculture, and gold exports. Zimbabwe's rulers imported luxury goods from as far away as Persia, India, and China. But Great Zimbabwe and the agrarian states that developed in the Great Lakes region were exceptions in a region with weak transport and communications. With no pack animals and few navigable rivers, central and southern Africa before 1500 had few cities and scant long-distance trade. Without horsemen, it had no large empires. Unlike the West African savanna, which had cities, markets, and empires, and thus approximated patterns common throughout Eurasia, East and southern Africa remained peripheral to the Old World Web.

Much of the Arctic north remained marginal too, where isolated communities of hunters, fishers, and gatherers pursued traditional ways. But in the Russian lands, where temperatures were somewhat milder than in Siberia, slowly but surely agricultural populations infiltrated the northern forests. Slash and burn farming predominated, always supplemented by hunting and gathering. The far-ranging river network of Russia provided convenient transport, thanks to boats in summer and sleighs in winter. That in turn meant that even a distant ruler could hope to collect taxes in kind—furs, not grain, in this case—from forest dwellers. Itinerant fur traders also distributed easily portable items like metal axes and traps among local peoples in return for more furs. The rise of the state of Muscovy in the fifteenth century and the wealth of the city of Novgorod, where the fur trade centered, registered this initial penetration of the northern forests.

The American Webs

Meanwhile in the Americas, new peoples erected powerful military empires in Mexico and Peru, and eagerly expanded the webs in the Americas through war and trade. Farmers continued to infiltrate hunting-and-gathering communities, and bow-wielding warriors widened their domain in the Caribbean Islands and wherever else bowmen encountered peoples with less effective missile weapons.

The effort required to build the Aztec capital of Tenochtitlán (founded on an island in 1325) required mobilizing massive numbers of laborers to maintain raised fields in the lake shallows, and build a dam to protect its fresh water from encroaching salt. The Incas (ruled 1440–1532) dragooned even larger numbers of their subjects for building roads, terracing mountain slopes, and constructing vast stone fortifications to defend their Andean empire. The size and number of the ceremonial mounds raised at Cahokia, Illinois, between about 1050 and 1250 also required the concerted effort of many thousands of persons. Religious and military ideas and organization combined to make these feats possible; and we can be sure that military and priestly demand for luxury goods kept long-distance traders busy and sustained an active American web that embraced much of North and South America by the time the Spaniards arrived.

Political-ceremonial centers and surrounding networks had existed in the Americas for more than 1,000 years, and while much undoubtedly was new, fundamental features did not alter very much between 1000 and 1500. No transformative intensification like that occurring in the Old World Web in response to improved water transport could take place since limits on transport and communication remained as before. As far as human occupancy of the Americas was concerned, the gradual advance of agriculture toward remote regions like New England and the Rio de la Plata Valley (today's Argentina and Uruguay) was probably more important than anything occurring in the centers of Mexico and Peru.

Conclusion

What happened in the rest of the world between 1000 and 1500 pales beside the transformations of the core areas of the Old World Web. Five centuries of increased interaction, specialization, intermittently rising production, and intensified mobilization of human effort—both in response to market prices and in response to political command—raised the power and wealth of the Old World Web's core areas to unprecedented heights. Simultaneously, the Old World Web had become increasingly unstable, especially in its westernmost European segment. Drastic consequences would ensue, transforming all the earth in the centuries to come.

VI

SPINNING THE WORLDWIDE WEB, 1450–1800

As of 1450, the 350–400 million people on the face of the earth spoke several thousand languages, followed several hundred religions, and recognized several hundred political rulers (although a few million people recognized no rulers at all). Despite the effects of four millennia of civilization, portable and proselytizing religions, and empire building, humankind was not in any deep sense a community. Tremendous diversity still prevailed. And 60–120 million people in Oceania, the Americas, and Central and Southern Africa lived almost completely isolated from the main theater of history to date, the Old World Web.

In the three and a half centuries after 1450, the peoples of the earth increasingly formed a single community. From this point forward, it makes less and less sense to treat different regions of the earth separately, as hitherto we have sometimes done, but will do no more. Henceforth we will increasingly approach themes globally—including the process of globalization.

Early modern globalization was a painful, sometimes brutal process. Peoples, languages, and religions vanished, while a handful of successful imperial societies spread their power and cultures to new lands. As tens of millions of people (together with their resources and ecosystems) joined what was now becoming a worldwide web, the process of specialization of labor and exchange became truly global, yielding greater wealth but also greater inequality than ever before. All these trends were continuations of—indeed, they were built upon—the homogenizing impacts of the spread of civilizations within Eurasia and Africa. But now things happened faster, and almost no one was left out—though many were left behind.

The World's Webs as of 1450

THE OLD WORLD WEB

By 1450, the Old World Web encompassed some three-fourths of humanity. Its western frontier abutted the Atlantic Ocean, from the West African savanna to Britain and Scandinavia. To the north, its reach extended into the vast forests of Russia and along the southern fringe of vaster ones in Siberia. Its eastern frontier stood at the Pacific Ocean, from Korea and Japan in the north to the archipelagoes of offshore Southeast Asia. Java lay firmly within the web, but participation shaded off further south and east. New Guinea and Melanesia remained (as yet) outside the web. Its southern frontier was the islands and coasts of the Indian Ocean world, from Sumatra around to northern Mozambique. The web extended some tendrils into the interior of East Africa, but for most purposes it stopped (as yet) not far behind the coast. The forest dwellers of West and Central Africa and the inhabitants of Southern Africa took part in the life of the web only sporadically. Thousands of years of migration, trade, missionary work, technology transfer, biological exchange, and military conquest had created this huge web.

The Old World Web was a homogenizing force, but it was far from homogenous. It could never be fully so, because geography and climate dictated some differences: sorghum will not grow in Sweden, nor rye in Bangladesh. The web was lumpy and inconsistent. Some places and people squarely within its boundaries did not take part: some forest peoples in Southeast Asian highlands, for example, remained self-sufficient, spoke their own local languages, worshiped their own local gods, and scarcely had any more contact with the outside world than did Easter Islanders. At the other end of the spectrum, parts of the web served as nodes of daily interaction, cosmopolitan centers where ideas, goods, infections, and people constantly mingled and left their mark: Venice, Cairo, Constantinople (Istanbul), Samarkand in Central Asia, Calicut in southern India, Melaka (Malacca) in today's Malaysia, among others.

Thousands of caravan tracks and sea routes held the web together. Two great trunk routes stood out. The first of these spanned Asia, from North China to the Mediterranean and Black Sea coasts. The old Silk Road, in reality a series of connected caravan routes, had carried travelers regularly since Han and Roman times. It also carried, at times, Islam, Buddhism, and Christianity; cotton, melons, cherries, and grapes; smallpox and bubonic plague; guns, gunpowder, and stirrups. Its traffic peaked when political conditions permitted peace and rulers had the power and foresight to suppress bandits and keep protection costs low. The Mongols had created such conditions in the thirteenth and four-teenth centuries, but the breakup of their empire, and the struggles of competing khans in Central Asia, had reduced caravan trade and all the contacts and exchanges that went with it. A smaller, successor empire forged by Timur briefly fostered contacts and trade, but by 1510 his suc-cessors succumbed to Uzbek and other conquerors, and enduring frag-mentation followed. In the long run, this trunk route gradually declined, and the great caravan cities of Tabriz, Khiva, Bukhara, and Samarkand slowly withered.

The second great trunk route was by sea. To some extent it com-peted for traffic with the first. It extended from the ports of Korea, Japan, and (especially) China south through the archipelagoes of South-east Asia, around the Malay Peninsula, and into the Indian Ocean to the ports of the Persian Gulf and Red Sea. Mastery of the monsoon winds had opened this trunk route in very ancient times. Few people sailed from one end of it to the other, just as few trekked the full length of the Silk Road. Rather, the Indian Ocean route was in most cases a collection of smaller links, with dozens of port cities serving as transfer and trans-shipment points. But it functioned as a single trunk route for goods, ideas, technologies, and diseases. Traffic fluctuated here too, depending on (among other things) the risks posed by pirates and the tolls demanded by political authorities able to control "choke points" along the way. It was along these trunk routes, and their countless feeder channels, that Ming porcelain made it to East Africa, Spanish silver to Chinese coffers, Chinese silks to Venetian grandees, West African gold to Indian princes.

The Rise of Maritime Links Within the Old World Web

By the fifteenth century, the eastern and western extremities of the web were thickening and consolidating quickly. This was mainly a result of advances, shared (if unevenly) throughout the web in ship design and navigational skill, but which bore different consequences in different settings. In earlier centuries, the domestication of camels and the refine-ment of caravan skills had disproportionately benefited the central seg-ments of the web, where these advances applied. Now new maritime knowledge and technology had a similar effect on the flanks of the web. Sturdier ships allowed fuller exploitation of the dangerous seas of the western Pacific, from Japan to Java, and of the northeast Atlantic, from Norway to Spain, and soon to Senegal. Both maritime environments were stormy and treacherous, but both featured numerous bays, peninsulas, and islands with plenty of good anchorages, and both were large enough to encompass a wide spectrum of resources and crops. This made the rewards to exchange, even of bulk goods such as grain, salt, and timber, appealing. In both cases the maritime worlds connected to waterborne inland transport, important in making transport costs low enough to permit bulk trade. The European rivers—the Rhine, Elbe, Danube, Po, and many smaller ones—flow fairly evenly throughout the year and are easily navigable. The East Asian rivers—Yellow, Yangzi, Pearl, Mekong, and many others—are more seasonal because of monsoon rains, but with painstaking construction of canals and irrigation works, the river and canal network of East Asia had become an effective means of extending waterborne transport and exchange into the interiors.

In South Asia, and even more so in southwestern Asia and East Africa, the river regime proved much less favorable (hence the prominence of caravan traffic). First of all, rivers were fewer, because rainfall was sparser. Further, most of the rivers fluctuated sharply with the seasons, and often carried too much or too little water for easy navigation. Moreover, the maritime world of the Indian Ocean had developed very early, and had long had ships well adapted to its comparatively gentle conditions. Hence it was less affected by the fifteenth-century improvements in ship design. So, within the giant web, maritime connections were acquiring greater weight, and the littorals of the Atlantic and Pacific prospered from these changes more than did the shores of the Indian Ocean.

THE PACIFIC AND AMERICAN WEBS

Two smaller webs existed in the fifteenth century, or perhaps one existed and another was still being spun. The least developed was the Pacific web. The extraordinary maritime skills of the Polynesians that had brought them to most of the habitable islands between New Zealand, Easter Island, and Hawaii also served to keep some Pacific islands in frequent touch with one another. The sailors of Micronesia had comparable maritime skills and, if anything, better sea craft than the Polynesians. The admittedly thin evidence suggests that in the fifteenth

Map 6.1 The World's Webs, ca. 1450–1500

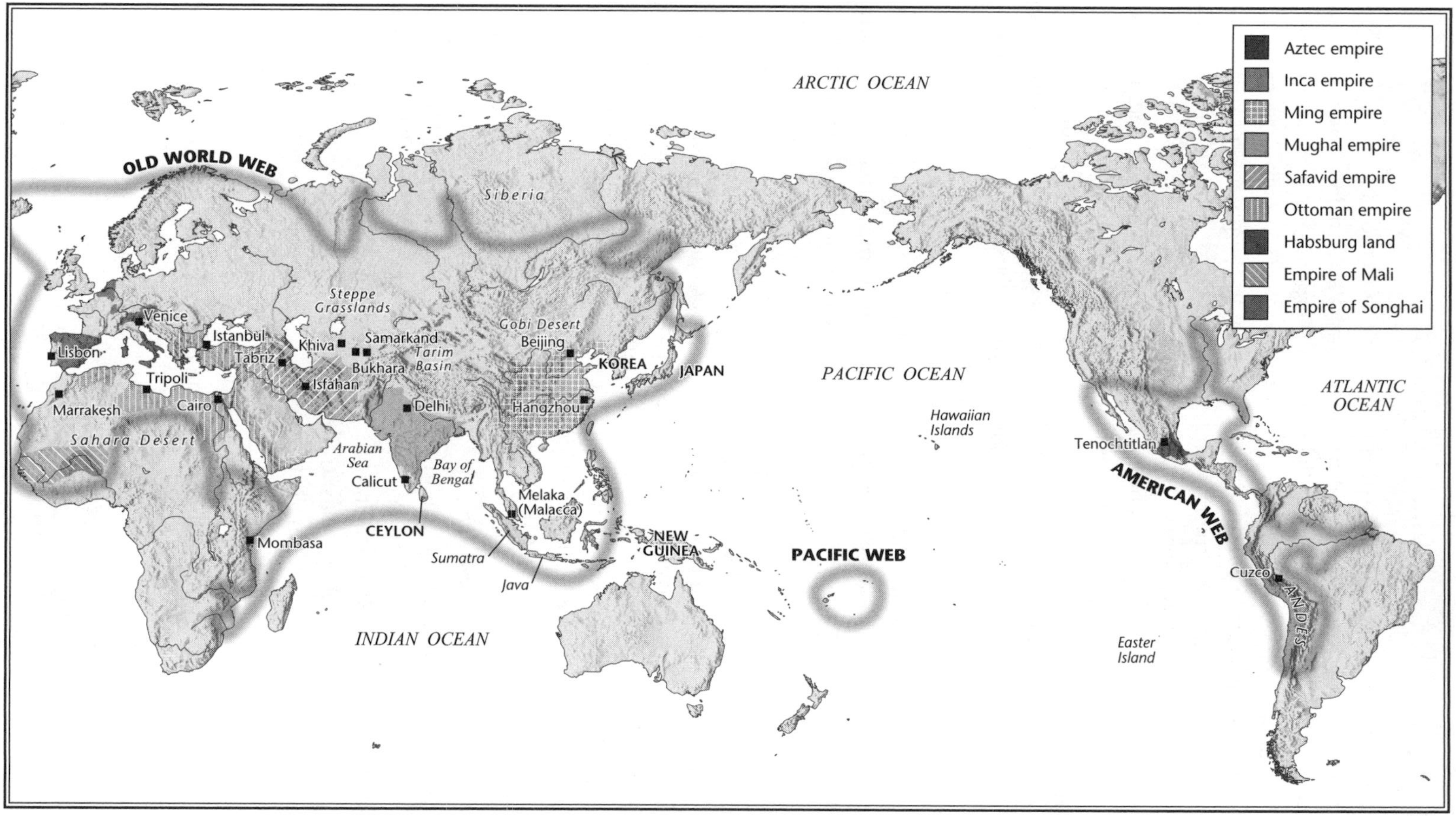

Legend:
- Aztec empire
- Inca empire
- Ming empire
- Mughal empire
- Safavid empire
- Ottoman empire
- Habsburg land
- Empire of Mali
- Empire of Songhai

ATLANTIC OCEAN

ARCTIC OCEAN

AMERICAN WEB

ANDES

Cuzco

Tenochtitlan

Easter Island

PACIFIC OCEAN

Hawaiian Islands

PACIFIC WEB

OLD WORLD WEB

Siberia

Gobi Desert

KOREA

JAPAN

Beijing

Hangzhou

NEW GUINEA

Melaka (Malacca)

Java

Sumatra

Bay of Bengal

Delhi

CEYLON

Calicut

INDIAN OCEAN

Arabian Sea

Tarim Basin

Samarkand

Bukhara

Khiva

Isfahan

Tabriz

Istanbul

Venice

Tripoli

Cairo

Mombasa

Steppe Grasslands

Lisbon

Marrakesh

Sahara Desert

century regular trade circuits centering on the island of Yap (in the Caroline Islands) extended as far as Guam and Palau, using stone discs as money. The Melanesian and Polynesian chiefdoms on Fiji, Samoa, and Tonga also maintained regular contacts. Tonga, an archipelago of small but fertile islands, was a maritime chiefdom, in the process of becoming a maritime empire. Its rulers built kinship networks and exchanged prestige items over long distances. This was the core of a web under construction in the fifteenth century. It was more political than commercial. Populations were scant—at most a few million people counting all the Pacific islands—and the ecological similarity of the islands north of New Zealand combined with the great distances to limit trade and other forms of interaction. This was a large but very loose web, with only slender threads beyond Tonga and its neighbors.

The second separate web, in the Americas, included far more people. The whole of the Americas in 1450 contained perhaps 40 to 60 million people. (Estimates range from 5 million to more than 100 million, but lately seem to be converging.) The great majority of these people lived in a loosely interactive web stretching from the North American Great Lakes and upper Mississippi south to the Andes. In the absence of pack animals (aside from the Andean llama), water transport played a large role in keeping this web together. Canoes carried people and goods efficiently on the rivers of the Mississippi basin. The same held for the Orinoco and Amazon basins of South America. Seagoing canoes containing up to thirty people and cargo rafts hugging the coastlines of the Caribbean and the Gulf of Mexico linked the two continents, as did traffic along the Pacific coasts between Mexico and Peru.

This American web had two nodes, one in central Mexico where the Aztec state was based, and the other in Peru, home of the Inca. The Aztecs had built on the traditions of earlier civilizations in Mexico and inherited a leading position in networks of trade and cultural influence that extended well north into the heartland of North America. These networks consisted of relay trade, overland and in coastal and river boats. Merchants and markets played a major role in Mesoamerican society, and formed the basis of the loose web of North American peoples. Politically, the Aztecs dominated only central Mexico, but culturally central Mexico influenced a broad belt from the drylands of northern Mexico through the Mississippi basin and on into the southeastern woodlands of North America. Although Mexican northward trade and cultural links seem to have weakened after the thirteenth century, they still existed in 1450. At the center stood Tenochtitlán, a city of perhaps a quarter million, with markets that in 1519 amazed and awed Spanish conquistadors who had seen the great cities of Naples and Istanbul.

Between about 1440 and 1520, the Inca built an empire stretching from southernmost Colombia to northernmost Argentina and Chile. It was extraordinary for the rapidity of conquest (like the contemporary Ottomans) and the high degree of political and cultural integration it imposed over 7–12 million people. The Inca held their conquests together with a network of roads in the Andes and along the Pacific coast, helping to make up for the lack of useful transport rivers. The road network included some 15,000–25,000 miles (25,000–40,000 kilometers) of engineered roads, arranged in two great trunk lines with innumerable feeder roads. This stands among the world's great public works achievements. Their imperial religion, in which a sun god played the central role, spread widely and quickly wherever their armies held sway, as did their distinctive monumental stone architecture, textile patterns, pottery styles, and the Qechua language. Coastal shipping fostered economic integration too, more under the guidance of the state than of merchants and markets. In contrast to the Aztecs and their predecessors, Inca influence seems to have reached little beyond the areas subject politically to Inca domination—which may reflect the limited role of merchants and markets in Andean society.

Outside the Inca domain, the American web was much looser, a matter not of political control so much as of migration, trade, and influence. Crops such as maize and manioc had spread quite widely. Some cultural practices, such as ball games played on outdoor courts, existed on the Caribbean Islands, in Mexico, and in northern South America (but curiously not in some of Central America). Some peoples, such as the Maya around Cozumel, traded very widely, but others seem to have taken little part in exchange beyond their local communities. Canoes regularly moved among the Caribbean Islands, but apparently only rarely from them to the mainlands of North and South America.

The nature of the evidence does not permit confident assessments, but it is best to conclude that the American web was large but thin when Columbus arrived in American waters. Many people existed quite outside it, in the far north and far south of the Americas, and in other pockets as well. Great cultural diversity persisted—some 2,000 mutually unintelligible languages were spoken in 1492—despite the centuries of contact and exchange, and the successful empire building. That would soon change.

SIMILARITIES AND DIFFERENCES AMONG THE WEBS

These webs, in Eurasia-Africa, in the Pacific, and in the Americas, were very different in scale, in both extent and density of interconnection. But, large and small, tightly or loosely integrated, they were all zones of comparatively low transport and information costs, in which it was comparatively easy to learn about conditions elsewhere, to travel, and to exchange goods, ideas, and, inadvertently, infections. Consequently, best practices diffused more quickly inside these webs than outside them—whether the best ways to rig a ship or to achieve a satisfactory afterlife. This reduced cultural diversity considerably, as people conformed, voluntarily or not, to a smaller set of standards. At the same time, however, the webs promoted specialization of production and division of labor, fostering a measure of economic diversity as different communities specialized in different activities. More important, specialization and exchange allowed more efficient exploitation of resources (including people), creating wealth. That wealth was distributed very unevenly. All this meant that societies within the webs were richer, more powerful, and more hierarchical than those elsewhere. Further, societies within the webs were epidemiologically more formidable, because their greater density and speed of interaction circulated infections more efficiently, causing (over time and at great cost in child mortality) disease resistance to spread more widely (among surviving adults). All this distinguished participants in the webs from more isolated societies.

But the world's webs were not equals. The biggest and densest was the Old World Web. Its constituent societies included the most formidable on earth, in terms of military and transport technology, in terms of their ability to focus political power at chosen times and places, and in terms of their disease resistance. They may not have been the world's most pleasant to live in—certainly not if one chooses child mortality or social equality as one's indicators—but they were the most formidable.

Fusing and Extending the World's Webs, 1450–1800

Adam Smith, the great Scottish moral philosopher of the eighteenth century and architect of modern economic thought, wrote that the greatest events in the history of the world as of 1776 were Christopher Columbus's voyage to the Americas in 1492 and Vasco da Gama's around Africa in 1497–98. He was half-right.

Prior to Columbus (1451–1506), large parts of the world existed in complete ignorance and isolation from one another. Sporadic contacts across the Atlantic and Pacific, such as the voyages of Norsemen to Labrador or (perhaps) Polynesians to South America, had very minor consequences. Columbus's voyage stands as the most crucial step in undoing that ignorance and isolation, in fusing the world's webs into a single, global one, the most important process in modern history. But that step was merely part of that journey, an outcome of widespread changes in ship design and navigational skill pioneered by mostly anonymous figures all across the Old World Web.

REVOLUTIONS IN SHIP DESIGN AND NAVIGATION

During the fifteenth century, the science and craftsmanship of Eurasia converged to produce in Atlantic Europe two crucial changes. One was a strong, swift, maneuverable ship, cheap to build and operate, capable of sailing anywhere on the world's seas and oceans, and capable of carrying plentiful heavy cannon. The second was navigational knowledge, an understanding of the general circulation of the winds and oceanic currents, combined with the capacity to convert astronomical observations into a good idea of where one was. With these developments, maritime connections became the guiding force in human history for some 300 years.

The innovations in ship design culminated in the fully rigged ship, the first evidence of which comes from about 1420. Expanded shipping between the Mediterranean and the North and Baltic seas brought a fertile cross between hitherto different traditions in hull design and rigging. The result featured the sturdy and economical "carvel" construction typical of the Mediterranean, in which planks were nailed to a skeletal rib, rather than, as had prevailed in northern waters, nailed to one another in overlapping fashion like house clapboards ("clinker" construction). This used less wood yet made for a stronger hull. The sternpost rudder (first developed in Chinese waters but probably a second time in the Baltic) improved maneuverability over the previous practice of trailing a steering oar. Combination of Northern European and Mediterranean practices in rigging brought both better maneuverability and speed. The fully rigged ship had three masts and carried both square sails (good at exploiting a favorable wind) and lateen sails (better at sailing into the wind). With improved maneuverability, ships could do without oars and oarsmen, formerly needed as insurance against uncooperative winds. Hence, the fully rigged ship was cheaper to operate as well as to build.

Further, the new hulls and rigging made it possible to build much larger, yet still seaworthy, vessels. The biggest were called carracks, which by 1450 attained 500 and, by 1590, even 2,000 tons burden, the largest wooden ships ever built. A sixteenth-century French king had a tennis court installed in one. The fully rigged ship was maneuverable in almost any wind, and strong enough to withstand the battering of rough seas. A good ship, however, was only the hardware.

In the fourteenth and fifteenth centuries, a parallel fusion of knowledge brought the software needed to unite the world. In Iberia, the traditions of Arab astronomy and mathematics, often buttressed by Jewish scholars, combined with the observations and practical experience of Spanish and Portuguese sailors to generate a truly mathematical science of navigation. With suitable instruments, charts, and tables, this allowed sea captains to know their latitude with considerable precision, permitting reliable return voyages to Atlantic islands, such as Madeira, the Azores, and the Canaries, by the 1420s. Portuguese and Spanish mariners began to master the Atlantic triangle between Iberia, West Africa, and the Azores. By 1442 (if not before) they were using a small, speedy, two-masted lateen-rigged vessel, the caravel, to venture southward along the West African coast. Its particular virtue was that it could sail close to the wind, permitting a return to Portugal sailing against the trade winds. When the Portuguese figured out that they could safely depart the African coast, sail into the mid-Atlantic, head north, and then catch the prevailing westerlies to get home again, they began using larger vessels for their voyages to Africa. By 1482, they established a post in what is today Ghana; by 1488, they had reached the Cape of Good Hope and figured out that the winds in the southern hemisphere followed a pattern that was a reverse mirror-image of those in the northern hemisphere. By 1498, Vasco da Gama (ca. 1460–1524) ventured into the Indian Ocean, where he retained the services of a local captain who piloted da Gama's carrack from the East African coast to India. The Portuguese quickly acquired the common knowledge of the monsoon wind patterns of the Indian Ocean; but their own knowledge, of Atlantic winds and mathematical navigation, they tried hard to keep secret.

Ships and Politics

So, by the 1490s the Portuguese had the knowledge and the equipment to go anywhere they might wish on the high seas. To do so in safety, and to get what they wanted from their voyages, they needed a further innovation, shipboard cannon. The big and sturdy carracks could carry a large complement of cannon, which the other ships of the world could not. Even the big ships of the Indian Ocean and the South China Sea did not have the sturdy rib construction of carracks, and tended to shake apart if subjected to the recoil from heavy cannon. In 1510, off the Indian port of Diu, the Portuguese won the first naval battle that did not involve ramming or boarding enemy ships. By 1530, they (and others) built ships tailored to the requirements of cannon, with gunports and gundecks just above the waterline. After 1550, naval and merchant ships in Atlantic Europe became structurally different, and any monarch or city-state hoping to survive on the seas had to come up with the money to build warships. That would affect European politics ever after.

Politics also affected the process by which Europeans brought the world's webs together. To bring together the scholars and sea captains who jointly created the decisive navigational knowledge required state sponsorship. Prince Henry the Navigator (1394–1460) energetically achieved this, using family ties to ensure the support of the Portuguese crown and the papacy. He embraced Jewish scholars from Spain, maintained a school of navigation at Sagres, and in his crusader zeal to combat Islam cheerfully made use of Muslim science. Portuguese state support for overseas voyaging slackened somewhat after Henry's death, but revived strongly by the 1480s, so that it was Portuguese captains who first rounded the Cape of Good Hope, and who first directly linked the Atlantic with trading circuits of the Indian Ocean.

Other Atlantic European kingdoms soon acquired the requisite maritime knowledge to imitate the Portuguese. Spain, a political rival of Portugal, sponsored Columbus after the Portuguese had rebuffed him (a Portuguese-supported captain, Ferdinand von Olmen, had sailed off to the west in 1487 and never returned). England supported John Cabot, an Italian like Columbus, who sailed to Newfoundland in 1497. Over the next century, the Atlantic European states sent scores of maritime expeditions across the high seas, seeking trade, plunder, geographical knowledge, and souls in need of salvation. By 1580, they had accumulated a fairly accurate geographic knowledge of most of the world's coasts. The wide Pacific hid a few secrets from them until the late eighteenth century, when, with the added advantage of instruments that could fix longitude with precision, mariners such as Captain James Cook and George Vancouver—both sponsored by Great Britain—mapped coastlines and currents from Australia to Alaska. By 1794, when Vancouver's survey of the Pacific coast of North America was complete, Atlantic Europeans had charted every inhabited coastline on earth and brought every coastal community around the world into a single interactive web. Columbus's 1492 voyage, which began the integration of the Americas into this worldwide coastal web, was the single most important step, but only one in a long cumulative process that began with the Portuguese voyages to the nearby Atlantic islands and ended with Cook and Vancouver. The process required state support.

CHINESE SHIPS

Zheng He (ca. 1371–1435), the admiral who led six Chinese armadas into the Indian Ocean between 1405 and 1433, had had such support on a scale the Atlantic Europeans could not approach. In the summer of 1415, when Prince Henry the Navigator was taking part in a Portuguese expedition against the Moroccan town of Ceuta, Zheng He was in Hormuz, at the mouth of the Persian Gulf, on the fourth of his six expeditions. Prince Henry was about 200 miles from home, while Zheng He had sailed some 5,000 or 6,000 miles from his base. Zheng He's biggest ships were six to ten times the size of the largest Columbus later commanded, and thirty times the size of John Cabot's lone vessel of 1497. On Columbus's largest expedition (the second of his four) he had 17 ships and about 1,500 men, whereas Zheng He's first expedition counted 317 ships and about 27,000 crew. Columbus's 1492 voyage had only ninety men; Cabot had about eighteen. Ferdinand Magellan, the Portuguese mariner who (in the service of Spain) led the first expedition to circle the globe, shipped out with a crew of 270, just 1 percent of Zheng He's. Prince Henry's Portugal contained about 1 million people (Spain in 1492 had 6 million), while in 1415 China had about 115 million, and its state revenues were probably more than 100 times those of Portugal's. Yet state support vanished in China and flourished in Portugal. After the 1430s, the Ming emperors had other priorities, and by 1470 the skills needed to build great ships were lost.

But the Chinese voyages yielded some dividends. Navigational and geographic knowledge accumulated despite the efforts of the Ming to suppress it. Zheng He's voyages reaped immense amounts of information about the Indian Ocean and Southeast Asian waters, which found its way into route maps, route manuals, star charts, and the like. These circulated in private hands even after the minister of war had official copies burned. Such knowledge was constantly refined by reports from (illegal) voyages and in 1537 some of it was published in a book called

Route for Crossing the Ocean. Many similar books, maps, and route guides followed. By the 1570s, the Ming relaxed prohibitions on maritime trade. Trade flourished, bringing the goods of Japan, Korea, China, and Southeast Asia firmly into a single giant maritime marketplace.

But by this time the Atlantic Europeans were well on their way to global maritime knowledge. In 1793, when Vancouver was completing that job, a British emissary to Beijing, in search of a trade agreement, was told by the emperor (Qianlong, reigned 1736–95) that China had no interest in a small country "cut off from the world by intervening wastes of seas." This outlook was an indication of China's genuine power, but also of the elderly emperor's failure to recognize that it was the seas that united the world into a single web by 1793.

EXPANDING THE WEB IN AFRICA

The first major maritime expansion of the web involved Africa. In 1450, Mediterranean Africa, Ethiopia, the sudan region, and the East African coast were already part of the Old World Web, but the rest of the continent was not. A dangerous disease environment, a paucity of navigable rivers, and considerable military skills helped keep outsiders out of tropical and Southern Africa until after 1800, with few exceptions. New maritime connections had begun to alter this after 1440, but only selectively. In East Africa, between the Zambezi River and Ethiopia, interaction with the web via the Indian Ocean expanded only a little. Portuguese mariners took over several coastal ports (1505–20), but these towns for several centuries had already communicated closely with the Arab, Persian, and Indian worlds. The Portuguese, and their Afro-Portuguese offspring, voyaged inland, up the Zambezi and also into Ethiopia, but they did not overthrow kingdoms or settle in any numbers. Nor did Christianity or Islam infiltrate far into inland East Africa (until later). A modest slave and ivory trade, to Arabia and India mainly, involved at a very rough guess 1,000 slaves a year before 1720, after which time Portuguese slavers in Mozambique stepped up the scale. Most of East Africa behind the coast remained almost unaffected by long-distance contacts, overwhelmingly rural, focused on the slow struggle to occupy the land with villages, crops, and cattle.

The tip of Southern Africa, however, joined the web suddenly and completely. Portuguese—and after 1600, Dutch—ships bound for the Indian Ocean commonly stopped at the Cape of Good Hope for water, food, and recuperation. The Cape has a Mediterranean climate with winter rains, but is surrounded (on the landward side) by arid zones. In 1652, the Dutch East India Company (known by its Dutch initials VOC) established a permanent post there and inaugurated regular contact with the local population. For millennia South Africa had been home to pastoralists, called Khoikhoi, and hunter-gatherers, the San. In the Cape region they numbered perhaps 50,000. The VOC found that the Khoikhoi and San could not provide the supplies they needed for their long voyages, and by the 1670s brought farmers to the Cape, making it into an agricultural colony. From the beginning it depended largely on slaves, purchased or seized from among the Khoikhoi, or brought from India, Indonesia, Madagascar, or, by the eighteenth century, increasingly from Mozambique. The economy evolved to fit the needs of passing ships, so wheat, meat, wine, and prostitutes featured prominently. In 1713 a ship, putting its linens ashore for laundering, brought a nasty strain of smallpox from some Indian Ocean shore. It killed a quarter of Cape Town's residents and as many as 90 percent of the Khoikhoi, whose society was already reeling from slave raids. Smallpox struck again in 1755 and the 1780s, affecting not merely the Khoikhoi but also the Bantu-speaking peoples to the east of the Cape, in parts of South Africa now called Transkei and Natal.

The Dutch language and the Calvinism of the Dutch Reformed Church slowly spread into the slave community and remaining free Khoikhoi population. By 1700, there were enough Muslims to petition VOC officials for a mosque. By 1800, the Cape contained about 20,000 European settlers, mostly Dutch, and 25,000 slaves, mostly of Southern African origin. The Cape was a tiny island of cosmopolitanism in a Southern Africa as yet outside the worldwide web.

In most of Africa, increased participation in the web came chiefly in the form of the slave trade. Sub-Saharan Africa had exported slaves for over a millennium before the Atlantic slave trade began. But the trade across the Sahara, the Red Sea, and the Indian Ocean had been of modest proportions. The significance and size of the slave trade changed when the Atlantic Europeans unified the world's coastlands. Portuguese sailors first seized black Africans in 1441, and began a small slave trade to Portugal and later to Madeira and the Canary Islands. The success of slave-raised sugar there (and in Morocco, where the Saadian dynasty built up a sugar plantation economy with slave labor) inspired imitation first in São Tomé and other offshore African islands, and then in Brazil. Transatlantic slave voyages began (to Brazil) in 1534, first mainly from the coasts of modern Senegal and Ghana. Eventually slave exports for the Americas came from the whole western coast from Senegal to Angola, and by the eighteenth century from Mozambique and East Africa as well.

Before it ended (1850–80), some 11 to 14 million slaves departed Africa, of whom about 85 percent survived the "middle passage" to reach American shores. About 40 percent went to Brazil, an equal number to the Caribbean, and about 5 percent to what would be the United States. The balance ended up in Mexico, Colombia, Peru, and the rest of mainland Spanish America. Traffic peaked in the 1780s at nearly 80,000 per year. Over its 400-year career it was, on average, about ten times the size of the trans-Saharan, Red Sea, and Indian Ocean slave trades.

With their newfound global reach, European slavers had much to offer their African counterparts. At first the Portuguese bought African slaves in order to trade them for African gold on the Gold Coast. But when they had found more profitable uses for slaves, they traded horses instead. By the seventeenth century, the slave trade was part of an intercontinental and interoceanic trade network lubricated by two monies, silver and cowrie shells. American silver allowed European slave traders to buy South Asian goods for the West African market. Cloth from India and Europe was the chief West African import, supplemented by hundreds of other items, including raw iron, copper, tobacco, alcohol, guns, and cowrie shells—harvested around the Indian Ocean, principally in the Maldive Islands, and purchased, typically with American silver, expressly for use in West Africa where they served as the main currency. In 1720, Indian Ocean cowries served to purchase about a third of the slaves sold from West Africa's coast. To get these goods and the cowrie shells, African coastal traders bought slaves and gold from the interior.

This gave merchants, raiders, and princes in the interior every incentive to enslave more people. On account of the Atlantic trade, they enslaved about 25 million people, of whom many died before they could be sold to coastal traders. These millions had been captured in war, kidnaped, or had become slaves by judicial decision when they or someone in their lineage were convicted of a crime.

But the ultimate reasons so many met this fate lay elsewhere. Sugar commanded a strong market in Europe, and tobacco did so almost everywhere. To grow these in the Americas, which lay conveniently upwind of Europe's markets, required a lot of strong backs. The plunging population of Amerindians (see below) did not suffice, and anyway

Amerindians could easily run away in familiar landscapes. Plantation owners tried European indentured laborers (and a few Irish and Scottish slaves), but after 1640 found these too expensive and too short-lived. They died very quickly once malaria and yellow fever became entrenched in the American tropics by 1650. African slaves were cheaper, although not cheap, and their life expectancies in tropical America were much longer. Hence they were bought. But why were they sold?

In Africa, men usually calculated wealth in terms of people—children, wives, retainers, and slaves. This is because in Africa people were scarce, more so than land. A large number of dependents meant status, power, wealth, and security. To achieve this, paradoxically, it made sense to sell slaves. If one could get them cheaply, through capture, and sell them for guns, cowries, or iron, one could accumulate wives and children, one could raid for further slaves—in short, one could amass wealth through reinvestment. Keeping the slaves made less sense, because they could easily run away if not sold far from home; because wives, children, and dependents were more valuable since they were less disaffected and more cooperative than slaves; and because extended family provided more emotional rewards than did a collection of slaves. Furthermore, Africans mainly wanted women and children as slaves, because in most societies they did agricultural work. The Atlantic market paid more for male slaves, so it made particular sense to sell them to coastal dealers. Through market connections made possible by the expansion of the web in the fifteenth and sixteenth centuries, many Africans got rich and gained status by (indirectly) converting slaves into family and followers. They sold some people to get more useful people.

Politics also figured. African rulers fought wars for their own purposes, and in so doing acquired captives. Keeping them around invited trouble. Selling them to the coast made better sense. Attacking one's enemy, seizing as many of his soldiers as possible, and selling them made excellent political sense. Underlying all this was the reality that African slavers had no attachment to the fate of African slaves, because there was then no shared sense of African identity.

The slave trade's impact on Africa was mainly indirect. The 25 million enslaved over 400 years accounted for a very small (but unknowable) share of the population. Even in Angola, where the impact was probably greatest, five to ten times more people died from natural causes every year than were enslaved. Angolans ran a lifetime risk of enslavement about five times greater than the one Americans currently run of death from traffic accidents. Although at certain times and places it was devastating, the demographic impact of the slave trade upon Africa as a whole was probably small.[1]

Yet the full impact was substantial. Politically, the slave trade encouraged the creation and expansion of states. Stateless societies, such as the Igbo of southeast Nigeria, stood at particular risk; they had to keep weapons handy when working in the fields, and lock children in fortified enclosures. The slave trade militarized African societies in many parts of the continent, promoting warlord-entrepreneurs, who challenged the existing order with their quick wealth and violent methods. It favored predatory states, such as the West African Asante (Ashanti) or Dahomey, which specialized in seizing slaves from less well defended neighboring societies. Economically, it favored predatory people who lived from the rewards of slaving and invested the proceeds in horses and guns (perhaps 20 million guns entered Africa in the slave trade) for further raiding, rather than in something that might have yielded greater benefit in the long run. It also quickened the commercialization of African societies, adding much traffic to long-distance trade routes. Culturally, it may have promoted Islam: Muslim law forbids the enslavement of believers, so conversion offered the hope of exemption from the ravages of Muslim slavers in the West African savanna. Socially, it proved divisive. Successful slavers became very rich and powerful; ordinary folk had to tread carefully. Some societies and some merchants chose not to traffic in slaves, while others calculated that they must, lest they themselves be enslaved. To this day in many parts of Africa, people remember whose ancestors were slavers and whose were slaves.

The slave trade's impact was also uneven. Some peoples were wiped out. Those poorly organized for defense and within reach of armed horsemen were the most vulnerable. The West African savanna, where horses were of great importance, was particularly violent, as was Angola, where horses scarcely mattered. By 1800, the tentacles of the slave trade had reached far into the interior, but not everywhere. The central rainforest region—thinly populated in any case—remained little affected.

Through the slave trade, the coasts of Atlantic Africa entered the web. African coastal slavers became fluent in European languages and

---

[1] A contrary view (one of several) on the demographic impact of the slave trade upon Africa appears in Patrick Manning, *Slavery and African Life* (Cambridge, 1990). Angola data from Joseph Miller, *The Way of Death* (Madison, WI, 1988), 154.

some adopted European dress and manners. Trade goods and food crops from around the world entered Atlantic Africa. Behind the coasts participation in the web also expanded through the slave trade.

The East African coast changed rather little under the impact of the web's globalization precisely because it was already deeply enmeshed in the Old World Web. The central sudan (just south of the Sahara between Lake Chad and the Nile) changed only a little more, because it was far from the Atlantic and slaving had long been important there. But in the western sudan, in the West African forest, in Angola and the Cape Colony, initial inclusion in the cosmopolitan web was disruptive and definitive.

FUSING THE AMERICAN AND OLD WORLD WEBS

Seaborne connections brought the Americas into the web shortly after the integration of Atlantic Africa began. Once across the Atlantic in 1492, Europeans forged their way inland in both North and South America, sometimes looking for gold, sometimes for furs, sometimes for souls to save, and sometimes for a route to China. Where they found unified empires, as in Mexico and Peru, they quickly took these over through military conquest or, in the case of the Inca, something more akin to a coup d'état. The Spanish adventurer Hernán Cortés, with a few hundred men, the help of the Aztecs' enemies, and a raging epidemic of smallpox, brought down the Aztec empire in 1519–21. In 1532 his distant kinsman, Francisco Pizarro, with 167 comrades, happened on the Inca empire ravaged by a smallpox epidemic and riven by civil war. By a combination of deft diplomacy, deceit, war, and murder, Pizarro soon became its master. Such events quickly extended the web, because existing systems of tax, tribute, and trade were tweaked a bit to suit Spanish purposes and continued almost as before, but now fused to the Old World Web. For example, the Inca labor-tribute system, the *mita*, by which roads and other public works had been maintained, became the system by which Spanish authorities assured sufficient labor to work the silver mines of the Andes that financed so much of Spain's empire.

Where no unified empire had existed, as in most of North America, Central America, Brazil, and the "southern cone" of South America, the extension of the web proceeded more slowly. New links had to be forged. Conquest of or accommodation with one people and polity had, initially, only local consequences. In Yucatán, for example, where centralized political control had vanished centuries before, Spanish power took centuries to establish, despite the same weapons and germs that had reduced the Aztec empire in two years. The cultural conversion of the Maya was correspondingly slow, and never complete. The Portuguese also took centuries to impose their power, economic linkages, and culture on the wide and politically fragmented spaces of Brazil. So did the English and French in North America, despite, in the English case, uniquely large flows of immigrants after the 1620s, and, in both cases, comparatively healthy populations that reproduced abundantly.

The greatest consequence of uniting the American web with the Old World Web was the catastrophic loss of population in the Americas. None of the American populations had any experience with the "crowd diseases" that had become routine, endemic infections within the Old World Web. Their ancestors had come to America before the domestication of herd animals. This meant none of the diseases derived from herd animals (smallpox, measles, influenza, among others) existed in the Americas, and no immunities to them either. Hence, when the dense, intercommunicating populations of the Americas first encountered these diseases, terrible epidemics resulted. Furthermore, the populations of the Americas all descended from comparatively few ancestors, and their genetic variation was correspondingly small. This meant that a given pathogen, if able to escape the immune system of one person, could very likely do the same to all (whereas among genetically diverse populations pathogens would encounter more people whose immune system shielded them effectively). The Americas recapitulated, on a grand scale, the experience of many peoples previously incorporated into webs. This brought one of the two greatest population disasters in recorded history (the fourteenth-century plague pandemic was the other). At least half, and perhaps as much as 90 percent, of the Amerindian population was lost between 1492 and 1650 to repeated epidemics.

By 1800, most of the Americas, like South Africa, had entered the web. Some 25 million people lived there, still rather less than in 1500. A quarter of them lived in the fledgling United States, and about a fifth in Mexico, still Spanish territory (until 1821). The economy nearly everywhere was run by Europeans or people of European descent, who, through literacy, enjoyed greater knowledge of global markets and political conditions. Silver from Mexico and the Andes circulated all round the world. Almost all American polities, whether European colonies or Amerindian chiefdoms, were enmeshed in global politics. The Iroquois federation, for example, figured in the Seven Years' War (1756–63) in which France and Britain fought in India, in Europe, on the high seas, and in North America. The great majority of people in the Americas followed a globalized religion, Christianity, although practices did not always conform precisely to standards set in Rome or Geneva. And a smaller majority spoke European languages, although in many cases as a second tongue. Only a quarter or a third of the population spoke Amerindian languages, while perhaps a tenth—some slaves and a few free blacks—spoke African ones. Culturally, as economically and politically, the Americas had joined the nascent worldwide web. Only sparsely populated areas, Amazonia or the intermontane west of North America, remained outside by 1800.

EXPANDING THE WEB IN SIBERIA AND THE SUBARCTIC

In the sixteenth and seventeenth centuries, although the seas united the world, the web expanded overland as well. The largest continental interior in the world as yet outside the web lay in the forest and taiga zones of Siberia. In 1500 this vast space, roughly a quarter of Eurasia, probably contained no more than half a million people. They constituted about one hundred linguistic groups, Tungus, Samoyed, Chukchi among them. Their social organization was based on kinship. Most lived as hunters, fishers, gatherers, or reindeer herders with little agriculture and scant interaction with the rest of the world. Some, on the southern fringe, traded and fought with neighbors to the south, Turkic and Mongol steppe peoples.

Siberians shared Siberia with several million fur-bearing animals, foxes, ermine, squirrels, and sable. In the early 1580s, members of the Russian Stroganov family, rich from their monopoly position in the Russian salt trade, convinced Tsar Ivan IV ("Ivan the Terrible") to form a public-private partnership by which the Stroganovs would recruit men and build a fur trade business in western Siberia. Since English merchants had begun to trade for furs at the Arctic port of Archangel, it seemed to the tsar a good idea to get a piece of the action for himself. The Stroganovs found many Cossacks—a rough, frontier population of southern Russia and the Ukraine, skilled in the ways of war—willing to venture into Siberia in search of their fortunes, and in 1582 began a campaign of frontier conquest. The Cossacks and Russians had all the advantages of life inside the web. They had firearms and cannon (which they mounted on river boats) and they had the support of the Russian state, whenever it could spare men and supplies from its western wars with Sweden, Poland, and Ottoman Turkey. They had writing, with which they could communicate over long distances and coordinate the actions of far-flung groups. They also had resistance to many routine infectious diseases, to which many of the Siberians carried few or no immunities. One small group, the Yukagir, was reduced by more than two-thirds, mainly by smallpox.

By 1640, Cossacks had mastered the rivers and portages of Siberia and reached the shores of the Pacific. By 1652, they, and others in the service of the tsar, had clashed with Chinese forces in the Amur River valley. Those struggles ended in a peace treaty of 1689, which set Russian-Chinese frontiers until the mid-nineteenth century. By the 1730s, Russians had taken to the Pacific and extended their settlements to Alaska, and by 1810, to northern California. They built a network of dozens of blockhouses and trading posts, from which they tried to control their sprawling empire.

What animated them was fur. They imposed a tribute system on the Siberians, demanding furs from every able-bodied adult male. They traded for furs too, offering tobacco, alcohol, tools, and flour. For some southern Siberians, in touch with steppe peoples, this was a familiar arrangement, simply with new tribute collectors. For all Siberians—as for many peoples before—this was a rude introduction to life in the web, full of violence, disease, social disruption, and the dispiriting effects of dealing with people more powerful than they. Sooner or later most of them found resistance unrewarding and accommodated themselves to the new regime. Men paid their tribute, women took Russian and Cossack men as husbands and masters. Many Siberians went to work for the Russians, extending the web by enlisting their neighbors in the trade and tribute system. For most of the seventeenth century, the Kremlin got 7–10 percent of its revenues from the 200,000–300,000 pelts it received annually from Siberia.

The inclusion of Siberia in the web was, as everywhere, a cultural as well as an economic process. By 1621, Siberia formed its own (Russian Orthodox) archbishopric. Missionary work converted most Siberians during the eighteenth century. They learned to speak Russian, and several of their native tongues vanished. Thus the peoples, and the ecosystems, of Siberia were added to the economic and cultural web.

The ermine, sable, fox, and squirrels grew scarce—as did the Siberian tribute payers—so the Russians pushed the fur frontier eastward to Alaska. There they did not get far. It took a year or more to travel from Moscow to the Pacific, and the cost of supplying forts and expeditions in the North Pacific was daunting. The broad expanses of northern North

America, thinly inhabited by people but with plenty of fur-bearing animals, were easier to reach from the Atlantic side.

Norsemen had come to Atlantic Canada around the year 1000 but made no lasting imprint. Nor did Basque mariners, who had located the great cod fishery off of Newfoundland sometime in the fifteenth century. Even a century or more after Cabot's 1497 voyage, the Atlantic Europeans still had little impact on North America; but soon after 1600, they established settlements and fur trade posts on the major waterways, the Hudson and the St. Lawrence rivers, and Hudson Bay. They set to work establishing a network of fortified posts, much like the Siberian ones, and induced Amerindian peoples to provide them with beaver pelts. They too had guns and infectious diseases, and the number of Amerindians plummeted as the fur traders spread their system of blockhouses and trading posts throughout the beaver's natural habitat. By 1800, they had reached the Rocky Mountains and, by sea, the Pacific coast of North America, where they found Russians clubbing fur seals and trapping beavers.

Although it took place on two continents, the whole epic was a single circumpolar quest for fur. The Cossacks and Russians, English and French all knew that they could sell as many furs as they could lay hands on. They had at least a general knowledge of the demand for furs in Europe and China (where a lot of Siberian furs ended up). Interestingly, when in 1793 the Scots explorer and fur trader Alexander Mackenzie became the first European to cross the North American continent, he was looking for a commercially viable route by which to sell Canadian furs to China. The expansion into Siberia and northern North America shows the web at work, circulating information, people, goods, and infections over great distances, bringing distant populations into cooperation and conflict, shuffling the fortunes of millions, making some rich, killing or impoverishing others, eliminating some languages and cultures (for example, Yukagir) while spreading others (Russian, French, English).

Expanding the Web in Australia and the Pacific

The far-flung, thinly populated expanses of Australia and Oceania remained outside the worldwide web until late in the eighteenth century. The increasingly lively maritime world of Southeast Asia occasionally brought vessels to northern Australia and Melanesia, but with only trivial consequences. New Zealand probably was entirely cut off from the wider world, even from the Tonga-centered mini-web. This splendid isolation was decisively broken in New Zealand's case in 1769 and in Australia's in 1788.

While population figures are only rough guesses, New Zealand in 1769 had perhaps 100,000 Maori, descendants of the small party of Polynesian pilgrims who arrived around 1300. For a few centuries they had enjoyed boom times, battening on large, protein-rich seals and huge flightless birds called moas. As these creatures grew scarce (and extinct in the moa's case), Maori turned more to horticulture and evolved more militaristic societies, organized into often mutually antagonistic tribes. Soon after Captain Cook began charting New Zealand's coasts in 1769, a swarm of British, French, and then American sealers and whalers arrived, followed by missionaries and traders. By 1820, they had created rough, cosmopolitan ports where Maori and European cultures mixed uneasily. Alien diseases worked their havoc here, although not as severely as in the Americas or elsewhere in Polynesia. Rapid European settlement, political annexation, land wars, and wide conversion to Christianity came only after 1840.

Australian Aborigines numbered perhaps 750,000 in 1788. Estimates vary greatly. They did not engage in agriculture, although they systematically burned vegetation to create conditions favorable for plants and animals they liked to gather and hunt, a practice dubbed "firestick farming." They lived in small, highly mobile groups, loosely confederated into some 500 or 800 "tribes" which, at least in the arid interior, maintained ties of trade, bride-exchange, and reciprocal support over distances of hundreds of miles. They also fought one another routinely. Their sparse numbers, their wood and stone weaponry, their small-scale social organization, their internecine struggles, and their inexperienced immune systems made them vulnerable to massacre, displacement, and disease when shiploads of British convicts, at first mostly petty thieves from London, began to arrive in 1788. By 1845, the settlers' rising population outnumbered the Aborigines' falling one.

Between 1769 and 1850, the worldwide web had stretched out over almost all the Pacific world, from Australia to Hawaii. The seals, whales, sandalwood of the Pacific entered a larger economy, mainly driven by Chinese demand. The few million people involved entered into a larger cultural world, dominated by Europeans and Christianity. They also entered a political-military realm in which they enjoyed few advantages, and a microbial common market in which they had none. It was, for all the peoples of the Pacific, a greater or lesser catastrophe, as it had been for the peoples of the Americas, Siberia, and South Africa not long before, and as it had been for countless peoples long ago, obliterated or absorbed, often with no trace, in the process of creating the large metropolitan webs. By 1850 the falling populations of all the thickly inhabited Pacific island groups—Hawaii, Samoa, Tonga, Fiji—had definitively joined the worldwide web.

The unification of the world's webs, and the extension of the new worldwide web into new lands, was chiefly the doing of the Atlantic Europeans. They were the Mongols of the sea.[2] Like the Mongols, they had a military edge (in their case shipboard cannon after 1450) and were not slow to use it. Like the Mongols, they found it easy enough to enlist allies who saw at least short-term advantage in making common cause. And like the Mongols, their conquests, slaughters, takeovers, co-optations, and absorptions of other peoples laid the groundwork for unprecedented consolidation of the webs of social and ecological interaction.

The World the Web Made, 1500–1800

The forging of a worldwide web disrupted and destroyed, but it also transformed and created. With the creation of a single web, it is as if history speeded up. Innovations and inventions, booms and depressions, pests and plagues rippled through a unified system, spreading wherever local conditions allowed. Human lives increasingly were molded by events and processes originating far away, acting in combination with evolving local realities, making for historical forces that few contemporaries understood. Silver production in the Andes, Mexico, and Japan would strongly influence the economic and political trends of Southeast Asian archipelagoes; Brazilian food crops, such as cassava, and Mexican ones such as maize, would exert sway over demographic trends in Central Africa, China, and the Balkans; guns would reshape geopolitics almost everywhere. So, as human history grew more unified, it grew more unstable and chaotic than ever, a condition with which we still live.

In this turbulence we discern some long-term trends that shaped the centuries from 1500 to 1800. In intellectual and cultural terms, the process of unification of the webs helped drive major challenges to existing patterns of thought and religion, leading to reformations, revivals, schisms, and to modern science. In political terms, the process led to

---

[2] This phrase is borrowed from Arnold Pacey, *Technology in World Civilization* (Cambridge, MA, 1990).

fewer, more powerful states and a huge increase in the gap between strong and weak. In economic terms, it led to a great reshuffling of fortunes, by and large in favor of the merchant classes everywhere. In social terms, it brought population growth, more complex social hierarchies, and an increase in inequalities. In ecological terms, it led to numerous biological exchanges, a partial homogenization of the planet's flora, fauna, and diseases. And in geographical terms, it led to new regional communities united by maritime transport, water worlds. These trends would continue beyond 1800 to the present day.

INTELLECTUAL AND CULTURAL CURRENTS

The cross-currents of ideas and information in these centuries challenged existing intellectual, religious, cultural—and political—orders. The challenge was perhaps most strenuous in Atlantic Europe, because of the role of Atlantic Europeans in uniting and traveling the worldwide web. But it was felt everywhere, and met with the usual range of reactions, from adoption of new outlooks to vigorous reassertion of ancient systems of knowledge and wisdom.

Information and Communication

Circumstances conspired to favor faster and wider movement of information. First came the matter of oceanic voyaging and the simultaneous expansion and tightening of the web. More trade and travel, faster urbanization, higher literacy rates, and more missionary work (by Muslims and Christians) all combined to enhance the speed and volume of communication. Beyond that (considered in its own right below) was the political climate, specifically the formation of great empires on land and at sea, each of which organized communication networks. And of crucial importance within Europe was the printing press, which drastically reduced information costs and made the political control of information surpassingly difficult, although it made propaganda easier.

Printing was the most revolutionary of these developments, although for centuries the most local. Around 1430 a metalworker in Mainz (Germany), Johannes Gutenberg, started working on casting type for use in printing. At that time, printing usually involved woodblocks, which could only be made painstakingly by skilled woodcarvers. Many texts were instead reproduced by hand, and of course copyists often introduced errors. But soon Gutenberg had invented movable and reusable metal type and a better press, with which he printed a Bible in 1455. Gutenberg's press remained standard until 1800, and his method of casting type prevailed until 1838. A creditor sued him in 1455, leaving Gutenberg with little to his name until a bishop appointed him to a sinecure in 1465. He died in 1468.

Koreans had invented movable metal type in the thirteenth century. (Indeed, it is possible, although there is no evidence, that Gutenberg had learned of the Korean achievement and drew inspiration from it.) When they added an alphabet in the early fifteenth, they touched off a small boom in printing and intellectual life generally. But it did not extend much beyond Korea, which in any case remained a highly stratified society in which only a tiny elite could read. In most of Europe, literacy was probably more common. Gutenberg's invention, one of the most significant in world history (and among the first for which we know the inventor's name), allowed printers to manufacture far more books far faster and cheaper than ever before. He ignited an explosion of printed works. By 1500, 236 towns in Europe had Gutenberg-style presses and had printed 30,000 titles, about 20 million books in all, in more than a dozen languages. By 1483, type had been cast for the Cyrillic alphabet (used in Russian and some other Slavic languages) and by 1501 for the Greek. By 1605, regular newspapers had appeared, at first specializing in business news. By 1693, the first women's magazine circulated, in England, and by 1702, the first daily newspaper. By 1753, British publishers sold 20,000 newspapers daily, each one probably perused by several people.

But all this did not go beyond Christendom. Presses were set up in Spanish America by 1533 (and in English North America by 1639), in Portuguese Goa by the 1550s, but the great states of Asia resisted the printing press until the nineteenth century. The Spanish crown used printing presses to hasten the flow of official state information after 1476. But the Ottoman Empire, the Mughal Empire in India, and the Ming in China continued to rely on scribes. Perhaps the scribes were too powerful to offend, perhaps printing looked too difficult to control, or—in the case of languages with ideographic rather than alphabetic script—printing seemed not much of an improvement over handwriting or woodblock printing. Until the eighteenth century, Muslim authorities objected to printing on the grounds that it amounted to desecration of the sacred text of the Qur'an. For all these reasons, from 1450 to 1800, printing made the information landscape in Europe and European colonies different from anywhere else. In particular it lowered information costs, and it encouraged the democratization of intellectual debate, notably vicious religious quarrels.

Religions and the Web

With or without printing, the changing world of information and ideas presented vigorous challenges to received orthodoxies everywhere. With the swirl of commerce, and burgeoning cities all around the world, new ideas found their way more often to receptive audiences. Many of these ideas were too bizarre to last long, and are now forgotten. But some took root. The successful ideas were those most compatible with contemporary social, economic, and political trends, specifically with greater social fluidity, with the uncertainties of the market, and with the rise of towns and cities. These ideas, on the whole, esteemed experience and observation above tradition and authority, and offered greater scope for individuals to fashion their own interpretations of all the big questions about life, society, and the divine. And, on the whole, they were moralistic, offering guidelines for virtuous conduct and (at least implicitly) condemning the moral lapses of those who supported established orthodoxies.

In some ways the religious and intellectual tumult of the fifteenth to seventeenth centuries was a reprise of the era in which the world's great religions first took hold. Then, too, increasing urbanism had driven people to consider religions that offered moral guidelines, that claimed to be universal, and that promised smoother relations with people outside their immediate community. The teachings of Buddha, Confucius, Jesus, and Muhammad were moral teachings suitable for mobile, urban populations, and more appealing to urbanites than nature worship or tribal religions. By 1400, these religions (to varying degrees) had accreted layers of bureaucracy that invited careerism; their cozy relations with political potentates required compromises here and there; and their worldly wealth invited corruption. Less and less, in a new age of commerce and cities, did they satisfy emerging classes and restive souls in general. This provided an opening for new intellectual and religious movements.

In China, for example, after the Ming took power in 1368, a revived Confucianism had become the basis for the civil service examinations and the intellectual orthodoxy of the empire. But Confucian orthodoxy seemed rigid and misguided to Wang Yangmin (1472–1529), an influential thinker who held that truth, knowledge, and virtue could be achieved by ordinary people without lengthy instruction in Confucian lore. Experience and innate knowledge could lead one to a virtuous path. Wang's followers took this as legitimation for greater individualism and even egalitarianism, radical notions indeed for those raised in the traditional Confucian context. The late Ming period in general featured unusual dynamism and diversity in intellectual and religious matters, including a flirtation with Christianity.

In India, Nanak (1469–1539), a sometime accountant working for an Afghan prince, educated in the Hindu Vedas and in the rudiments of Islam, literate in Sanskrit, Persian, and Arabic, sparked a new religion. Sikhism, as Nanak's creed is called, was based on Hindu scripture, but rejected the clerical authority of the Brahmin caste, injecting some elements derived from Sufi Islam, and advancing a strict moral code for all followers, rather than one that varied for different castes. Guru Nanak (the first of ten gurus, or "great teachers," in Sikh history) preached toleration, saying there is no Hindu, no Muslim, only God. Sikhism spread widely in northern India, appealing at first to worldly urban classes, to low-caste Hindus, and to women. It had an egalitarian, or at least meritocratic, streak, and was originally pacifistic. It so impressed the Mughal emperor Akbar (1542–1605) that he granted land for its Golden Temple in Amritsar.

The great emperor Akbar went so far as to encourage intellectual and religious ferment in the Mughal Empire. The Mughals were a Muslim dynasty from Central Asia. After 1526, they ruled the predominantly Hindu land of northern India. Akbar's solution to the problems this raised was a policy of toleration. He gave lands to scholars of several religious faiths, abolished the standard tax Muslim states levied on non-Muslims, commissioned translations of philosophical and religious texts between Persian and Hindi, and even hired a Jesuit to tutor his son. He successfully quashed a revolt endorsed by the *ulema*, the learned guardians of Muslim Sacred Law (1579–80). Although illiterate himself, Akbar supported a rainbow of philosophical and religious scholars.

Elsewhere in the Muslim world, challenges to orthodoxy bubbled up as well, and several rulers also engaged in measured religious toleration, if not quite as radical as Akbar's. In the Ottoman Empire, Mehmet the Conqueror (1432–1481) explored various religious doctrines for himself and promoted lenient treatment of Christians and Jews. But the Ottomans proved less tolerant of Shi'a Muslims, because the Shi'a movement constituted a real challenge to Ottoman power, which Christians and Jews did not.

A version of the Shi'a branch of Islam became the official faith in

Iran after 1501, thanks to the military success of the Safavid clan (thereafter Safavid dynasty). After 1501, the Shi'a faith received state support in Iran, and became a perpetual challenge to Sunni authority in general and to the Ottoman sultans—who after 1517 claimed the title of caliph—in particular. Initially, the Safavids established a very embattled theocracy, struggling against the Ottomans and Uzbeks, but by the reign of Shah Abbas I (1588–1629), they adopted a policy of religious toleration, and encouraged Armenians and Jews to settle and trade in Iran. Abbas helped pay for a Christian church in his capital of Isfahan, built by Portuguese Franciscans from Goa. Abbas derived a good deal of his revenue from international trade (especially of silk), and he cultivated the linkages the web provided to improve his position with respect to his hostile Sunni neighbors. As it was in India for Akbar, a policy of intellectual openness became good politics in Iran.

In Europe, the sternest challenge to the orthodoxy of the Catholic Church came from the Protestant Reformation, born in 1517. Christianity had spawned many heresies, but most had been stamped out or confined to backwaters or mountain fastnesses. That changed when Martin Luther (1483–1546), the German Wang Yangmin, concluded that Christianity was at heart an inward personal commitment, and that salvation came from faith alone. Luther, a miner's son, monastic priest, and university lecturer, made his views public in 1517. He had the printing press on his side. Cheap pamphlets spread his criticisms of church practices far and wide, and found receptive readers, especially in the towns of Northern Europe. No authority could halt this spread: information and people moved too freely. Soon variations on Luther's themes sprang up in Holland, Hungary, and elsewhere, such as Calvinism in Switzerland and France, and Anglicanism and Presbyterianism in Britain. Like the Shi'a Muslims, Protestants felt the religious hierarchy was a stolid, legalistic, and often corrupt barrier standing between believers and God. Like the Shi'a in Iran, Protestants found political support: among German princes, who for their own reasons wanted autonomy from the Holy Roman Empire. Protestants even found toleration in the Catholic kingdom of France, when the crown in 1598 granted Huguenots (as French Protestants were called) considerable freedom of worship.

The papacy and its supporters did not opt for toleration, but nonetheless had to come to terms with Protestantism because they couldn't stamp it out. This required new thinking in the Roman Catholic Church: in trying to keep things the same, the church had to change. It supported a spiritual renewal within Catholicism, embracing mysticism, encouraging missionary work, and underwriting art and architecture on an expanded scale. Its efforts, called the Catholic or Counter-Reformation, involved both suppression of deviants and research about exotic peoples and religions. On the one hand, the church tried to enforce established belief and practice by energetic persecution of all heretics. On the other hand, it sponsored scholarly inquiry into matters philosophical and religious, and even supported Dominicans, Franciscans, and—hesitantly—Jesuits who spent lifetimes studying Islam, Hinduism, or Buddhism.

The intellectual and religious effervescence, from China to Europe, had many causes. Some were local and particular. The schools of thought and religious doctrines involved varied greatly in their particulars from place to place. The movements probably had no influence upon one another: Luther did not take notice of, let alone inspiration from, Safavid success or Wang Yangmin. Nonetheless, it seems fair to say that the general climate of intellectual and religious tumult was favored by the expansion, consolidation, and quickening of the web, and its attendant commercialization, urbanization, and rise of literacy. Further, the challenges to orthodox thought, from China to Europe, often involved the promotion of more personal, individual creeds of conscience. This, of course, is the sort of objection that bureaucratized, established religions normally provoke.

Religious Clampdowns

This effervescence, and the ages of toleration that went with it, did not last. In Japan, where after 1543 Christian missionaries had gathered a following and provoked a reconsideration of Japanese Buddhism and Shinto, the state clamped down in 1614 and by 1630 had reconverted or killed about 300,000 Japanese Christians. In China, Wang Yangmin's challenge eventually provoked a vigorous reassertion of Confucian orthodoxy and renewed emphasis on classical texts. The laxity of the late Ming, it seemed to many, had permitted the collapse of the empire and the incursion of the barbarian Manchu (or Qing). The violence and chaos surrounding the Qing conquest (ca. 1630–83) persuaded many intellectuals to get back to basics. The Qing themselves, once firmly in power, encouraged this Confucian counterreformation, because it enhanced their credentials among the literati whose support they needed to govern China, and because classical Confucian doctrines, with their emphasis on order and hierarchy, are very agreeable to rulers generally. In India, later Mughal emperors reversed Akbar's policy of toleration. His son promoted hostility toward Sikhs, to which they responded by developing a formidable martial tradition. His great-grandson, Aurangzeb (reigned 1658–1707), recast the ideological basis of the Mughal state, insisting on adherence to Islam among all high state officials and restoring differential taxation that favored Muslims (1689). Revolts and restiveness among Sikhs, Hindus, and others only confirmed the Mughal state in its twinning of loyalty and Muslim identity. In Europe, the clampdown failed. The Catholic Church did win over the French crown and secure the revocation of toleration for Huguenots (1685), and it reversed Protestantism's spread in Polish and Czech lands. But in Britain, Scandinavia, Holland, Germany, Switzerland, Hungary, and elsewhere, Protestantism in various forms survived, ensuring a future of intellectual diversity and sectarian violence. In Europe, political fragmentation and comparatively cheap and free-flowing information made religious and intellectual conformity a hopeless goal.

In general, strong and confident rulers, like Akbar and Mehmet, could pursue a policy of religious and intellectual toleration, and did so both out of political calculation and from personal preference and curiosity. But successors beset by enemies within and without, like Aurangzeb, found it expedient, and congenial to their personal temperament, to clamp down on what they deemed heresies, and enforce as best they could adherence to official ideology and religion. This worked best in Japan and China, least well in Europe, where the Catholic Church could not prevent nearly half of Europe from opting for Protestantism.

Religious Expansions: Islam, Christianity, and Buddhism

While the major intellectual traditions of Eurasia underwent these storms, those of the Americas, much of Africa, and Oceania faced typhoons. Many local religions disappeared. Others were submerged into Christianity where, as in the Americas, political power fell quickly into the hands of Christian Europeans. Catholicism as practiced in Mexico or Peru retained features of pre-Columbian religion, recast so as to be (usually) acceptable to the church. In Africa, both Christianity and Islam expanded rapidly between 1450 and 1800, always incorporating local practices and belief, creating distinctive versions of these religions. As noted above, the climate of the slave trade encouraged some to adopt Muslim identity for protection. Where Portuguese and their

Afro-Portuguese offspring were active, as in Angola and Mozambique, Christian converts proliferated. The king of Kongo, seeing advantage in closer ties to the Portuguese, embraced Christianity early in the sixteenth century. In general, the political and social disruptions associated with the expansion of the web made fertile fields for the expansion of Christianity and Islam.

Christianity and Islam made converts within backwaters of the Old World Web, too. With the establishment of an official Spanish presence in the Philippines (1571), missionaries recruited most of the islands' population to Catholicism. In Bengal, Islam expanded at the expense of local religion in step with forest clearance and the spread of settled agriculture, which replaced the more mobile life of hunters, gatherers, and swidden farmers. Indeed, around the world, the interconnections of the web favored the portable religions at the expense of local ones, for membership in a larger community conferred many practical and perhaps psychological benefits. Strict adherence to local traditions and belief left one isolated, and invited political annihilation wherever militant Christians or Muslims were nearby.

Buddhism, too, underwent a significant expansion in the sixteenth and seventeenth centuries. Tibetan Buddhism had long had a minor role in the religious life of the Mongols, who mainly followed local, shamanistic traditions. But after the conversion of a khan in 1578, Buddhism gradually became dominant among the Mongol tribes, which helped consolidate trade and other linkages between India, Tibet, and the Mongol steppe. By 1601, a Mongol was chosen as the Dalai Lama, and soon Mongolia sprouted Buddhist monasteries like spring flowers. Thus, in religious terms, the Old World Web consolidated by spreading portable, evangelical religions at the expense of local, community ones.

Science

Ultimately the most consequential element in this intellectual swirl of the sixteenth to eighteenth centuries was the so-called Scientific Revolution. In effect, it has not ended, because at its heart was the notion that experiment and unfettered reason are appropriate methods of inquiry, and that observation and experience need not bow to received authority. Such views were (and are) inherently subversive, and hence were always under attack from religious and political authorities.

That attack usually succeeded in checking innovation in science, but not always. For instance, when their conquests put Arabs in possession of the written heritage of Hellenic, Hebrew, and Indian scholars, this sparked a remarkable spurt of scientific inquiry during the seventh to twelfth centuries as Arabs (Turks and Persians too) tried to reconcile the differences they encountered, and had little in the way of their own scientific traditions to protect. They combined the harvests of the past, exposure to contemporary science from Spain to India, and an institutional structure (the madrassas attached to mosques) that often permitted scholars to follow their inclinations. This spurt stalled in the fourteenth and fifteenth centuries, perhaps because the Muslim scientists, especially mathematicians, astronomers, and physicians, had by this time produced a formidable body of work that, almost like religious truth, acquired authority and demanded protection from new ideas.

In the event, the Scientific Revolution took place in Europe, not in the Muslim lands, India, or China. There were two chief reasons for this, one internal to Europe and one not. During the twelfth and thirteenth centuries, Europe spawned the autonomous university (see chapter 5), which had a corporate legal existence that marked it off as a community where scholars were usually free to dispute as they saw fit. They of course hatched countless harebrained ideas, most of which vanished quickly.[3] Religious and political authorities tolerated this only because they could not quash it in a fragmented Europe. The survival of universities gave European scientists a supportive community not quite paralleled elsewhere in the world. Europe had more than one hundred universities by 1500, and by 1551 new ones had also sprouted in European colonies in Mexico City and Lima.

Into this archipelago of intellectual liberty after 1450 came information from all over the world. Like the Arabs before them, Europeans now faced a rash of contradictory, competing information. Voyages below the equator yielded observations of heavenly bodies previously unknown (to Europeans); the Americas raised all sorts of questions (were Amerindians descended from Noah too? were llamas on the ark?). From India came botanical treatises testifying to unimagined worlds. Expanded contact with Islamic centers of learning brought a great legacy of medical, astronomical, and other scientific work, some of it based on ancient Greek predecessors, whose works soon received increased attention. Nicholas

---

[3] A favorite is that promoted by the vice chancellor of Trinity College, Dublin, James Ussher (1581–1656), who calculated on the basis of scripture that the earth had been created in 4004 B.C.E., a view that retained adherents through the nineteenth century. This, incidentally, was not so different from a calculation made by Gregory of Tours in the sixth century.

Copernicus (1473–1543), the Polish astronomer who is credited with recognizing that the sun, not the earth, is at the center of the solar system, read Ptolemy's original works and almost certainly drew inspiration from work produced two centuries before him at the Maragha observatory in northwestern Iran, where Ibn al-Shatir (died 1375) and others had challenged Ptolemy in much the same ways that Copernicus did later.

Compiling, contemplating, and systematizing this global harvest was demanding but only occasionally dangerous work. It inevitably provoked challenges to existing ideas, but no power could suppress these challenges. Instead, in the universities, they found institutional support.[4] And thanks to the printing press, new ideas spread quickly and cheaply. The Catholic Church made intermittent attempts to extinguish aspects of the Scientific Revolution. (For that matter, Luther unsuccessfully discouraged the publication of Copernicus's work.) In 1559 the papacy began to proscribe particular books it deemed subversive, a practice abandoned in 1966. After a religious trial, the astronomer Galileo Galilei (1564–1642), who had championed Copernicus's views, was confined to house arrest in Florence in 1616. But these measures proved pitifully inadequate. Galileo could publish his offensive thoughts in Protestant Holland—and he did.

Like the refinement of the arts of navigation, the Scientific Revolution in general required the combination of a political landscape that gave protected space to thinkers and broader circumstances that favored the long-distance flow of ideas and information. The political (and after 1517 increasingly religious) fragmentation of Europe, combined with the peculiar institution of universities, achieved the requisite political landscape. The information flow came via the printing press and oceanic voyaging.

This confluence of circumstances explains why the Scientific Revolution happened in Europe and not elsewhere. In China from the Ming dynasty until the early twentieth century, the examination system focused education on moral, literary, and aesthetic attainment. Chinese scientists found very little institutional support, and free inquiry and radical ideas usually aroused successful state opposition. The harvest of knowledge accruing from Zheng He's expeditions made only a modest imprint on Chinese science, and failed to beget a continuing program of overseas scientific research.

---

[4] About 87 percent of the European scientists for two centuries (1450–1650) included in the *Dictionary of Scientific Biography* had studied at universities, and half were employed by universities. Toby E. Huff, *The Rise of Early Modern Science: Islam, China, and the West* (New York, 1993).

Hence Europeans alone developed a culture of scientific inquiry that after 1500 provided immense practical knowledge. Navigation and astronomy came first. Physics and ballistics—useful in artillery—followed, as, more slowly, did systematic sciences of medicine, botany, and chemistry, among others. Slowly, these sciences yielded practical advantages in military affairs, agriculture, mining, metallurgy, and elsewhere. These, particularly the military sciences of fortification, artillery ballistics, and mathematically precise organization of men and supplies, made even small European states increasingly formidable from the late sixteenth century. By the mid-nineteenth century, science in Europe (and the United States) systematically informed technology, generating a self-sustaining process of technological change to which no end is in sight.

POLITICAL CURRENTS

All power comes from the barrel of a gun, said Mao Zedong, and by the sixteenth century this was almost coming true. The period 1450–1800 was as turbulent politically as intellectually. The general trend, a very marked one, showed the big fish devouring the small fish. States and rulers that managed to tax efficiently, retain the loyalty of their military men, and adapt to the changing basis of warfare enjoyed increasing returns for a century or two: the bigger they got, the easier it was to get bigger still. That process of political centralization and expansion reached its limits when big fish rubbed up against one another, or where great distances made logistics so difficult that even the biggest fish had little effective power.

Power of course comes from moral authority, charisma, wealth, and other sources. But often, in the end, it comes down to force and the threat of force. In the years 1420–1700, the use of force underwent sharp changes that made it more expensive to deploy, making new demands on states and societies, and giving the big fish an edge they ruthlessly exploited. There were four main components of this: oceanic navies; cannon and fortification; disciplined standing armies forged through close-order drill; and finely tuned logistical organization to support armies of up to several hundred thousand men (and tens of thousands of horses).[5] Taken together, these comprised a military revolution, the most important driving force in world politics in this era.

---

[5] This component is sometimes underrated by military historians, but any parent who has tried to coordinate the movement and feeding of a few children and a car can appreciate the staggering complexity of trying to supply a large army on the move.

The Big Fish

All of the big fish shared to some extent in these revolutionary developments: that is what made them big fish. The biggest, in declining order of population size, were the Qing Empire in China and its borderlands; the Mughal Empire in India; the Ottoman Empire in Southwest Asia, southeastern Europe, and North Africa; and the Habsburg Empire in Europe and the Americas (and the Philippines).

The Qing began as a Manchurian family which intervened in a civil war in Ming China, played one side against the other, and suddenly captured the capital of Beijing in 1644. They faced another forty years of struggle before they pacified all of China. Simultaneously they consolidated their maritime frontier, suppressing pirates, one of whom, Zheng Cheng-gong (died 1662), commanded thousands of followers. The Qing took Taiwan in 1683. They then turned their energies to the Inner Asia frontier, to Mongol confederacies and the Tibetan empire, where matters had been complicated by the emergence of Russia as a participant in steppe politics after 1640. By and large the Qing were very successful in ruling China, in ruling the eastern steppe, and in maintaining a mixed identity as steppe warlords and Chinese emperors. At their accession, their empire included some 140 million people; by 1800, more than 350 million, more than a third of humankind. Two great and long-lived emperors, the Kangxi emperor (reigned 1662–1722) and his grandson the Qianlong emperor (1736–95), gave the Qing extraordinary continuity and freedom from succession struggles. The dynasty lasted until 1911.

The Mughals were originally a group of Muslim Turks from the Ferghana Valley in today's Uzbekistan. After taking a beating from Central Asian and Afghan armies, on their fifth invasion attempt they entered India and overthrew the sultanate of Delhi in 1526, using field artillery to good advantage. After a succession crisis, an empire was formed under Akbar, beginning in 1556. His was a delicate balancing act, because of the Hindu majority in India, but when things went well for the Mughals they went very well, because northern India was a fertile and populous land. About 100 or 150 million people lived under Mughal control in the seventeenth century, and state revenues were four times those of France. Succession crises were routine because there were no set rules. Every emperor had to worry about all his sons, each of whom was trying to prepare himself for the throne by building power, making alliances, assassinating rivals. When an emperor died, civil war usually followed, and the victor took pains to kill off or otherwise destroy his brothers, and maybe his nephews too. This political system, widely followed in the Muslim world, characterized the Ottoman Empire too until the mid-seventeenth century. It assured frequent crises and civil wars, but it also assured strong rulers: few weaklings or military incompetents withstood this selection process. The Mughal Empire lasted officially until 1857, but its real power evaporated after 1707, when Hindu forces developed too much power for any Mughal emperor to control.

The Ottoman Empire, also a Muslim and Turkish dynasty, had its origins in northwestern Anatolia. Its early career is described in chapter 5. Despite a severe setback at the hands of Timur in 1402, the Ottoman Empire grew very rapidly from about 1415, and conquered Constantinople in 1453. The judicious use of field artillery and infantry with firearms permitted further expansion for a century or more, assisted by policies of conciliating defeated leaders and enrolling them in the higher ranks of Ottoman society. By 1550, the Ottoman Empire extended from the Euphrates in the east to Hungary in the northwest to the Sahara in the south. Its population then stood at about 20–25 million (and grew to perhaps 30 million by 1800). After 1517, it included the cash cow of Egypt, which accounted for about a quarter of Ottoman revenues for a while, and the holy places of Mecca and Medina, protection of which provided the Ottoman sultans with justification for their claim to be caliphs, earthly leaders of Islam. Despite repeated succession struggles of the sort that plagued the Mughals, and frequent warfare against Iran, Russia, Venice, and the Habsburgs, the Ottoman Empire lasted until 1923.

The house of Habsburg, the last of the big fish, began its career in Switzerland. Its head, Rudolf I, became Holy Roman Emperor in 1273 and installed his son as ruler of Austria. Through marriage and inheritance the Habsburgs subsequently acquired the Netherlands in 1477, Spain in 1516, and several other territories (Luxembourg, Burgundy, Bohemia, Hungary, Sicily, Naples, Milan) in Europe. Their claim to the title of Holy Roman Emperor paralleled the Ottomans' claim to be caliphs. In any case, they allied themselves with the Catholic Church, led the military crusade against Protestantism and Islam, and tried vigorously to assert dominion over all Christendom, as the Ottomans did within the Islamic world. In Europe, their domains included about 20 million people in 1550, about 18–20 percent of the European total, and in the Americas several more millions (although falling fast). Like the Ottomans, they enjoyed their greatest edge over their neighbors in the sixteenth century, when their early adoption of new military and fiscal methods boosted their power. They also enjoyed a subsidy in the form of silver from the Americas, which by the 1540s provided some 10–20 percent of their revenues. The Austrian branch of the house of Habsburg lasted until 1918, destroyed—again like the Ottomans—only by the tumult of World War I.

Each of these great empires took part in the military revolution to greater or lesser degrees, and gobbled up their smaller neighbors until they bumped into another big fish, or reached the ends of their logistical ropes. This left some room for medium and small fish, like Japan (17 million people in 1500, 28 million in 1800—a big fish in terms of population but not territory or resources) or Iran (4–6 million). Often the medium ones who adopted some of the military innovations gobbled up the small fry. In this way, modest empires arose in places around the fringes of the great powers. Indeed, eventually, some of the new military techniques helped build small empires—in Madagascar, Ethiopia, northern Sumatra, Hawaii—far from the centers of power. They too were part of the military revolution.

The Military Revolution

The story of the emergence of oceanic navies we told in the pages above. What is crucial to note is that Atlantic Europeans built such navies and refined and expanded them, the Chinese built one and abandoned it, and almost no one else built one until the nineteenth century. The sultanate of Oman constructed a formidable navy in the western Indian Ocean in the eighteenth century, and the sultanate of Aceh (northern Sumatra) also had a considerable local navy. But they did not roam far and wide. Even a big fish such as the Mughal Empire trained its sights on territorial objectives and never built a navy to speak of, although Akbar showed interest in naval technology in the 1590s. The Ottomans did build one, but they stuck to oared galleys, which while quite effective in the Mediterranean and other enclosed seas, could not project force across the high seas. None of these powers before the eighteenth century built ships strong enough to use as cannon platforms. This meant that the Atlantic Europeans' innovations in seapower did not spread quickly throughout the world, giving them a lasting military advantage wherever they could sail their men-of-war.

From about the 1420s Western European armies used field cannon. Soon thereafter, Ottoman armies did too. In the 1480s, in the context of Christian Spain's successful war against Muslim Granada, armies learned how to move and use dozens of cannon pulled by hundreds of horses. In 1494, a French force entered Italy with similar equipment, and showed how a mobile artillery force could quickly batter down the vertical walls of castles, destroying one stronghold after another. To counter this new weapon, Italian architects by the 1520s had begun to devise new fortifications, with sloped, earthen walls that could absorb the impact of cannonballs. For a while, both Michelangelo and Leonardo da Vinci worked on designing fortresses, using the same geometry that lay behind their painting and civil architecture. The new fortresses had to be big, painstakingly designed and built (it often took twenty years to do it right), garrisoned with 1,000 to 3,000 men, packed with supplies, and bristling with cannon of their own: very, very expensive. But the cost of not building such fortresses, if one's enemies had capable artillery, was defeat or surrender.

The third element in the military revolution came later. By the 1550s some European armies had fairly reliable muskets, and by the 1590s they found it effective to arrange musketeers in ranks (parallel lines) so as to fire volleys. Some Japanese armies actually did this by the 1570s, but they did not take the decisive next step. Between 1590 and 1610, Dutch captains, having read Roman military manuals about how to train legions for battle, began to create the elaborate choreography of close-order drill (and soon wrote their own manuals). They made their soldiers spend endless hours on the parade ground, practicing repetitive, synchronized movements. The point was to make a large group of men act as one, to make them automatically responsive to commands, to make them able to load, fire, and reload their weapons quickly and without injuring or killing their comrades. It also probably had the added effect of heightening group cohesion and loyalty: synchronized movement, it seems, promotes bonding among humans. Well-drilled men would, in the heat of battle, stand still, load, and wait for the command to fire, even as their closest comrades were falling left and right. Without drill, no army in the world could do this. Close-order drill was costly, too: it took years of training to make units thoroughly disciplined, and to keep them that way required a standing army of men kept separate from civilian society. They had to be fed, clothed, and housed or else they would turn their skills against that civilian society. So this too was expensive, but again, the cost of not doing it, if one's enemy did, was defeat.

The final element was sophisticated supply and logistics. As armies grew larger, as cavalry, infantry, and artillery had to be used in effective combination, as strings of fortresses had to be built and maintained, and as (with success in war) all this had to be done further from home, and over greater varieties of terrain, the problems of supply for war became exponentially more complex. A successful war machine needed men, horses, and their food, together with iron, steel, leather, gunpowder, and much more. It needed infantrymen and cavalrymen, artillerymen, smiths, guncasters, cooks, engineers, sappers, muleteers; it needed cavalry horses and draft horses, and perhaps mules, oxen, camels, and war elephants. It needed all this in great quantity, at the right places and right times, needed to get it across rivers, over mountains. To achieve this required a numerate and literate military bureaucracy, people with desk skills normally despised by men at arms.

Since all this was so expensive, the military revolution imposed great strains on rulers and societies. Victory, as one Portuguese commander put it, went to the king with the last *escudo*. The only ways to get the money needed were to borrow it, seize it, or build a tax system—techniques that overlapped in many cases. Borrowing meant having a banking system, something that developed prominently in Italy, the Low Countries, and later in England. The Habsburg war machine depended on the ability of monarchs to borrow money, as did the rather modest English one. Seizing wealth of course created enemies, but if it could be seized from one's existing enemies, it made a very satisfactory method. The early Ottoman Empire and the Mughal Empire did very well at this, amassing booty from wars of frontier expansion, which in turn financed the state and war machine. Seizing it from within one's borders risked rebellion, but at times proved irresistible, especially where religious establishments were sitting on great wealth. Establishing a reliable tax system was preferable both for rulers and ruled (although rarely popular). For rulers it was most convenient to have tax paid in money rather than in kind. The Chinese in the sixteenth century imposed a tax payable only in silver; the Mughals tried to monetize their tax system with some success; the Ottomans did too. The Habsburgs' tax system was comparatively efficient and buttressed by the revenues from American silver production, but they needed bankers frequently because their military ambitions were so grand. By 1550, the Habsburgs had to pay annual interest rates of nearly 50 percent for ready cash from bankers, an indication that the bankers lacked confidence in Habsburg finance. A ruler who wanted to keep abreast of the military revolution needed a cutting-edge financial system too. Most of the big fish spent 70–90 percent of their revenues on their war machines.

This package of innovations, to summarize, consisted of a hardware of ships, cannon, muskets, gunpowder, and fortifications, and a software of drill, military engineering, logistical-bureaucractic apparatus, and financial systems.

Effects of the Military Revolution

The package developed and spread very unevenly around the world. Military machines and financial systems were formed in the contexts of existing (and evolving) societies and ecologies. The incentives and obstacles to adopting parts of the package varied. Egypt, without timber, could scarcely build an oceanic navy. Illiterate societies could not create a supply bureaucracy on any scale. Nomadic pastoralists could not build fortresses. Societies where chivalric traditions were especially strong perhaps could, but often did not, build infantry and artillery armies, and engage in the "mole's work"—as one Polish nobleman called it—of fortification. Muslim societies, where adherence to the Qur'an inhibited lending at interest, could not easily build banking systems.[6] These ecological, social, and cultural constraints help explain the military revolution's uneven spread.

The inclinations and talents of individual rulers had a good deal to do with it too. Recall Prince Henry the Navigator. Mehmet the Conqueror embraced artillery eagerly. Gustavus Adolphus (1594–1632) made Sweden a regional power after 1611 by mixing drilled infantry and field artillery. In Japan, the warlord Oda Nobunaga (1534–1582) in the 1560s adopted musketry and his successor Toyotomi Hideyoshi (1536–1598) in the 1580s absorbed both field artillery and cannonproof fortification into the Japanese military system. The Manchu leader Hong Taiji (1592–1643) reacted to a crushing defeat in 1626 by developing artillery forces, which helped the Manchu take power in China. These men might have done differently, but they did not: they mattered too.

Most of the package evolved first in Europe and the Ottoman Empire: field cannon, artillery fortresses, infantry with firearms. Europeans invented close-order drill and developed the oceanic, cannon-equipped navy. Innovations spread very quickly in Europe. The Dutch military manuals, for example, were translated and published in a dozen languages. Information costs were low, and the incentive to learn the new methods was high. The software spread widely but not universally

---

[6] Muslim bankers could engage in joint ventures, which worked well in commercial banking but did not help rulers as much as lending at interest could. Christian scripture forbade usury, but by the fifteenth century lending at interest had become routine in Christian communities.

within western Eurasia. The hardware was so expensive only a few rulers could afford it, and the rest were destroyed or became vassals. The most successful were the Habsburgs, France, Holland (which lacked many raw materials for war but made up for that with seapower and commerce), Sweden, and eventually (by 1690) England and Russia.

The Ottomans participated fully in much but not all of the military revolution. They used artillery, built artillery fortresses, and created perhaps the world's best logistical apparatus. The famous Janissary corps used firearms to great effect, but they did not adopt regular drill. Their navy remained a galley navy. Their financial system relied on booty (seizure) and taxation, and never allowed banking to thrive, although they often extorted forced loans from their subjects. They had full access to information about every component of the military revolution in Europe, from fighting experience, from renegades, and from European books. They made informed, deliberate choices when not creating a navy of sailing ships and avoiding drill.

The Mughals also made good use of field cannon from at least the 1520s and muskets too. They relied on cavalry, especially early on, and took pains to control the horse supplies of South Asia. Their military was never bureaucratically organized to the extent the Ottoman was, remaining more factionalized, as fighting men followed their captains, not the emperor. When those captains chose to follow the emperor, the Mughal army was a formidable instrument of several hundred thousand men, and nothing between Persia and the dense forests of Bengal could stand in its way. But when they did not, Mughal power almost evaporated, and civil wars and rebellions ravaged India. The Mughals had no seapower and no banking system. This helps explain the rapid rise of the Mughal Empire, its irresistible strength when unified, and its tendency to crumble quickly under weak emperors or during succession struggles: in general, its sudden oscillations in strength between 1526 and 1707.

The Qing Empire was much more stable, despite no shortage of rebellions. The Qing adopted cannon before coming to power in 1644. Indeed, they could not have defeated the Ming forces had they not mastered the art of siege warfare in the 1630s and woven siegecraft into their steppe war-fighting techniques, creating a flexible military equal to any task on land. They studied artillery carefully when in power, making full use of Chinese skills in metallurgy and mathematics. They got some help from Jesuit missionary priests, who managed cannon foundries for the Qing (indeed, they had done this for the Ming too), and did much to acquaint them with the latest military innovations of Europe. The Qing inherited fortifications on their northern frontier and around important cities that were already cannonproof, by dint of sheer thickness (the walls around Beijing were some 50 feet thick). Their armies relied on size more than drill and firearms, although they adopted both for use in some contexts. That their comparative advantage lay in numbers made logistics especially difficult, but here the Qing, like the Ottomans, excelled. Their enemies, mainly steppe peoples, could not adopt much at all of the military revolution, and hence the Qing did not have to, and needed only parts of it to prevail.

The ultimate effects of the military revolution were threefold: it concentrated power, building states and empires and laying the foundation for the modern international system; it prepared the way for the emergence of Western European states as the most formidable in the world; and it destroyed nomad power forever.

First, it strengthened central power and assisted in the rise of modern states. Rulers used field cannon to knock down castles and intimidate local nobles. Japan before the 1580s was divided into dozens of fiefdoms frequently at war with one another in shifting coalitions. One central authority emerged in Japan, when Nobunaga and Hideyoshi deployed field cannon to defeat their rivals, destroy their castles, and build a unified state that enforced a monopoly on the use of firearms. In France, the Valois kings did the same thing, crushing resistant dukes and rebellious cities, then tearing down their defenses. They replaced this with a system of fortresses around the frontiers of the country. The Safavid dynasty in Persia unified the country by slow degrees with the help of similar methods, although the Safavids retained a dislike of guns and cannon as unworthy of true warriors. Like the Mughals, the Safavids built their empire initially mainly on the basis of cavalry, but used cannon to destroy centers of resistance. On larger scales, the success of the Habsburgs, Ottomans, Mughals, and Qing in taming local power and unifying their domains owed much to their complete or partial adoption of the military (and fiscal) revolution. This state-building and empire-building process was a very violent business, bitterly resisted, but ultimately triumphant. It reduced the number of polities very considerably, putting more power in fewer hands. It prompted a geopolitical shakeout: large numbers of competing units following a broad variety of military, political, and fiscal practices were reduced to a much smaller number practicing a narrower variety of proven methods.

Second, it prepared Western European states for a surge to global power after 1750. That surge, as we shall see, depended on several things that happened only after 1750. But the military strength on which it rested developed gradually after 1420. The key to this lay in the inability of any European ruler to monopolize the power generated by the military revolution and create a pan-European empire. This was not for lack of trying. The Habsburgs sought to dominate all Europe, but their cause was hopeless: the French, Dutch, and Ottomans knew all the tricks of war and finance, and moreover could make common cause. Thus, the consolidation of power in Europe foundered, a competing states system evolved, large-scale warfare became chronic, and in this crucible of ruthless competition, the surviving states developed very efficient fiscal and military machines that could, by 1800 or so, project power around the world so successfully as to menace even the great land empires in China and India. This was in part an accident: it could have turned out differently, more like the rest of Eurasia. But it was related to the open information society of Europe. Details about shipbuilding, mining and metallurgy, guncasting, fortification, and drill circulated freely, thanks in part to the printing press, so that no single ruler could monopolize this knowledge and the power it conferred.

Third, the military (and fiscal) revolution spelled the end of nomad power. Nomad confederations on the Eurasian steppe and in North Africa had long played a prominent role in politics. Their empires came and went suddenly, because confederations were based on unstable alliances rooted in tribal social structures. When united, their mastery of horse or camel transport, their prowess at archery, their martial society in which every man, and some women, were fully versed in military skills, made them highly formidable. Settled cultivators had lived in fear of nomad power for over 2,000 years. But the military power of nomads, indeed, of tribally organized societies in general, ended around 1760. The reasons lay with guns and money. Nomads could and did make use of firearms. They could and did occasionally use field cannon (small pieces were mounted on camels by Mongols in the eighteenth century). But they could not make these things in quantity, and could not easily repair or supply them. As settled societies had always lacked for horses and had to trade for them, mobile societies now lacked guns and powder, and had to trade for them. From West Africa to Mongolia, this tipped the balance of power in favor of agricultural societies, who could more easily generate more firepower. Beyond this, pastoral and nomadic societies could not come up with financial systems to undergird new ways of warfare, or buy all the firearms they might need.

In the 1740s, the last gasp of tribal warfare in Europe came with the final defeat of Scottish highlanders. At Culloden in 1746 they charged with swords drawn into volleys fired by British infantry. In the 1750s, the last gasp of nomad power in Eurasia came with the defeat of the Zunghar confederacy (made up of Mongol tribes) in what is now northwestern China. The Zunghars had firearms, even cannon (which Swedes helped them to use). But the Qing armies had more of them, and, more decisively, developed between 1670 and 1750 a precise logistical system that allowed them to supply large armies in arid lands. This was enormously expensive, but the Qing had a taxation system that could finance it, and the cost was worth it because it ended, once and for all, serious threat from Inner Asia (although the expanding Russian Empire would provide a minor threat). Like the Scottish highlanders who soon served the power that had defeated them, Mongols increasingly enrolled in the banners (as their military units were called) of the Qing. Nomadic, tribal peoples retained military power in North America until 1890, when the greatest confederation, that of the Sioux tribes of the Great Plains, was finally defeated by the U.S. Army. This was a mere footnote, however, as here nomad power had existed only briefly, after 1680, when the horse was introduced to the grasslands of North America. Similarly in South America, mobile societies whose military strength rested on skill with horses were overpowered in the Chaco and Pampas of Bolivia and Argentina in the eighteenth and nineteenth centuries.

The military (and fiscal) revolution transformed the political landscape of Eurasia. It left horrible wreckage in its wake. Centuries of ever more lethal warfare killed millions, terrorized millions more, destroyed crops and cities, and devoured capital that might have been invested elsewhere. It created a world dominated by a handful of big fish. The Qing expanded to the point where even their logistical capacity could carry them no farther, and achieved (approximately) the borders of today's China. The Mughals did the same to their south, eventually gobbling up almost all the little states of the Indian peninsula. To the northwest they bumped up against Safavid power (and occasionally powerful Afghan states). The Ottomans expanded to the limits of their logistical reach, and fought continually against the Safavids in the east and the Habsburgs in the west, not to mention the Russians to the north.

In the Americas and Africa, the military revolution came with outsiders, and only small parts of it were adopted by local peoples. Their swift incorporation into the web (still incomplete by 1800) was indeed hastened because they scarcely took part in the military revolution. Amerindian societies adopted some of the hardware, notably firearms, but not all of it, and none of the software. Their own martial traditions made adoption of new ways hard, as did their limited access to the knowledge in question, and their limited experience with metalworking. In any case, epidemics were thinning their ranks and loss of land was destroying their economies: adopting innovations that required huge commitments of manpower and money was out of the question for Amerindians. Their polities shrank back and disappeared, defended only by courage, tenacity, weapons of wood and stone, and, eventually, muskets and rifles. This was not enough in the face of Portuguese, Spaniards, French, Dutch, and English, all full participants in the military revolution.

In sub-Saharan Africa, too, the military revolution made only a faint imprint. Guns made their presence felt. Artillery and fortification did too, in the cities of the Indian Ocean coast, and to some extent on the Atlantic coasts also. Turks and Omanis, as well as Portuguese, introduced some of the new techniques. But regular drill, large-scale bureaucratic-logistical apparatus, and financial systems—the software of the military revolution—never took root in Africa south of the Sahara, not even in the Dutch settlement at the Cape. Existing ways of war suited African contexts, where dense bush often made arranging musketeers in ranks impossible. Without an African firearms industry, muskets and ammunition had to be imported, and remained scarce except among slave raiders. Local economies were often not monetized, making efficient taxation impossible. Without draft animals, there could be no widespread use of field artillery, hence no spur to further development of defensive fortifications. As we saw above, large parts of Africa felt the full measure of violence that characterized Eurasia in these centuries, but acquired only a small part of the enhanced military capability. This set the stage for an unequal encounter in the nineteenth century.

ECONOMIC AND SOCIAL CURRENTS

Although there were no truly fundamental changes in the techniques of agriculture or industry, the world's economy in these centuries changed in crucial ways. In the first place, it became a genuinely global economy for the first time. Second, long-distance trade, cities, and merchants assumed larger roles. This produced strains in all agrarian societies, but probably the greatest strains were felt where the economic dynamism was greatest: around the shores of the Atlantic and the western Pacific.

The world's economy between 1450 and 1800 grew very rapidly by the standards of previous ages, although very slowly by the standard of the twentieth century. The best estimates, which are no more than informed guesses, suggest that the global economy grew between two- and threefold (which is less than one-quarter of 1 percent annually). The world's average standard of living in 1450 was about the same as it is today in the poorer countries of Africa, and it did not rise much at all: maybe by 20 percent over 350 years. Almost all the economic growth came simply from population growth: more people meant more tilled land, more fish landed, more sheep herded, more of almost everything. Agricultural and manufacturing techniques stayed much the same, using muscle power for almost everything. This imposed stringent limits on how much work could be done, and how much wealth created. Most of the people alive in 1450 would have easily recognized the tools, the chores, the opportunities and risks, trials and tribulations of economic life in 1800. Yet within this overall picture of glacial change, a closer look reveals some important shifts that (although no one knew it at the time) would pave the way for fundamental transformations of economic and social life in the nineteenth and twentieth centuries.

One crucial change was the globalization of trade. For the first time, the Americas took part. And the old Eurasian trade intensified, as the Cape of Good Hope route around Africa allowed cargo to move from one end of Eurasia to the other entirely by water. Sailors could avoid pirates and other risks by staying well out to sea, because with the new navigational knowledge they knew roughly where they were even on the trackless oceans. In this situation, the volume of goods traded grew. More and more people specialized in producing for the market, and by producing only one thing refined their skills and productivity.

Thousands and thousands of different items were bought, shipped across oceans, and sold, but in very general terms world trade in these centuries featured a half dozen major specialties. China sold silk and porcelain, and at times gold. Southeast Asia sold spices and peppers. India sold cotton cloth. Africa sold slaves and gold. The Americas sold silver, furs, sugar, and tobacco. Japan sold silver and copper. Europeans sold protection on the high seas and increasingly served as middlemen, carrying everyone's goods. Until about 1750, China remained at the center of this system. Most of the spice trade went directly to China. More than three-fourths of the silver went to China or India, often after several stops. But, in the course of the eighteenth century, the Atlantic economy came to rival the China-centered economy of the western Pacific.

Intercontinental trade assumed a larger profile in part because of the technological changes in ships and the new science of navigation. But there was more to it than that: silver. Trading economies need money because barter is terribly inefficient. Intercontinental trading economies need a money that is acceptable everywhere. Gold and silver fit this description from ancient times. But they exist on earth in limited supply, and that limit put a constraint on long-distance trade (local traders who know and trust one another can get along fairly well without silver or gold, working on the basis of promises of future payment). In the middle of the sixteenth century, miners in Japan, Mexico, and above all in Bolivia dramatically relaxed that constraint. They found new silver mines, applied the world's best technologies to old mines, and sharply increased world silver production. Most of this happened in Spanish America, where German techniques to separate silver from rock were transplanted to the world's richest silver veins at Potosí in the 1540s. Some three-fifths of the world's silver came from Potosí in its heyday. Japanese mines raised their output from the 1560s. The world adopted a de facto silver standard, and every major port city accepted the Spanish peso.

Most of the Japanese silver went to China in exchange for silk, ceramics, and other manufactures. When the Ming restricted shipping and overseas trade (before 1567), some of this trade funneled through overseas Chinese communities in Batavia (modern Jakarta), Malacca, and elsewhere. The American silver went in one of two directions. As much as a fifth of it went across the Pacific, from Acapulco to Manila via Spanish ships called Manila galleons—the world's longest-running shipping line (1565–1815). The remainder went to Spain, but little of it stayed there long. The Habsburgs spent it, on war and debt service, spreading the silver around Europe. Much of it went, via Holland, to Russia for grain and timber, and thence to Iran and India; some went to the Ottoman lands, especially Egypt and Syria, and from there, often to India for cloth. And a lot of it went via Portuguese, Dutch, and English ships to the East Indies for spices. In general, silver flowed toward China.

The reason so much silver (perhaps two-thirds of global production) went to China was that China valued it more highly than elsewhere and gave more for it, either in the form of gold or goods. This was because the Chinese economy was growing fast and needed silver to lubricate its exchanges. The Ming decision in the 1570s to impose the "single-whip tax," payable only in silver, meant that every Chinese liable to taxation, even peasants, had to sell something to get silver. This mobilized goods for the market as never before.

The monetization and mobilization of the Chinese economy helped spur trade in Japan, Korea, and Southeast Asia. Chinese, Japanese, Malay, and other East Asian merchants plied the waters of the western Pacific in greater numbers. A furious boom took place between 1570 and 1630, after the Chinese relaxed their restrictions on overseas trade and before Japan imposed any. A surge in Potosí's production and Spanish shipment of silver to the Philippines helped fuel the boom in the western Pacific. By the early seventeenth century, Japanese foreign trade accounted for perhaps 10 percent of Japan's economy. Japan's cities grew to the point where they accounted for 15–20 percent of the population in the eighteenth century, perhaps double the world average. Everywhere the Asian merchants went they encouraged specialized production for the market, the refinement of skills, and hence greater wealth. Southeast Asian agriculture, for example, grew much more specialized and market-oriented. Large tracts turned into plantations, often worked by slaves, and growing cloves, nutmeg, cinnamon, or peppers. At the same time, Southeast Asian cities grew quickly, attracting merchants and mariners from near and far. One Portuguese observer in the 1520s claimed more than eighty languages were spoken on the streets of Malacca.

Soon the Asian merchants were joined by Portuguese and then Dutch traders, who often used their superior firepower to get a share of the trade. They sold protection to Asian traders, agreeing not to use their cannon for a suitable fee. But the Portuguese and Dutch could compete in this distant business for another reason: not only did they enjoy a firepower edge but they had an information edge too. Because the Asian merchants did not sail all around the world, they did not have valuable market information that the Portuguese and Dutch sometimes had. Knowledge (even, as it often was, two-year-old knowledge) of prices in Brazil, in Europe, in Egypt gave these globe-spanning merchants occasional opportunities that others could not see. Cowrie shells, mentioned above, are an example. These came from the Maldive Islands, and were used as currency for small-scale transactions in nearby India. But they were standard money in West Africa, so Portuguese, Dutch, and English merchants bought them in Bengal or Ceylon, used them as ship ballast en route home to Europe, then traded them on African coasts to buy slaves for shipment to the Americas. The opportunities of globalization accrued most to those who knew the most about the world.[7]

The other part of the world with especially dynamic commerce was at the other end of Eurasia: the Atlantic coastlands. Here the Atlantic Europeans organized a new economy, the heart of which was plantation agriculture. This grew out of the sugar plantation system of the Mediterranean, Morocco, and the Atlantic islands of Madeira, the Canaries, Cape Verde Islands, and São Tomé. The Portuguese transplanted this to Brazil, beginning in the 1530s, as we saw in connection with the slave trade. A variant emerged in the Caribbean, initially on the basis of tobacco and indentured laborers mainly from the British Isles. However, in the 1640s and 1650s, sugar came to the Caribbean in a big way, and it soon rivaled Brazil in sugar production and shared all the features of the plantation system: slavery, an African majority, very high mortality (of both slaves and masters), and consequent high immigration (both via the slave trade and from Europe). At the same time, plantation production of tobacco came to Virginia and the Chesapeake, although only in a small way by Brazilian or Caribbean standards. So from Bahia in Brazil to the colony of Maryland a huge system of plantations arose, based on slave labor. It produced sugar, tobacco, rice, indigo, and eventually cotton.

Sugar and tobacco are addictive drugs that created their own markets. Neither grew well in Europe north of the Mediterranean lowlands, and the low production costs in the Americas allowed the plantation system to capture most of the European market. That proved a fast-growing one, as population grew, prosperity grew, and consumption patterns changed. Sugar had once been an expensive medicinal drug that cost several weeks' wages for a teaspoonful. By 1780, urban workers routinely consumed it. Sugar and tobacco were so profitable that Brazil and the Caribbean Islands imported many foodstuffs (and wine) from Europe and North America. The great fisheries of the North Atlantic sent salted fish to the Caribbean to feed slaves; Caribbean salt was shipped to Europe to salt Dutch herrings. The Atlantic economy, and especially its heart, the plantation economy, was from its origins thoroughly commercial, where specialization and exchange reached great heights: hence its profitability.

It remained until the nineteenth century a lethal economy. Slaves

---

[7] In the time of Ibn Battuta (1304–1368), one of the few people to visit both the Maldives and West Africa, cowries were worth 350 times more in West Africa. This was an arbitrage opportunity that he could not exploit, but European sea traders later could.

died faster than new slave children were born until about 1830 (more like 1730 in the southern colonies of North America). This kept the slave trade going. Whites also died at high rates; in the Caribbean they died even faster than the slaves. European immigrants to the Caribbean normally hoped to make money fast and return home before malaria or yellow fever killed them, and treated slaves accordingly. Slaves had no such hopes.

Atlantic Europeans kept control of the Atlantic economy to themselves. They put down slave revolts consistently until 1791. No one else on earth had the seapower to intrude upon the Atlantic economy the way that the Atlantic Europeans could intrude on the commerce of the Indian Ocean and the western Pacific.

SOCIAL STRAINS AND SHIFTS

As the role of commerce grew, the distribution of wealth and income changed. This happened most conspicuously in the places where trade expanded most: the western Pacific and the Atlantic. Here men of commerce (there were few women) came to rival the old landed elites in wealth. With a single lucky voyage one could make more money than in years of squeezing rents from peasants. In an afternoon Pizarro acquired bullion equal to a half century of Europe's production. This was of course rare. But over the centuries, urban merchants, especially those involved in long-distance trade, emerged as wealthier and more influential, chiefly at the expense of aristocratic landlords. Eventually the rising commercial class would insist on a share of political power, provoking crises around the world, but especially on the shores of the Atlantic.

Simultaneously, the landed classes were (reluctantly) surrendering their military roles. Knights in Europe, samurai in Japan, timar-holders in the Ottoman Empire all specialized as fighting men, serving an emperor or king in exchange for the right to the income from specified lands. But with the military revolution, their skills were less in demand. Princes needed masses of infantrymen, gunners, sailors, fortress builders. But they did not need swordsmen and lancers much. All this amounted to a loss of social position for a class that had dominated both war and rural society in Eurasia for millennia. Aristocratic ways retained their cachet, however, and rich men of commerce normally sought aristocratic status, if not for themselves, then for their offspring. So the process took several centuries and was complete only by 1950 or so.

The gradual rise of cities and commerce affected ordinary human relations too. As more goods were bought and sold, fewer changed hands through customary, tributary, or symbolic exchanges. People's status, at least in cities, rested more and more on money, and less and less on honor, ancestry, or piety. Decisions to marry, to have children, or to kill children (infanticide) became more economic calculations, although by no means fully so, even in Europe, Japan, and China, where these developments seem to have been strongest.

Economic inequalities probably increased too. They usually do in times of economic expansion because some people take advantage of new links and new technologies better or sooner than others. Long-distance trade brought fabulous wealth to a very few, as did successful banking operations. At the same time, the number of slaves around the world grew markedly, reaching perhaps 20 to 50 million by 1800 (2–5 percent of humanity).

Inequalities of wealth among regions of the world probably grew as well. These of course always fluctuate over time. In this period, average incomes in China and Japan, in Southeast Asia, in northwestern Europe, and in colonial America grew faster than those elsewhere. These judgments about the world's inequalities are quite rough, and the comparative statistics on which they are based are open to doubt.

All these social changes were parallel developments arising from the commercialization that arose from, and in turn helped propel, the fusion and expansion of the world's webs. Unlike the use of artillery, which was in the main a matter of deliberate imitation, social changes were unconscious adaptations to the demands of a new age.

Ecological Shifts and Biological Exchange

In linking up the world's webs, and expanding the resulting worldwide web into almost all the nooks and crannies of the globe, oceanic mariners reshuffled the world's ecology. Creatures of all kinds appeared in places they had never existed in before. In particular, the ecosystems of the Americas were put in contact with those of Africa and Eurasia in what historians now call the "Columbian Exchange." This was a larger and more important echo of the "Monsoon Exchange" (between South Asia and Africa) of previous centuries. On a smaller scale, Austronesian and Pacific island ecosystems were also brought into the global mix by the end of the eighteenth century. The most important consequences involved what people ate, and what fed upon them.

People had transferred crops with their migrations for many millennia, but after 1492 they did so much faster. American food crops quickly proved their usefulness in Africa and Eurasia. Maize, which grows fast, withstands drought fairly well, stores very well, and gives high caloric yields, traveled to Morocco and West Africa early in the sixteenth century. It soon became important in Egypt, and in many parts of the Ottoman Empire, especially (by the eighteenth century) its European provinces. Maize also arrived early in Angola, and in the course of the seventeenth and eighteenth centuries spread widely throughout Southern Africa, becoming the staple food of the region. It yielded about nine times as much grain (per unit of labor) as either millet or sorghum, which it often replaced. In the same centuries maize traveled to Southeast Asia and China, where it complemented rice and in some regions became the mainstay of peasant diets.

Cassava, or manioc, is a native of Brazil. It grows in almost any tropical environment, wet or dry, mountainous or seaside. It handles drought well and flourishes even on poor soils, and its starchy tubers could keep for as long as two years underground. In the violent context of tropical Africa during the seventeenth and eighteenth centuries, keeping one's food underground rather than where it might be seized by raiders often made sense. Moreover, cassava yielded as many calories per acre as rice or maize (twice as many as wheat). It arrived in Angola in the sixteenth century, and spread throughout Central Africa. It gradually became the main food there. It made some headway in tropical Asia too, especially in Indonesia, but its impact was limited because irrigated rice already did well in many environments suited to cassava.

The third great gift of the American farmers to the world was the potato, originally from the Andes. Its high yields and success on sandy soils made it most useful in Ireland and Northern Europe generally. By the nineteenth century it became a staple food in Russia as well as Ireland, and an important food nearly everywhere in Northern Europe. It also made an impact in mountain areas around the world, where cool conditions inhibited many other crops. Like cassava, it recommended itself to farmers wherever raiders and soldiers might loot, pillage, or requisition food.

The sweet potato, several kinds of beans, peanuts, cocoa, pineapple, squashes, tomatoes, and several other American foods also spread around the world. In many cases, their different soil, temperature, and moisture requirements allowed new lands to be farmed, such as the mountain slopes of southern China. The eventual effect was to raise the variety of foods eaten, and the total food supply in most parts of the world outside the Americas. Africa, Indonesia, China, and Europe felt the effects more strongly than India, Iran, or Central Asia. African farmers were probably the most innovative: they were frontier farmers par excellence, willing to experiment and with few good crops of their own.

In the exchange of food crops, the Americas acquired a few helpful ones from Eurasia, mainly grains such as wheat, oats, and barley, but also citrus fruits. Just as there were large areas in Africa and Eurasia better suited to maize or potatoes than to wheat or rye, in the Americas broad prairies existed where wheat or rye did better than anything the Americas had to offer. With the new grains, farming became more practical on the Argentina grasslands known as the Pampas, and on the northern plains of North America as well. In both these settings, it was not until the nineteenth century that great transitions took place, because until then Amerindians controlled these spaces. They preferred a way of life based on livestock (normally using Eurasian breeds), supplemented by long-standing patterns of gardening.

In addition to the movement around the world of food crops, the oceanic voyaging brought some other important plants to new environments. Sugar, coffee, and cotton came to the Americas. Generally speaking, they were raised as cash crops, for markets overseas (mainly in Europe), and worked by forced labor, usually African slaves. By the eighteenth century, they accounted for a large share of the agriculture of the Atlantic coast of the Americas. Brazil in particular found its niche in the world agricultural markets thanks to Asian and African crops: very little of the native flora and fauna commanded much of a price, but Brazilian conditions proved excellent for sugar and coffee. Tobacco, a South American plant, also formed part of the plantation economy of the Americas. But it too traveled the world's oceans, and by the seventeenth century was raised in Atlantic Africa, in India, Southeast Asia, and China. A few other economically important plants also made intercontinental migrations. Spices such as cinnamon and cloves (native to Southeast Asia) commanded high prices. Consequently, people made great efforts to grow them, in Brazil, in East Africa, on tropical islands everywhere. These met with modest success, although East African islands eventually became major clove producers. The movement of economic plants was often a very deliberate affair, organized by royal authorities seeking to maximize their revenues or advance the cause of science. The

Portuguese, who held tropical territories on every continent, were especially active. So was the Jesuit order of the Catholic Church, which had priests all around the world, some of whom took a strong interest in economic botany.

Animals bounced around the world, too. Cattle, horses, pigs, goats, and sheep all came to the Americas after 1492 (an earlier horse had gone extinct in the late Pleistocene). By and large, these animals were of more use to Amerindians than were the new food crops. In the Andes and in Mexico, sheep became the basis of a new way of life, one that offered more meat, more protein, more wool. Herding sheep and goats made child labor more productive than before. Cattle too proved useful, especially on the wide grasslands. Horses allowed the efficient management of cattle and made buffalo-based nomadism possible in North America.

But the new animals proved a mixed blessing. Without effective fencing, they often went where they pleased, which sometimes included maize fields and bean gardens. Farmers and herders often found their interests in conflict, notably in Mexico. Furthermore, the new animals' hooves put new pressures on soils, and probably sharply increased levels of soil erosion in the Americas.

The last major component of the Columbian Exchange came in the form of the disease-causing microbes that provoked widespread disaster in the Americas. No reciprocal effect emerged: the Americas donated no major lethal infections to the rest of the world, although it is likely that syphilis originated there and spread far and wide thanks to oceanic mariners.

Another biological exchange took place when the ecosystems of Australia and the Pacific were brought into regular contact with those of the rest of the world. Although historians do not use the term, this might be called the Cook Exchange, in memory of the sailor who did most to break the ecological isolation of Australia and Polynesia. Here the exchange was more one-sided. Australia gave the world the eucalyptus tree, a fast-growing drought-resistant species that now flourishes on every continent. But no crop, animal, or disease of world-historical importance originated in this part of the world. In the other direction, the traffic proved immense. Between 1780 and 1900, Australia and the Pacific Islands acquired scores of new plants, both crops and weeds, and dozens of new animals, both useful livestock and irksome pests. The linking up of the world's ecosystems altered Australia and the Pacific Islands more drastically than any other parts of the world.

Effects on World Population

Big changes in food supply and in disease regimes naturally affected world population. Between 1450 and 1800, human numbers more than doubled, reaching about 900 million. Certainly a large part of this came from the exchange of food crops. With new areas coming under cultivation, there was more food for more people. In frontier areas, people often married young and had very large families. Famines still periodically stalked villages and towns everywhere, but nonetheless numbers climbed. Food supply was only part of the story, however.

The other part was a shift in the toll of infectious diseases. The initial impact of linking up the world's populations was to expose millions of people to infections with which they had no prior experience. The result, especially in the Americas, Australia, and the Pacific, was catastrophic. The result elsewhere was quite different. Gradually, the circulation of diseases became so rapid that all the major centers of population hosted all the major infections all the time. This meant that they ceased to come periodically as epidemics, scything down millions in the prime of life. Instead, they became endemic diseases that carried off mostly infants and toddlers. Families often had more babies to compensate for this. While the sixteenth and seventeenth centuries saw repeated severe epidemics in China and Europe, and probably in India and Africa as well, by the eighteenth century epidemics began to wane, and the rate of population growth began to climb almost all over the world. The Americas began to recover from their demographic disaster: population doubled in the eighteenth century, with the fastest growth among European and African migrants. In India and Europe, population rose by about half. Chinese population more than doubled, reaching 350 million by 1800, accounting for one-third of humankind (today China accounts for only one-fifth of world population). In Africa, population appears to have grown much more slowly, although the figures are only educated guesswork. In Australia and the Pacific, the post-linkup disaster was just beginning, but because the total numbers there were never high, it scarcely affected the world pattern. The eighteenth century was a turning point in the world's population history, the beginning of the modern age of very rapid population growth. The global ecological shifts in crops and diseases were the main reasons.

Population growth combined with greater mobility to create new settlement frontiers where ecological change was especially swift. The eastern seaboard of the Americas from Argentina to Newfoundland is a case in point. So is the Dutch settlement around the Cape of Good Hope, and Indian settlement eastward into Bengal. Japanese farmers moved north to the island of Hokkaido in these centuries, and the Chinese government encouraged a settler frontier along its northern and western borderlands. Sometimes these movements were spontaneous, like the Puritans in Massachusetts, but often they received state support, as in the Chinese case. All these migrations brought new systems of human ecology, typically involving the elimination of native peoples, great reductions in edible wildlife, widespread deforestation, and the establishment of cultivation and pasture. Sagas of frontier settlement continued as a major theme in world history into the nineteenth century.

Conclusion

In the three and a half centuries after 1450, the world's separate webs fused. Beyond that, many lands hitherto outside any of the webs now became enmeshed. By 1800, only a small proportion of the 900 million people on earth remained outside the worldwide web.

The process of web fusion and expansion changed the world. Bolivian miners could put Bavarian ones out of business. Bengalis smoked Brazilian tobacco. The process made the world slightly richer, because it furthered the division of labor and specialization. It made the world somewhat more unequal, in that some people could take advantage of the new connections and exchanges much more thoroughly than others. It slowly homogenized the world's disease pools, so that more and more people were exposed to the same range of infections, and developed similar sets of antibodies, which restricted the scope for epidemics. It slowly reduced the frequency and severity of famines, because commercial links, and in China's case state distribution systems, could move grain around more quickly to where its price was highest. It powered a convergence in world agriculture, in that the same crops spread over larger portions of the globe, and more and more parts of the world followed the trend toward commercial agriculture, especially to plantations with cash crops raised by coerced labor. It speeded the transfer of technologies, so that, for example, seventeenth-century Caribbean sugar plantations adopted a rolling mill based on Chinese precedents. More and more people lived in cities, enrolled in larger and larger social networks. Information circulated faster and more cheaply, fomenting new intellectual outlooks. Military competition with new and expensive techniques led to the elimination of large numbers of states (and of stateless societies), while a smaller number grew larger.

In effect, the web fusion and expansion turned the world inside out. The port cities and their hinterlands became dynamic and prosperous, more so than before and much more so than landlocked regions. Millions migrated to the coasts. New communities were created around the world's bodies of water. The Mediterranean Sea and the Indian Ocean had for many centuries functioned this way, bringing people together. But between 1500 and 1800, this process extended to the Atlantic world. It intensified somewhat in the Indian Ocean, and strongly in the western Pacific from Japan to Java. Indeed, the makings of a Pacific world emerged, with the trans-Pacific links of the Manila galleons. In every case these maritime worlds consisted of communities of commerce, of information, and of infection. They did not crystallize as political units, and their existence as cultural units was always weak. Nonetheless, this prominence of the sea in defining human communities was unprecedented and represents a distinguishing characteristic of the world between 1450 and 1800.

And yet much had not changed. The majority of people in 1800 (perhaps 80–85 percent) still lived on the land as farmers. They worked with their own muscle power, with a little help from animals and less from wind or water power. They lived in poverty and insecurity, fearing famine, sickness, war, and old age. They took solace in religious faith. They knew little about the world beyond their own experience, because they could not read and they only occasionally met strangers.

In 1800, it still took well over a year for people, goods, or information to circle the globe. It took a year to ride the monsoons from China to Java and back, or from India to Mozambique and back. It took about a month to cross the Atlantic Ocean; three to six months to cross the Pacific; a month or more to cross the Sahara by camel; and a year to walk from one end of Eurasia to the other. The world's web had indeed become worldwide, but people, goods, ideas, and infections still moved only slightly faster than they had when the first metropolitan web formed around Sumer. Webs had grown and fused into one, but the velocity within it had grown only a little. In the nineteenth century, the pace of intercommunication within the web would accelerate dramatically: the web would get faster. It would get thicker too, as threads extended into more communities, connecting not just port cities and their hinterlands, but all the world's towns and villages as well.

VII

BREAKING OLD CHAINS, TIGHTENING THE NEW WEB, 1750–1914

In the eighteenth and nineteenth centuries, humankind broke loose from long-standing constraints on human numbers, food supply, mobility, and economic output. The single most important development in all this was the Industrial Revolution, and within that, the harnessing of fossil fuels. This permitted a basic change in the human condition, equaled in importance only by the transition to agriculture many millennia before. Just as the unified worldwide web helped make the Industrial Revolution happen, so the Industrial Revolution helped extend, tighten, and quicken the web. These transformations, similarly, furthered social and political changes, such as the rise of nationalisms and the abolitions of slavery and serfdom, crucial processes in the formation of the modern world.

In breaking loose from old constraints, humankind set some new ones. By 1914, a growing proportion of people depended on fossil fuels, on food raised on distant continents, in short, on the maintenance of global linkages. Long-distance trade increasingly involved items basic to human survival, such as food and fuel. In the nineteenth century, the worldwide web attained such efficiency that great gains followed from erecting an economy based on massive daily flows of energy and materials over great distances, a feat that required huge technical skill, investment, and constant maintenance. The transition to agriculture had—long ago, and rather gradually—locked humankind into certain routines and risks, such as continual toil and epidemic disease. But there was no going back: everywhere it was adopted, farming permitted more people, and greater numbers required the continuation of agriculture. The transition to fossil fuel–powered industry—rather suddenly—locked us into a high-energy society, in which we must continue to mobilize, transport, and use vast quantities of basic items.

The Progress of the Web

In 1750, indeed in 1820, information and goods moved around the world only a little faster than in the heyday of the Sumerian web. Animal muscles and sails still powered all transport. That changed dramatically by 1914, by which time the web was held together by steel and steam and cables, and messages that had formerly taken a year to deliver could be sent in minutes. By contrast, further geographical extensions of the worldwide web, into the isolated interiors of the American and African continents, were less epochal than the earlier ones that linked the world's coasts and hinterlands. The web became much tighter and faster, but only a little larger.

ENLARGING THE WEB

After the British colonization of Australia, beginning in 1788, no habitable landmasses remained outside the worldwide web, and very few people. The few outsiders lived mainly in tropical rainforests in Africa, America, or Southeast Asia, or in the most isolated reaches of the Arctic, Australia, and North America. They numbered a few million people at most, and soon far fewer. In the 1830s, a youthful Charles Darwin (1809–1882) noted in his journal, "Wherever the European has trod, death seems to pursue the aboriginal."[1]

Some of them disappeared leaving little trace. In 1803, when Britain set up a penal colony there, some 5,000 Tasmanians lived on their sizable island some 200 kilometers south of the Australian mainland. Their ancestors had arrived on foot about 35,000 years ago, but when sea level rose at the end of the last Ice Age, they were cut off from the rest of humankind. Thoroughly isolated for 10,000 years, they lost the capacity

[1] Quoted in Roy Porter, *The Greatest Benefit to Mankind: A Medical History of Humanity from Antiquity to the Present* (London, 1997), 466. It was of course not the fact that they were Europeans that made them agents of disease, but that they were participants in the Old World Web. Japanese or Indians would have spread smallpox, measles, influenza, and the rest just as effectively.

to make bone tools, to make fire, and to catch fish. Their technological decay is striking evidence of the penalties of long isolation from the world's webs. After 1803, prisoners and their keepers brought new infections, new weapons, and a very casual attitude toward lethal violence to Tasmania. By 1830, some 300 Tasmanians remained. The last person who was culturally and genetically entirely Tasmanian, a woman named Trucanini, died in 1876.

Other long-isolated peoples fared only slightly better. Easter Island, the easternmost outpost of Polynesia, acquired its first settlers around 400 C.E., but they soon lost contact with the rest of humankind, and eventually lost all memory of others, believing themselves to be the only people on earth. That illusion lasted until 1722, when a Dutch ship stopped off for a day (Easter Sunday). But Easter Island remained so far off the beaten track that the islanders were left almost to themselves for the next 140 years. Then, in 1862–63, the world caught up with them. In Europe and the United States, farmers needed more fertilizers because of soil depletion, and they got it from the coastal guano deposits of Peru. Peruvian slave raiders, scouring Polynesia for men to work the guano fields, carried off some 1,400 people, a third of the population of Easter Island. When a few managed to return, they brought smallpox and other diseases with them, and soon epidemics scythed down much of the island's remaining population. The first missionary arrived in 1864 and found the survivors in need of comfort. By 1868, the few Easter Islanders left had embraced Christianity. Their former religion, which probably held the secret to their distinctive statuary, vanished.

The extension of the web to Tasmania and Easter Island wrought havoc on totally isolated populations. Lesser catastrophes befell those who were less isolated. In Amazonia, whose scattered populations had never been fully cut off from the rest of South America, the scale of interaction with the wider world increased dramatically toward the end of the nineteenth century, when the world's markets paid well for rubber, which at that time came only from a tree native to Amazonia. Rubber tappers fanned out across promising tracts of Amazonian forest, and soon made deals with indigenous Amazonians to gather more rubber. Epidemics inevitably followed upon these contacts, and a certain amount of violence too. Similar encounters took place in the Canadian and Alaskan Arctic, where communities of Inuit met intruders in the form of fur trappers, sealskin traders, or gold seekers; in New Zealand, where Maori met with sealers, whalers, missionaries, and then farmers, mainly from Great Britain; on the grasslands of South and North America, where Amerindians encountered ranchers and farmers of European descent.

These encounters resembled those of ages gone by in which the diseases and technologies of peoples involved in metropolitan webs destroyed the lives and societies of more isolated peoples. In this era, however, tuberculosis joined the deadly list of diseases, because fast urbanization and crowded conditions, especially in Europe, had created environments favorable for that breathborne infection. And the technologies of violence included more sophisticated weapons, such as repeating rifles. So the blows administered to long-isolated societies, both by disease and by violence, were probably sharper than those sustained by the Yukagir or Khoikhoi in the seventeenth century, or any of the countless peoples incorporated into metropolitan webs in earlier times. In any case, the worldwide web expanded further, and the range of human genetic and cultural diversity narrowed.

Even peoples already enmeshed in the world's web sometimes suffered disastrous effects. Dzungar Mongols, for example, living on the steppe north and west of China, had long partaken in exchanges and contacts with their neighbors. But in the early eighteenth century they had somehow managed to stay free of smallpox for a generation or more, and thus rendered themselves vulnerable to it when in the 1750s closer contact with the Chinese reintroduced smallpox to the Dzungars. Similarly, the numerous peoples of Central Africa had by the 1870s had long, if intermittent, contact with outsiders. But between 1880 and 1920 these contacts intensified because European imperialism, in the form of soldiers, traders, and missionaries, reached Central Africa, bringing sharp bouts of warfare and violence, forced labor migrations, exposing people to diseases to which they carried no immunities. The local population fell by perhaps a quarter.

The reason such fates befell Dzungars and Central Africans is not that the worldwide web suddenly embraced them, as happened to the Tasmanians and Easter Islanders. Rather, it was because the web tightened, strengthening links that changed disease patterns and brought the militarily weak into systematic contact with the strong. In the process, some of the strong got stronger, because they oversaw the tightening of the web, they built and owned the infrastructure that did the tightening, and they benefited disproportionately from the faster and greater flows of information and goods. Those who became strongest, by 1914, were the societies of the North Atlantic.

Tightening the Web

Communications prior to 1815 proceeded, if not at a snail's pace, then at a horse's. The ancient Persian Empire had pioneered systems of roads and post-horses, a scheme widely imitated throughout Eurasia. Some governments also invested in systems of beacons and hilltop fires to transmit signals even faster, at the cost of content because only a few prearranged messages could travel this way. During the French Revolution (discussed below), when national unity seemed of the utmost importance, the French built a system of mechanical semaphore signals, called *le télégraphe*, which with telescopes and enough relay stations could send short messages the length and breadth of the country in a few hours. Still, bad weather, dark of night, and human error hampered its usefulness. This, like earlier rudimentary telecommunications systems, served state interests, not commercial ones.

Modern telecommunications arrived in 1844 when the first electric telegraph messages moved between Baltimore and Washington. Morse Code, invented for the telegraph, could convey any range of meaning that words can capture. The telegraph system in the United States grew along with the railroad network it served. Around the world it grew with British imperial power, which it also served. In general, telegraphy provided a tremendous edge in information costs, reliability, and speed to those who used it, which in practice meant mainly Europeans and Americans.

By 1851, submarine cables linked Britain to continental Europe, and by 1866, a transatlantic cable united Britain and America. Contemporaries, including an anonymous optimistic poet, saw a new era dawning:

> *Two mighty lands have shaken hands*
> *Across the deep wide sea;*
> *The world looks forward with new hope*
> *Of better times to be;*
> *No more, as in the days of yore,*
> *Shall mountains keep apart,*
> *No longer oceans sunder wide*
> *The human heart from heart,*
> *For man hath grasped the thunderbolt,*
> *And made of it a slave*
> *To do its errands o'er the land*
> *And underneath the wave.*[2]

---

[2] Quoted in Peter Hugill, *Global Communications Since 1844* (Baltimore, 1999), 25.

Telegraph cables made the acquisition and management of empire much easier. When a telegraph line from Britain to India was completed in 1870, messages that formerly had taken up to eight months to transmit now took five hours. By 1902, Britain had a worldwide telegraph system using undersea cables and outposts in the British Empire. Rivals, such as France, used British-owned and -controlled cables, so that when British authorities listened in they knew what was happening around the world, even in the French Empire, before Paris did. In 1914, at the outbreak of World War I, Germany found its modest undersea cable network cut, and had to send coded messages over lines to which British codebreakers could listen. This was how they found out about Germany's bid to get Mexico to attack the United States, a major reason behind the American decision to enter the war, which itself decided the outcome of the war. This privileged position in telecommunications helped Britain immensely in diplomacy and geopolitics as late as the 1950s.

The capacity of telecommunications increased rapidly and their cost declined just as fast. The French mechanical telegraph might send 150 words per day. By 1860 the electric telegraph could handle 10 words per minute, by 1900 about 150 per minute (about the pace at which English is spoken), and by 1920 about 400. In the 1860s, a message cost $10 per word, but by 1888 only 25 cents, within the reach of small businesses and private citizens. Buy or sell orders from London could reach the New York Stock Exchange in three minutes by 1900. Businessmen and investors with access to the telegraph could make instant profits. Those without it found it harder to stay in business.

The telegraph revolutionized communications, with major consequences for geopolitics and business, but it was only one of the technologies that tightened the web. The others were in transport. The steamship and the railroad launched a transport revolution, but improvements in older transport systems—canals and roads—helped make the steamship and railroad possible. By the eighteenth century, the best transport networks in the world lay at the opposite ends of Eurasia, in coastal China and adjacent waters, and coastal Europe, the regions where the maritime web had had the strongest effects in previous centuries. In the course of the eighteenth century in Europe, and especially in Britain, roads, bridges, and canals grew more numerous, their engineering improved, as did the efficiency of carters, stagecoach, and postal services. Turnpike trusts formed to build and maintain roads for profit. By 1770, Britain had 15,000 miles of turnpikes and almost no one in England lived more than a day's walk from one. Between 1760 and 1790, the time needed for a stagecoach journey between London and Manchester fell from three days to one. Such advances allowed the postal service to provide daily service throughout the country, permitting firms to keep in close touch with suppliers and customers. Between 1660 and 1830, Britain straightened and widened enough river channels to triple the length of navigable waterways within the country, and added an equal length of canals. All this was important because faster and cheaper movement of information, people, and goods made the Industrial Revolution possible. Moving all the coal, iron, raw cotton—and market information—necessary for booming industries was feasible in Britain by 1780 but not in 1720.

Steamships and railroads were offspring of the Industrial Revolution, made possible by the earlier improvements in British transport, but they in turn enabled and encouraged further industrialization. They erased some of the constraints of nature. Contrary winds could not delay steamships for months, nor could any but the harshest weather slow trains. They seemed to annihilate distance, making reliable shipment of bulk goods over thousands of miles routine. They made it economic to produce on gigantic scales, because superior or cheaper goods found buyers all over the world. And merely building steamships, locomotives, and rails created demand for vast quantities of iron, steel, and coal.

The first paddlewheel steamships, built in Scotland and the United States, proved commercially useful on rivers and in coastal traffic after 1801. By 1860 or so, they started to leave sailing vessels in their wakes on the high seas. Subsidies from post offices (which wanted prompt and reliable mail delivery) and technical improvements (better engines, screw propellers) brought great savings in time and money. A journey from Holland to Java in the spice trade took a year in 1650, three months by sail with favorable winds in 1850, and three weeks by steamer in 1920. Similar savings in time took place on all oceanic routes. Savings in freight rates mattered just as much. Long-distance trade before 1700 had involved mainly precious goods such as spices, sugar, and silks. By 1800, costs had fallen enough to make it worthwhile shipping mass quantities of tobacco, opium, cotton, tea, among other commodities. In the nineteenth century, especially after 1850, freight rates fell faster as steamship technology improved and shipping lines emerged to manage the business efficiently. During the California gold rush, San Francisco even imported prefabricated houses from Hong Kong.[3] Soon scores of other

---

[3] We thank Dennis Flynn for this information.

commodities, including coal and grain, floated across the oceans and world shipping increased fourfold (1850–1910).

While steamships tightened the web across the sea, railroads did the same overland. They too made good use of the telegraph, of new forms of large business organization, of cheaper iron, steel, and coal. The first public railroad, opened in 1825, served the British coal industry. The railway age began in 1830 with a link between Manchester and Liverpool, a great commercial success. British companies built a dense network of railways in the next decades. Germany, France, Belgium, and Switzerland quickly laid plenty of track too, but it was the United States that railroads affected most. Long distances, natural resources, and political unity allowed full scope for all the advantages of railroads. By 1845, the United States had twice as much track as Britain, and by 1870 four times as much. In 1869 the Americans completed a transcontinental rail link and after 1880 had at least seven times as much track as any other country. Canada (1885) and Russia (1903) also knitted their lands together with transcontinental threads of steel, becoming railroad empires. By 1914, European countries had built most of the track they would ever build; the highest densities were in Germany and Britain. But North America had nearly half the rail track in the world. Rail networks, like steamships, drastically reduced time and costs in transport, and thus opened the way to great extensions of specialization, division of labor, and economies of scale in production. In many cases, they also helped unify nations, not merely economically, but politically, culturally, and socially as well.

Table 7.1

Length of Railroad Networks, 1850–1930 (in kilometers)

YEAR	USA	RUSSIA	CANADA	INDIA	GERMANY	FRANCE	GREAT BRITAIN
1850	14,500	500	100	—	2,100	900	3,900
1870	85,000	11,000	4,000	9,000	19,000	16,000	21,000
1890	335,000	31,000	23,000	27,000	43,000	33,000	28,000
1910	566,000	67,000	51,000	53,000	61,000	40,000	32,000
1930	692,000	78,000	91,000	71,000	58,000	42,000	33,000

Source: Based on Daniel Headrick, Tentacles of Progress (New York, 1988), 55.

In Africa and Asia, railroads usually served colonial purposes, encouraging export trades. Trains by 1900 traveled twenty times the speed of human porters, thirty times as fast as oxen, and they carried heavier loads. Overland freight rates declined by 90–97 percent when rails replaced porters or bullock carts in Africa and India. Suddenly it became economic to ship fiber crops, minerals, and other bulk goods from the interior of Africa or India. In South America, colonialism ended before railroads began. But foreigners financed most of the railroads with the export of coffee, wheat, or copper in mind, so the tracks usually led from plantations and mines to the nearest port, just as in Africa or South Asia. Argentina built the most track, and had more than Britain by 1913– mostly financed from Britain.

By 1914, world trade had become a matter of fairly routine transactions. The days of merchant-adventurers had passed. Businesses and bureaucracies managed trade flows in huge quantities over vast distances—and information, people, and goods circulated faster and cheaper than ever before, thanks to telegraphs, steamships, and railroads.

Igniting the Population Explosion

The world's population grew very slowly for most of human history. By the time the first metropolitan web was forming around Sumer some 5,000 years ago, the earth hosted perhaps 10 to 30 million people. By 100 C.E., when the Old World Web had formed, global population had reached about 150 million (about what Brazil has today). And in 1500, when the modern worldwide web was taking shape, the world had roughly 450 million people. By 1700, that total had climbed to about 610 million.

Population growth remained slow and unsteady before 1700 because death rates were high—sometimes very high. In agrarian societies, babies were born at rates around 30 or 40 per 1,000 per year (about three times higher than the U.S. birth rate today). But half of them did not live past their fifth birthday, because of routine, endemic diseases, often compounded by malnutrition. Child mortality was the main check on population growth. The other was occasional demographic crisis. In ordinary years, people died at rates around 25 to 35 per 1,000 per year (the death rate was a little lower than the birth rate), but every few years epidemic, famine, violence—or all three—killed larger numbers, pruning back population growth. These crises were usually local or regional in scope, but with the extension of webs epidemics could become very widespread catastrophes, like the Black Death that ravaged most of the Old World Web in the mid-fourteenth century. Cities remained particularly dangerous places, where people died faster than others were born, sustained only by in-migrants from surrounding villages. Naturally variations existed from place to place and over time, but in general this was the outline of the demographic regime in agrarian societies before 1700. In the sixteen centuries before 1700, world population grew, on average, by about 12 percent per century.

In the 1700s, this regime began to crumble. Death rates fell, and in some places birth rates rose. China's population doubled, and Europe's almost did so. In the Americas, population grew even faster, rebounding from the disasters that had followed the linkup to the Old World Web. Evidence is sparse for India and Africa, but their growth apparently lagged behind the pace set by China and Europe. The world's total by 1800 was probably around 900 million. Population growth in the 1700s reached 30 percent per century, nearly three times as fast as in the centuries before 1700. Epidemics and famines did not disappear, but they became less frequent and less severe. By 1900, world population had reached 1.6 billion, a growth rate of nearly 80 percent per century. A fundamental transition was underway.

The reasons behind this modern surge of population derive from changes in the web. Better, faster, denser transport and communications made more diseases endemic and reduced the scope for epidemics. Better transport made it easier for food to reach those most eager to pay for it, checking lethal famines, although this did not help the penniless. The global dispersal of food crops continued, and probably had more effect in the 1800s than in any previous period. Medicine had very little to do with the first stages of this population surge, although the diffusion of the knowledge of inoculation against smallpox, a venerable folk practice in China, India, West Africa, and elsewhere, lengthened many lives. Warmer climate in the northern hemisphere after the 1690s may also have improved harvests, and therefore food supply, disease resistance, and life expectancies.

Whatever its root causes, this surge came in the course of what historians call the demographic transition. In that pattern, death rates decline first, followed at some interval by a fall in birth rates, ultimately reaching a point where the rates are in rough balance again and population growth (or loss) is again slow. But during that interval population grows very rapidly. This transition proceeded at different paces in different places. Some societies may not follow this script, but it captures the experience of most of the world's peoples.

In Britain's case, the interval of brisk growth lasted from about 1750 to about 1910, an era in which the British population grew from 7.5 million to 40 million, despite the emigration of perhaps 20 million. Death rates declined in the 1700s and birth rates stayed high for several generations; indeed, they climbed a bit higher, before falling sharply in the 1890s. The demographic transition was slow enough that contemporaries, such as T. R. Malthus (1766–1834), the great and grim analyst of population, did not notice it.

In France, fertility decline began earlier, between 1780 and 1840, truncating France's high-growth stage and ending its career as the most populous country in Europe. Japan followed a special course. Its population stagnated from 1700 to 1860 or so, a result of unusually low fertility. It then surged to 1940 before making a transition to very low birth and death rates. In most of the rest of the world demographic transitions happened later, and thus will be taken up in chapter 8. The fact that it happened first in Atlantic Europe meant that Europeans accounted for a larger share of humanity around 1900 than before or since.

Rapid and uneven population growth brought new strains and pressures. These helped drive new patterns of migration, including faster movement to cities. Half of Britain's population in 1850 lived in cities, an unprecedented situation which required that the countryside provide huge numbers of migrants. Rapid and uneven population growth also affected politics, encouraging overseas imperial adventures on the part of Western Europeans and Japanese, and overland ones on the part of Russians, Chinese, Americans, and Canadians. It threatened the stability of multinational empires, in which some nationalities increased far faster than others. It affected the natural world too, because more people meant more farms, more cities, and hence less space for forest, grassland, and wild creatures. Indeed, the rapidity, and unevenness, of population growth after 1750 affected almost everything—and continues to do so today.

New Foundations for Politics

Since the creation of the first states 5,000 years ago, the most common and durable political arrangement has been monarchy. A single individual, normally a man, claimed the right to rule, normally on the basis of heredity and divine approval. In practice, kings and emperors had to compromise with religious authorities and with local magnates, usually big landowners in regions where rents and land taxes provided the source of wealth. In places where land was plentiful and people scarce, say Russia, tropical Africa, or Southeast Asia, magnates might be distinguished by their control of people or commerce rather than land. Monarchies also varied considerably in the degree of freedom and political voice granted to subjects. A few societies departed from the monarchical norm, creating democracies in which every citizen (however defined) took part in politics, or republics in which representatives of privileged groups did so. These arrangements tended to be small-scale, brittle, and short-lived. To most people, monarchies seemed part of the natural order of things.

But the growing integration of the web transformed the basis of politics, beginning in the seventeenth century. Rapid growth of trade and cities produced communities of merchants and commercial landowners who resented the taxes levied on them by monarchs. This happened throughout the worldwide web, especially in its maritime regions such as coastal China, West Africa, and Atlantic Europe. Where literacy and communications were most developed, these men of property (very few were women) found it easier to organize themselves into coherent factions. Simultaneously, in the seventeenth century, monarchs in many places struggled with their finances because of decades of bad harvests and lower revenues (partly a matter of adverse climate change) and higher expenditures because of the military revolution. They needed to increase taxes just when a crucial source of revenue, men of property, were organizing themselves to protect their own interests.

The great Asian empires of the Qing, Mughals, and Ottomans contained these pressures, albeit with difficulty. Where states were numerous and combative, as in much of Europe and Atlantic Africa, chronic warfare exacerbated the strains on monarchies. In cases, the old order fell apart, as in Kongo, an autocratic kingdom of some half a million people as of 1650, situated to the south of the Congo River. There slave traders and vassals ousted the hereditary king after 1665, leading to civil wars and eventually to a reconstructed, less autocratic, more decentralized kingdom by 1710. The old order fell apart in Holland and England too, where hitherto politically excluded men of property (including a few slave traders) banded together to seize power. In Holland it happened when the urban elite cast off Spanish Habsburg authority in a long war. In England it came as a result first of Civil War between King and Parliament in the 1640s and a coup d'état in 1688–89 which installed a new weakened monarchy, one accommodating to the new men of property and Parliament. This laid the sociopolitical foundation for the economic and technological revolutions that England later launched upon the world.

In Europe—as in Kongo—these revolutions proceeded in tandem with new political ideas that justified the new order. These ideas, about the limits of kingly privilege, found brilliant spokesmen such as John Locke (1632–1704), who argued that legitimate government can come only from the consent of the governed. The web circulated these ideas widely, overwhelming efforts at censorship, and they found favor wherever men of property chafed under monarchs' rule. They became powerful where men of property were growing richer fast, and became revolutionary where monarchs teetered under fiscal pressures.

This happened next in the North American colonies in the 1770s. Men of property, mostly merchants in the northern colonies and slave-holding landowners in the southern ones, joined together to resist heightened taxes levied by the British Parliament. As usual, war debts made higher taxation seem necessary, this time arising from the worldwide struggle between Britain and France known as the Seven Years' War, fought in Europe, America, India, and on the seas. In effect, men of property in Britain hoped to shunt some of the expenses of running an empire onto men of property in North America. Many of the Americans objected, raised an army by taxing themselves, and organized the American Revolution (1775–81). They won because fighting in America was terribly expensive for Britain, and because the French intervened on their side.

The French king soon had cause to regret it. The American example invigorated advocates of liberty everywhere, and the eloquent expression of ideas of freedom achieved by Americans such as Thomas Jefferson (1743–1826) proved contagious, adding to the mix of subversive views already in circulation in France. By the 1770s, the French elite had already fractured: a large proportion of landed aristocrats, urban merchants, and professionals no longer supported the monarchy, wanting freedom from laws, taxes, and restraints on business that the king would not and could not grant. That might have come to nothing, except that population growth led to land hunger among the peasantry, the American war had drained the treasury, and bad harvests injured everyone. In the 1780s, bankers, the Catholic Church, and rich aristocrats refused further loans so the king summoned a long-dormant body called the Estates-General to help him raise taxes, inadvertently opening the flood-

gates of revolution. Those summoned—mostly men of property—
declared themselves representatives of the people, from whom true sovereignty flowed. When attacked, they received support from the urban
poor of Paris, and this alliance toppled the monarchy (1789-91). Near
chaos ensued as revolutionary factions struggled against one another and
war erupted with neighboring monarchies. But soon an army man,
Napoleon Bonaparte (1769–1821), captured the revolution for his own
purposes, leading France on an extraordinary series of military adventures in Italy, Austria, Germany, Egypt, Spain, and Russia, and ultimately
to defeat in 1815. The monarchy was then restored, but without much
legitimacy, and further revolutions followed in France, until a more
durable republic emerged after 1871.

The French explosion ignited others across the Atlantic, first in the
French sugar colony of Saint Domingue. The events of 1789-91 weakened colonial control there, and when a slave revolt broke out, it quickly
became a revolution. A large proportion of the slaves in Saint Domingue
came from Kongo, and Kongolese ideas about limited monarchy combined with French ones to shape the revolution. The French, British,
and Spanish took turns trying to suppress it, but all failed. A former
slave, domestic servant, and cattle manager, Toussaint l'Ouverture (ca.
1743–1803), organized an effective army, conducted a guerrilla war, and
prudently allowed yellow fever to destroy his enemies between 1791 and
1803. In 1804, Haiti became an independent state, the second republic
established in the Americas, and the first and only one based on a slave
revolt. Here the men of property, some of whom had originally wished to
secede from France, were overwhelmed by men who had formerly been
their property.

The French Revolution also brought independence to Spanish
colonies in the Americas. Again, the example and ideology of revolution,
both in the United States and in France, resonated with men of property
throughout Latin America. The Spanish Empire's constraints on trade,
although widely flouted, irked merchants and landowners alike. They
enjoyed rising prosperity based on population and commercial growth,
but saw Spanish rules preventing still greater gains. When Napoleon
invaded Spain in 1808, the Latin American colonies rose in revolt, and
Spain could do nothing about it. After Napoleon was ousted from Spain,
the new Spanish government tried by force of arms to reconstitute the
empire, but failed, its largest expeditionary army falling victim to yellow
fever. By 1826, Spanish America had splintered into several independent

countries, leaving Spain only Cuba and Puerto Rico, where sugar planters remained loyal to their best customer.

These revolutions reverberating throughout the Atlantic world all had local and specific causes. But they also had causes in common: clamor for representative government or popular sovereignty, the rising power of commercial classes, population growth, fiscal woes of embattled monarchs. All these derived, to some degree, from the tighter linkages of the worldwide web. Because that tightening took place most strongly and quickly around the shores of the Atlantic, the Age of Revolution was at first an Atlantic affair.

But not for long. All the revolutions except the Haitian had advanced the notion that men of property should be free to seek their fortunes as they saw fit. The French Revolution in particular had also advanced the notion that sovereignty rests on the consent of the governed, that the state is the expression of the will of the people. Both these ideas traveled well, especially the latter. In France it proved practical as a basis for a new type of army, the "nation-in-arms"—new at least to Europe since the Roman Republic 2,000 years before.[4] When combined with masterly organization, a skill Napoleon had in full measure, this mass army proved a formidable instrument of land warfare. It also helped forge a collective consciousness, a sense of nationhood, among the French, who in 1790 were a diverse lot. By 1815 they were somewhat less diverse, somewhat more French, and hence, somewhat more compliant to any government that could convince them it embodied the will of the people. There was magic here.

Nationalism, the sense of solidarity among people who believe themselves to comprise a nation, could make the art of government a lot easier. In this respect, it served as religions had long done, reconciling the ruled to their fate. Where the entire population shared the attributes held to distinguish a nation—usually language and culture, but in some cases supposed ancestry—the state could easily portray itself as the embodiment of the nation. Thoughtful governments used military service, mass education (especially heroic and nationalist history lessons), and patriotic literature to instill nationalist sentiments; drama, music, museums, marches, and ritual celebrations carried the message to the unlettered. People almost everywhere, especially city folk and educated classes, proved enormously responsive to the lure of nationalism. It

---

[4] Neglecting Europe's tribal societies in which every man was a warrior.

made people feel part of something larger and nobler than their families or parishes. While nationalism functioned a bit like a secular religion, and in some cases (Italy, France, Mexico, Turkey) allied with anticlerical elements, it often harmonized with the dominant religion, as with Catholicism in Poland and Ireland, with Orthodoxy in Russia, Greece, and Serbia, or with Shinto in Japan. It sometimes delivered tangible rewards, to schoolteachers, journalists, army officers, and many others who helped spread the message. And it satisfied what is probably among the deepest human cravings, the urge to solidarity and community, the urge to divide humanity into "us" and "them." This urge probably had survival value in the long apprenticeship of human history, when group solidarity meant more successful hunting and self-protection, and is perhaps hard-wired into human brains. Modern nationalism is the convergence between such group solidarity and state sovereignty. In any case, nationalism caught on.

It helped upset the world political order. First, nationalism conferred greater power on those states that could marshal it in their service. This meant those where borders of language and culture coincided neatly with political ones—such as Japan. But it also applied to those where political borders could be adjusted to accommodate emerging senses of nationality, such as Italy and Germany, which became powerful states through diplomacy and small-scale wars between 1859 and 1871. France and Britain also benefited from nationalism once their linguistic and cultural diversity were suppressed, a project that in both cases took a century or more. After the Civil War, free schooling and an appealing political ideology of freedom made nationalism work in the United States, despite its ethnic and religious diversity. Followers of many religions find freedom in submission to God: rulers of reasonably homogenous states found power in submission to the will of the people, because submitting to it, or appearing to, inspired nationalist support.

But where populations were too diverse, nationalism generally weakened the state. This proved the case in the Habsburg and Ottoman domains in the nineteenth century, where great cultural and ethnic variety resisted amalgamation, despite no shortage of state efforts to capture the elusive magic. Instead, the many nationalities pursued their own agendas of liberation, making those empires increasingly awkward to govern. Indeed, centralizing and consolidating policies helped provoke further minority nationalisms. Imperial Russia suffered too, as many of its subjects, Poles in particular, developed lively nationalisms. "Russification" projects aroused bitter resentments. In the twentieth century, nationalism would travel well around the world, upsetting political arrangements everywhere, lumping and splitting peoples and countries relentlessly. With the rise of national identities, politics and culture would never be the same.

In the nineteenth century, the emergence of representative government and nationalism spread only so far. The Russian Empire showed little inclination to widen the basis of politics, nor did the great Asian empires or the hundreds of African states, although in several cases some small steps were taken. By the end of the nineteenth century, as we shall see, much of Asia and nearly all of Africa fell under European control, and colonial government (except in settler colonies like New Zealand or Australia) usually proceeded by fiat or in consultation with local, unelected rulers. The independent states of Latin America after 1826 usually adopted republican constitutions (although Brazil styled itself an empire until 1889). But often as not they were run by their armies, because in most cases the army (and in some cases the church) was the chief institution that survived and prospered during the wars of independence. It was not until about 1950 that the principle of representative government became so generally accepted that almost every polity at least pretended to adhere to it.

The new politics had another limit too. In republics and constitutional monarchies alike, the revolutions broadened political participation mainly to the men of property who had led them. Poor people remained excluded for a few generations and women for a bit longer. In the 1830s, the United States extended the vote to poor white males, and Britain in 1884 to almost all tax-paying males. France and Imperial Germany widened the franchise to all adult males in the 1870s. But in Italy in 1881, only 6 percent of the populace could vote. Women did not vote in national politics anywhere until 1894, when New Zealand opened the franchise to them, and nearly everywhere women took little part in politics until after 1918. So, in most polities, as late as 1914, no one could vote; and in those where men could vote, women normally could not. Further, in the American republics, even after the abolition of slavery, various rules and threats often kept black people from voting. The principles of the Age of Revolution remained only principles for most of the world until the twentieth century, and even where they became practice, they usually widened the basis of political participation only by slow degrees. Nonetheless, these new principles, however inconsistently applied, formed part of the foundation of the modern world.

The Industrial Revolution

Yet there was something even more fundamental going on in the world: the Industrial Revolution. Although focused first on England, it too was a worldwide transition, partly because even the initial industrialization of England required new connections to places such as India and America, and partly because, once started in England, industrialization spread. Like the demographic transition and nationalism, it spread quickly and unevenly. This produced further pressures provoking migrations, revolutions, imperialisms, imperial collapses, and much else.

First and foremost, the Industrial Revolution transformed the energy base of human society. Energy is essential for making things, for transport, and for bodily survival. Before the use of fossil fuels, people could harness only a tiny fraction of the energy available on earth. By eating plants, people acquired chemical energy that photosynthesis had captured from sunlight. By eating animals, and using the muscle power of draft animals, humans tapped further energy. Wind and water power, available only in favorable locations, also harnessed a fraction of the annual energy delivered to the earth from the sun. Each of these methods tapped only the annual flow of energy generated by the sun, which although abundant, was very inefficiently converted into useful forms. By burning wood or charcoal, people could tap energy stocks accumulated in trees over a century or two. But ultimately all these methods provided a very limited energy harvest, which meant that almost all people would always be poor, dependent upon grinding toil for their daily rice or bread.

Fossil fuels changed all that. The first people to make them central to their economy were the Dutch, who burned peat to heat their homes and fuel industries such as brewing, brickmaking, sugar refining, or glassmaking (but not metallurgy, for which a peat flame was not hot enough). Peat is accumulated vegetable matter, preserved by water. The Dutch cut it out of bogs, dried it, and burned it to harvest energy that plants had captured over a few millennia. This gave the Netherlands a unique advantage (until coal) in energy-intensive industries. To a considerable extent, the prosperity of the Dutch in their Golden Age (ca. 1580–1700) depended on low energy costs.

While wood allowed access to stores of energy captured over centuries, and peat to energy captured over millennia, coal represented energy stocks accumulated over eons. People around the world had known of coal's uses for a long time, and Song China had used it on a large scale in its iron industry. London had burned coal for home heating from at least the thirteenth century. Britain had abundant coal deposits, part of a "carboniferous crescent" that stretched from the Scottish lowlands through England to northern France and Belgium and the Ruhr region of Germany. This would become the industrial heartland of Europe, a region as important for modern history as the fertile crescent was for ancient history. Before 1750, only the coastal coal of northeastern England could travel economically for more than a few miles. But with canal construction in the eighteenth century, Britain's larger inland coal deposits entered the marketplace. By 1815, annual British coal production yielded energy equivalent to what could be garnered from a hypothetical forest equal in area to all of England, Scotland, and Wales, twenty times what the actual woodlands of Britain could then produce.[5] In effect, coal substituted for land. Britain was on its way to becoming the first high-energy society. Table 7.2 shows the difference in energy use before and after fossil fuels:

Table 7.2
Average Annual Per Capita Energy Use

Basic requirements of the human body	1*
Hunting-and-gathering societies	3–6
Agrarian societies	18–24
Industrial societies	70–80

*The unit here is the average basal metabolic requirements of an adult human body, about 3.5 gigajoules per year.

Source: Rolf-Peter Sieferle, Der Europäische Sonderweg: Ursachen und Faktoren *(Stuttgart, 2001), 18–19.*

The harnessing of fossil fuels, like the transition to agriculture a hundred centuries before, ratcheted up energy supplies available for

---

[5] The 23 million tons of coal produced in 1815, even if burned in inefficient steam engines, could do the work of perhaps 50 million vigorous men. The total population of Britain was about 13 million, so the number of vigorous men was perhaps 3 million.

human use, thereby permitting a vast increase in human numbers and wealth. Where the demographic transition (in its latter stages) slowed population growth, the expanded energy harvest meant that for the first time in history, mass poverty became unnecessary.

With cheap British coal it became easier to stay warm in winter and to stoke the energy-intensive industries that the Dutch had specialized in. But matters in Britain went much further than this, thanks in part to two technical changes. Most coal seams were of no use to the iron industry because coal's impurities made iron brittle. But after 1709 this no longer mattered, because an ironmaster named Abraham Darby (1678?–1717) figured out that coke, a purer carbon derived from coal, served admirably. This resolved an energy bottleneck in iron production, allowing an expansion that could not have happened using the traditional fuel, charcoal. The second technical innovation came in the form of steam engines, which had existed in rudimentary forms in China and France as well as in England. The problem of draining water from coal mines inspired several advances in steam engine design, the most important one credited to the Scotsman James Watt (1736–1819) in the 1770s. Where coal was almost free, at pitheads, coal-powered steam engines pumped out groundwater, which allowed miners to dig deeper and deeper.

Getting the water out of the way opened a new subterranean energy frontier. This was a momentous achievement roughly analogous to what happened in agriculture when farmers succeeded in cultivating the damp lowlands of northwestern Europe with the moldboard plow, or further afield, when East Asian rice paddies or Mesoamerican raised fields opened up new food-producing opportunities. Regulation of water was the key, and in the case of coal mining it was machines, not peasants, who did it.

By 1800, Britain had about 2,000 steam engines, most of them employed pumping water out of coal mines. This made coal cheaper still. Soon it became practical to use coal, and stationary steam engines, in many other applications, such as textile and pottery manufacture, and to work the bellows in iron foundries. Mobile steam engines, on locomotives and ships, eventually became standard, with results noted above. This was the technological heart of the Industrial Revolution in Britain.[6]

---

[6] And contemporaries knew it: steam engines in the early 1800s often had decorative flourishes derived from ancient classical architecture, and engine houses and pumping stations sometimes looked like churches. The steam engine was the symbol, as well as the substance, of the Industrial Revolution.

But there was more to it than technological innovation and cheap energy. Within Britain an emerging social, political, and economic environment rewarded, and eased, innovation. Compromises put in place by the so-called Glorious Revolution, the coup d'état of 1688–89, helped establish a more predictable tax regime, more secure property rights, and policies more favorable to businessmen, such as the prohibition of imports of Indian cloth (1721), which made the English cotton industry more viable. British manufacturers enjoyed high tariff protection from foreign competition until the 1820s. Employers in the mining or textile industries could also rely on the government and its army to support them in struggles with laborers. Moreover, the transport improvements noted above permitted a national market, thereby rewarding large-scale production. Britain's three major wars between 1756 and 1815 also made the government a good customer for large production runs of clothing and iron goods: Britain built a military-industrial complex.[7] Britain also developed a financial system that more efficiently put the wealth of savers at the disposal of businesses needing to borrow, although this apparently mattered little in the early decades of the Industrial Revolution. Abraham Darby turned to family and friends for funds to expand his ironworks, as did James Watt for his business. But after 1780 entrepreneurs could borrow from so-called country banks and sell shares on the London Stock Exchange (est. 1773). So the social and political landscape, together with coal's resolution of the energy bottleneck, allowed and encouraged innovations.

Beyond Britain's shores other circumstances helped shatter the old constraints. While coal substituted for forest land, overseas fields substituted for British farmland, improving the food supply, especially to the cities. Britain's manufactures allowed it to trade for grain from Russia and North America. Britain's colonial power allowed it to obtain, at favorable prices, sugar from the Caribbean, which supplied urban workers with some of their calories. It also brought cheap tea from China and India, a stimulant that helped those workers last through their shifts. And the export of manufactures and exercise of colonial power both helped Britain obtain all the raw cotton its mills could use, from the American South, from India, and later from Egypt and elsewhere in Africa. The expansion of America's cotton belt after 1790 proved essential to the

[7] The significance of military production in the Industrial Revolution is disputed by Joel Mokyr, *The British Industrial Revolution* (Boulder, CO, 1998), 56.

British textile industry; dyestuffs and dyeing techniques from India and Turkey were also helpful. The worldwide web of trade brought Britain's population, and its industries, all they needed—thanks to the advantages conferred by British coal and steam. Here is the economist W. S. Jevons in 1865:

> [U]nfettered commerce . . . founded on the material basis of our coal resources, have [sic] made the several quarters of the globe our willing tributaries. . . . The plains of North America and Russia are our corn-fields; Chicago and Odessa our granaries; Canada and the Baltic our timber-forests; Australasia contains our sheep-farms, and in Argentina and on the western prairies of North America are our herds of oxen; Peru sends her silver, and the gold of South Africa and Australia flows to London; the Hindus and Chinese grow tea for us; and our coffee, sugar and spice plantations are all in the Indies. Spain and France are our vineyards, and the Mediterranean our fruit-garden; and our cotton-grounds, which for long have occupied the Southern United States, are now being extended everywhere in the warm regions of the earth.[8]

Historians have long tried to figure out why the Industrial Revolution happened first in England, and why it happened when it did. A short answer is that internal characteristics (lots of coal and iron) and developments (the sociopolitical environment after 1688) combined with tightening of the web both within Britain (roads, canals, railways, postal service) and worldwide (overseas trade and colonies, and population growth) to create the necessary conditions for industrialization, ones in which both the freedom and incentive to innovate attained unusual proportions.

The resulting innovations resolved old bottlenecks, but created new problems that cried out for solution. In textiles, for example, long a small-scale but widespread business, before 1733 it took three or four spinners to produce enough thread to keep one weaver busy. But the invention of the flying shuttle made weavers twice as fast, and raised the incentive to figure out a way to make spinners faster—accomplished in 1770 with the spinning jenny. Hence, at least in retrospect, major inno-

---

[8] W. S. Jevons, *The Coal Question* (New York, 1965 [1865]), 410–11.

vations came in clusters. These involved both technical and organizational elements, and evolved together with social and political arrangements. The first cluster, which took shape around 1780–1830, involved primarily the textile and iron industries. The key technical achievements were the flying shuttle, spinning jenny, and power loom in cotton production, and coking furnaces in the iron industry. Crucial advances in transport were turnpikes and canals. Decisive organizational innovations came together in the factory system, which brought workers under tighter supervision and made quality control more feasible. The central sociopolitical development was the reconciliation of political and economic power, manifested in the compromises of the Glorious Revolution.

The second cluster of innovations (ca. 1820–70) centered on iron, coal, and steam engines. Joint-stock companies, which provided a legal mechanism for a limitless number of investors to pool their investment funds, and a newly liberal state (meaning one that regulates economic activity as little as possible) evolved in step, providing the software innovations and sociopolitical environment compatible with the technical components of this cluster. That the newly liberal state also engaged in empire building, creating military and overseas markets, helped too.

The third cluster (ca. 1850–1920) featured coal and steel, railways and telegraphs, chemicals and electricity—and giant firms that took advantage of economies of scale and operated internationally. For the first time, most of the innovations came not in Britain, but in Germany and the United States, especially the large-scale bureaucratic business organization, pioneered by American railroads. Equally new, the Industrial Revolution now acquired further momentum from science. Previously, the important innovations had come from tinkering by people who worked in foundries, mines, or mills. But after 1860, organized science played a growing role. Universities developed research programs that cooperated with businesses, especially in chemistry and engineering, and especially in countries keen to catch up with Britain. Big firms also started funding their own research departments. These arrangements paid dividends and eventually became standard around the world wherever industrialization spread.

With each successive cluster, the Industrial Revolution became increasingly global. From its outset, it drew on food and fiber from afar, and this dependence on distant sources of raw materials grew over time. But the Industrial Revolution was a worldwide process in two other respects: its impacts and its spread.

Impacts of the Industrial Revolution

The Industrial Revolution was the most important factor in generating the inequalities in wealth and power that shaped world politics after 1800. One of its early effects was to put less efficient industry out of business.

DEINDUSTRIALIZATION IN ASIA, AFRICA, AND THE AMERICAS

In 1700, the world's only great exporter of woven textiles was India. But by 1860, Indian weavers could not match British competition, because they did not have the cheap energy, or the standardization and quality control, of the factory system. Of Dhaka, a textile center in today's Bangladesh, Sir Charles Trevelyan said in testimony before the House of Lords, "the jungle and malaria are fast encroaching . . . the Manchester of India, has fallen from a very flourishing town to a very poor and small town." Its population shrank from about 120,000–150,000 in 1750 to 40,000–60,000 in 1850.

Before the British textile invasion, weavers around the world had produced a wide range of finished cloths attuned to local fashions. In Iran, for example, cotton and silk industries flourished before 1820, providing a living for thousands of weavers (mostly men) in cities like Isfahan and Tabriz, and for spinners (mostly women) in the surrounding countryside. British cotton cloth began to enter the Iranian market in the 1820s, and in ensuing decades British cloth became cheaper, better, and more appealing to Iranian tastes. Eventually British cottons became more popular than Iranian silks. By 1890, Isfahan had only one-tenth of the silk looms that it had had in 1830. Iran stopped exporting silk and cotton cloth, and began to export raw cotton and silk. In 1850, Iran exported twenty-three times as much cotton cloth as raw cotton; by 1910, it exported twenty times as much raw cotton as cotton cloth. Street urchins were singing:

> Everyone who earned his bread by weaving
> Would be better off dead than living.[9]

---

[9] Quoted in Willem Floor, *The Persian Textile Industry in Historical Perspective, 1500–1925* (Paris, 1999), 119.

Similar refrains, no doubt, were sung on the streets of Kyoto, Shanghai, Calcutta, Bukhara, Cairo, Tlemcen, Timbuktu, Cuzco, and Mexico City. In villages around the world (England included) where spinning helped make ends meet, the efficiency of British factories also brought distress.

In Iran, the Ottoman Empire, Mexico, and elsewhere, governments tried new measures to protect their weavers and spinners. Iran tried banning foreign-made cloth and requiring subjects to wear Iranian fabric, until the shahs saw their interest in higher customs revenues from textile imports. The Ottomans and Mexicans financed new steam-powered factories, using machinery and expertise imported from Europe. Such measures probably worked best in the Ottoman Empire, where after initial collapse the textile industry by 1900 had returned to its approximate size as of 1800. But even after its revival, it accounted for a much smaller share of the cloth sold within Ottoman borders: its absolute size was the same as before but its relative share much smaller. It was also different, focused much more on carpet production—and by 1910 a British consortium owned most of the carpet factories in the Ottoman Empire.

By the middle of the nineteenth century, the Industrial Revolution in Britain produced so much so cheaply that other industries around the world suffered the same fate as textiles. British iron, steel, and metal goods outcompeted the products of Asia, Africa, and Latin America. So did British shipbuilding, pottery making, and for that matter, British banking and insurance. Britain even exported coal around the world in the late nineteenth century. The hardware and software innovations of the Industrial Revolution conferred an enormous comparative advantage on many enterprises within Britain, especially those that were energy- or knowledge-intensive. This launched an enormous reorganization of the world's economy in which most parts of the world found their comparative advantage shifted to land-intensive production, mainly of food and fiber crops. In some cases this reorganization derived not merely from shifts in relative productivity and comparative advantage: Britain used enhanced military power to impose tariffs, taxes, and treaties that furthered the interests of its manufacturers. India, for example, became a net cloth importer by 1816 in part because many Indian states were obliged to accept free trade in textiles.

IMPERIALISM AND SELF-STRENGTHENING

Before the Industrial Revolution, the Atlantic Europeans had created maritime empires. In most cases these consisted of strings of fortified trading posts or sugar islands. The Spanish and Portuguese claimed vast territories in the Americas, but genuinely controlled only about a quarter of what they claimed. Britain had growing colonies of settlement in North America, but only east of the Appalachians. The Dutch grip on today's Indonesia extended only to a few ports and their hinterlands. Outside the Americas, Siberia, and Australasia, where demographic catastrophes made imperialism easy, the political balance did not permit overseas imperialism on any scale. European power melted away beyond the range of ships' cannon.

Industrialization changed this situation fundamentally, making European, especially British, imperialism cheap and easy, and therefore more inviting. Factories churned out new, more deadly weapons; indeed, the modern methods of mass production, based on standardized, interchangeable parts, first emerged in the arms industry. Ironclad, steam-powered gunboats could project power inland, along rivers such as the Ganges or Yangzi, previously arteries of Mughal or Qing power. From the 1840s, a great imbalance in weaponry and communications systems prevailed, making European armies victorious in war even against far more numerous foes. Despite occasional objections at home, industrialized states often fought wars and acquired territory rather casually, in response to a diplomatic slight, an unpaid debt, or a failed negotiation for a commercial treaty. Nationalism and improved state finance helped strengthen European states too, but at root this was industrial imperialism, a result of the power imbalance that prevailed between about 1840 and 1945.

By the end of the 1800s, this imbalance grew far greater, what with repeating rifles, the first machine guns, exploding ordnance, and other arms innovations. After 1875, industrial countries made their gun barrels of steel using new techniques; no longer could clever smiths in Africa or Indonesia imitate and build modern weaponry. Industrial states could wage war in Africa and Asia at extremely low cost. By the 1890s, military doctors met considerable success in checking the diseases that formerly had done so much to keep outsiders at bay in tropical Africa and Southeast Asia. Moreover, by training local troops and equipping them with modern weapons, Europeans could fight and win wars of conquest in which most of the fighting was done by Africans or Asians. This further blunted the impact of tropical diseases.

Industrial imperialism proved a jarring experience for societies on the receiving end of European power. Courage, spears, arrows, and muskets could achieve little against a modern military force. People every-

Map 7.1 Imperialism in Asia, Pacific, and Africa, ca. 1910

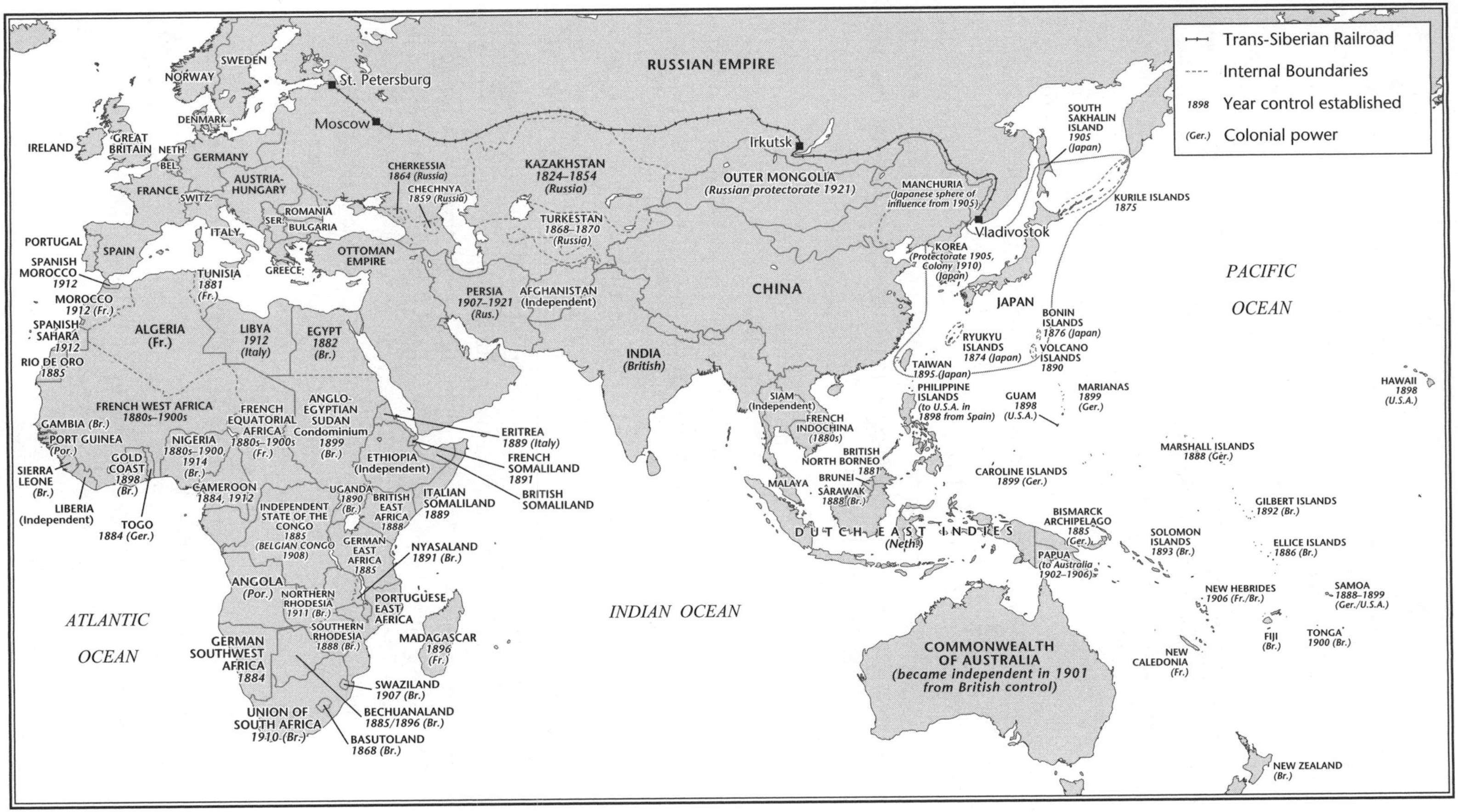

where turned to the supernatural for help. All manner of new prophets cropped up to lead resistance against imperial advances, mixing elements of local religion with aspects of Christianity or Islam. In many cases, the new prophets promised magic that would defend their followers against bullets, a prospect that appealed mightily to some Plains Indians resisting the U.S. Army in the 1890s, to the peasants of North China who raised the Boxer Rebellion in 1900, and to the Maji-maji rebels fighting German colonialism in East Africa in 1905–06. But even magic could not stop bullets.

Thanks to their edge in military strength, the industrial powers carved up much of the rest of the world in the decades before 1914. Their power convinced Europeans that they were inherently, racially, superior to Africans and Asians, and thus suited—indeed, intended by God—to govern the world. Even when the economic or strategic benefits of acquiring a given territory were unclear, imperial expansion proceeded apace because the costs were so low. Britain took the lion's share. Having lost the United States in 1783, it acquired an empire that spanned the globe by 1914.

India, the most populous and important colony, became British by degrees between 1750 and 1860. At first it was a commercial matter, in the hands of the East India Company. The Mughal Empire had lost its vitality by 1710, and the numerous Hindu states that emerged from its shadow remained at odds with one another, as well as with Muslim ones. In this situation, the company found that it could shape Indian politics advantageously by training and equipping Indian armies of cooperative princes who could then defeat the uncooperative ones. By 1818, its lands contained fifty times as many people as Britain had lost in the American colonies in 1783. Eventually the British crown annexed some territories, and after a great rebellion in 1857–58 the crown liquidated both the East India Company and the Mughal Empire, and consolidated British power throughout India, including what are now Pakistan, Bangladesh, and Sri Lanka. In this process, as subsequently in Africa, a very few British soldiers and administrators could conquer and govern huge territories, because of the equipment and knowledge available exclusively to them and their chosen local allies.

Other states that enjoyed some of the advantages of industrial power seized smaller empires. France acquired colonies in Africa and Indochina. Germany, a unified country only after 1871 and a latecomer to imperialism, seized scattered territories in Africa and some islands of the western Pacific. Russia expanded its territorial empire into the Caucasus region and Central Asia. Even second-rank European states, such as Italy, Belgium, Portugal, and Spain, acquired or extended empires in Africa after 1880. By recruiting, training, and equipping African armies of their own, they could defeat almost any African power. The great exception was Ethiopia, where King Menelik (1844–1913) had the foresight to import European officers to train his army, to buy modern weaponry (including a few machine guns), and to build a modest railway and telegraph system. This allowed Ethiopia to become an imperial power itself on a regional scale and repulse an attempted Italian conquest in 1896.

What Ethiopia did within the Horn of Africa, other states did elsewhere, and sometimes on larger scales. By 1815, observant rulers had noticed that industrialization brought wealth and power, and often concluded that if they did not wish to succumb to industrial imperialism they needed to industrialize themselves—or at least undertake some rigorous "self-strengthening" program, as the process was known in China. Self-strengthening was a deliberate effort by elites in and out of government to transform their military, their economy, and (if necessary) their society to face the challenges posed by the industrial powers. Normally, governments wanted as little social transformation as possible, hoping to do no more than modernize their militaries. But to do so required an armaments industry, an iron and steel industry, an industrial labor force, and in most cases more higher education, freer circulation of information, and a better tax system. In other words, meeting the industrial imperial challenge required, it turned out, a broad set of changes that sometimes threatened the government and its supporters. This helps explain why such self-strengthening efforts often failed.

The first outside Britain to industrialize were neighboring states in Europe and Britain's offshoots across the Atlantic. Britain did its best to prevent technology transfer and to keep its industrial secrets. But people, ideas, and machinery moved about too freely for Britain to retain its monopoly. European governments paid British industrialists to set up shop in their countries. European and American entrepreneurs hired British workers, and in a few cases even kidnaped them for their skills and knowledge. Businessmen such as Alfred Krupp (1812–1887), the great German steel baron, went to Britain to study new techniques. And so the Industrial Revolution spread to Europe and the United States, especially after 1815. Belgium with its coal, and Switzerland with its water power, led the way at first. Fast-flowing rivers sufficed to generate power for textile mills. But efficient iron and steel production required coal (and iron ore). Governments throughout Europe tried to encourage these industries, with subsidies, tax breaks, free infrastructure, and suppression of rebellious workers, but ultimately the geography of European industrialization depended most on the location of large coal seams. France had too little coal, and had to import it by 1848. Germany built by far the largest iron and steel industry, centered in the coal-rich Ruhr region. By the 1880s, German industry had outstripped British.

American industrialization followed the European pattern. At first it depended heavily on European immigrant labor and direct imitation of British methods. Water power drove the textile industry, which flourished first in New England. Pennsylvania coal powered heavy industry, located chiefly in the Ohio River valley. American industrialization also got plenty of government help, notably in the form of tariff protection from the 1790s on. American industrial firms, like the German, were sometimes very large, employing 1,000 or more workers. As cheap passage brought millions of immigrants to American shores from the 1840s, American factories became more bureaucratic and hierarchical, partly because workers often could not communicate easily with one another. Americans contributed a few important technical innovations before the 1880s, but in business and factory management they were true pioneers. Their most consequential achievement, known at the time as "the American system of manufactures," involved mass production of interchangeable parts, followed by simple assembly. The federal government did this first, in weapons production, and the technique spread widely throughout American—and ultimately the world's—manufacturing. By 1890 if not before, U.S. industry outpaced Germany to become the world leader, a position it still holds.

The power and wealth generated by industrialization attracted the notice of political and business leaders elsewhere around the world. In Egypt, where Mehmet Ali (1769–1849), an innovative Albanian in Ottoman service, had set himself up as pasha in 1805, state-sponsored industrialization began in the 1830s. In Brazil, entrepreneurs used steam engines in sugar refining as early as 1815. The Tagore family in India set up textile mills with equipment from Britain. The Chinese tried to create a modern arms industry after their defeat at the hands (and guns) of the British in the First Opium War (1839–40). But none of these initiatives got far. The societies in question lacked a sufficient concentration of people with the new skills, and in most cases their businessmen could make more money by selling grain, timber, sugar, or cotton—that is, by expanding existing operations—than they could by upsetting existing arrangements through industrialization.

By the 1860s, the political costs of relying on a low-energy, agrarian economy had grown painfully obvious, and some countries redoubled their efforts to industrialize. The most successful were Russia and Japan. Both learned agonizing lessons in the mid-1850s. The Russians met defeat in the Crimean War (1854–56), when Britain and France joined forces with Ottoman Turkey. This provided the stimulus for a series of reforms in Russia, notably the abolition of serfdom, which made the legal system and the labor regime more flexible, opening the way for a state-sponsored industrialization effort. Russia had certain advantages: lots of iron ore and coal, recently conquered lands in Central Asia that could grow cotton, and an elite versed in European languages and accustomed to borrowing foreign ideas. It also had, like the United States, wide open spaces that railroads could unite. Russian industrialization emphasized railroad construction; Russia even built the world's first laboratory for locomotive research (1882). Also like the United States (and Japan), Russia needed foreign investment capital and skills. Converting ex-serfs into disciplined factory workers proved a challenge for employers, one only slowly surmounted. Starting from a low base in 1860, Russian industrialization grew, leisurely at first, then very quickly from 1890 or so, when it became a top priority for the finance minister, a former railroad official. By 1910, Russia had the world's fourth or fifth largest heavy industry complex.

Japan's industrialization was a much more unlikely development. In 1853, Japan received a shock when an American armada steamed into Edo (Tokyo) Bay and demanded a commercial treaty and the rights to build a coaling station. At that point, Japan had for 220 years deliberately let its ties to the rest of the world wither. Its economy remained agrarian. With its countryside fully packed after 1720 or so, families tried hard to limit the number of their children and population growth proceeded extremely slowly for about five generations. The forests were almost gone—as in Britain. But unlike Britain, Japan had little coal, and less iron ore, and no access to lands well suited to cotton. It was, in the 1700s, colonizing territorially, but to the north, on the island of Hokkaido, useful for its forests and fish, but not for raw materials for industrialization. But to its good fortune, Japan's population was unusually literate, habituated to hierarchy, group loyalty, and discipline. After a political struggle highlighted by the installation of the Meiji emperor (reigned 1867–1912), Japan acquired a ruthless elite firmly committed to learning the tricks that made foreigners so formidable. Occasional bombardments of Japanese ports by British, French, Dutch, and American ships emphasized the urgency of self-strengthening, lest Japan become a colony.

The decisive element in Japan was the state and its unstinting support for big business, especially shipbuilding, mining, railroads, iron, and steel. As in Germany, military considerations played a major role in investment choices. A modern military required endless iron and steel. The government left the textile industry to private hands, but carefully nurtured heavy industry. It owned a lot of the shipyards, arsenals, and mines itself, and supported private shipbuilding and railroads with subsidies, credit, tax breaks, and with violence against disgruntled laborers and peasants—whose taxes financed all this and whose fields suffered from industrial pollution. Successful firms nurtured political connections to get their share of state support, an arrangement that favored big businesses like Mitsubishi and Kawasaki, giant firms still powerful today. The state also undertook imperial conquests at the expense of China from 1894, securing access to coal and iron ore in Manchuria. Furthermore, the state supported technical education and scientific agriculture, helping the rice harvest double between 1880 and 1930. Population growth, long stagnant, soared, providing plenty of young people for the factories—and the army. Japan's industrialization came very suddenly by previous standards and by 1914 vaulted it into the front ranks of industrial—and military—powers.

The German, American, Russian, and Japanese industrializations all took place in the context of self-strengthening efforts. In the United States, for example, the government explicitly recognized the economic and military threats posed by Britain. It responded with tariff protection from the earliest years of the republic, a postal system, a system of military arsenals, and postal and military roads. When British forces repelled an American invasion of Canada and burned the White House in the War of 1812, the United States redoubled its efforts. It built an infrastructure for riverboat traffic, dredging sandbars and harbors. It reorganized its new military academy at West Point in the 1820s and established a naval academy in 1845. It embarked on territorial expansion westward, using the army, government surveyors, and various incentives including free land for settlers, to forestall British interest in the Oregon Territory and Texas. Its state governments constructed networks of canals and roads. After 1862, it provided free land for railroad companies and universities. This sustained self-strengthening project succeeded spectacularly.

The Germans, Russians, and Japanese undertook similar programs. The German effort involved the abolition of serf labor, political unification of most of the German-speaking lands, canal and railroad building, tariffs, heavy investment in education and the army, and much more. The same elements, in differing proportions, were present in Russia and Japan too, producing a more flexible society, a stronger state and military, and, as the crucial piece, an industrial economy. In large measure, the great powers of the twentieth century were those that succeeded in meeting the self-strengthening challenge of the nineteenth.

Some self-strengthening efforts failed. The Ottoman Empire undertook reforms of its military and tax system from the 1790s, spurred by observation of French and British practices in the wars of the French Revolution. After uprisings by disgruntled military units, the program stopped in 1806, only to be revived, more forcefully, in 1826 by Sultan Mahmud II. He slaughtered the segments of the Ottoman military that resisted his reforms, and set a course that under his successors would entail a new financial system, new educational institutions, a new legal system, a new conscript army and factories to supply it, recourse to foreign experts, and reduced authority for religion within Ottoman society. This package, which went by the name of *Tanzimat* ("ordering" in Turkish), helped the empire survive serious strains in the mid-1800s, including the loss of much territory. But it offended powerful elements (landowners, religious authorities) who put a brake on reform in the 1870s. Wars and growing debt undermined Ottoman finances, limiting the government's capacity for further initiative. Struggles against rebellious subjects in the Balkans and Armenia, and policing an increasingly worldly and revolutionary officer corps, further sapped Ottoman strength. An officers' coup d'état in 1908 promised to rejuvenate the empire, but soon World War I destroyed it: Ottoman self-strengthening was too little too late.

Qing China faced up to the challenge of industrial imperialism later and less successfully than the Ottomans. By 1800, population growth in China pressed against resources, and peasant rebellions erupted frequently. An accelerating loss of forests and soils, and a general ecological decline—interpreted, as was customary, as a sign that the emperor had lost the Mandate of Heaven—added to peasant restiveness. Pressures heightened when British and American merchants found they could profitably smuggle opium from India into China, which by the 1820s produced widespread addiction. When the Qing acted to check the opium influx, Britain regarded the measure as an infringement on free trade, and subsequent failure in negotiations led to the First Opium War. British gunboats and rifles proved superior to the Qing forces, many of which had no firearms, and so China in 1842 had to accept a treaty that opened doors to foreign traders and missionaries and surrendered chunks of Chinese sovereignty. This was a humiliation for the Qing, but one they did little about. Things soon got worse, thanks to Hong Xiuquan.

Hong Xiuquan (1814–1864) was a member of an ethnic minority in South China called the Hakka. From a poor family, but one with pretensions to gentry status, he sought success as clever youths did by taking the civil service examinations that opened a career in government. His whole village made sacrifices to support many years of study. Hong failed four times, and in despair took solace in the millenarian teachings of an American Baptist missionary, Issachar Roberts, a self-taught Tennessee preacher who had learned the Hakka dialect. Hong had a creative way with Christian doctrine. He concluded on the basis of dreams that he was the younger brother of Jesus, sent by God to bring about heaven on earth and rid China of corrupt, foreign rulers in the bargain. His preaching attracted followers especially among those at the bottom of the Confucian hierarchy, and in the later 1840s an armed utopian uprising took shape. The Taipings, as they came to be called, denounced the Qing as foreigners and agents of the devil. They encouraged peasants to ignore taxes and obligations to landlords, and rejected private property. They encouraged women to reject men's authority (except that of the Taiping leaders), recruited women as soldiers, and proclaimed the equality of the sexes. They promoted a simplified language and mass literacy to undermine the position of the scholar-bureaucrats whose ranks Hong had failed to enter. Their religion was puritanical, proscribing opium, alcohol, tobacco, adultery, concubinage, prostitution, and even sex. Their God was the wrathful, vengeful sort, demanding obedience and meting out, through the Taipings, brutal punishments.

This program attracted millions of followers, voluntary and otherwise, and therefore also attracted the wrath of the Qing. At first the Taipings were too strong for Qing forces. They almost took Beijing. Meanwhile, because the Qing had fallen behind in some of their obligations arising from the First Opium War and subsequent treaties, in 1856 they were attacked by Britain, and soon by France. The dynasty almost collapsed. But by 1860, after the European powers had occupied Beijing and sacked the emperor's summer palace, they got what they wanted in a new treaty. Britain and France then lent their support to the Qing and made common cause with local gentry and bureaucrats who had raised their own armies to fight the Taipings. These forces, together with quarrels and assassinations within the Taiping leadership, which spectacularly betrayed the puritanical morality it preached, brought victory to the Qing and mayhem to a close in 1864. But 20 or 30 million people had died in history's largest civil war.[10] Fighting had laid waste large parts of the country. The treasury was bare.

The dynasty never truly recovered, but the shock did inspire a self-strengthening effort. The Qing overhauled the customs service. Provincial governors, who had organized the defeat of the Taipings, launched efforts to reform agriculture, education, and armaments production. After 1867, the biggest factory in China was an arsenal. They also built shipyards and railroads. Reformers sought sufficient military technology to defend China against "barbarian" aggression, and recognized that a certain amount of industrialization was required, although they hoped not to disturb the fundamentals of an agrarian, Confucian society. But their modest initiatives aroused opposition from more tradition-minded members of the gentry, and eventually from the imperial family too. One provincial governor decreed that a railroad, the first built in China, should be ripped up. China's military remained undereducated in technical subjects, underequipped, and unsuccessful in war. China could not prevent the loss of tributary kingdoms to France (Vietnam) and Britain (Burma) in the 1880s. In 1895, it lost another tributary kingdom (Korea) and, most gallingly, an island province (Taiwan) in war with Japan. After the Boxer Rebellion of 1900, a failed antiforeigner rising supported by the imperial family, China was left with a crushing indemnity and the humiliation of foreign troops in Beijing. The dynasty made one last effort at reform. It abolished the centuries-old examination system for civil service, experimented with local self-government, approved railroad construction, created new military schools, and mounted a war on opium, among other initiatives. But, like the Ottomans, the Qing inadvertently produced a revolutionary officer corps. The dynasty tottered until its final collapse in a series of uprisings and mutinies called the Chinese Revolution, in 1911–12. Self-strengthening in China had failed decisively.

The changes in the web that fomented the demographic transition,

---

[10] For comparison, the American Civil War (1861–65) cost about half a million lives.

nationalism, and industrialization created new geopolitical winners and losers. Lands that turned population growth to a force for industrialization and urbanization fared well, while those in which it served mainly to impoverish peasants fared poorly. The web permitted the sudden spread of industrial knowledge and technology, which some countries exploited as they recast their societies and economies. But elsewhere the challenge of industrialization proved too strong, or provoked self-strengthening programs that divided the elite against itself, bringing low once mighty empires.

SOCIAL CHANGES

Industrialization also reshuffled the fortunes of hundreds of millions of ordinary people. Daily life changed first and most thoroughly where industrialization progressed furthest. But because the world in the 1800s was increasingly a tightly unified web, the Industrial Revolution changed lives everywhere.

In the industrial heartlands of Europe the changes reached to the core of life: family, work, village. With the population surge after 1750, villages everywhere were overflowing with young people, many of whom had scant prospects of maintaining their parents' standard of living. Despairing of their futures at home, they streamed into industrializing cities, fueling a rapid urbanization such as the world had never seen. Small towns in 1780, Birmingham and Berlin became metropolises by 1880. Villagers increasingly acquired urban tastes. Many spent at least parts of their lives in big cities. After 1890, when birth rates in the villages began to decline, they no longer had surplus youths to export and began to shrink in size. This trend gathered force in the twentieth century, sealing the dominance of cities in the modern world. The factory system also took spinning, weaving, and other handicrafts out of the villages, leaving them more purely agricultural, and less self-sufficient, than before.

Industrialization forever altered the nature of work. From the natural rhythm of the days and seasons that governed farm work, people shifted to schedules controlled by the clock. Factory work demanded new forms of discipline—workers could not take a break when they felt like it—as well as tolerance of noise, heat, dust, and sometimes danger. Factory workers generally performed very specific tasks, and did not produce goods themselves in the way that a cooper produced a barrel or a farmer produced a crop. On the farm, families usually worked as a unit, but in factories an individual worked as part of a far larger team. Most of the new jobs demanded only modest skill, which anyone could learn in a few days or weeks. So, unlike a family member, a worker could easily be replaced if he drank too much or worked too little. Employers often preferred to hire women and children, who seemed less inclined to resist factory discipline. (Their nimble fingers also made them better at many tasks.) Husbands and fathers had to cede part of their authority over wives and children to factory bosses.

These basic shifts in working conditions and social life created new intellectual and emotional needs, met by new faiths including various revolutionary creeds, the most influential of which was Marxism. Karl Marx (1818–1883), a learned German philosopher and journalist, worked out a complex interpretation of history and vision of the future, which promised that eventually workers would succeed in revolution, ending the rule of capitalists and kings, and inaugurate a permanent era of equality and harmony, called communism. The theory appealed mostly to educated people at odds with the status quo, but the millennial promise attracted many people impatient with theory. As we shall see, Marxism in Russia and China had a dramatic career.

Christianity spawned new creeds too. Many of them, like communism, predicted that things would have to get worse before they got better. American fundamentalist Protestants, for example, believed that Christ would return to set things right only after a dark period of strife. Urban workers could find comfort in that message. Many also were drawn to newer versions of Protestantism, such as Seventh-Day Adventism or Christian Science, both successful in urban, industrial America (and both led at times by women). Methodism, although born in the eighteenth century, proved especially successful in adapting to industrialization in Britain. It emphasized small, mutually supportive communities, the possibility of self-improvement, the need for frugality and study, but made no strict doctrinal demands of believers. Catholicism, in Europe and America, responded to the needs of industrial communities (and the challenge of Marxism) with an urban outreach program based on Catholic schools, labor unions, youth groups, and community organizations.

Until industrial workers organized themselves into trade unions, they worked hard in unpleasant conditions for low wages. They ate poorly, suffered bad health and stunted growth, and developed strong grievances against their employers. Only people with few options chose the life of a mill worker or miner, but as long as the villages overflowed with youth, the factories found willing, if grudging, recruits. Many of them took refuge in what drink and debauchery they could afford, or solace in those religions that made their travails easier to bear. Others planned revolutions that would upset the social order and put workers in the saddle. Despite a few insurrections, these revolutions never happened. The main reason is that early in the industrialization process peasant conscript armies proved willing to fire on urban workers, suppressing revolts; later on workers' unions wrung concessions from employers in the form of safer conditions, shorter hours, higher pay, sharply reducing workers' appetite for revolution. The unions occasionally had the help of reformers in government, who passed legislation restricting child labor or permissible punishments of workers.

The restriction of child labor, coupled with the provision of free education, marked another turning point. Industrialization rewarded literacy and basic education as never before, so increasing numbers of people sought it, and many states saw fit to subsidize it. For the first time, millions of children spent several years in formal schooling, learning to read and write, to love the father- (or mother-) land, and to accept discipline from people outside their families. Hitherto, in rural or urban settings, children contributed economically to their families from a young age. But these new arrangements converted children from economic assets into liabilities, and so parents preferred to have fewer of them. The demographic transition described above proceeded fastest where industrialization altered this economic calculus. This made a vast difference in the lives of wives and mothers, who acquired new options and flexibility as they invested less in offspring.

In short, the initial stages of industrialization brought wrenching changes in working lives, subjecting people, families, and, to a lesser extent, communities to great stresses. Only the diminished prospects of rural life convinced people to accept the bitter lot of a German coal miner or Massachusetts mill girl in 1850. But after two or three generations, conditions slowly improved in industrial societies, especially for unionized workers. By 1900, workers in the industrial heartlands on average lived healthier, longer, and easier lives than either their rural cousins or their great-grandparents.

Outside the industrial heartlands, the Industrial Revolution brought deep changes in working lives and families as well. In Russia and Japan, not quite industrial heartlands but still industrial powers by 1914, the social experience took quite different courses, although both industrialized at roughly the same time and speed. The rapidity of industrialization in both countries meant that the majority of factory workers were transplanted peasants. In Russia they found the giant factories alienating, and the sharp inequalities of urban life unjust. Many had come from villages that periodically reallocated land among families so as to ensure a general equality, and had a low moral tolerance for inequality. Russian workers were mostly men. They moved frequently back and forth from factory to village, keeping in touch with their country cousins. They saw little improvement in pay and conditions, and their efforts to unionize were vigorously suppressed. In these circumstances, many of them found that revolutionary ideas such as anarchism or Marxism spoke to their condition. Russian workers developed a strong sense of grievance, of solidarity, and of sympathy with peasant complaints. This produced agitation, strikes, violent suppression, and, when Russia lost a war with Japan in 1905, an uprising. Later, when Russia was losing a much larger war to Germany, Russia's urban workers would provide the shock troops of the Russian Revolution of 1917.

In Japan, factory life was no sweeter than in Russia. But most of the labor force (62 percent in 1909) was female, young women drawn from the villages who hoped to return home and marry after a stint in the city. They had been taught from a young age to put up with what life offered them, and by and large did so. They were accustomed to obeying men, including factory bosses and their fathers and brothers who had often instructed them to take factory work to help their families before they married. They often lived closely supervised lives in factory dormitories, to ensure that they should remain marriageable despite the temptations of the city. Japan had very little in the way of unions or strikes, and what there was the state ruthlessly suppressed. Workers developed little solidarity, and socialism got nowhere.

But new religions did. Japan's industrialization inspired a religious reorganization, as in Europe and America. The state's feverish nationalism, which justified the people's sacrifices, rested on a new emperor cult woven into the traditional Shinto faith. But rival religions emerged too. In the case of Tenrikyo, started by Nakayama Miki (1798–1887), adherents found comfort in her promise of a coming world free from corruption and greed, and in the emphasis on community and selflessness. The Omoto sect, also started by a woman and also messianic in flavor, explicitly rejected industrialization and modernization, preferring the aesthetics, harmony, and purity of rural life. The state persecuted leaders of both these religions, but could not stamp them out. Although Japan's industrialization was late, fast, and state-sponsored just as in Russia, the social and political outcomes differed radically.

Abolition of Slavery and Serfdom

In the interconnected world of the 1800s, industrialization also changed the daily lives and outlooks of millions who lived in lands far from the nearest factory. The initial stages of industrialization intensified hardship, but time brought improvements, if less visibly than in the centers of industry. We have already seen how the world's weavers and spinners suffered from and in cases adapted to industrial competition. Far more numerous were the food and fiber producers, whose labor made possible the mass shipments of sugar, tea, coffee, wheat, and cotton to industrial cities. The early stages of industrialization intensified demand for all these commodities. This rewarded the expansion of the farms and plantations on which they were raised. Informed, market-savvy entrepreneurs took the initiative to buy more land, clear more forests, and hire more workers, or—as was often the case—buy them. Early industrialization inspired a great expansion of slavery and serfdom.

The extension of forced labor was most obvious in the Americas but not confined to them. In the American South, the cotton economy responded to the appetites of the textile mills of New England and Britain. Between 1800 and 1860, the slave population quintupled to 4 million, spreading cotton and slavery as far as Texas. In the Caribbean, planters bought more slaves to maximize the sugar, cotton, and coffee crops. In Brazil, where sugar and coffee were the major slave crops, a similar expansion took place. In Southeast Asia, imperial powers and independent states alike presided over a rapid extension of plantations and slavery, by which peppers and sugar came to market. In Russia and Eastern Europe, where serfs raised grain for export, entrepreneurial landowners sensed profit in the rising food demand in industrial cities. They expanded their operations, buying more serfs and encouraging a maximum birth rate among those whom they already owned. In Egypt, where most slaves came from the Nilotic sudan, the military undertakings of Mehmet Ali and his successors—they used a lot of African slaves in their armies—and the expansion of cotton growing inspired an upsurge of slavery after 1805. In the Indian Ocean islands of Mauritius and Réunion, a new cotton, coffee, and sugar plantation system emerged from about 1780, importing slaves from Madagascar, East Africa, and

India. In West Africa, slavery expanded in the nineteenth century, partly in response to European demand for palm oil, an early industrial lubricant. Wherever labor was too scarce to make the most of the commercial opportunities presented by the tighter web and by industrialization, the economic logic of slavery or serfdom improved.

But just as the world's systems of forced labor attained their maximum historical size, something strange happened: the systems were dismantled. Slavery, which had existed for at least 5,000 years, and had seemed part of the natural order of human affairs, in many societies came to be seen as immoral. Simultaneously, its economic logic began to weaken, its political support waned, and its opponents organized. All these developments show the worldwide web at work.

Moral opposition to slavery originated in the Atlantic world. In the 1780s, just as the Atlantic slave trade reached its apogee, religious and intellectual opinion turned against it. English Quakers first led this movement, concluding that slavery was un-Christian. They joined forces with more secular thinkers influenced by the ideals of the Enlightenment, in particular, notions of the rights of man. Antislavery soon became a popular cause in England, and hundreds of thousands of people signed petitions calling for abolition. An antislavery society emerged in France in 1788. The revolution in Haiti proved a setback: powerful people deduced that freedom for slaves brought violent chaos. But British antislavery advocates proved masterful in the political and parliamentary arts and in 1807 achieved the abolition of the slave trade. This was just the beginning.

Other Atlantic countries continued to permit slaving, but not for long. Under moral and economic pressure from Britain, and from indigenous antislavery movements, the United States, Denmark, the Netherlands, and France outlawed slave trading between 1808 and 1830. Britain used part of its fleet to intercept slavers on the high seas, returning captives to Africa, usually to Sierra Leone, a newly established colony for freed slaves. When Brazil (1850) and Spain (1867) outlawed the slave trade, the transatlantic trade ended, except for a few illegal voyages, the last recorded one coming in 1864.

Moral qualms about slavery only partly explain these events. The other parts of the equation were economic and political. The moral objections to slavery flourished where slavery was only indirectly important to the economy—Britain, France, the northern United States. Where it formed the basis of production and the social order, moral qualms remained unpersuasive. But some slaveowners accepted the abolition of the slave trade willingly, because they expected that natural increase among slave populations could perpetuate slavery. Indeed, this was the case in the United States and Barbados where slave populations were biologically self-sustaining. The prospect of further population growth among slaves everywhere undermined the economic logic of slavery. If people were plentiful enough, plantations could flourish on the basis of cheap wage labor. This helped reconcile some plantation owners to the idea of the emancipation of slaves.

Not all agreed, however. One planter in Mauritius viewed the prospect of emancipation as a "rascally stroke of the most base and most infernal fanaticism."[11] In South Africa (which had become British territory in 1815), the slaveowning Boers, descendants of the early European settlers, resisted abolition and other impositions by migrating out of reach of British rule in 1833–34. Slaveowners in the United States so objected to proposed restrictions on slavery that they led a rebellion that became the American Civil War (1861–65). Even where slaveowners conceded that slavery's economic logic was weak, they often clung to it fearing that reform would open the floodgates of revolution, as in Haiti.

Others saw in rebellions the best reason to be quit of slavery. With the expansion of slavery in the Atlantic world after 1750, the number and size of slave rebellions grew. The Haitian Revolution, by far the largest, proved the only successful one. But frequent rebellions, even if suppressed, raised the costs of slavery to the planters and diminished their profits and security. Communities of runaway ex-slaves (called maroons in English-speaking settings) menaced some plantations. The example of Haiti, the lure of maroon communities, and the ideology of freedom reverberating around the Atlantic world all made slaves more restive. But that did not necessarily convert ex-slaves to the principle of antislavery: maroons in Jamaica sometimes helped the colonial government to suppress rebellions on plantations, and in Brazil a maroon community bought and owned slaves.

The first major abolition of slavery after the Haitian Revolution came in 1833 when in Britain an enlargement of the franchise brought new middle-class elements into Parliament, permitting the passage of an Act of Emancipation.[12] Some 750,000 colonial slaves acquired their freedom over six years, during which they were legally obliged to work three-

[11] Quoted in Deryck Scarr, *Slaving and Slavery in the Indian Ocean* (London, 1998), 198.

[12] Smaller abolitions had already occurred where slavery was not important, for example, in some northern U.S. states in the 1780s.

quarters' time for their former masters for free. The government paid the masters a sum equivalent to about one-third or one-half of the annual budget of Britain as compensation. Thus an ancient institution came to its legal end in the British Empire, thanks to the combined efforts of abolitionists and slaves, and the intellectual currents and demographic trends circulating throughout the world.[13]

Over the next century slavery came to an end almost everywhere. It happened first in Europe and Latin America, where political revolutions eventually brought to power liberals sympathetic to the antislavery cause. Chile and Mexico abolished slavery in the 1820s, immediately upon winning independence from Spain. Abolition in the French Empire came with the revolution of 1848, freeing a third of a million slaves. In the Dutch Empire abolition came in 1867, in Spain's (which in practice meant Cuba and Puerto Rico) in 1886. In Brazil slavery lasted until 1888, when sufficient Portuguese and Italian immigration made wage labor a promising basis for coffee plantations formerly worked by slaves. The biggest emancipations in the Americas took place in the United States (4 million freed) when the South lost the Civil War and in Brazil (1.5 million).

Emancipation in Russia dwarfed all the slave emancipations put together. Although Russia did have slaves, its chief form of forced labor was serfdom. In the late 1700s, the position of Russian serfs deteriorated and came to approximate that of slaves. They were the legal property of landowners or the state. They were subject to brutal discipline. They could be bought and sold as individuals, families, or as entire villages. They married when and whom their owners chose. In Russia in 1797 there were about 20 million serfs owned privately, and another 14–15 million state peasants owned by the government, whose lives were somewhat more free but subject to frequent labor conscription. Most state peasants worked in the fields, some in forests or mines, a very few in cities.

The abolition of serfdom in Russia derived from the same factors as the abolition of slavery in the Atlantic world, although in differing proportions. The intellectual currents of the Enlightenment and French Revolution had their effects, and indeed led directly to abolition in Prussia and parts of Poland before 1810. Some Russian intellectuals decried serfdom from the 1790s, inviting persecution and exile when they did so publicly. Over the next sixty years, serfdom lost almost all intellectual

---

[13] In India and Ceylon, slavery remained legal until 1843.

and moral support in Russia. It seemed backward to Russians conscious of the growing political freedoms of Western Europe. Its economic logic for the Russian elite declined with rapid population growth, which made wage labor more inviting. It impeded technological progress, because serf labor was almost cost-free to landowners (or mine owners) and because serfs had no incentive to handle machinery with care. It prevented the modernization of the Russian army, specifically the creation of a reserve system, because the government dared not release serfs with military skills to their home villages; with serfdom, Russia was stuck with a huge, expensive, standing army.

And serfdom condemned Russia to living with the specter of revolt. In 1773, in the middle of a war against the Ottoman Empire, a huge revolt broke out along the Volga, led by a Cossack named Emilian Pugachev (1726–1775). He claimed to be the recently murdered tsar (Peter III, husband of Catherine the Great), proclaimed the abolition of serfdom, and led a ragtag army on a violent spree that killed 1,000 landowners, took the city of Kazan, and shook the foundation of the Russian state until his capture and execution in 1775. The memory of Pugachev's revolt led Russia's rulers to fear the continuation of serfdom but also to fear its abolition. They felt they were riding the tiger, much as did slaveowners in the Atlantic world after the Haitian revolution: the status quo entailed dangers, but dismounting seemed riskier still.

Thus, emancipation in Russia was contemplated for decades and secretly planned for years before it was announced in 1861. The humiliating defeat in the Crimean War convinced the tsar that the time had come to risk it. He and most of the ruling class anticipated a violent uprising from the 23 million serfs in private hands, but in fact few incidents occurred—despite the terms. Serfs, now peasants, got their legal freedom, the right to marry as they pleased, to acquire property, to migrate, and they got land—but gradually. Like the ex-slaves in the British colonies, they had to work for their ex-masters, in this case for nine years: they bought their freedom with more unpaid labor. They also had to buy their land from the state, which had paid landowners for it. These terms applied to the 23 million serfs held privately. In 1866, another 27 million state peasants were given the lands on which they worked in exchange for tax payments. Some 50 million people thus acquired greater freedom in the Russian emancipation, albeit by degrees and on terms that left them disappointed.

With gathering momentum the intellectual and demographic changes of the 1800s rolled back the domain of forced labor. In Southeast Asia, legal abolitions took place between 1868 (the Dutch East Indies) and 1926 (Burma). European colonial pressure produced these changes, even in independent states such as Thailand. There King Mongkit (ruled 1851–68) adopted the antislavery gospel, and decreed that men could not sell their wives and children without wifely consent; full abolition of slavery came in 1915. Throughout Southeast Asia, abolition was a political matter: forced labor remained economical. But a tsunami of Chinese "coolies"—indentured laborers recruited by both the carrot and the stick—flooded into Southeast Asia in the nineteenth and early twentieth centuries, providing the workforce to expand plantations and mines, and making the end of slavery a smoother adjustment.

In Southwest Asia and the Ottoman lands, slavery also came under pressure from European governments. The Ottomans succumbed and banned the slave trade from Africa in 1857, except along the western coast of the Arabian Peninsula (the Hejaz), where it was most important and local elites most invested in it. The other Ottoman slave trade, from Circassia on the northeast shores of the Black Sea, lasted until the late 1860s. The Ottomans never banned slavery itself, hoping to extinguish it by cutting off the supply. Slavery was recognized in Muslim law, and the sultans had no authority to change the word of God. In Saudi Arabia legal slavery lasted until 1962, and de facto slavery on a small scale persists to this day.

In Africa, legal abolition also came from European intervention, although that came in part from pressure applied by slaves themselves. Ironically, the suppression of the Atlantic slave trade in the early 1800s helped expand the scope of slavery within Africa itself. Slave prices declined with the closure of the transatlantic market, so the economic logic of using slaves in Africa improved. African entrepreneurs responded by establishing new slave plantations in West and East Africa, raising peanuts, cassava, cloves, and other crops. Furthermore, in the sudan region, wars launched by Muslim reformers who felt that African Islam did not conform fully to Muslim scripture led to the enslavement of many captives, and eventually the slave population there reached a third or half of the total. By the late 1800s colonial powers, chiefly Britain and France, actively suppressed the slave trade within Africa, often citing that as moral justification for extending their rule. By 1914, large-scale slave trading had ceased. Suppressing slavery took longer, because the colonial powers dithered. To govern in Africa they needed the cooperation of prominent men, many of whom owned slaves, more than they needed the gratitude of millions of poor people. They also judged that slavery in Africa often was not terribly oppressive, and in any case was often important to agricultural and textile production. Additionally, in Muslim Africa, abolition invited the opposition of clerics who often saw it as an impertinent human effort to revise divine law.

But from the 1890s slaves forced the issue. They deserted in droves, sometimes killing their masters, especially in the western sudan region, weakening the rulers through whom the colonial powers had hoped to govern. The British and French after 1900 switched their policy, withdrew their support of slaveowners, and reluctantly imposed abolition, mainly between 1905 and 1936, formally ratifying what was happening anyway. The numbers are very uncertain, but taken as a whole, it was probably history's second largest emancipation, after the Russian. In the Sokoto Caliphate (northern Nigeria) alone, abolition freed 1 or 2 million people. As in Arabia, slavery on a small scale survived its legal abolition in colonial Africa. After independence, Mauretania banned slavery again in 1980, and it has yet to disappear entirely, expecially in the country of Sudan.

Even if never totally extirpated, the abolition of slavery and serfdom represents a great liberation for humankind. Between 1790 and 1936, an arrangement that for millennia had seemed normal, moral, indeed natural and necessary to most societies, came to seem immoral, uneconomic, and/or politically imprudent. What the harnessing of fossil fuels achieved in the sphere of work itself—a historic liberation from muscular toil—abolition achieved in the social sphere. They were connected events and roughly simultaneous. The use of inanimate energy gradually made labor less scarce, and forced labor less appealing. It made communication of antislavery ideas easier. It made the imposition of European antislavery morality upon Asia and Africa easier. In some settings the abolition of forced labor made the use of machinery and inanimate energy more economic. Worldwide currents of demographic growth, industrialization and energy use, and egalitarian morality all flowed together to refashion the human condition.

Globalization in the Age of Imperialism

These and other currents swirled around the world faster as the worldwide web tightened. A great pulse of globalization took place between 1870 and 1914, part and parcel of the demographic, political, and economic changes described so far.

The first pulse of globalization had united the world's seacoasts and

river basins via maritime shipping. The second one, 1870–1914, intensified the first and extended it inland. The technological basis for this
(steamships, railroads, telegraphs) we noted above. The political basis of
it was mainly European imperial power, but also the growing power of
Japan, the United States, and a few smaller states, all able to consolidate
their control over internal populations and in many cases expand at the
expense of others. But the most important dimensions of the second
pulse of globalization were economic: the heightened mobility of people,
goods, and money.

The new systems of transport and communications made it more
tempting for people to move around the world. The great migrations of
the past had usually been the wanderings of nomadic peoples, mass
movements of refugees from violence or persecution, or slave trades.
These were all significant, but they usually involved modest numbers
until the rise of the Atlantic slave trade. Even that would be dwarfed by
the migrations of the nineteenth century. These were mainly economic
in motive. People typically moved to regions where land could be had on
easy terms, or where wages were higher than at home. Cheap and abundant information on foreign lands allowed people to compare their circumstances at home with distant possibilities, encouraging tens of
millions to gamble on migration.

The end of slavery helped provoke major streams of migration. In
some former slave societies, ex-slaves found other options than taking
wages for the same work they had formerly done. In Martinique (a sugar
island in the Caribbean), for example, when slavery ended in 1848 two-
thirds of the former slaves left the island within three years. Yet, with the
rapid growth of demand for industrial fibers and metals, and for food,
the world's plantations and mines needed millions of strong backs. So a
recruitment business emerged in poor regions, especially in India and
China, to enlist laborers to go to places where no one else would. Most
went freely, but over 2 million migrated as indentured laborers, owing
three to seven years' work in exchange for their passage. Most of these
bonded laborers went voluntarily, hoping to return better off once their
term was up, although some were in effect kidnapped. Worsening
prospects for poor peasants in India and China explain why so many
chose to leave. Peasants from South India had excellent reason to try
their luck abroad: rural rents increased very sharply after 1850.[14] Many

[14] In Nellore District, north of Madras, peasant rents increased ninefold in real terms in
1850–1927. David Ludden, *An Agrarian History of South Asia* (Cambridge, 1999), 219.

never came home, either because they died—unfamiliar disease climates were the main reason—or because they chose to remain in their new lands.

About 1 million Indians went to Mauritius, Trinidad, Guyana, Natal (South Africa), or Fiji to work in canefields, mostly as bonded laborers, and 4 million (mostly free migrants) to Malaya's rubber plantations and tin mines. Some 2–3 million, mostly Tamils from southern India, went to Sri Lanka to work on tea plantations. Several million more went to Burma; most, like most migrants to Sri Lanka and Malaya, came home again. Indians supplied the bulk of the labor needed to keep the mines and plantations of the British Empire going until the contract labor system was ended in 1917. Some 30–40 million Indians migrated in all (1830–1913), and 3–6 million stayed put overseas.

Chinese had emigrated to Southeast Asia since at least the eighth century, but in very large numbers only after 1870. Entrepreneurs in southern China developed a business called the "coolie trade" in which they advanced money for the passage of willing (and not so willing) migrants and sold their debt, and therefore their labor obligation, to planters and mine operators, mainly in Southeast Asia. They went mostly to Malaya's tin mines and rubber plantations (about 6 million in 1881–1914), but also to Thailand and Indonesia (then the Dutch East Indies), to plantations in the Philippines, Cuba, Peru, and Hawaii, and to South African mines. Others helped build the railroads of the western United States and Canada. Perhaps 10 to 15 million Chinese coolies emigrated (1830–1914), and they were far less likely than Indians to return home.

Much smaller flows of unskilled labor, often indentured labor, took place within the southwest Pacific, to the canefields of Fiji and Queensland in Australia. A few hundred thousand Japanese moved to Hawaii, Brazil, or Peru. And a few smaller currents of indentured Africans went to the Caribbean, following in the wake of the Atlantic slave trade. All of these migrations involved far more men than women, generally young men.

Another flow, this one a torrent, left Europe. It was almost entirely voluntary in nature, although many fled to escape famine, military conscription, or prison, and a few hundred thousand left Europe precisely to go to prisons in Siberia, Australia, or French Guiana; and the flow of indentured laborers to the Caribbean included a few thousand Europeans, mostly Portuguese, but also some Norwegians and Germans. Some 50–60 million people left Europe between 1840 and 1914, of whom perhaps a third returned home. Five or 6 million came from Ireland, which in 1840 had 6.4 million people but by 1900 only 3.9 million: one of the few countries in modern times to sustain long-term population loss. One million left during a great famine in 1845–47 alone; the official response to the Irish famine was to repeal tariffs in imported food, opening Britain to cheap food from abroad, which ruined many a farmer in Britain. Subsequently, 13–16 million migrants sailed from Britain and Ireland between 1845 and 1914. Some 6 million Germans left for the Americas between 1820 and 1913. More still left Southern and Eastern Europe, mainly after 1890, because fertility remained high to 1914 and industrialization slow, so most young people faced poor prospects at home. About 70 percent of Europe's emigrants went to the United States. But some 4 million Russians went to Siberia, and about 11 million Italians, Spaniards, and Portuguese went to South America (1824–1924), mainly Argentina and Brazil. Meanwhile, more British and Irish also departed for Canada, Australia, New Zealand, and South Africa.

This mass migration reached its peak around 1890–1913, for three main reasons. First, between 1815 and 1850 most Europeans countries removed all legal obstacles to emigration. Second, passage got cheaper and quicker: in 1894 one could sail from Ireland to the United States in ten days for $9, only a week's wages at American rates. Third, conditions for European farmers and peasants got worse: cheap grain from the North American and Argentine prairies undercut Europe's producers. Millions went to those prairies to farm, making American grain cheaper still, and uprooting still more Europeans. Only World War I stopped this cycle.

Taken together, the gigantic migrations from India, China, and Europe between 1830 and 1914 involved over 100 million people. Millions more migrated within China and India to frontier regions such as Manchuria and Assam, and within Europe to industrializing regions such as the Ruhr or Silesia. This massive movement of people contributed mightily to the world's economic growth, because people went from places where their labor did not produce much to places where it did. It reshaped the countries that received migrants, making their economies the most dynamic in the world and making their societies far more religiously and ethnically diverse. That sometimes led to enduring tensions that continue to bedevil politics today, as in Fiji, Malaysia, or Sri Lanka. And it served as a safety valve for rural population pressure in the sending societies, which otherwise might have suffered greater turmoil.

Goods and money moved even more easily than people (although greater caution must be applied to the figures). In monetary terms, world trade increased by three- or fourfold between 1870 and 1913, with the growth coming fastest in trade between North America and Atlantic Europe. The proportion of all production exported, perhaps 2 percent in 1820, reached 12 percent by 1913 (some estimates go as high as 33 percent)[15]—18 percent in Latin America, but only 1–5 percent in East and South Asia. Falling freight rates account for much of this zest for trade, and low tariffs helped too.

Investment capital flowed even more freely, thanks to the telegraph and the gold standard. The gold standard, formally established in 1878, fixed the value of currencies in gold, reducing the uncertainties of international investment and trade. Whereas formerly only financiers had dabbled in foreign investment, now banks and bond dealers mobilized the savings of barristers and barmaids for such purposes. International investment grew by about five- or sixfold (maybe as much as eightfold) between 1870 and 1914, with half the total coming from Britain. France and, after 1890, Germany were the other big capital exporters. Their investors preferred government bonds, mainly from other European countries. British investment went mainly to the United States, Canada, Australia, and Argentina. In the latter three countries foreign investment accounted for half of the total, meaning that their prosperity and growth was very dependent on these flows. Far less flowed to China, India, or Africa.

These massive movements of people, goods, and money—far greater and faster than the world had ever seen—had three notable effects. First, they reflected and helped create a tighter world market. Prices for some goods, those most often traded, converged somewhat across markets. Interest rates (the price of borrowed money) converged even more, especially in those lands most involved in capital flows. For the first time in history, economic slumps quickly became worldwide. Before 1850, economic crises had come mainly from bad harvests. But by 1870, a financial collapse could instantly ripple through the economies of dozens of countries: the world's financial system now mattered more than all but the worst weather for those lands enmeshed in the web. Second, these movements help account for the fastest economic growth the world had ever seen, about 2 percent or 2.5 percent annually from 1870 to 1913, for a total expansion of around two- or threefold over these

[15] A. G. Kenwood and A. L. Lougheed, *The Growth of the International Economy, 1820–2000* (London, 1999), 79.

decades. This rate was two or three times as fast as that of the preceding fifty years (1820–70) and something like six to eight times as fast as in the centuries 1500–1800. On a per capita basis, the world's economy grew by only about 1.3 percent annually or 1.6-fold in all (1870–1913), but even so incomes rose far faster than ever before. But they rose very unequally: the third great effect of this pulse of economic globalization was to widen inequality around the world. Prosperity arrived fastest in the industrial regions and a few fertile farm regions in the United States, Canada, Argentina, and Australia. Elsewhere, it remained elusive.

Late nineteenth-century globalization also had cultural and ecological dimensions. The power, prosperity, and confidence of Atlantic Europe and America helped inspire tens of thousands of missionaries to spread versions of the Christian gospel around the world. They met their greatest success where the extension of the web was most disruptive, for instance, on Pacific islands, in Southern Africa, and the interior of South America. But they made many converts in Korea and China too. As always, the resulting beliefs were syncretic, and in effect new religions were born, Korean or African forms of Christianity. Local, indigenous religions disappeared, as they had done for centuries.

Something similar happened with the world's languages. Some disappeared, while a few imperial languages—Chinese, Arabic, Spanish, Russian, French, English—spread. Local languages died out fastest on the world's imperial frontiers, in Australia, the Americas, Siberia, and Central Asia, but it also happened in Europe: the local tongue of Cornwall, in southwest England, went extinct in the 1800s. Languages sometimes vanished because their speakers did, as in Tasmania. But usually it happened voluntarily, as parents urged children to learn the language that would serve them best in life, the language of power and prestige. Thus, over two or three generations cosmopolitan languages replaced more local ones. Missionaries who went to great troubles to learn aboriginal languages in Australia, New Guinea, or Amazonia often regretted that by the time they finished their translation of the Bible, no one needed it.

As with religions, the swirl of people and power produced new amalgams in languages. Imperial languages acquired new words as their speakers experienced the world: English adopted hundreds of Hindi or Urdu words (e.g., *pajama, jungle*) and others from Amerindian tongues (*moccasin, powwow*). The world's mines and plantations, where people from many lands came together to work, often proved crucibles of entirely new languages, called "pidgins." Pidgins are stripped-down languages with minimal grammar, created by people who are thrown together with no language in common. Most pidgins in the modern world draw their vocabulary mainly from Portuguese or English. Children who grow up hearing a pidgin language as native speakers invariably give it a grammar and enormously expand its richness and flexibility, making it a "creole" language. The Caribbean, because of its history of labor migration from many quarters, has about twenty-five or thirty creole languages, most of which took shape in the eighteenth and nineteenth centuries (although like all languages they continue to evolve). On rare occasion, a creole language could become an imperial one. Swahili, invented as a pidgin among traders on the East African coast, became a rich creole tongue, and in the nineteenth century expanded inland to the Great Lakes region because of the success of coastal traders. The pace of globalization struck some thoughtful observers as so fast that the world needed a new international language, and they invented several, the most successful of which was Esperanto, created in 1887 by a Polish Jewish ophthalmologist (it claims a million speakers today). On balance, of course, the number of religions and languages fell: the world's cultural diversity declined, and faster than ever before.

Ecological Change

The expanding and tightening web, the globalizing currents of migration, trade, and investment, disturbed and sometimes destroyed ecological arrangements almost everywhere. Industrialization, with its intensive use of coal, created urban air pollution of an unprecedented intensity. The famous London fogs derived their yellowish, sulfurous quality from combustion of coal. In 1873 pedestrians stumbled into the Thames because the fog was so thick, and in 1879–80 some 3,000 people died in London from lung ailments during a siege of fog. Air pollution sickened and killed millions in the industrial cities of Europe, North America, and Japan.

The Industrial Revolution and growing population required much more fiber and food from the world's farms and plantations. Between 1750 and 1910, the area under crops almost tripled, with the fastest expansions in North America, Russia, and Southeast Asia. Pastureland more than tripled in this same period, growing fastest in the Americas, Africa, and Australia. The world's forests shrank by about 10 percent, mainly in North America. The space and nutrients available to wild creatures declined. At the time almost everyone regarded these changes as beneficial, and millions of people worked hard to achieve them.

Even this massive conversion of land to crops and pastures did not suffice to grow all the needed food and cotton. To make the soil yield more, people in parched lands turned more and more to irrigation. European empires promoted this keenly: British investment and Indian muscles built huge irrigation systems in India, and the Russians built large ones in Central Asia. U.S. westward expansion involved bringing irrigation to drylands on the high plains and in California, as did the Chinese frontier movement into Xinjiang and Mongolia. The population growth and improved transport networks made it rewarding to reorganize the earth's plumbing almost everywhere that rain-fed agriculture could not prosper.

The tightening web carried plants, animals, and diseases around the world too, although with less revolutionary results than in the wake of Columbus. American food crops continued their spread throughout Africa and Eurasia. In one corner of Tanzania, by the late 1800s about one of every three cultivated plants was American in origin. Maize probably had its biggest impact on China in the eighteenth and nineteenth centuries. Simultaneously, Old World food crops extended their colonization of the Americas, notably wheat on the former grasslands of the prairies and Pampas. The Columbian Exchange continued to bring Old World pathogens to new groups of Amerindians throughout the eighteenth and nineteenth centuries. Great disruptions occurred in Oceania and Australasia, where new diseases brought to people with inexperienced immune systems had their usual catastrophic consequences after 1750, and livestock refashioned soils and flora, notably in New Zealand and Australia. Introduced species, such as the rabbit in Australia, ran wild, nibbling vegetation to the point where local creatures starved. Competition and predation by newcomers drove hundreds of native species extinct in Australia, New Zealand, and Pacific islands.

Faster transport and mass migration brought new diseases even to populations with experienced immune systems. Cholera, a disease that kills quickly, had long existed in South Asia. But it did not travel well, partly because it disabled and killed its victims before they could move far. Yet with better transport, it regularly accompanied Muslim pilgrims to Mecca. It arrived in Europe, via troop movements, for the first time in the 1830s, and returned in several subsequent epidemics. Tuberculosis also became an important disease worldwide after about 1820. Healthy people could often carry the infection without falling ill, but when malnutrition weakened their resistance, as was frequently the case among the industrial working class, the disease sometimes overwhelmed them. Like many infections, it also caused havoc among peoples with no prior exposure, killing millions in the Pacific, the interior of the Americas, and in Southern Africa.

The terrible toll of cholera, typhoid, and other waterborne diseases inspired medical researchers, beginning in Britain in the 1840s, to unravel the means of communication of some of these infections. It eventually became clear that systematic separation of drinking water from waste water could make a huge difference. A "sanitary revolution" followed, at first mainly in Northern Europe, North America, and some European colonies around the world, in which cities acquired sewage systems and cleaner drinking water. Between 1880 and 1910, urban life became much safer thanks to water filtration plants. Where municipalities built such plants, life expectancy of city folk soon outstripped that of their country cousins: for the first time since they emerged 5,000 years before, cities were no longer demographic black holes. Their political and cultural domination of rural areas would therefore only increase in the twentieth century.

Conclusion: Lock-In

The tightening web between 1750 and 1914 helped produce and spread a demographic explosion, more representative forms of politics, nationalist identities, and industrialization. All of these things spread unevenly, generating great tensions within and between societies. Old constraints cracked and old orders tumbled, to be replaced not by any new stability but by tumult and uncertainty. The world has still not settled down from the upheavals begun in the eighteenth century.

In 1910, it was just possible in London or Paris to maintain the view that the world was an orderly place, with durable empires sure to last for centuries, with free trade among nations, with science unswervingly serving the public good, with men firmly in charge of their families, and so forth. But it was an illusion then, as anyone in Beijing or Mexico City would have said. And it would be revealed as an illusion to everyone else by the course of events after 1914.

The vast changes of the years 1750–1914 created acute tensions and vulnerabilities around the globe. In effect, humankind made new unconscious commitments on unfirm foundations. World population and urban growth required the maintenance and expansion of commercial agriculture, but some people and nations had less land and water than they needed. The prosperity delivered by economic globalization required the maintenance, if not the expansion, of free migration of people, capital, and goods, but this system did not mesh well with nationalist sensibilities. The new high-energy economy required ever more fossil fuels, scattered inconveniently around the world. The growing inequality of wealth and power required either that the less well off remain in ignorance, that they meekly accept their fate, or that they be bludgeoned into accepting it. In retrospect, the world at the beginning of the twentieth century was a big tinderbox in which many people were carrying lighted torches.

VIII
STRAINS ON THE WEB:
THE WORLD SINCE 1890

In the spring of 1930, an Australian gold prospector named Mick Leahy ventured up into the interior highlands of New Guinea. He did not find the El Dorado he was after, but he did close a long chapter in human history. The New Guinea highlands were home to several tens of thousands of people, mainly subsistence farmers, who lived in near-complete isolation from the rest of humankind. Their ancestors had been farming the fertile highlands for about 9,000 years. In the decades after 1930, prospectors, missionaries, colonial officials, traders, anthropologists, and others would bring the highlanders into systematic and sustained contact with the outside world. This was the last time a substantial population joined the worldwide web. Henceforth, the web would quicken and tighten but it would not entangle new territories and new populations.

While technology and other forces hastened integration within the web in the twentieth century, politics at times brought disintegration. In general, the pulse of globalization that came after 1870 ended with the outbreak of World War I in 1914. International migration, trade, and capital flows fell, recovered partially after the war, then fell again. Only during another great war, World War II, did momentum gather for renewed integration of the world's economies and societies. The rise of the United States to economic and military preeminence after 1945 made globalization often appear as Americanization. As always, the process of tightening the world's web reshuffled the fortunes of states, populations, and individuals, creating new dissatisfactions, inequalities, and tensions—as well as new comforts and freedoms for about a quarter of humankind.

Communications and Ideas

The great technological shifts in communications and transport in the 1800s (steamships, railroads, telegraphs) helped knit the world together more tightly, but some aspects of life remained untouched. The great distinction of the communications and transport technologies that shaped the twentieth century (telephone, radio, TV, movies, automobile, airplane, Internet) was that they altered the everyday lives of billions of people, enlarging their range of experience and their access to information. These new technologies democratized the transmission of information in prosperous countries, and until about 1975 helped narrow gaps between rich and poor within them. But at the same time, because they conferred wealth and power upon those who used them, they helped widen the gap between the prosperous and the poor around the world. In 2000, about 60 percent of the U.S. population regularly used the Internet and about 35 percent in South Korea. But in Brazil only 6 percent did and in Nigeria less than 0.1 percent. We shall return to this matter at the end of this chapter.

Roughly speaking, the technological transformations came in three waves. Although the telephone was invented in the 1870s, the automobile in the 1890s, and radio around 1900, they became widespread only in the 1920s, and even then mainly in the United States. Their spread around the world came in fits and starts thereafter. The second wave came in the 1940s and 1950s, when television (invented in the 1930s) and commercial aviation became routine in the United States and soon in much of the rest of the world. Like telephones and radio, the airplane had been important in war well before it became commercially viable. The third wave, networked computers, originated in the 1960s but took off in the early 1990s. All of these new technologies worked as networks, which meant they were slow to catch on but once over a threshold they spread very rapidly. It made little sense to have a telephone before lots of other people had them, but once they did it made scant sense to be without one. Similarly, it made no sense to have a car before there were gas stations and passable roads, but once there were, having one proved irresistible to almost all who could afford it. So these technologies, once established, transformed daily life very quickly and raised the intensity and velocity of traffic within the cosmopolitan web.

The cumulative effect of all these changes (and some others such as mass circulation newspapers) was to bombard people with new information, impressions, and ideas, and to allow more of them to travel further, faster, and more frequently than ever before. This proved disconcerting and disorienting, as well as seductive. It invited people to suppose that their circumstances need not be as they were, but could be improved—through emigration, revolution, education, hard work, crime, or some other initiative. With radio, movies, and TV in particular, hungry illiterates could catch a glimpse (accurate or not) of how more fortunate people lived. This information, combined with massive urbanization, inspired both ambition and resentment, providing potential recruits for an array of political movements.

Radio, movies, and TV had another important effect, this one more clearly political. They allowed skilled speakers to reach millions. Orators who could convey excitement, anger, or authority with their impassioned voices built broad political movements more easily than before. Among the effective radio politicians were Adolf Hitler (1889–1945) in Germany, Franklin D. Roosevelt (1882–1945) in the United States, and Gamal Abdel Nasser (1918–1970) in Egypt. Many successful politicians came out of radio and TV broadcasting, notably Eva Perón (1919–1952) in Argentina, whose popularity as an actress proved invaluable to her own and her husband's (Juan Perón) political careers, and the American president Ronald Reagan (born 1909), an actor whose TV persona underpinned his electoral success. After a generation or so these media became harder to exploit, partly because audiences grew more sophisticated and partly because so many politicians mastered the requisite skills that no individual could easily outshine all rivals. The new communications technologies, when first introduced to a society, probably made it easier to manipulate the masses—certainly to mobilize them. But over time they probably had the reverse effect, making it harder for a government to control information and people.

CULTURE, RELIGION, SCIENCE

The new information infrastructures intensified competition in the marketplace of ideas. In 1890, most Chinese had never encountered anyone who held views not shaped in the Chinese cultural context; most Irish had never met anyone who was not Christian and Irish. And because most Chinese and Irish could scarcely read, their outlooks on life, if they did not travel far, could easily remain parochial, unreflective, and bound by custom. To be sure, some Chinese and Irish had relentless curiosity, some did read, and some traveled. And, equally, in some parts of the world cultural clashes and competition were the rule, for example, in South Africa, where Indians, Chinese, Zulu, Xhosa, Tswana, Khoikhoi, San, Afrikaners, British, and dozens of other peoples with different languages, religions, and styles of life jostled one another on a daily basis. But for the majority, only with radio and TV, literacy and newspapers, movies and airplane travel did it become unusual to go through life without encountering radically different ideas and ways of life. In this respect, the new technologies made the world more like South Africa: more people encountered more cultural diversity more often.

The results—so far—amounted to a cultural shakeout: the elimination or marginalization of many competitors and the conspicuous success of a few. We touched upon this process with respect to languages in chapter 7. Those trends continued and intensified, to the point where by 2000 a language went extinct every two weeks or so. Most of the world's people spoke as a mother tongue one of the top fifteen languages,[1] while more than half of the world's languages had fewer than 10,000 speakers. The same process held sway over styles of dress, music, sport, or cooking. Some local variants vanished as people saw advantages in assimilating to urban, national, or international standards. At the same time, those national and international standards evolved, and sometimes reflected or absorbed local influences that thereby became widespread. Under the influence of radio, for example, local variation almost disappeared in Brazilian popular music beginning in the 1920s, replaced by a very few styles that became national—including Rio de Janeiro's *samba*, which soon became internationally popular and emblematic of Brazil. Through the international success of (mainly) American and British popular music, West African–derived rhythms percolated into music in Japan, Algeria, and indeed almost everywhere. Under the influence of TV, basketball became an international game after the 1970s, transcending its American origins. Architectural styles converged, so that increasingly a new airport, office tower, or apartment block looked much the same in Manila, Madras, or Montreal. Youth culture took this conformist tendency the furthest. Those aspects of it that were inexpensive—

[1] In descending order by number of native speakers: Mandarin Chinese, English, Spanish, Bengali, Hindi, Portuguese, Russian, Japanese, German, Wu Chinese, Javanese, Korean, French, Vietnamese, Telegu. Daniel Nettle and Suzanne Romaine, *Vanishing Voices* (Oxford, 2000), 29. (Nettle and Romaine seem to have missed Arabic in their list).

baseball caps in the 1990s—became well-nigh ubiquitous in the cities of the world.

Political culture too converged on fewer and fewer standards. Through both imperialism and imitation, the law codes of a handful of Western and Central European countries, based often on Roman law, became the basis for legal systems on every continent. Muslim law (*shari'a*) had spread far and wide in prior centuries, and retained its position after 1890, although sometimes in uneasy combinations. Nigeria and Pakistan, for example, drew on both English and Muslim legal traditions. Hybrid legal codes, roughly analogous to creole languages, increased the variety of legal traditions in force. But local, clan, and tribal legal traditions, lacking prestige and state support, went extinct. Similarly, the variety of political systems shrank. Tribal chiefdoms, city-states, pastoralist confederacies, and other historic political forms did not entirely disappear, but examples became fewer and weaker. Meanwhile, more and more societies, willingly or not, accepted bureaucratic empire or the nation-state as their political format.

In the realm of religion, the easy communication of ideas worked to the advantage of portable creeds and against local ones. Religions everywhere had to adjust to the new means of communication, to the new shape of the world economy, in many places to imperialism, and everywhere to urbanization. The period after 1890 therefore saw unusual dynamism and instability in religious life. Indeed, since in the past the anonymity, rootlessness, and conspicuous sinfulness of urban life regularly provoked religious quests for meaning, belonging, and morality, the contemporary rush to the cities implies a very turbulent and fertile time for religion in the century ahead.

In Peru in 1900 people had a choice between Catholicism (with local features, of course) and local religions that had survived in the shadows during the 400-year period when first Inca (ca. 1440–1532) and then Catholic (ca. 1540–1840) faiths had been state religions. In 1915, a third choice appeared when Protestant evangelicals began to make converts in Peru. With urbanization and improved health care, the local religions lost out, since they were intimately tied to features of the natural environment and specialized in the healing arts. Catholicism struggled, having lost state support in the nineteenth century. Protestantism converted perhaps 10 percent of Peruvians by 1995. Its messages of mutual aid, self-discipline, and hard work appealed to the millions who had left their villages to make their way in the grim shantytowns ringing Lima, Cuzco, or Arequipa. Evangelical Protestants found fertile fields in other urbanizing Latin American countries too, accounting for over 20 percent of the population in Brazil and Chile by 1990.

In Africa also, migration to the cities, exposure to new ideas, and the pressures of imperialism revolutionized belief. Local religions lost followers. In the colonial period (ca. 1890–1960), Christianity prospered mightily, promoted by thousands of missionaries, generally with encouragement from colonial authorities. But so too did Islam precisely because it was not the religion of colonial power. (Christianity flourished in Korea for similar reasons when Korea was a Japanese colony and Buddhism received Japanese support.) African Muslims also became more aligned with the dominant variants of Islam, as more of their leaders studied in seats of Muslim learning such as Fez and Cairo, and more Muslims could make the pilgrimage to Mecca. Radio and TV eventually brought the words of Egyptian or Saudi religious authorities directly to the masses. Christianity, on the other hand, became less orthodox in Africa. To flourish there it had to make some accommodation with ancestor worship, polygamy, and ritual healing. Africans also had to see in it something that spoke to their spiritual—or material—needs. Christianity, like all the portable religions, contained messages that addressed the condition of the downtrodden, whether in the Roman Empire of the third century C.E. or in Kenya in 1925. So millions of Africans adapted Christianity to suit their circumstances. Many European missionaries saw superstition and sorcery in these adaptations. Some Africans agreed and became orthodox Anglicans, Methodists, or Catholics, but others responded by forming their own independent churches, of which there are perhaps 10,000 today. Among them was Simon Kimbangu (1889–1951).

Kimbangu was born in the southern part of what was then becoming the Belgian Congo, the son of a healer. He became a Baptist as a young man, but—a bit like Hong Xiuquan—failed his examinations for the ministry. But he soon heard the voice of Jesus instructing him to lead his flock from temptation and sin. In 1921, a time when Central Africa was beset by epidemics, Kimbangu began to acquire fame as a healer. His popularity and his unorthodox preaching worried the Belgian authorities, who had him imprisoned and sentenced to death. The Belgian king commuted the sentence, and Kimbangu spent the rest of his life in prison, while his most prominent followers were arrested, imprisoned, or exiled. But in the colonial setting, persecution only enhanced his stature. Kimbangu's followers pointed out that his career echoed that of Jesus: a divine call, a ministry of healing, popular preaching, and persecution by an imperial regime. The Church of Jesus Christ on Earth Through the Prophet Simon Kimbangu was accepted into the World Council of Churches in 1969 and today claims about 4 million adherents. By the 1990s, Africa counted about 350 million Christians, a few of whom undertook missionary work in darkest Europe, where millions of souls had drifted away from Christianity and needed salvation in the worst way.

Imperialism produced diverse religious reactions. For many people, adopting the religion of the imperialists seemed prudent, as in Africa, or in British Hong Kong, where many Chinese became Christians, or in Korea, where some took up Buddhism during the Japanese occupation. But for many others, especially Muslims and Hindus, three different options prevailed. One was to seek some sort of accommodation between religious belief and the practices, habits, and science that seemed to make the imperialists so powerful. This was perhaps easiest for Hinduism, which was very fluid at its edges. In the nineteenth and twentieth centuries it acquired greater consistency (sacrificing some variety) under the impact of figures such as Vivekananda (1863–1902), a social and religious reformer who sought to reconcile science, Western humanistic values, and the Vedic traditions of Hinduism. A second religious response was to harken back to a golden age of purity, rejecting almost everything new and alien—except perhaps useful communications technologies. This was tempting for Muslims, such as those who joined the Muslim Brotherhood (founded in Egypt in 1928) and those who led the Iranian revolution of 1979–80 putting a religious regime in power. A third course was to abandon nominal religion altogether in favor of secular ideologies. The most popular of these were nationalism and socialism, which at times held great appeal in many lands. These secular and overtly political ideologies will be treated below.

The ideas and information reverberating throughout the web in the twentieth century, combined with the pressures of urbanization and imperialism, brought a swirl of conversion, syncretism, and novel religions, creeds, and cults. The dominant trend, a recurrent one in world history, was the elimination or marginalization of local religions and the spread of major evangelical faiths to new ground. But additional trends emerged as well: the retreat of Christianity in Europe and North America in the face of secular outlooks; the accommodation of Protestant churches to feminism by the 1980s; and the retreat and suppression of Confucian and Buddhist faiths in China under Nationalist and Communist regimes.

In this confusion, the notion that all religions are in essence one acquired new appeal. The Ramakrishna movement in India found avenues to the divine in all faiths. Its most effective apostle, Vivekananda, dazzled audiences at the 1893 World Parliament of Religions in Chicago, preaching a global, unified religion. The Baha'i faith, a nineteenth-century offshoot of Persian Shi'a Islam that also emphasizes the underlying unity of all religion, acquired a few million followers in the twentieth century—and adopted English as its preferred language. In its own wacky way, the Theosophist movement also exemplified the appeal of religious unity. Founded in 1875 by a Russian noblewoman and an American lawyer, later led by an Englishwoman but most influential in India, the Theosophist Society dabbled in occult and psychic phenomena, and proved hopelessly schismatic. But Theosophists found a common core in all major religions and a common unity of all humankind: a true creation of the worldwide web. They were also victims of it.

Theosophy, and many other mystical beliefs, came to seem faintly ridiculous with the advent of modern science. The great religions also faced a challenge from modern science, one to which they generally adapted successfully, surrendering a few points of doctrine but retaining most of their followers (except in Europe where disbelief flourished), if not always their former influence on public life.

In some respects, science underwent a shakeout too. Fewer and fewer distinct ideas about, say, the origins of the universe, the contents of the deep oceans, or the causes of disease survived the twentieth century's rapid exchange of information and ideas. More and more people accepted a narrower range of ideas, and educated scientists came to accept a fairly consistent set of truths, whether they were based in Boston, Berlin, Bombay, or Beijing. The chief reason for this was the increasing global exchange of scientific data and ideas. International congresses and journals proliferated from the 1880s on. Young scientists from around the world went to study in Europe (Russia included) and North America. The power and prestige of Europe and the United States—and eventually Japan—were such that scientific ideas generated there swept the world.

The evolving scientific worldviews had several core features in common. First, the approaches to science that emerged in seventeenth-century Europe, emphasizing observation and experimentation, acquired nearly unimpeachable authority, even in lands such as China with their own long and distinguished scientific traditions. Second, science increasingly abandoned the principle of timelessness and adopted evolutionary models of the natural world. Third, good science did not come cheap.

Geology became a distinctly historical science by the 1830s. Fossils of marine animals indicated that places now high and dry were once oceans and that the earth must be millions of years old (today's geologists estimate the earth's age at 4.5 billion years). Mountain chains, it seemed, were born and then slowly eroded away over the eons. By the 1960s, geologists accepted the idea that continents drifted slowly across the earth's surface, a notion ridiculed in 1915 when first proposed.

Biology also became historical after the publication in 1859 of Charles Darwin's theory of evolution by natural selection. He argued that all species were descended from earlier ones, and that all creatures were locked in a struggle for existence which selected for the traits most advantageous for survival at a given time and place. Darwin's ideas were the most revolutionary and powerful scientific propositions of modern times, and posed a direct challenge to religious accounts of the origins of life and humankind. For this reason his views attracted vigorous opposition, especially from those who took the Bible as the literal word of God. They also aroused the enmity of ideologists in the USSR, who felt that the strong element of chance in Darwin's scheme—random mutations directing evolution, for example—violated the laws Marx had discovered, according to which progress toward communism was a historical necessity and humankind perfectible. But gradually Darwin's view became—with modifications—universally accepted among the world's scientifically educated.

The other great departure in biology came in genetics, mainly after 1950. The basis was laid by the experiments of Gregor Mendel (1822–1884), an Austrian monk whose work on peas showed how heredity worked. His writings went unnoticed until 1900, after which geneticists around the world busily elaborated upon his work, yielding practical results in crop breeding. Just why heredity works the way it does remained mysterious until the work of academics Francis Crick (born 1916) and James Watson (born 1928). In the 1950s, they offered a persuasive model of the genetic code, indicating just where and how genetic information was stored in DNA molecules, a feat that nailed down the Darwinian vision in biology.

Physics followed suit after the 1920s, when the American lawyer and astronomer Edwin Hubble (1889–1953) proposed that the universe was not stable, as earlier astronomers had supposed, but growing. Stars, including our sun, had life spans and were not permanent fixtures of the heavens. By the 1960s astronomers believed in the big bang, a theory according to which the universe was born about 12 billion years ago in an instantaneous expansion from an unimaginably dense blob of matter and energy. Physicists from the 1890s also investigated the hidden world of atomic and subatomic particles, a quest that by the 1940s brought nuclear weapons and by the 1950s led to nuclear power stations. Instead of the timelessness and universality of physics and astronomy that Isaac Newton and his heirs had understood, it now appeared that conditions on earth, indeed in our solar system and galaxy, were local and temporary.

The Marriage of Science and Technology

The sciences, while they grew more historical, also grew more expensive, more bureaucratic, and more closely linked to technology. Throughout most of human history, science and technology had had little to do with each other. Scientific changes affected ideas but rarely practices. Technological change came from tinkerers, people with little to no scientific education but plenty of hands-on experience. By 1860 or so, this began to change.

"The greatest invention of the nineteenth century was the invention of the method of invention,"[2] noted Alfred North Whitehead, the English philosopher. What he observed bore even more fruit in the twentieth century. From the 1880s the great powers, chiefly Germany and Britain, competed to develop superior navies and increasingly organized scientists and engineers into teams directed to generate useful military technology. Scientific expertise gradually became a crucial component of military security. In the 1870s, industrial firms in Germany and the United States had created their own research laboratories and maintained small flocks of scientists assigned to solve particular problems. Chemical firms in particular developed ties with universities, financing research and assuring a stream of skilled graduates. As governments and firms became more involved in funding science, the thrust of inquiry shifted toward applied science that could help win wars, improve health, and expand wealth. Almost all science, pure or applied, required expensive technologies and educational systems. This helped keep the inter-

[2] A. N. Whitehead, *Science and the Modern World* (New York, 1925), 98.

national landscape of science dominated by a few countries, notably Germany until the 1930s and the United States thereafter.

After World War II, the Americans built a sprawling scientific-industrial-military complex involving coordinated research and development by firms, universities, and the Pentagon. Britain had a much smaller one, dating back to the late nineteenth century. The Soviet Union embarked on a similar venture, with the additional feature of specially designated, often secret, science cities, where small armies of physicists and engineers lived and worked in near isolation from the broader society. The Cold War was the driving force behind these developments. But the implications of these investments in science and technology touched every aspect of life. Industrial chemists developed plastics, now ubiquitous. Solid-state physics research yielded the transistor in the 1950s, making radios cheap and portable. Plant geneticists created new strains of wheat, rice, and maize that, in favorable conditions, doubled or quadrupled crop yields (ca. 1960–80), dramatically raising the world's food supply. The pace of invention and innovation accelerated as governments, universities, and businesses competed and cooperated in supporting hordes of engineers and scientists. This helped make science more bureaucratic.

In Darwin's day, science remained an occupation for gentlemen (rarely gentlewomen) of leisure or academics. They typically worked alone, although thanks to post offices and scientific societies they communicated frequently with fellow researchers. In 1900, the two most scientifically advanced nations, Germany and Britain, each had about 8,000 working scientists. By 1940, American businesses employed some 70,000 scientists in research and development. The demands of World War II led to the emergence of larger-scale, more institutionalized and bureaucratic science: the atomic bomb project alone employed 40,000 people. The success of that and other efforts showed what abundant funding and scientific manpower could do, and thereafter governments and businesses generously bankrolled scientific research, a large share of which was connected to military projects. By 1980 the United States boasted over 1 million scientists, and Western Europe employed still more. While their backers were prepared to pay for a modest amount of pure science—disinterested inquiry about, say, the fate of the dinosaurs—what they most wanted was applied science that would help build a better mousetrap—or, after the rise of biotechnology in the 1980s, a better mouse. Science could not do without state funding and, increasingly, states could not do without the technological fruits of science.

Modern science took on some of the authority formerly held by religions. It seemed to offer plausible answers to some of the cosmic questions, although it did not help much with moral ones. Science acquired ever greater prestige as it became more closely tied to technological innovation and to medical advances. Almost every school system in the world included its methods and insights among those things that children must be taught. But science could not answer everything, leaving religions room to adjust their messages. Many of them eventually accepted modified Darwinism. Believers made their own accommodations with modern science, seeing, for example, the big bang as a version of divine creation. Only a few rejected it altogether.

The very success of twentieth-century scientific and technological advance eventually brought public unease and suspicion, especially in those societies most transformed by it. Whereas at the beginning of the century the great New Zealand scientist Ernest Rutherford maintained that all good physics could be explained to a barmaid, a hundred years later no one supposed anything of the sort. Physics and genetics especially were well beyond lay understanding. Even the irreligious found some aspects of nuclear physics or genetic manipulation morally or politically repugnant, an attitude sometimes abetted by some scientists' apparent disinterest in the social consequences of their work. But even the suspicious were entirely dependent on the smooth functioning of immensely complex technological systems and the continuing work of an elite cadre of highly skilled people.

Population and Urbanization

One of the most distinctive features of the twentieth century was its population history, a tale of boom and partial bust in which both science and social change played major roles. In 1900, the earth supported some 1.6 billion people, about a fifth of them in China. By 2000, the total had quadrupled to 6.0 billion (China still accounted for a fifth, and India a sixth). Nothing like this had ever happened before, nor will it again. Most of this surge took place after 1950. The world's population growth rate peaked around 1970, at around 2 percent per annum. It has fallen, irregularly, ever since, and demographers expect it will slow to zero by 2050 or 2070. What might happen after that is anyone's guess.

The main reason for this extraordinary burst was the transfer of successful death control measures to most populations on earth. Before

1914, effective public health systems existed in only a few regions. But after 1950, vaccinations, antibiotics, and sanitation measures, the fruits of decades of scientific research, cut death rates everywhere. Life expectancy at birth, which globally had been less than thirty years in 1800 and about thirty-five years in 1900, reached forty-five in 1950 and sixty-seven in 2000. This constituted a radical change in the human condition. Japanese, currently the longest-lived people on earth, can expect to live twice as long as their great-grandparents' generation. Even the least long-lived, Sierra Leoneans, enjoy perhaps twenty extra years compared to their forebears in 1900. Worldwide, most of the progress in death control took place between 1945 and 1965. Until birth rates fell too (which has not happened everywhere), populations grew by as much as 4 percent per year in some African and Central American countries, fast enough to double in sixteen years. In some countries, the transition from high birth and death rates to low ones took as little as twenty years, with a correspondingly modest leap in total population. South Korea, Taiwan, and Thailand all achieved this after 1960, and not coincidentally got comparatively rich in record time.

Science helped in birth control as in death control. The first contraceptive pill became available in 1960. It, incidentally, was a product of the cosmopolitan web: based on chemical feedstock from a Mexican yam formerly used as fish poison, the first pill was financed mainly by rich American women and researched by Central European Jewish scientists who had fled Nazism for Mexico. By 1995, some 200 million women around the world had used pills to prevent pregnancy.

The tremendous human slaughter of the twentieth century had little effect on population trends. If one adds up all the premature deaths from wars, genocides, state terror campaigns, and human-caused famines, the total comes to perhaps 180–90 million. This accounts for about 4 percent of the total deaths in the twentieth century.[3] The acceleration of death from political causes did not nearly match the deceleration of death from public health measures and improved nutrition.

The inequality in population growth rates, so important in the eighteenth and nineteenth centuries, remained disruptive after 1890. Fertility stayed high in Eastern Europe until 1914, which assured heightened tensions within the Russian and Austrian empires, despite high rates of emigration. But this was the twilight of rapid population growth in Europe. By 1920, almost every corner of Europe had reduced its fertility

[3] See the arithmetic of Matthew White at http://users.erols.com/mwhite28/20centry.htm

sharply, and the fastest growth now occurred in India, Latin America, and, after 1930 or so, in Africa. Whereas in Europe in 1900 emigration took away about one-third of the natural increase, in India, China, Latin America, and Africa emigration did not notably reduce pressures. Instead, population growth promoted political unrest, urbanization, and desperate state efforts to industrialize overnight. Africa's population history was especially dramatic—and traumatic—a six- or sevenfold increase to roughly 750 million in the course of one century.

The stresses and anxieties caused by rapid population growth motivated states to craft population policies. In the past, rulers did not often concern themselves with population, and when they did their position was simple: the more people the better. This attitude persisted in the twentieth century, especially among dictators who wanted more men for cannon fodder and wanted women to concentrate on child rearing. Hitler and Joseph Stalin (1879–1953) both rewarded fertile mothers with state decorations. But after 1950, population growth rates that seemed too high provoked concerted efforts to lower them. The most important efforts to curb population growth came in the world's two most populous countries. India, independent after 1947, by 1952 encouraged citizens to limit their family size. In the 1970s, India even specified a fertility rate (25 per 1,000) as a target in its five-year plan, and in 1976 attempted to impose mandatory sterilization for those who already had three children. This proved very unpopular, and the official population control effort achieved only modest results. By the 1990s, India had reduced its overall fertility rate by about one-third from the 1952 level, yet its population had more than doubled in forty years. It was set to overtake China as the world's most populous country early in the twenty-first century.

In China, population control emerged as a sustained policy only after the death of Mao Zedong (1893–1976), who usually, but not always, took the view that there could never be too many Chinese. After tentative steps toward a sustained policy in the early 1970s, Mao's successors in 1979 instituted a one-child quota on families in most of the country, with enough incentives and penalties to alter fertility fundamentally. Owing to the strength of China's state, China's rapid urbanization, and perhaps to the long history of managed fertility in Chinese families, this quota had remarkable impact. Between 1970 and 2000, China's fertility fell by two-thirds, approximately to replacement level, the fastest such reduction in world history. By the mid-1980s, 94 percent of humankind lived in countries with population control policies, although none but China made it a central plank of national ideology.

A few countries facing population decline adopted an opposite policy, providing incentives for childbearing, as Hitler and Stalin had done. France offered baby bonuses from 1939, and several other European countries followed from the 1970s, and Japan from 1993, although with very little discernible effect. Communist Romania in 1965 banned all forms of birth control and deployed its secret police to make sure women did not shirk their reproductive duty. These extreme measures doubled the birth rate in 1966, but when the regime fell (1989–90), Romanian women went on a reproductive strike. Pro-natalism also suffered from resemblance to the programs of discredited authoritarian regimes in Spain, Italy, Germany, Russia, and Japan. In any case, it ran counter to the impact of an irresistible trend, urbanization.

Exuberant growth of cities was another defining characteristic of the twentieth century. In 1900, about 12–15 percent of humankind lived in cities; by 1950, some 30 percent did; but by 2001, more than half did. This also represents a great turning point in the human condition. Prior to 1880, cities everywhere were demographic black holes, mainly because of endemic childhood diseases but also because of recurrent epidemics. London in 1750 killed children and newcomers so quickly that it canceled half of the natural increase of all of England. But after the 1880s, public health measures made city life safer, first through the provision of clean water. By the 1920s, Chinese city dwellers, for example, outlived their country cousins. Henceforth, cities grew and grew, from natural increase as well as from in-migration.

In 1900, about 225 million people lived in cities. But by 2001, about 3 billion did, a thirteen-fold increase. Broadly speaking, this surge to the cities came first in Europe, eastern North America, and Japan during their eras of industrialization (ca. 1850–1930). Britain was the first large country in which more than half the population lived in cities (by 1850); a proportion reached in Germany in 1890, in the United States by 1920, and in Japan by 1935. Next came the USSR and much of Latin America, where state-sponsored industrialization helped propel a rush to the cities between 1930 and 1970. By the early 1960s, the 50 percent urban threshold had been reached in both the USSR and Latin America (taken as a whole). Chinese policy kept people in the villages until 1980, after which peasants stampeded to the cities in the largest, fastest urbanization the world has ever seen; China will probably surpass the 50 percent mark between 2005 and 2010.

Cities became both more numerous and larger. Villages became cities almost overnight in regions where iron ore and coal could be found together, as in Germany's Ruhr region. Frontier settlement also brought forth great cities, such as Buenos Aires, Melbourne, or Chicago, each of which counted about 100,000 citizens in 1858 and more than half a million by 1900. (Chicago was then the fifth largest city in the world with 1.7 million.) Where industrialization occurred in a capital city, the growth was often greater still: Mexico City had a third of a million people in 1900, some 5 million by 1960, and 20–25 million by 2000. Indeed, by 2000, sprawling megacities such as São Paulo, Shanghai, Cairo, and Delhi each contained more people than the entire world did when agriculture was first invented, and about as many as Great Britain counted at the time of the Industrial Revolution.

This basic change in the human condition affected almost everything: morals, religion, identity, politics, ambitions, education, health, recreation, and much more, in ways that are as yet far from clear. In most places people had gradually worked out ways of living together in village settings, where every transaction took place in the context of personal encounters, where everyone's reputation was known to all, where customs had evolved to constrain conflict. In urban settings such customs and constraints melted away, leaving only law, police, and moral education to discourage predatory behavior. A smorgasbord of social organizations sprang up to meet the needs of urban life, from street gangs to cults to neighborhood associations. But, as yet, no one has found a satisfactory moral code or a way to ensure smooth or stable social relations in urban settings.

Despite all its distresses, urban life offered great advantages. Opportunity for upward social mobility and more excitement for the young had always tempted migrants. Increasingly after 1890, cities also provided better access to education, health care, clean water, and electricity. After 1950, the easily acquired skill of driving a motor car could ensure an income without backbreaking labor. In many countries governments feared urban insurrections and consequently used their power to assure cheap food for the cities, sometimes by fixing prices, sometimes simply by confiscating it from the peasantry. All this helps explain the continuing magnetism of the cities.

Urbanization was also the main reason that world population growth began to slow after 1970. In cities, at least where child labor is uncommon, children are costly to their parents for fifteen or twenty years, whereas in rural settings, especially where there are goats or chickens to tend, children from the age of five or so are economically useful. In cities, girls are more likely to get formal education, and more educated women generally have fewer children. So, wherever cities predominated, people within a generation or two abandoned the normal agrarian emphasis on fertility and had far fewer children. This became most apparent in Central Europe after World War I. Around 1930, Viennese reproduced so slowly that, without in-migration, the city's population would have declined by three-fourths within a generation. Berliners were almost as reluctant to bear children. By the 1970s, urbanization (and city habits among the country folk) had spread so far that in Germany and Japan the national populations had subreplacement fertility.[4] In Russia and Ukraine after 1980 birth rates fell, while death rates (especially for men) climbed, so that population decay set in very quickly.

This pattern, if it persists, means that cities are resuming their historic role as demographic black holes. Before 1880, they consumed population because their death rates were so high; after an interval of growth by natural increase, they began to consume population because their birth rates were so low. London today, as in 1750, would shrink without in-migration. (Since the 1950s, London has drawn many migrants from the Caribbean and South Asia, not merely from the rest of Britain.) Will life in Lagos and Lima eventually make people as reluctant to bear children as has life in London? Will urban conditions always persist in discouraging people from parenthood? The answers are by no means clear. Unforeseeable developments in biotechnology, for example, could revise the procedures of reproduction and family life.

Energy and Environment

One of the central reasons why human numbers could grow fourfold in the twentieth century, and why urban population could grow thirteenfold, was the phenomenal success our species enjoyed in harnessing fossil fuels. The use of coal smashed old constraints on transport and industrial production. By about 1890, half the energy deployed around the

---

[4] That is, less than about 2.1 children per woman over her lifetime. In such situations, population will eventually fall without immigration. It will not normally fall instantly, because usually there are enough people of childbearing age to keep the birth rate above the death rate for perhaps ten or twenty years. The data on Vienna and Berlin are from Dudley Kirk, *Europe's Population in the Interwar Years* (Princeton, 1946), 55. In Oslo, Stockholm, and Riga, maternity wards were nearly as empty; several European countries briefly had subreplacement fertility in the 1930s.

world came from fossil fuels, mainly coal. In the twentieth century, the crucial development in energy history was the emergence of cheap oil.

The United States led the way in building its economy and society around oil. The first successful hard-rock drilling came in Pennsylvania in 1859, but the first American gusher came in southeastern Texas in 1901, heralding a century of cheap energy. Big oil finds came later in Mexico, Venezuela, Indonesia, Siberia, and—by far the greatest of all— around the Persian Gulf, exploited heavily since the late 1940s. In global terms, the shift to oil came mainly between 1950 and 1973, during which time world oil production climbed from 10 million to 65 million barrels per day. It has since risen to 75 million. Oil revolutionized transport. Cars and airplanes could not run on coal. It transformed agriculture too, powering farm machinery and serving as the chemical feedstock for fertilizers, making it possible, for example, for 3 percent of Americans to feed all the rest. The rice, wheat, and potatoes that feed the world's population stem from oil as much as from soil, water, and photosynthesis.

With oil, and smaller contributions made by natural gas, hydroelectric power, and nuclear power, the world's energy harvest grew ever more bountiful after 1890. The average global citizen used three to four times as much energy in 2000 as in 1900. This average, of course, conceals great differences. Just as the Industrial Revolution widened inequalities of wealth and power around the world, so did the accelerating transition to high-energy use. The ordinary Canadian or American, for example, by 1990 used fifty to one hundred times as much energy as the average Bangladeshi. That was because in Bangladesh most energy still came from biomass. For those who enjoyed it, the transition to a high-energy society amounted to a great liberation from drudgery and toil. It made people far more mobile, productive, and richer than their ancestors—or their contemporaries who did not share in the transition. In short, the harnessing of fossil fuels, especially oil, simultaneously eased life for a large fraction of humanity and deepened the inequalities between the haves and have-nots.

The fourfold expansion of human numbers and the thirteen- or fifteen-fold expansion of energy use in the twentieth century provoked an unprecedented disruption of the environment. It was—and is—a gigantic, uncontrolled experiment on the biosphere. The conversion of forest and grassland to farms and pastures continued, although a bit more slowly than in the nineteenth century. The land devoted to crops roughly doubled between 1900 and 2000, from an area the size of Australia to the equivalent of South America. The scene of the fastest land use shifts moved from the temperate zones to the tropics: the last great plow-up of temperate grasslands occurred in Russia and Kazakhstan in the late 1950s. Thereafter the expansion of cropland proceeded most quickly in Central America, West Africa, and Southeast Asia, especially after 1950, mainly at the expense of rainforests. Inserting larger numbers of people into the complex ecosystems of tropical rainforests carried unforeseen risks. The AIDS virus apparently jumped to humans from Central African chimpanzees shortly before 1959, and circulated within tropical Africa for twenty years before becoming a worldwide plague. By 2002, it had killed nearly 20 million people, two-thirds of them Africans. But AIDS did not change the larger pattern of increasing human colonization of the biosphere.

All this left less and less space for wild creatures. Many of them—there are no reliable estimates—went extinct when their habitats were converted to farm or pasture, or when newly introduced predators or diseases wiped them out. Many others, while not driven to extinction, came close, such as blue whales. The earth has seen five great extinction spasms in its history: the twentieth century showed signs of starting a sixth, the only one caused by humanity. Meanwhile other species, ones directly useful for human purposes such as cattle and chickens, found the earth refashioned in ways calculated to raise their populations. And still others, such as rats and dandelions, while not useful to humans, also found the world as remade by humans very suitable to them. Altogether, by 2000 the proportion of life on earth that served human ends, directly or indirectly, approached 40 percent on land and 10 percent in the seas, probably five to eight times as much as in 1900. So, in the process of trying to feed ourselves, make money, and protect ourselves from our fellows, we recast the biosphere dramatically, inserting ourselves as the main force shaping biological evolution. In the short run this unconscious process brought far more people, less famine, more wealth, and longer life than ever before in human history. How it will play out in the long run remains to be seen.

In addition to recasting the biosphere, human actions inadvertently altered the basic biogeochemical cycles of the earth. This was not entirely new, but after 1890 its scope attained far greater proportions. For example, the burning of coal and oil created thicker clouds of urban air pollution in thousands of cities. At its worst, as in London in December 1952, this killed 4,000 people in a week. Happily, in societies where citizen agitation could make itself heard, urban air pollution was easily reduced through substitution of oil or natural gas for coal, or through cleaner technologies in factories and power plants. Checking urban air pollution was a major plank in the program of the environmental movement as it took shape in North America, Japan, Western Europe, and elsewhere in the 1970s. But where the goals of industrialists or of states trumped the health of citizens, lethal pollution persisted. This was especially the case in poor industrializing countries, such as China, India, Thailand, or Mexico, and in the Communist countries of Eastern Europe. In Mexico City, where 4 million cars operated under geographical conditions ideal for brewing smog, the municipal government estimated in 2002 that air pollution killed 35,000 people annually. In Krakow in southern Poland, by the 1980s pollution had measurably reduced the oxygen content of air and (presumably) accounted for cancer rates twice the national average, itself very high by world standards. In all, urban air pollution killed perhaps 25–40 million people in the twentieth century.

Loading the atmosphere with carbon dioxide was less immediately dangerous but a more fundamental change—and harder to reverse. Carbon dioxide is one of the so-called greenhouse gases that exist in tiny proportions in the air, but play a major role in regulating the earth's temperature. By burning fossil fuels and forests, since 1750 people have increased the amount of carbon dioxide in the atmosphere by almost one-third. Almost all of that increase came after 1900, and three-fifths of it after 1950. Concurrently, the earth warmed up, slowly at first, but more rapidly after 1980. As a result, sea level has risen by about a foot since 1900. So far, these changes have had only a modest effect on life on earth. But unlike urban air pollution, it is a trend that will be impossible to check quickly, even if the will to do so exists, because carbon dioxide once in the atmosphere stays there for about a century. The range of plausible consequences includes some dire possibilities, such as shutting down the Gulf Stream, something that apparently happened in the distant past during warm eras. That would be, if it happens again, a gigantic disaster for Europe. The range of certain consequences includes further sea-level rise, perhaps enough to swamp a few island nations and some of the world's most fertile farmland in coastal river deltas.

Our political institutions, which evolved over millennia to cope with other challenges, proved ill suited to this and other large-scale but slow-moving environmental problems. The competitive international system impels states to maximize their wealth and power in the short run, assigning low priority to other concerns. Economic systems, whether capitalist or Communist, encouraged similar attitudes and conduct. The impetus for effective response to environmental ills came mainly from citizen agitation. That agitation typically focused on problems whose solution did not require any material sacrifice from the citizenry, nor much trust and cooperation across national boundaries. In rich countries in the 1980s, for example, it proved easy enough to reduce sulfur dioxide pollution from power plants or lead emissions from automobile exhausts by switching or altering fuels. But few people desired the sacrifices that seemed necessary to check carbon dioxide emissions or fertilizer runoff. The general approach in the twentieth century was to make the most of resources, harness nature to the utmost, sacrifice ecological buffers and tomorrow's resilience if need be, and hope for the best.

It may one day appear that this ecological tumult, particularly climate change and the reduction in biodiversity, was the most important development in the period after 1890, more so than ideological struggles or world wars. But one can reliably make that judgment only decades—or centuries—hence. In the meantime, let us turn to political and economic tumults, which the twentieth century had in full measure.

Retreat from Globalization: War and Depression, 1914–41

The rapid integration of the world's societies and economies after 1870 led many to suppose that war had become obsolete. In 1914, the outbreak of World War I shattered such fond hopes. The proximate cause was trivial: the assassination in Sarajevo of the heir to the throne of Austria-Hungary. The underlying reason for the war was the emergence of Germany as a great power. Its population grew far faster (1871–1914) than France's or Britain's. German urbanization and industrialization rates outstripped its neighbors' as well. That brought Britain and France, historic rivals, together after about 1900, and rival alliance systems soon formed involving all the major powers of Europe. At the same time, the Germans worried that Russia, with its vast resources, might soon overtake them as they had just overtaken Britain. The vigor of nationalism in every society made war easier to accept, as did ignorance of what war might entail.

An alliance of France, Britain, Russia, Italy, and eventually the

United States narrowly prevailed over Germany, Austria-Hungary, and the Ottoman Empire, and at great cost. Military medicine had progressed to the point where doctors could keep gigantic armies free of epidemics long enough that they could engage in the prolonged slaughter of trench warfare. Heavy artillery and poison gas made life in the trenches living hell, while the machine gun made climbing out of them extremely lethal. The war killed about 9–10 million combatants in all. Millions more civilians died, from hunger, disease, or violence. European imperial interests ensured that the war spread to Africa, Asia, and the Pacific, although without the mass butchery of the European battlefields. The war became one of attrition, of both men and morale. All armies except the German underwent mutinies within thirty-five months after the onset of heavy casualties. In the end, the contribution of fresh American men and resources decided the war.

As they poured more and more men into this meatgrinder, governments concluded they had to mobilize every aspect of their societies for the war effort, a practice now known as "total war." War production became too serious a business to be left to the market, so official planning boards took over most decision making in industry, transport, and agriculture. Factories recruited millions of women to make weapons, munitions, and uniforms. Despite frustrating bottlenecks, it turned out that war economies could quickly ratchet up levels of production. This record of success offered an example of government management of national economies that proved appealing afterward, in both war and peace.

The war shook the political and economic foundations of Europe, and reverberated throughout the world. The peace treaties created new countries out of Austria-Hungary's multinational empire, shrank Germany slightly, and imposed a large indemnity upon Germany for causing the war (as had been done on a smaller scale to France in 1815 after the Napoleonic Wars). They awarded some Ottoman territories to the victors —not directly, but through the mechanism of the League of Nations, an international body created in 1919–20 to manage future conflicts and prevent war. The Ottoman Empire collapsed in revolution (1919–23), as a secular, nationalist Turkey was born (see below). The Turks promptly abolished the caliphate of Islam, leaving the Muslim world without a religious head or political center. But the world of the victors came apart too.

The Russian Empire was the first to go. By 1917, the strains of industrial warfare proved too much for Russia. It had sent men to the front ill-prepared, sometimes even unarmed, and its army mutinied en masse. Urban populations protesting harsh conditions, especially bread prices, and the bad management of the war, met with repression. These discontents fused into revolution in the spring of 1917, bringing the abdication of the tsar. A new, provisional government fatally chose to continue the war effort, and in the fall of 1917 fell in a coup d'état known as the Bolshevik Revolution, organized by Vladimir Lenin (1870–1924). Lenin had been expelled from university, studied law on his own, but became a revolutionary by profession. He had educated himself in Marxist doctrine and once in power sought to recast Russia as a Communist society. He first had to make peace with Germany (March 1918) and win a Civil War (1918–21), which he did using command economy methods he had admired in the German war effort—Lenin spent World War I in Zurich, a good observation post. The country he created, the Soviet Union or USSR, remained ever after indebted to methods of economic management pioneered by Germany during World War I. It also emulated a Russian tradition of secret police and political repression, inherited from the tsars but carried to self-destructive extremes by Lenin and his followers.

Others among the Allies felt the strains of war too. Italy's government collapsed amid strikes and street violence (1919–22) giving rise to the fascist dictatorship of Benito Mussolini (1883–1945). Fascism repudiated democratic politics, rejected socialism, sought to mobilize the masses through a single political party, exalted the nation, and extolled martial virtues and the purifying effects of war. It appealed to millions who had suffered during the war and its aftermath, notably to war veterans who felt betrayed by (and scornful of) civilian authorities who had sat out the war in safety, and to victims of currency inflation who lost their life savings.

To millions in Europe and around the world, Russia and Italy seemed to offer appealing solutions to the troubles of the postwar age. The booms and busts of the market meant constant risk of unemployment or, for peasants, of ruinously low prices for the food they sold. Churches, political parties, labor unions, business associations, newspapers, universities—all had supported the war, and all suffered, to greater or lesser degrees, loss of prestige as a consequence. With the public appetite for new economic and political arrangements whetted, communism and fascism found many supporters in Europe, and a few in China, colonial India, the United States, and elsewhere. The Chinese Nationalists or Guomindang, heirs to the 1911 revolution of Sun Yat-sen, admired both Italian fascist economic policy and Leninist political organization, and tried to adapt them to China. Chinese Communists, the main rivals of the Guomindang, preferred the pure Soviet model. In this respect, internal power struggles in China (ca. 1925–40) echoed ideological struggles in Europe.

Part of the appeal of the Soviet and Italian models lay in the buffer they promised to provide against the buffeting of international markets. Both made economic self-sufficiency a high priority (although Italy never came close to achieving it). In World War I, international trade had fallen sharply. The combatants ceased trading with one another and energetically set about sinking one another's merchant ships, which the invention of the submarine made much easier. So shortages affected all participants, especially those most in need of imported food. Devising substitutes for lost imports became a crucial part of the war economies, but no one found a substitute for food. The USSR and Italy, determined not to suffer such shortages again, made autarky a peacetime policy. They also restricted emigration. Moreover, the peace treaties created a half dozen new countries in East-Central Europe, thus erecting new barriers to trade and migration. New, weak states, including the Weimar Republic of Germany, resorted to printing money to balance their budgets, bringing hyperinflation to the point where, in Germany in 1923, money became worthless and ordinary Germans could import nothing. So, although capital and trade flows recovered substantially in the 1920s, the fragmented political landscape and ambitions for autarky prevented the full resumption of the globalizing economy of the pre-1914 era.

What remained soon collapsed. After 1924, American loans allowed Germany to pay some of its war reparations to Britain and France, and soon Germans, British, and French resumed their imports from around the world: the international economy flickered back to life. But American loans dried up in 1928 when a stock market boom absorbed all available capital. Financing for exports from Latin America, Australia, and other agricultural regions evaporated too, bringing an agricultural depression. Then the American stock market crashed in 1929, loans were called in, and banks and firms suddenly went bankrupt. The fact that banks were linked in worldwide networks of loans ensured that the New York crash and the subsequent failure of 40 percent of American banks set off a chain reaction around the world. Soon millions of people lost their jobs in the industrial countries, and farmers around the world could not sell their crops. Given the memory of successful economic management during World War I, governments had to do something.

They did: they shattered the world economy in trying to save themselves. They put up tariffs, quotas, and other obstacles to trade. They devalued their currencies, raised taxes and lowered public spending to balance budgets, and some defaulted on bonds, bankrupting a few more enterprises. They abandoned the gold standard, making all international transactions more difficult. Each state tried to minimize imports so as to maximize production and employment at home. In short, by seeking national escapes from the depression, they deepened it internationally. By 1932, the world economy had shrunk by a fifth, world trade by a quarter. Unemployment levels in hard-hit countries like the United States, Canada, and Germany reached 20 to 30 percent. Food and raw material prices fell by half. Farmers and peasants around the world lost much of their incomes, and if they were in debt, often lost their lands.

The policies followed after 1929 sounded a retreat from globalization. The most autarkic economies seemed to weather the storm best. Italy suffered less than other countries, and the Soviet Union also appeared to, although in reality it was undergoing an acute economic crisis of its own. Lenin's successor, Joseph Stalin, sought to extend the revolution to the countryside by replacing family farms with collective and state farms. This aroused bitter opposition, which Stalin answered with desperate brutality. About 10 million peasants were killed or starved to death in 1932–33, and the Soviet economy contracted by perhaps a fifth. All this Stalin kept from the outside world, however, while trumpeting simultaneous—and very real—Soviet achievements in industrialization. Stalin aimed to end Soviet dependence on imported industrial and military goods. A planned national economy, which the USSR became after 1928, could not easily mesh with unpredictable swings in supply and demand normal in international markets. Autarky was the answer. State-sponsored industrialization also became policy in Mexico, Argentina, and Brazil, without Stalinist terror. Japan's military government renewed the emphasis on heavy industry and agriculture, hoping to make the country self-sufficient in weaponry and food. Almost everywhere governments aspired to build more autarkic national economies.

This proved fateful. Few of the governments in question survived the early years of the Great Depression. Mussolini and Stalin did, but voters turned out incumbents in every country where voting mattered, and in Germany, Hitler was appointed chancellor (1933) and soon put an end to voting. Dictatorships sprouted in most European countries, as well as in several Latin American ones. Colonial rule survived in Africa and Asia, although the depression years were lean ones for export trades; the hardships of peasants and miners added momentum to anticolonial agitation (discussed below). But the most important consequence of the turn to autarky in the 1930s was that it made states expansionist, particularly those without overseas empires. To be free from imports that seemed ruinously expensive in peacetime and would (the experience of World War I suggested) be unreliable in war, it made sense to acquire more territory and resources, or, in the case of imperial powers, to squeeze more out of what one already had.

Britain and France tried to get more from their existing empires. They wanted to develop the mineral and food exports from their African and Asian colonies, which required deeper interventions in daily life. These ranged from greater resort to forced labor to higher taxes (so as to oblige peasants to raise cash crops) to more benign but often unpopular measures to combat soil erosion or animal diseases. In general, colonial governments became more "developmental," that is, concerned to restructure society so as to maximize economic growth, usually through exports that could be taxed. This deepening intervention created classes of loyal Africans, Indians, and Vietnamese, who benefited from it. But it also created new centers of resentment against colonial rule, including many educated and politically conscious people. Some of the seeds of decolonization were sown in the 1930s.

While Britain and France sought to squeeze more from their overseas empires, the United States and USSR tried to develop their land empires. The U.S. government built big dams throughout the West, irrigating vast expanses and tapping the hydroelectric potential of all the big rivers. The Soviets built big dams too, and tried to harvest the mineral resources of Siberia and the Arctic, often with forced labor, and develop the agricultural potential of Central Asia. These American and Soviet efforts, both involving major environmental transformations, proved useful in the war years soon to come.

Meanwhile, Italy, Germany, and Japan pursued empires of their own. They all lacked crucial resources necessary to an autarkic economy, especially oil. Italy sought an empire in the Mediterranean and in the Horn of Africa, a quest that led to the conquest of Ethiopia in 1935–36, erasing the humiliation of 1896. Germany built an economic empire in southeastern Europe, luring smaller countries into exclusive trade agreements, and in 1938–39 annexed Austria and Czechoslovakia politically. Japan from 1931 seized Chinese territory, especially in Manchuria, a region rich in coal and iron ore. It also tried to harness Korea and Taiwan more tightly, and, on a smaller scale, to tap the agricultural potential of the Micronesian Islands it had acquired from Germany through the League of Nations after World War I. These quests for empire to make autarky more feasible brought on World War II.

On balance, the period from 1914 to 1940 saw a great disintegration of the world economy. As noted above, trade plummeted. Capital flows, never fully recovered from World War I, dwindled after 1929 and did not reach 1913 levels again until after World War II. The great era of migration stopped, partly because some countries forbade emigration and partly because the largest recipient of immigrants, the United States, adopted tight quotas in 1924. Brazil also restricted immigration in the 1920s. Germany cut back on immigrants (mainly Poles) in 1922. The flows of Indian and Chinese laborers to colonial mines and plantations slowed to trickles. Only France, with its low birth rate, made immigration easier. These were deep changes, and very disruptive to prosperity based upon free movement of goods, capital, and people. They undermined the politics of liberalism and advanced the idea that governments should direct economic life. They also provoked disillusionment with accepted cultural and religious ideas and thus a new willingness to experiment with new forms. In a nutshell, globalization after 1870 and war after 1914 generated resentments and fears that fed nationalism and the quest for autarky, thus undermining the cooperation and restraint necessary for a global economy, and for peace.

But the cosmopolitan web did not unravel. Links remained in place: that is precisely why the depression spread worldwide. Tariff wars bound governments together more tightly than before. And in some respects the velocity and intensity of interaction within the web increased, even as the international economy disintegrated. Radio and the automobile began to make deeper impacts in this period. Many business firms, especially American and Japanese ones, grew more international in the 1920s. In many countries, politics became more participatory. Communist and fascist parties in some cases became genuinely mass parties, and Communist ones attempted international cooperation. Trade unions became more politically active, as did employers' associations. The greatest expansion of political life came with female suffrage. With the participation of women in the war effort in World War I the logic of excluding women from political rights became unpersuasive, and from 1918 more and more democracies permitted women to vote.

Moreover, although international migration slowed after 1914, military migrations quickened. Millions moved around during World War I, expanding their horizons and absorbing new influences. Britain and France drew heavily on the manpower of their empires, bringing Indians, Arabs, and Africans to the battlefronts. Legions of Canadians, Australians, New Zealanders, and South Africans fought in Europe and elsewhere, as did Americans. When these troops returned home they spread the first truly global pandemic in history, the influenza of 1918–19, which killed about 40 million people—many more than died in the war itself.

In international politics, war and its aftermath also promoted tighter interaction, both competitive and cooperative. The pitiless military competition of World War I brought a closer interaction, both among allies who had to integrate their planning and operations, and among enemies who had to study one another closely and copy successful innovations quickly. Communism after 1918 also fostered political cooperation of a sort, because Communists believed that ultimately revolution had to succeed globally to succeed at all, so they tried hard to coordinate activities across boundaries, mainly through an international body known as the Comintern. This Communist cooperation diminished in the late 1920s when Stalin reversed official doctrine and launched the slogan, "Socialism in one country." But he continued to support Communists here and there, and by the late 1930s did so actively during the Spanish Civil War. For that matter, the Nazi persecution of Jews in the 1930s provoked an exodus of learned refugees (such as Albert Einstein) to Britain, the United States, and elsewhere, thus bringing an additional measure of integration to the intellectual sphere.

World War I also inspired new institutions intended to broker competition. A handful of international organizations had arisen in the 1800s, mostly with specific mandates such as the International Telegraph Union (1868) or the Universal Postal Union (1874). But in 1919 several more were hatched. The League of Nations was the most important, including as it did several subsidiary bodies charged with regulating labor standards, refugees, agriculture, and so forth. National soccer federations cooperated to launch the World Cup tournaments, first held in Uruguay in 1930. So the breakdown of the world economy reversed the globalizing momentum of the decades before 1914, and slowed but did not halt the advance of integration in other spheres.

Resurgent Globalization:
War and the Long Boom Since 1941

The League of Nations proved unequal to the tasks it faced. The United States, which had done the most to create it, refused to join, as did the USSR until 1934. The League lacked the power to check the expansionist ambitions of Italy, Japan, and Germany, who formed a loose alliance in 1936, known as the Axis. The combination of their belligerence and the League's impotence obliged the USSR, France, Britain, and the United States to prepare for war.

WORLD AT WAR, 1937–45

World War II was the largest, most destructive struggle in history. Dozens of countries took part, but at root it combined four distinct conflicts. Chronologically, the first conflict pitted Japan against a disorganized and divided China, where large-scale warfare began in 1937. To pursue its war in China, Japan needed oil from Indonesia, then controlled by the Dutch. When the United States, Britain, and the Netherlands combined to restrict oil sales to Japan in August 1941, the Japanese embarked on a desperate gamble, attacking Pearl Harbor and opening a second conflict across the Pacific. The Japanese had little hope of defeating the United States, but thought they might hobble the U.S. Navy long enough to build an impregnable imperial position in East Asia, from which the United States could not dislodge them except at costs unacceptable to a democratic and supposedly soft society.

Meanwhile, in Europe, Hitler's Germany, emboldened by its peaceful annexations of Austria and the Sudetenland in 1938, and its unobstructed occupation of the rest of Czechoslovakia in 1939, attacked Poland in September of that year, precipitating declarations of war from Britain and France. Germany quickly overran Poland in 1939 and France in 1940, but Britain held out. Britain, and soon the United States, fought German and Italian forces in the Atlantic, the Mediterranean, and Western Europe (the third conflict). The fourth conflict came when Hitler attacked the USSR in June 1941, another desperate gamble, further widening his war. Hitler harbored deep personal hatred of Slavs and Jews, and by attacking the USSR he intended to obliterate them, creating empty lands in the east for German settlement, a plan that would make an autarkic greater Germany possible.

All these conflicts lasted until 1945. The Japanese and the Germans had to win quickly if they were to win at all, because the Allies' economies could handily outproduce the Axis. The USSR was pre-adapted to a war economy. It had used command economy methods from 1918 and economic planning since 1928. It specialized in hasty improvisation; its culture extolled frantic mobilization of the sort that built factories from scratch in a week, and encouraged (some might say obliged) women to work in field and factory. And its peasants and prole-tarians had developed a high tolerance for spartan conditions. The United States was also pre-adapted to a war economy by its "genius for mass production,"[5] its huge production runs, its tradition of entrepre-neurial innovation and ruthless quests for efficiency. The United States created a huge military-industrial complex in one year, 1942, during which it alone outproduced the Axis in quantities of war materiel by about two to one. In 1944, the Ford Motor Company assembled a B-24 bomber every sixty-three minutes on a mile-long assembly line outside Detroit; Ford alone outproduced Italy in the war. The shipyards of the Pacific coast, using electricity made available by the newly built large dams, assembled cargo ships in eight days. The United States built six-teen warships for every one launched in Japan. The USSR, despite much lower skill levels in its labor force and great disruptions due to lost territory, outproduced Germany in every year of the war. Germany and Japan had a head start of several years in armaments production, but their militaries insisted on high-quality goods and, unwisely, despised the shoddy fruits of mass production. They could not quickly ratchet up their armaments output. They did not have enough men to staff factories and battlefronts simultaneously (and the Nazis did not approve of women doing factory work), and they did not have enough oil. The Allies had more raw materials, almost all of the world's oil, more men, and they eagerly recruited women for war work, even for combat in the Soviet case. In addition, thanks to clever decipherment, the Allies could read their enemies' secret codes. Finally, the Axis never achieved anything like the degree of economic and strategic cooperation that the Allies, especially Britain and the United States, managed. So, once the Allies had withstood the initial assaults of 1940–41, their chance of winning improved daily. They won when the Soviet Army smashed its way into

---

[5] Franklin Roosevelt's words. Hermann Goering derided American industry as capable only of producing razor blades.

Berlin in May 1945, and when American airmen dropped atomic bombs on Hiroshima and Nagasaki three months later.

World War II killed about 3 percent of the world's 1940 population, some 60 million people, including large numbers of civilians. It was a war of movement, mainly because of new technologies such as the tank and aircraft. So armies and civilians came in routine contact, with sometimes horrible consequences, especially in China, and in Eastern Europe where the Soviet and German armies fought. The Germans and their accomplices also murdered about 6 million Jews. Most of the fighting, and especially the dying, took place in eastern China and the western USSR. The USSR lost perhaps 25 million to the war, two-thirds of them civilians, Poland lost 6 million (half of whom were Jews), Germany 4.5 million, Japan 2.4 million, Yugoslavia 1.6 million, and China maybe 15 million, although that figure is only a guess. The Americans, whose factories did so much to win the war, lost 290,000 in battle and 400,000 in all, about the same as Britain and Greece, rather less than France.

The Cold War World

The United States emerged from World War II as the first global superpower. Imperial Rome and China had held unrivaled sway regionally, but never before had any state exercised such global reach. The United States had the world's biggest navy, it had (briefly) a monopoly on nuclear weapons, it had (briefly) about half the world's industrial capacity, and all the world owed its bankers money. It also enjoyed great prestige. Some of these advantages were simply the result of victory and the prostration of the other major powers: the United States had not had its cities flattened, its industries blown up, its population decimated. But others derived from longer-term processes dating back to the 1800s. The United States had become the world's largest industrial power around 1890, and for the next forty years was the "tiger" of the world economy, growing at five to seven percent per year. The key to American power, amply demonstrated in World War II, was the efficiency of its heavy industry, symbolized by the moving assembly line, which made production faster and cheaper. Henry Ford installed the first electrified assembly line in a car factory in 1912. His workers hated it, and he had to pay double the going rate to keep them. This allowed them to become his customers as well: two months' wages could buy a Model-T Ford. The symbiosis of mass production methods and a comparatively well paid labor force amounted to a social contract (sometimes called Fordism) that undergirded American democracy after World War I. As millions of workers became consumers, businesses enjoyed larger and larger production runs, lowering their costs further. Cheap energy and mass production made U.S. industrial firms the most competitive in the world. This allowed them to export successfully and to build subsidiary plants using American-style techniques overseas, which they did energetically in the 1920s. The depression and World War II interrupted the emergence of American business on the world scene, but after 1945 American business enjoyed a double windfall. Industry elsewhere lay in ruins and the American government was prepared, as never before, to undertake management of the world economy.

Remembering the fiascos of peacemaking in 1919, the Allies in World War II insisted upon unconditional surrender so they could dictate terms to Germany and Japan. The Allies quickly quarreled, but nonetheless managed to reconstruct a stable order very quickly. The Americans did most of the managing. They sponsored and bankrolled a new slate of international institutions intended to make sure that the disasters of depression and world war did not recur. The United Nations was expected to look after issues of world politics. Agreements and institutions were hatched to attend to the world's financial system (the Bretton Woods Agreement giving rise to the International Monetary Fund or IMF, and the World Bank), international trade (General Agreement on Trade and Tariffs, forerunner of the World Trade Organization), health (World Health Organization), and much more. The point was to succeed where the League of Nations had failed: to check nationalism, autarky, militarism, and other evils by enrolling countries in a set of clubs with rules. This new regime was intended to reglobalize the world, but in a less anarchic way than had happened between 1870 and 1914, so that the resentments that experience generated would not erupt again.

Domestic policy in the United States and most of its allies followed this general goal: it was designed to soften the blows inherent in participating in the international economy. This took various forms, but usually involved commitments to full employment and/or unemployment insurance, pensions, and subsidies for farmers and some other primary producers (often the coal or oil industries). It obliged the state to regulate social and economic life, raise taxes to levels formerly reached only in wartime, and cultivate the arts of economic management. As ancient states had rested on an alliance between throne and altar, and could not do without their high priests, modern ones came to depend on an alliance between cabinet and boardroom (government and business), with economists increasingly serving as the high priests.

So the United States, with a little help from its friends, organized a new international regime based ultimately on American economic and military power, but mediated by a set of international agreements and institutions. It was, in some ways, an extension of the wartime cooperation after 1941, and in other ways a reaction to the depression and its autarkic policies. It was, in essence, a search for security from the horrors of 1914–45 in a form compatible with American traditions and preferences.

This postwar arrangement nudged the world toward reglobalization. It raised the speed limits on the cosmopolitan web, as information, money, goods, and technology all began to move around much faster than before 1945. Thanks to its power and prestige, the United States achieved a high degree of political and military cooperation among its friends. U.S. allies found the rewards of taking part in this arrangement usually outweighed the irksomeness of American arrogance. Thanks to the new rules, the efficiency of its industry, and some occasional help from the government, U.S. businesses after 1945 spearheaded a rapid— but partial—economic reglobalization.

Stalin mistrusted the whole enterprise. He remembered that the United States, Britain, and Japan had tried to quash the Bolshevik Revolution by intervening in the Russian Civil War. He suspected that in World War II the Americans and British had delayed opening a second front (originally promised in 1942 but only delivered in June 1944 with the D-Day landings in France) so as to let the USSR bear the brunt of fighting the Germans. His ideological training told him that capitalism was communism's mortal foe. And he was by nature mistrustful to the point of paranoia.

He wanted a postwar order that ensured that the USSR would never relive the rigors of 1941–45. His highest priorities were a weak Germany and the creation of pliant buffer states between the USSR and Germany. He did not care about safeguarding the world economy from depression, since he could not expose his planned economy to its chaotic swings anyway. When the Americans showed an inclination to rebuild Germany and Japan in their quest for a revitalized world economy, this looked to Stalin like conspiracy against the USSR. Stalin had the largest army in the world in 1945, and because much of it was in Eastern Europe, he was able to get the pliant buffer states he wanted, including the eastern third of Germany. He joined the United Nations in 1945 but refused to take part in the institutions erected to manage the world economy, and declined to accept any share of the money that the United States offered to Europe for reconstruction through the Marshall Plan, begun in 1947. Stalin used the tool he had, the Red Army, to consolidate control over Eastern Europe, which included removing much of its industry to the USSR. The Americans, meanwhile, used the tool they had, money, to rebuild Western Europe's industry and thereby create bonds that assured voluntarily pliant states, especially Britain and West Germany. The U.S.-Soviet rivalry became the Cold War, in full career by 1948.

Chinese peasants and Soviet physicists improved Stalin's position in the Cold War in 1949. First, his physicists, with help from his spies, provided him with an atomic bomb, ending the American monopoly—a long stride toward military parity. Then, in October, a peasant army directed by the Chinese Communist Party, itself led by Mao Zedong, defeated the Guomindang in a civil war and reunified China. In World War II the Japanese had claimed they were going to stamp out communism in China, but they inadvertently helped bring it to power (as Hitler inadvertently helped make the USSR a superpower). Mao's forces had shown themselves more committed and heroic in fighting the Japanese, and usually abstained from the reckless abuse of peasant populations that the Guomindang troops engaged in. The Communists offered a program that bore strong resemblance to that of the Taipings nearly a century before: peasants should dispossess landlords, women should be free from male oppression, Confucian hierarchy should be replaced by social equality, discipline and morality should prevail—and foreigners should go home. It replaced the idiosyncratic syncretic theology of the Taipings with an ideology that accommodated Marxist principles, as refracted through Lenin's writings and Soviet experience, to Chinese realities. Whereas Marx had complained of the "idiocy of rural life," and the Soviets had ruthlessly exploited the USSR's peasants, Mao proclaimed that peasants (of which China had many, including Mao's parents), and not merely proletarians (of which China had few), could be a revolutionary class. With this program, good military organization, excellent lieutenants, a little help from Stalin and a lot from Guomindang ineptitude, Mao won control over mainland China (not Taiwan) by October 1949.

The Chinese Revolution briefly created a Communist bloc of a size to rival the American-led one. It showed its strength in the Korean War

(1950–53) when Chinese armies fought successfully against an American-led coalition, leaving Korea divided. But the Chinese and Soviets never achieved smooth cooperation. They had doctrinal differences about Marxism. They had a history of intermittent Russo-Chinese friction dating back to the 1680s. They both had strong nationalist leanings and favored economic autarky. They had conflicting ideas about how to confront the capitalist enemy: Stalin and, after his death in 1953, his successors took a cautious approach, whereas Mao thought there were enough Chinese that he could afford to risk nuclear attack by the Americans. This cavalier position understandably scared the wits out of the Soviets.[6]

So, ten years after they had become allies in socialist solidarity, China and the USSR had a falling out: this was the beginning of the end for the USSR. In 1968–69, their armies clashed along their long frontier. Henceforth, the Soviets felt they had to station a good chunk of their military forces along the Chinese border. Then, in the early 1970s, China played the American card, initiating diplomacy with the United States that left the Soviets feeling encircled. All this added to military costs that their economy could ill afford to bear. By the 1970s, they had approached the limits of what their command economy could achieve. They had shifted most of the peasantry into urban employment while mechanizing most agriculture. They had put women to work outside the domestic sphere on a large scale (obliging Soviet women to shoulder the double burdens of wage work plus domestic work, a powerful disincentive to childbearing). Both these shifts raised productivity significantly. But these were cards that could only be played once. The Soviet system discouraged technical and organizational innovation because there was no competitive market for goods, no rewards for innovators. So the Soviets extended an industrial system built on coal and steel, the cutting edge of the 1870s, instead of constantly reinventing it. This made it technically and financially difficult to maintain a formidable military-industrial complex. Soviet agriculture missed out on crop-breeding

---

[6] In 1957, Mao told Premier Nikita Khrushchev: "We shouldn't be afraid of atomic missiles. No matter what kind of war breaks out—conventional or thermonuclear—we'll win. As for China, if the imperialists unleash war on us, we may lose more than 300 million people. So what? War is war. The years will pass and we'll get to work producing more babies than ever before." *Khrushchev Remembers: The Last Testament,* trans. and ed. Strobe Talbott (Boston, 1974), 255. Or so Khrushchev claimed: he had reasons to disparage Mao.

developments, remained stagnant, and by the late 1970s could not feed the Soviet population.

In the 1960s and 1970s, Soviet rulers responded to these weaknesses by becoming a major exporter of Siberian oil and gas to Western Europe. Moreover, cheap oil helped bond the Eastern European satellites, who could not afford world prices, to the Soviet empire. When world oil prices tripled in 1973 and again in 1979, the USSR briefly became a giant oil sheikdom, able to import consumer goods, new technology, and, gallingly, American grain. This bubble burst when oil prices collapsed in 1984–86, undermining Soviet finances. The Soviet economy had become less autarkic, and found itself once again vulnerable to the whiplash of international price fluctuations.

Soviet political legitimacy suffered too. New contacts and communications undermined the Soviet social contract. The USSR had always justified daily hardships with extravagant promises of a rosy future. This seemed plausible for a while, especially when the economy grew briskly. Ordinary citizens by the 1950s knew they were materially better off than their parents and grandparents, and if they had to accept tight political control, that seemed acceptable to many. This was the social contract of the USSR. As long as the economy performed satisfactorily, it worked well enough that after Stalin's death the repressive police state could relax somewhat. But after the 1970s it became increasingly obvious that the USSR's economy could not continue to deliver the goods. When the tight grip on information was relaxed, some people learned—via travel, movies, or West German TV available in East Germany—the degree to which they were doing without. New information changed their frame of reference: it no longer seemed so relevant that they were better off than their grandparents when they were visibly worse off than Germans or Italians. To make matters worse, the Soviets invaded Afghanistan in 1979 to shore up a client dictator, but ended up fighting a long, vicious, and unpopular war. By the mid-1980s, almost no one believed in the Soviet dream any more.

With both finances and legitimacy crumbling, the leader who took over in 1985, Mikhail Gorbachev (born 1931), desperately allowed more freedom of information and expression, hoping to revive the economy by exposing Soviet society to new ideas and technologies. A fire in a nuclear reactor at Chernobyl in 1986, initially covered up by Soviet officials, became an embarrassing international disaster, sprinkling radiation throughout the northern hemisphere—and underscoring the necessity of a more open society. But openness let the genie of minority—and Russian—nationalisms out of the bottle and Gorbachev was not prepared to stuff it back in. He had been only thirteen years old when German troops left Soviet soil, and he did not feel the visceral attachment to the buffer states of Eastern Europe that all his predecessors had. In 1953, 1956, and 1968, Soviet troops had quelled uprisings in Eastern Europe. As late as 1981, when Polish workers led an uprising in Gdansk, Soviet authorities ruthlessly pressured the Polish government to suppress it. But Gorbachev saw things differently, and his views narrowly prevailed over hard-liners who wanted to rely on trusted policies of repression at home and adventurism abroad. In 1989, Gorbachev refused to intervene to prevent East Germans from fleeing to West Germany, and soon the entire set of buffer states had slipped from the Soviet orbit. Then in 1991 the USSR itself fell apart, largely because its Russian component sought greater authority, and its other fourteen constituent republics acquired their independence from Moscow. The Soviets lost the Cold War for the same reason the Axis lost World War II: they could not create an interactive, cooperative, innovative, international economy to match the American-led one. They remained too wedded to the autarkic economy Stalin had built, which could not sustain global political competition for long. The reason they lost the Cold War *peacefully* was that Gorbachev prevailed over his elders and rivals.

Yet the Cold War was not all competition. Although locked in struggle, the United States and the USSR cooperated too. The Americans and the Soviets had a strong mutual interest in preventing large-scale war. They succeeded in this, paradoxically, by building huge nuclear arsenals so that the costs of all-out war became unacceptable to sane people, and happily no insane ones came to power. They also unwillingly shared information by spying on one another so effectively that neither side could hide much from the other. By the 1980s, spy satellites could detect anything on the ground larger than a beer keg. The Americans and Soviets checked the belligerence of their most reckless generals, politicians, and overseas clients, allowing only proxy wars fought in poor regions (Angola, Southeast Asia) where defeat or victory mattered—to them at any rate—mainly in terms of prestige. From the late 1950s, the two superpowers engaged in academic and cultural exchanges. In the 1970s, such cooperation intensified, trade links developed, and leaders even revived the practice of summit meetings that Stalin and Roosevelt had inaugurated.

And of course the pressures of the Cold War encouraged unusually close cooperation among the United States and its allies. Not only did it underwrite the international institutions mentioned above, the United States oversaw the reconstruction of Japan and permitted access to American markets for Japanese business. It created numerous military alliances in Europe, South Asia, and East Asia. It financed academic exchanges on an unprecedented scale. Its corporations set up shop in dozens of countries and it allowed foreign firms to operate in the United States. Indeed, this sort of cooperation was a big part of what made the American side more formidable than the Soviet one. The Soviets, for their part, despite their rift with the Chinese and the uprisings in Eastern Europe, organized an economically loose but militarily tight cooperation among their allies. And several states of Western Europe, led by former rivals France and Germany, formed the European Economic Community (EEC) in the 1950s, intended among other things to prevent the United States and the USSR from fully dominating Europe. The EEC gradually embraced both more countries and more responsibilities. By the 1990s, now called the European Union, it functioned as something of a superstate, exerting strong pressures on members to conform in matters of economic, agricultural, and migration policy, and weaker pressures in matters of the environment, education, or technical standards. Thus, the Cold War, while on the surface an affair of relentless competition, furthered cooperation and integration, mostly on the American side, but also within the Soviet bloc and even between the two blocs.

DECOLONIZATION

While the great powers engaged in hot and cold wars, they lost their empires. By 1914, the industrial powers had acquired dominion over most of the globe, and in the 1930s, Japan and Italy extended their empires into China and Ethiopia respectively. But as early as 1918, the world's empires began to unravel under the strains of total war, the impact of nationalisms, the diffusion of information in general, and the arts of political mobilization in particular. By 1960, the technological and military gaps separating the weakest from the strongest were greater than in 1914, but even the weakest were becoming well enough organized to convince their colonial masters that imperialism did not pay.

World War I had broken up the Russian, Ottoman, and Austro-Hungarian empires in western Eurasia. The Bolsheviks quickly reconstituted the Russian one, equipping it with new ideology and accepting different borders, but restoring centralized bureaucratic empire. The Ottoman Empire vanished forever. It had lost most of its Balkan territory before 1914 to the surging nationalisms of Greeks, Serbs, and Bulgarians. It lost its Arab lands in the 1919 peace settlement, which awarded them to France and Britain through the League of Nations. A similar parceling out of Turkish territory was planned, but the Turkish nationalist revolution, led by Mustafa Kemal (1881–1938), prevented that. Kemal happily accepted the end of empire, preferring to found a Turkish nation-state, but he refused to let Kurds (a large minority in eastern Turkey) go their way, bequeathing a vexing problem to modern Turkey. The Austro-Hungarian Empire dissolved into four separate European states in 1919, each with its own restless ethnic minorities (bits of the empire were also awarded to other nearby states). So the initial burst of decolonization created only a few new states before it ended, and left plenty of problems for the future. Three of the new states (Poland, Czechoslovakia, Hungary) became Soviet satellites in the late 1940s, and thus had to achieve independence a second time in 1989–90.

Ireland, or at least most of it, also won independence from Britain after World War I. Irish agitation for freedom dated back centuries, motivated by economic grievance and Catholic-Protestant friction, but during World War I Irish nationalists took advantage of Britain's heavy commitment in France and organized a rebellion in 1916. British troops suppressed it, but after the war the British government decided that maintaining a grip on Ireland would be too costly. So after much negotiation the Republic of Ireland was born in 1922, leaving only the small territory of Northern Ireland, with its majority of Protestants, in British hands. This arrangement too left many problems for the future.

A second and larger burst of decolonization came between 1943 and 1975, liberating most of the world's colonies. The key to this process was the political restructuring of colonial societies. Original efforts at resistance to industrial imperialism had been violent and often suicidal. The struggle required new weapons. Africans, Indians, and others took advantage of the opportunities made available by the new communications and transport technologies. Some studied in Europe or the United States and learned about political struggles elsewhere. They formed political pressure groups, the first of note being the Congress (now the Congress Party), founded in India as early as 1885. These groups tried to harness the bonding power of nationalism, which worked well in ethnically homogenous colonies such as Vietnam or Korea. Elsewhere nationalists forged transethnic political alliances, trying to create a nation where none had existed before. This was especially important in Africa, where ethnic fragmentation prevailed, partly a result of divide-and-rule policies of colonial states. Anticolonial intellectuals made common cause across the world from the 1920s. The depression made life harder in most colonies, raising rebellious sentiments higher. Colonial economies generally had a vulnerability that well-organized anticolonial nationalists could exploit. State revenues depended on exports of crops or minerals, which passed through the bottlenecks of railroad lines and ports. So, when railwaymen or dockers went on strike, the colonial state risked insolvency, a fact eagerly exploited by nationalists from the 1930s on.

In many ways, World War II set the stage for the final drama. Millions of men from India, Indochina, Africa, and elsewhere had their horizons broadened by overseas military service. They learned modern military skills. They heard American and British propaganda explain that the war was fought for freedom. Some of them, especially in India and North Africa, heard Japanese and German propaganda tell them that the hour had come to cast off the shackles of colonial rule. Moreover, World War II completely destroyed the empires of Italy and Japan, soon freeing Ethiopians, Libyans, and Koreans from foreign control. It also weakened the finances and resolve of France, Holland, and Britain. In the course of the war Syria and Lebanon became fully independent from France. And, after decades of boycotts, strikes, and marches against British rule, in World War II Indians made considerable blood sacrifice on behalf of the British, rendering it possible for them to negotiate their independence in 1947.

Elsewhere after the war, France, Holland, and Britain tried to reassert colonial control, notably in Southeast Asia where the Japanese army had driven them out in 1941–42. But rising nationalisms in Southeast Asia now required a stronger commitment than the colonial powers could make. The Dutch gave up in Indonesia in 1949, turning the country over to men who had honed their political and military skills in cooperating with the Japanese occupiers. Vietnamese forces humiliated the French in 1954, but because the anticolonial nationalists were also Communists, the United States gradually made France's war its own. This led to a long and bloody struggle before the Americans gave up in 1975.

In Africa, the war mattered too, if less so than in Asia. Again, the underlying issue was the development of political organization, skill, and commitment on the part of anticolonial nationalists. They raised the costs of continued imperialism beyond the level that France and Britain could stomach. At first, as in Southeast Asia, the colonial powers tried to strengthen their control, and invested in new infrastructure and economic development schemes. In this they sought cooperation from among the educated elite, and also the blessing of the United States, which had its doubts about continued European colonialism, at least where Communists were not involved.

But events overtook these plans. A nasty and increasingly unpopular war in Algeria (1954–62) finally convinced France to give up its empire in Africa. Algerian and Moroccan manpower had become essential to the French colonial forces due to the scarcity of young Frenchmen, so with the loss of its North African colonies France could not resist mounting pressures for independence. The Suez crisis in 1956 exposed further weaknesses of France—and of Britain. In response to quarrels over the financing of the Aswan Dam project, Egypt's leader, Colonel Nasser, seized the Suez Canal, hitherto managed by the British. Britain, France, and Israel mounted a surprise attack on Egypt, but the United States threatened to cut off the oil and dollars that kept Britain and France afloat, forcing a humiliating withdrawal. France and Britain needed full American support to withstand the challenges posed by anticolonial nationalism, and they clearly did not have it. Partisans of African independence took note and took heart, redoubling their efforts. By 1963, almost all of Africa had acquired its freedom, though in Mozambique and Angola nationalists had to fight on until 1975 against Portugal.

The next stage of decolonization came with the collapse of the USSR, described above. Several small islands and enclaves remain colonies, dependencies, or UN trust territories today, although their combined population is tiny. China remains an empire of sorts, controlling Muslim and Tibetan populations that, if free to choose, would certainly go their own ways. So does Indonesia, an archipelago in which several populations would probably prefer to be free from Javanese control. But, unmistakably, the Age of Empire created by the great inequalities forged in the eighteenth and nineteenth centuries is now past. The subordination of the weak to the strong takes other forms.

The dismantling of empires since 1918 created well over a hundred new countries. Most of them remained weak and subservient to powerful outsiders. The political skills that hastened decolonization did not easily translate into good government. Transethnic unity proved elusive once the imperial master was gone. Successful industrialization required investment, skills, and markets that often scarcely existed. Rapid population growth made it hard to maintain living standards, especially in Africa. The most economically successful ex-colonies were both among the most brutally ruled (South Korea) and most gently (Cyprus, Hong Kong). They owed their good fortune to their comparatively well educated populations, to ethnic solidarity that made nationalism a force for unity (Cyprus excepted), and in some cases to their strategic location that inclined the United States to favor them. A prosperous and stable South Korea and Taiwan, for example, helped in the struggle against communism in East Asia, so financial assistance and access to American markets suited American interests there.

The de-Sovietized states after 1991 fared poorly too. Their economies shrank by 10–30 percent as their industries proved uncompetitive internationally. Uzbekistan, for example, had specialized in growing the world's lowest quality cotton, which after 1991 found few buyers. Many ex-Soviet states had little coal or oil of their own and after 1991 missed Soviet energy subsidies. Russia itself collapsed economically, in sharp contrast to the experience of Japan, Britain, France, Portugal, and Holland, each of which enjoyed record prosperity after dismantling empires. The Soviet years had saddled all the successor states with acute environmental problems, latent (and now resurgent) ethnic struggles, and singularly stodgy political elites. Of the former Soviet satellites, Poland, Hungary, and the Czech Republic seemed the best candidates to emulate South Korea and Taiwan, able to harness nationalism, create a stable polity with some legitimacy, and haltingly embark on the road to prosperity.

THE LONG BOOM AND REGLOBALIZATION

An American bluesman, John Lee Hooker, recorded a song in 1962 that began with the words: "Boom, boom, boom, boom." This serves as a good summary of the second half of the twentieth century. Population, energy use, and the production of scientific knowledge and technology all underwent long booms, as noted at the outset of this chapter. The fourth long boom occurred in the world economy. It was a result mainly of the other three, but it also helped advance each of them. The first three were in force for the entire century, and indeed before it, but the economic boom came only after 1950 or so. Thereafter, all four long booms co-evolved, mutually propelling one another.

Soon after World War II ended, the global economy entered its most remarkable era, growing sixfold between 1950 and 1998. Indeed, in the quarter century before 1973, the world's economy grew at nearly 5 percent per year, and 3 percent per year per capita. But even when economic growth slowed after 1973, it galloped faster than at any time before 1950. Taken as a whole, this era is the most unusual in the history of economic growth, although many people, having experienced nothing else, now imagine it is normal.

It happened because of oil and energy, medicine and population growth, science and technology—the three long booms. It also happened because married women had fewer children, and so entered (and stayed) in the paid labor force in unprecedented numbers, and because farmers left the land at record pace for urban jobs. Each of these was a singular, unrepeatable social transformation that added greatly to GNP numbers. More specifically, the long economic boom also happened because modern industrial techniques, such as electrified factories, spread to some very populous lands. In Europe, postwar reconstruction of the industrial landscape brought rapid growth from 1950 to 1973. But the two great examples of this were Japan, where economic growth between 1950 and 1973 averaged nearly 10 percent annually, and China, where from 1978 to 1998 it averaged nearly 8 percent. China's economic policies after the 1949 revolution had included truly disastrous components, notably collectivization of agriculture and an industrialization scheme (the "Great Leap Forward") intended to make China more autarkic, and to allow China to surpass Britain in steel production, a target of symbolic importance to Mao. The Great Leap Forward generated vast tonnage of very bad steel and a famine that killed 20–40 million Chinese. After Mao's death in 1976, China reoriented, ended the collective farms, and liberalized rules in industry and trade. Shifting hundreds of millions of people into more productive work yielded spectacular results in China: the original market society took to market liberalization with zeal. Equally impressive growth took place among some far smaller populations of East Asia after 1980—South Korea, Taiwan, Hong Kong, and Singapore, for example. All together, this amounted to a real great leap forward in East Asia.

The long boom also happened because of the reglobalization of the world economy, which yielded all the usual returns from specialization and exchange. The international institutions created in the 1940s helped in this regard, as, perhaps more fundamentally, did the American commitment to open U.S. markets to the exports of Europe and East Asia. That commitment wavered, and in any case never extended to some sectors (e.g., agriculture), but it was a crucial political ingredient in the recipe of post-1950 world economic growth. Reglobalization intensified competition among firms, and the fortunate ones responded with innovations that dramatically raised productivity so that, for example, steelmakers increasingly could wring more steel out of the same amounts of iron ore, coal, and labor.

Trade played a big part in the long economic boom. In 1950, the share of goods produced for export was about the same as in 1870, and much lower than in 1913. But that share doubled between 1950 and 1973, and tripled by 1995. The biggest increases took place in trans-Pacific trade, much assisted by the new technology of container shipping, invented in the 1950s but routine from the 1970s. Containers were big boxes of standard size that could travel by truck, train, or ship, and thus required far less handling, packing and unpacking, than had earlier methods. This reduced the time it took goods to get from Hong Kong to New York by two-thirds, cut labor costs sharply by putting legions of longshoremen out of work, and made the thorough participation of East Asia in the international trading economy much more practical.

As the world grew richer, the proportion of income spent on food declined. The export of food from places such as Argentina, Australia, Canada, or the United States, so important in the era 1870–1913, mattered much less, shifting world trade patterns. Now trade increasingly exchanged manufactures for other manufactures. During the long boom, about three-quarters of world trade took place among Japan, Europe and North America. Especially between 1945 and 1975, the integration of the world economy took place chiefly among the former autarkic blocs of the interwar period. After 1980, however, trade increasingly involved manufactures from Brazil, Mexico, China, India, Indonesia—big, populous countries with low wages. Most African countries remained on the margins and gained little from the expansion of world trade.

The resurgence of capital flows eventually became a still bigger part of the long boom. The Marshall Plan was but a start. In the 1950s and 1960s, capital moved faster and in greater absolute volumes than ever before (although as a proportion of total investment, at lower levels than in 1870–1913). A good chunk of it came as so-called direct foreign investment, whereby a firm in one country opened a factory or a mine in another, thereby becoming a multinational corporation or MNC. Direct foreign investment involved MNCs in the politics of host countries, as they wanted wages kept low, advantageous trade policies, tax breaks or subsidies if possible; in general, a generous host. Rich MNCs came to wield considerable clout within small, poor, or bureaucratically corrupt countries. In short, from the 1950s onward, MNCs, because their investments involved them deeply in host societies, became important conduits of information, money, and power within the cosmopolitan web.

Capital flows accelerated when a great "financialization" of the world economy began in the late 1970s. The difficulties of the 1970s (slower growth, higher unemployment and inflation) were mainly due to higher energy costs associated with the tripling of oil prices in 1973 and again in 1979, itself mainly a political matter. But among the responses was an intellectual and policy shift toward liberalization of the rules governing capital flows, beginning in the United States, the United Kingdom, Chile, and a few other countries. This newly relaxed regulatory environment combined with new technologies to make it far easier to make money in finance rather than in production or trade. Telecommunications and networked computers drastically changed the ways of doing business, allowing instantaneous transactions all over the world at negligible costs. A tiny rise in an interest rate could cause the overnight migration of huge sums.

Whereas in 1870–1914 the great majority of international capital flows took the form of long-term investment in bonds, railroads, or factories, after 1980 it increasingly was short-term, restless capital looking for the opportunity of the moment—a currency or stock whose value was likely to rise. The volume of such capital flows increased exponentially, dwarfing the value of world trade by the late 1990s; every week foreign exchange markets handled business equivalent to the annual GNP of the United States. In small and medium-sized countries, say Chile or Thailand, the ability of capital to flee instantly sharply restricted the range of policies open to them: if they departed from the preferences of investors, they courted swift retribution in the form of declines in their currency's value and the price of their bonds. So they tried hard to conform to the wishes of mobile capital, balancing budgets and restricting the money supply. This was a perilous course because it often meant firing government workers, trimming social programs, and other painful measures sure to arouse popular complaint. The choice between the Scylla of capital flight and Charybdis of popular unrest was eased, but not resolved, by the willingness of the IMF to lend money to governments that followed the new orthodoxy.

This brave new world of restless capital did help to tame inflation in the big economies, although it occasionally worsened inflation in smaller ones, such as Turkey or Argentina. It did little to solve persistent unemployment, and nothing to accelerate growth, which in the 1980s and 1990s fell well below the rates of 1945–73. Its principal effect, perhaps, was to help shift income from labor to capital, rapidly widening inequalities within and among societies (discussed below). This was a rising tide that lifted some boats but swamped others. People who could offer capital in the global marketplace enjoyed a tremendous advantage once capital could migrate instantly with few restrictions. People who could offer only labor prospered much less, because moving bodies remained more expensive and slower than moving money—and more regulated too. People with only unskilled labor to offer found it difficult to migrate across borders except illegally.

Nevertheless, although small in comparison to the growth in trade flows, and tiny compared to the oceans of capital sloshing around the world, the years after 1965 also saw a resurgence of international migration. Fast-growing economies with slow-growing populations had to import labor. Poor regions with fast-growing populations needed to export people. When Europe's postwar recovery gathered speed after 1955, its industrial regions began to attract millions of laborers from Southern Europe, Turkey, and North Africa. By the 1970s, even Southern European countries became importers of people, mainly from North Africa, but also from South America and elsewhere. Europe, for 400 years an exporter of people, now attracted immigrants from far and wide. So did the newly rich oil states around the Persian Gulf, which imported laborers from Palestine, Pakistan, Korea, and elsewhere in Asia. By 1990, in Kuwait or Saudi Arabia immigrants did almost all the manual labor. Nigeria's oil boom (ca. 1975–83) helped attract 2–3 million other West Africans—many of whom were forcibly expelled when oil prices collapsed. The United States, Canada, and Australia, traditional recipients of immigrants, liberalized their racist policies in the 1960s, accepting skilled or rich people from almost anywhere, which in practice meant largely from East and South Asia. The United States quintupled its intake of legal migrants between 1965 and 1995, and at the same time received millions of clandestine immigrants, chiefly from Mexico and Central America. Canada doubled its immigration rate in the same years. In absolute numbers, the United States and Canada had more immigrants than at any time in their history by 2000, although in 1913 the proportion of immigrants to native-born was much higher.

In general, cheap transport, cheap information about conditions elsewhere in the world, and relaxed quotas on migration encouraged scores of millions to uproot and try their luck elsewhere. By 2000, some 150 million people lived as immigrants, and the annual flow of legal migrants totaled about 2 million. Most, as in the past, were poor and unskilled, but a large minority had strong educations and marketable skills. One distinctive feature of the late twentieth century was the number of Filipina women who found work as domestic servants and nannies in prosperous households everywhere from Hong Kong to Athens to New York. This too was an index of globalization: in the past the labor market for domestic servants had almost everywhere been local.

This accelerating swirl of migration helped ease the stresses of rapid population growth in places such as Algeria or El Salvador. It provided willing laborers in France or the United States or Saudi Arabia, often in jobs that no native-born citizen would take. It took people from places where their labor would produce little to places where it produced more. In economic terms, it proved helpful to all but the laboring classes in recipient countries, whose wages were held down by the competition of immigrants. In cultural and political terms, the great swirl brought new tensions. Most Britons did not welcome large numbers of Pakistanis and Jamaicans in their midst, and Algerians in France, Turks in Germany, and Filipinos in Kuwait also met cold receptions.

The most serious political problems arose in Palestine, where Jewish influxes led to continual friction with local Arabs and after the establishment of Israel, to four genuine wars. The Arab-Israeli conflict involved several of the dominant trends of the twentieth century: nationalism, oil, and the Cold War; but at root it was a matter of Jewish immigration to what Palestinians considered their land. In the dark days of World War I, British and French diplomats had promised Palestine to both Arabs and Jews in exchange for support in the war. After the war the League of Nations awarded it to Britain, which permitted a trickle of further Jewish immigration. After World War II, rapid Jewish immigration and violent ágitation led Britain grudgingly to cede to American pressure and acquiesce in the creation of the State of Israel (1947–48). Many Palestinians fled after some were massacred. Neighboring Arab states immediately attacked Israel but were defeated, allowing Israel to expand its territory while more Palestinians fled. Meanwhile, the importance of Arab (and Iranian) oil to the United States made it seem prudent for the Americans to nurture and arm client states in the region, none of which enjoyed popular support. To counter that problem, their rulers normally posed as champions of Arab nationalism, allies of the displaced Palestinians, and implacable foes of Israel. So did the equally unpopular regimes that aligned themselves with the USSR. At the same time, partly out of sympathy for Jews in the wake of the Nazi Holocaust, and partly because of the political skills of American Jews, the United States also supported Israel handsomely with money and weaponry. The cosmopolitan web was at work here too: the indispensability of oil flows around the world, the intercontinental politics of the Jewish diaspora, decolonization, and American ascendancy all contributed to this dangerous standoff.

ELECTRIFICATION OF THE COSMOPOLITAN WEB

The most important reasons behind the long economic boom were cheap energy and population growth. But new technology helped too. Transport technology mattered much less (despite containerization) than it had in the growth spurt of 1870–1913, while communications and information technology mattered more. Underlying this of course was cheap energy permitting the continuing electrification of the globe. Electrification and the development of new telecommunications and computer technologies reduced information costs, sometimes to the vanishing point. In 1930, a three-minute telephone call between London and New York cost $300, and in 1970, about $20. Then commercial satellites, optical fibers, computer microprocessors, and deregulation of telecommunication markets in the 1980s quickly cut the costs of such communication much further. By 2001, a transatlantic phone call could cost as little as 30 cents, and an e-mail exchange was just about free.

Computers first became useful during World War II for codebreaking and the first Internet exchanges took place within the U.S. military. Civilian Internet traffic began in the 1960s, but developed fast only after 1990 with the emergence of networked personal computers. The United States had 1 million personal computers in 1980, 10 million in 1983, and 44 million in 1989. By the early 1990s, these were increasingly linked. This trend caught on faster than most earlier networked technologies, and by the 1990s the global electronic village was under construction. By 2000, the world had over 1 billion telephones (up from 0.5 billion in 1980), all connected; several hundred million computers with Internet access; and 1.6 billion web pages to choose from. Every minute, 10 million e-mail messages landed in the world's in-boxes.

The consequences of the electrification of the cosmopolitan web are hard to assess because the process is still in train. It has clearly played a large role in the "financialization" of the world economy. It has enriched the information-intensive service sector more than manufacturing and agriculture. It has strengthened the premium on education in the modern world, increasing the rewards for those who acquire schooling and shrinking the rewards for those who can contribute only a strong back or a good pair of hands. It has, so far, enhanced the status of English worldwide, because (as of 1999) 78 percent of Internet home pages were in English (Japanese came second with 2.5 percent). It changed the conduct of warfare for those who could afford it (mainly the United States), because satellites linked to computers allowed a level of precision with long-range weaponry previously impossible. The U.S. military won wars against Iraq, Yugoslavia, and the Taliban in Afghanistan with almost no American casualties. But it created new vulnerabilities as well as new capacities. A malicious, skilled, and lucky hacker could raise havoc with air traffic control, city water systems, banks, and everything else that is computerized. The electrification of the global web probably weakened state control over society in most cases, permitting other organizations—multinational corporations, pressure groups, academics, terrorists—to communicate more efficiently. But governments in the past learned to regulate and control new technologies of information, and they may learn in this case too. It is too soon to tell.

One consequence, which may not last, was the emergence of the so-called digital divide, the latest chapter in the history of inequality. Industrialization widened the gaps in wealth and power among the populations of the world from 1800 until about 1950. For a quarter century after 1950, economic inequality between the richest and poorest regions of the world narrowed. But after the late 1970s, that equalizing trend reversed. Economic inequality within industrial societies, after having diminished between 1890 and 1970, also grew sharply after 1980. Moreover, the richest tenth of the world's people, regardless of region or nationality, grew much richer while the poorest tenth got slightly poorer after 1980. These growing gaps had several causes, including the "financialization" discussed above, but among them was differential access to, and skill with, modern information and communications technology.

As of 2002, half the world's population had yet to make a telephone call, let alone surf the web. A vast international underclass of at least 1 billion people, mainly in Africa and South Asia, remained without electricity, largely cut off from the electrified web. But even they were much affected by it. Most of them knew, through TV glimpsed in a café or bar, or radio or word of mouth, what they were missing. They knew that most of the world was richer, better fed, healthier, and safer than they. When inequality within and among societies grew sharply during the Industrial Revolution, the effects proved socially explosive. In the late twentieth century, such widening gaps occurred in an electronically unified world, one in which information circulated freely. So the world's poor are far more aware of their position than were their predecessors 150 years ago. They are unlikely to accept that position meekly, as the messages of contemporary culture, spread so relentlessly via the electronic media, promote acquisition and consumption as the road to fulfillment. Conceivably, constant displays and occasional use of overwhelming force might suffice to protect the world's rich. So might the provision of modern-day bread and circuses: the entertainment industry excels at supplying music, sports, and sex. It may be, of course, that information and communications technology will soon help narrow inequalities by making education cheaper and more accessible worldwide. But that, should it happen, will be a slow process during which we all face the dangers of glaring economic inequalities in a world of full disclosure.

Conclusion

The cosmopolitan web grew ever tighter after 1890. Geographically, it expanded only very slightly, but the volume and velocity of communication increased markedly, mainly propelled by changes in technology—but also in politics. In cultural terms, this tightening was a fairly steady progression, continuing the long-standing process of homogenization around the world, or put more precisely, of greater conformity to fewer standards. But those standards evolved too, often absorbing influences from all over the world. In political terms, integration had its fits and starts; and in economic terms, it underwent a genuine reversal before gathering momentum again after 1950.

The surge of globalization between 1870 and 1914 generated inequalities and resentments that made nationalisms and war more likely. The war of 1914–18 discredited nationalism (and war) for some, but deepened its appeal for others. The political and economic pressures of the postwar world, and especially the depression, made nationalist autarkies seem sensible policy, leading directly to World War II. The new regime put in place after 1945 once again encouraged integration and globalization, helping generate unprecedented economic growth, and in ways that for a while reduced social inequality. After 1980, technology and policy combined to produce far faster globalization, this time combined with rapidly growing inequalities. The cosmopolitan web encompassed the habitable globe, all the world's peoples and ecosystems, in a swirl of kaleidoscopic interaction. This made it harder to conceal the ethnic frictions and economic cleavages that beset the world, and perhaps harder to control them. On balance it was an age of differentiation: the ever-tightening web helped concentrate wealth and power and highlight the differences between those who had it and those who did not.

The web also helped humankind as a whole to expand its niche on earth. The knowledge generated and distributed within the scientific community led directly to successful efforts to curtail disease and improve crop yields. These ongoing interventions allowed a surge of population growth and urbanization. In a sense this achievement remained precarious, because pathogens and crop pests—not to mention human conflict—always threatened to escape their bonds and destroy the conditions that allowed such expansion of human numbers. But to date the institutionalization of science, and of technological research and development, has kept humankind ahead in this ecological arms race.

Urbanization and population growth stands as the cardinal social change of the last century. For 5,000 years or more the typical human experience was village life, and human ideologies, institutions, and customs all evolved primarily in that setting, although the majority of cultural challenges and changes came from cities. Now the majority human experience is that of city life with its anonymity and impersonal character. Past eras of urbanization, all slow and circumscribed compared to the modern one, put great pressure on reigning religions, ideologies, and worldviews as well as on standing political structures. Among the acute challenges of our time, it seems sure, is the process of social, political, psychological, moral, and ecological adjustment to life in the big city.

IX

BIG PICTURES AND LONG PROSPECTS

by J. R. McNeill

Counting books and puzzle pieces, my family has a few thousand objects in our house, divided among nine rooms. Over time, the distribution of those objects tends toward a random one, including such possibilities as Popsicle sticks in the disk drive and stuffed animals in the oven. But my wife and I find only a few of the several trillion possible arrangements of these objects acceptable, so we routinely invest energy to attain and maintain order and structure. We are locked in a struggle with the forces (however lovable) of disorder. We can prevail while our energy lasts, but not forever and always at a cost: the energy applied to tidying up cannot be applied elsewhere. This is approximately the story of the universe, of life, and of human history.[1]

The universe, soon after it exploded in the Big Bang roughly 12 billion years ago, began to acquire islands of order, structure, and complexity such as galaxies, stars, and planets. These were created by flows of gravitational energy, and maintain their structure, their complexity, by further flows of energy. Stars, for example, were created by gravitational pull on dust and gas. They evolved structures and gradients so that par-

---

[1] Physicists use the term *entropy* to refer to the degree of randomness or disorder exhibited by a system. Their second law of thermodynamics, alluded to by metaphor here, states that entropy is inevitably on the rise in the universe as a whole, meaning that randomness and disorder are always growing. Locally and temporarily, energy flows can create and sustain order, structure, and complexity, but only by drawing energy from elsewhere and dissipating it, lowering the total amount of order and structure in the universe.

ticles and heat move around within them in regular fashion. But eventually they scatter (by exuding heat) so much of the energy they captured that they collapse and die. They can attain and maintain order only by capturing and using energy, and they cannot keep it up forever.

Living organisms, whether single-celled life or giraffes, follow approximately the same script. Their bodies are islands of complex structure (more complex than stars) that require energy to build and to maintain. They take in structured, usable energy (food) and in using it, convert it to less structured, less usable forms. The more complex such creatures are, the more energy they require. In the last half million years, life on earth has gotten very complex, building more and more energy-guzzling structures. The thirstiest to date is the human brain, the most complex object in the known universe, and the one that uses the most energy per unit of mass. The story of life is a story of evolving complexity, of creatures that compete successfully for niche space—for nutrients, for survival, and for opportunities to procreate—by grabbing more energy from the surrounding environment and using it more effectively.

Cultural evolution presents roughly the same story, with some wrinkles. Human society has evolved ever more complex structures over time, with ever greater energy requirements. Hunting-and-gathering societies were and (where they survive) are comparatively simple in structure. Farming villages were more complex, larger in population and with greater hierarchy and social differentiation. They, and the local webs that they sustained, required more energy to build and maintain too, because some went into the construction and maintenance of homes, tools, pots, and some into maintaining domesticated animals and the travel that maintained links among villages. Early civilization was yet more complex and more energy-guzzling. It rested on specialization and the division of labor, exchange and compulsion, and the metropolitan webs that underpinned it required great amounts of energy for the building of infrastructure and the movement of people and animals. Today's cosmopolitan web is feasible only because of the massive energy capture we invest daily in growing, transporting, and storing food, moving goods and people over vast distances, and—not least—the electricity that allows the transmission and storage of streams of data. So human history, like the history of the universe and the history of life, shows an evolution toward complex structures, created and maintained by energy flows, the sizes of which correspond to the degree of complexity and structure in question. But human history is not quite that simple.

In the evolution of the universe, and of life, while more and more complex structures and creatures appear with time, simple ones do not necessarily disappear. Indeed, some persist. There is still cosmic dust floating in space, unattached to any galaxy, star, or planet after 12 billion years, and there are bacteria (in my house, no doubt) little different from their ancestors of 3 billion years ago. But in human history, complex societies do not coexist easily with simple ones: they tend to destroy and absorb the surviving elements (the individuals) of simple ones. Complexity seems to have conferred a greater competitive advantage. Time and again, simple societies when brought into contact with more complex ones have gone under or gone complex. The selective pressure for complexity has been stronger than in biological or cosmic evolution, because the complex societies left little room for the simple. Giraffes have not appreciably reduced the opportunities for bacteria.

Perhaps the reason for this lies in the information-processing capacity of human brains and the social webs they created. Our ancestors lived in groups, as we do, so in order to survive and reproduce, they had to be savvy about alliances and competitions. The power to communicate and cooperate is what brought success in terms of survival and reproduction, especially when big-game hunting or fighting against other groups was involved—although peaceful food gathering also rewarded those skilled in communication and cooperation. Over time our ancestors got savvier at alliance building and alliance breaking because the savviest survived more often and reproduced more.

Beyond this, cultural evolution is Lamarckian, that is, acquired traits and skills can be passed on over generations. Information—how to speak a language or how to make people trust you—is transmitted from brain to brain, from generation to generation, without the slow process of genetic mutation and natural selection. This accelerated pace of cultural evolution made it possible for some groups of humankind to get the jump on others and to destroy their structures and appropriate their resources. This does not often happen in biological evolution because it is slower: even the most complex creatures evolve so slowly that others usually have time to adapt.

Armed with formidable communicative and social skills, our ancestors developed larger and larger webs of interaction in response to the rewards of exchange and the penalties of military inferiority: evolution toward complexity. As in the stories of evolution of the universe and of life, this process moved in fits and starts ("punctuated equilibrium," in the language of evolutionary biology). As in those stories, there were local and temporary reversals. Sometime around 900 C.E., for example, the southern Maya society grew less complex, abandoning cities and civilization for a simpler way of life without pyramids or writing, with less trade and (probably) less war—a local and temporary movement away from complexity, analogous to the extinction of a star or of a dinosaur. But episodes such as the Maya collapse are rather few; the general trend has been toward greater complexity, toward larger and denser webs of interaction, at the expense of simpler societies, which went extinct in droves.

Seen slightly differently, human history is an evolution from simple sameness to diversity toward complex sameness. Our remotest ancestors lived in simple, small groups, spoke only a few languages, and pursued a narrow range of survival strategies in East Africa. Eventually, as groups spread out across the world, broader cultural variety emerged—more languages, differing toolkits, and so on. Later still, people developed more social complexity, reflected in a broad range of political forms—tribes, chiefdoms, city-states, empires. The trend was toward cultural differentiation, toward heterogeneity, toward islands of complexity in a sea of near uniformity. But that did not last. At some point (I would guess between 1000 and 1 B.C.E.) the trend reversed. Interactive webs reduced cultural diversity—fewer languages and religions, fewer polities,[2] and fewer political formats. As the webs grew and fused, complexity became the rule—the new uniformity. Best practices spread; societies settled on a narrower range of traits, beliefs, institutions, all compatible with life inside far-ranging interactive webs. Societies that resisted were wiped out. Diversity declined. This process is not complete nor is it likely ever to become so. Nonetheless, it is a striking trend of the last two or three millennia and probably has far to go yet before it reaches its limit or is somehow reversed.

At present, human society is one huge web of cooperation and competition, sustained by massive flows of information and energy. How long these flows, and this web, might last is an open question. Ultimately, the limits are capacious. Information can exist in infinite quantity (although it requires effort and energy to segregate the useful from the useless, and the more abundant information gets, the more difficult

---

[2] In 1500 B.C.E., according to one estimate, there were 600,000 polities on earth; today there are less than 200. Robert Carneiro, "Political Expansion as an Expression of the Principle of Competitive Exclusion," in Elman Service, ed., *Origins of the State* (Philadelphia, 1978). In 10,000 B.C.E., some 12,000 languages were spoken, compared to 6,000 today and (perhaps) 3,000 a century from now.

this task becomes). The sun is scheduled to provide abundant energy for a few billion more years before its collapse and extinction (although soon we will need a more efficient way to capture it than burning fossil fuels that emit gases that threaten to warm the globe uncomfortably).

Solving these information and energy problems will take time, and in the meanwhile there will be other perils. Most obviously, human ingenuity has endowed us with the capacity for violent self-destruction. Further development of destructive technology seems inevitable and our capacity to restrain violence remains decidedly imperfect. The power of 6 billion (and growing) networked human brains is awesome to contemplate, but it can of course be harnessed for destructive as well as helpful purposes.

The tendency of complex society to generate and maintain social inequalities, evident throughout history, in combination with cheap information and thus greater knowledge of such inequalities, is a combustible mix. Add yet more dangerous weapons than those already in existence, and the chances of cataclysmic violence seem depressingly good. That makes it prudent to strive to reduce such inequalities, a goal that runs counter to long-term trends of recent centuries and perhaps to cherished notions of freedom as well.

In any case, if today's web survives, we will be, more than ever before, arbiters of our own fate. Our communication and cooperation skills have lately allowed us to join the editorial board of life on earth, deciding which species survive and which do not. For some time now we have influenced our earthly environment more than it influenced us, and shortly we may shape genes more than they shape us. We will have biological evolution, as well as cultural evolution, in our own hands. A great deal will depend on just whose hands.

by William H. McNeill

The central argument of this book is that throughout their history humans used symbols to create webs that communicated agreed-upon meanings and so, as time went by, sustained cooperation and conflict among larger and larger groups of people. Inventions and concerted efforts that enlarged individual and, more especially, collective wealth and power tended to spread through these webs, always and everywhere.

So despite innumerable failures and local disasters—environmental, biological, and sociopolitical—the net effect was to expand human life by sporadically enlarging our species' consumption and control of energy: food and fire, first and foremost, but also muscular energy in the form of domesticated animals, mechanical energy in the form of tools, and fossil energy in the form of fuels. The human career on earth is unique, since no other species, not even termites or ants, has ever deployed such a flexible and capacious web of communications to concert common effort on anything approaching the human scale.

Nonetheless, the human record conforms to larger evolutionary patterns. Exact and surprising parallels can, in fact, be surmised in the deep past, when bacteria first formed innumerable living cells in the earth's oceans, and sporadically exchanged genetic material by direct contact of one to another in much the same way that early human bands exchanged information by meeting and mingling together on festival occasions. Time and again, direct bacterial genetic exchange had the effect of permitting cells to propagate useful mutations and so adapt to altering environmental circumstances.

But, just like humans, bacteria also changed their environment, most notably when some of them hit upon photosynthesis as a way to make food from sunlight, air, and seawater and began to release free oxygen into the atmosphere. This eventually changed the natural environment in an even more drastic way than we have yet changed ours. For free oxygen was lethal poison to most existing forms of life. Yet life survived because as oxygen-intolerant bacteria retreated into the deep recesses of the earth where the poisonous gas did not intrude, persistent exchange of genes also propagated mutations that protected living cells against destructive oxidation. Eventually, genetic mutations even produced bacteria that breathed, that is, consumed oxygen in regulated ways, acquiring hitherto unattainable amounts of energy by doing so. These bacteria used part of that energy to move about more rapidly than before—making it easier for them to find food, escape from dearth and other inhospitable conditions, and so survive and flourish.

Parallels with the human record of inventing and propagating new skills and ideas, using them to alter the environment and thereby learning to control and consume more and more energy, are exact and obvious. The selective process sustaining both processes was surely the same. Genetic change may have been random among bacteria, while among humans change was initiated by often mistaken expectations and conscious choices. But, regardless of how they arose, some changes promoted survival and these were the ones that spread and shaped the future among bacteria and humans alike.

The emergence of large, nucleated bacteria and then of multicelled plants and animals introduced another close parallel between biological and human history. These more complex life forms needed far more energy to sustain constant flows of chemical and electrical messages within their bodies, and were correspondingly more successful in capturing energy from their environment by dint of greater flexibility, motility, and sensibility sustained by those internal flows. Moreover, some of the structures within nucleated bacteria and multicelled organisms were, almost certainly, once independent life forms. Initially, they either preyed upon or were eaten by their future partner in what became a patterned symbiosis, advantageous to both parties because it assisted joint survival. The eventual result of such symbioses and subsequent genetic adaptations was an almost unimaginable complexity of specialization and of functions within the tissues of multicelled organisms. Similar complexity and specialization among human beings, built initially upon modified predation and subsequently modulated by custom, was and remains the hallmark of cities and civilization.

Parallels are again obvious. Symbiosis arising from mutual adaptation of originally independent, often hostile organisms allowed multicelled forms of life to get access to more energy, so they soon dominated the biosphere. Civilizations, similarly, engulfed originally independent human communities—willy-nilly—creating new, more powerful bodies politic, economic, and cultural; and being more powerful, they persistently spread to geographically favorable new ground. Moreover, their spread, as we have been at pains to point out in this book, meant that across the past millennium, as communications intensified, what began as separate civilizations followed a familiar path by blending into an ever more powerful global, cosmopolitan web that now prevails among us.

The biosphere, with all its complex patterns of cooperation and conflict, also constitutes a global web, closely resembling the symbolic human web that now unites, and, we claim, has always united, humankind. Today, the web propagates change, complexity, specialization, and power far faster than ever before. But the human web was always one in quite the same way that the biosphere was always one, even when it took thousands of years for a really useful new skill or idea to spread gradually around the earth through sporadic face-to-face contacts among isolated human communities—as the bow and arrow was still doing in 1500 C.E.

Such parallels are comforting. They convince me that the human terrestrial career is natural, however exceptional it may be. For, when carefully observed, we really and truly do belong where we are, alive on planet earth, part and parcel of the biosphere sustaining us.

Yet my reassuring sense of belonging here on earth is countered by a heightened sense of insecurity. How long will all the complex flows sustaining us endure? Flows not just of food and energy but also of meanings, hopes, and aspirations, uniting and dividing humankind more forcefully than ever before? Will human life survive future catastrophes—political, military, biological, ecological? Will urban lifestyles disrupt cultural as well as biological reproduction? Can humankind, in short, somehow adapt to radically new circumstances, largely of our own creation, as our predecessors did in times past?

My personal hunch is that catastrophes—great and small—are sure to come and human resilience will prove more than we can easily imagine. But I think we also need face-to-face, primary communities for long-range survival: communities, like those our predecessors belonged to, within which shared meanings, shared values, and shared goals made life worth living for everyone, even the humblest and least fortunate.

If so, perhaps the most critical question for the human future is how cell-like primary communities can survive and flourish within the global cosmopolitan flows that sustain our present numbers, wealth, and power, without being disrupted by those flows and without disrupting them. In other words, we need a new symbiosis all over again.

In times past, most cities were demographic sinkholes, parasitic on rural villages since they imported both food and manpower from the countryside. Cities still fail to reproduce themselves and still depend on rural immigrants to do their dirty work. What then happens when city attitudes and expectations reach out and begin to disrupt the peasant communities upon which they depend? This, it seems to me, is the situation in which humankind now finds itself. Peasant patterns of life and labor are in full retreat. Urbanization swells, and city-style hopes and expectations flood across the countryside, thanks mainly to new, electronic communications.

Radical choices thus impend. Either the gap between cities and villages will somehow be bridged by renegotiating the terms of symbiosis, and/or differently constructed primary communities will arise to counteract the tangled anonymity of urban life. Religious sects and congregations are the principal candidates for this role. But communities of belief must somehow insulate themselves from unbelievers, and that introduces frictions, or active hostilities, into the cosmopolitan web. How then sustain the web and also make room for life-sustaining primary communities?

Ironically, therefore, to preserve what we have, we and our successors must change our ways by learning to live simultaneously in a cosmopolitan web and in various and diverse primary communities. How to reconcile such opposites is the capital question for our time and probably will be for a long time to come. The most obvious alternative is collapse of the existing web, which would bring radical impoverishment, catastrophic die-off, and perhaps, if humankind survived, a new start on the basis of local, broken fragments of the web. I conclude that we live on the crest of a breaking wave. Luck, intelligence, and awkward tolerance may keep the web from breaking. Let's hope so.

FURTHER READINGS

I

Richard Leakey, *The Origin of Humankind* (New York, 1994), Roger Lewin, *Human Evolution: An Illustrated Introduction*, 3rd ed. (Boston, 1993), and John Reader, *Africa: A Biography of a Continent* (New York, 1998), are good places to start. Peter Bogucki, *The Origins of Human Society* (Malden, MA, 1999), offers a recent and insightful survey of the archeological record around the world. On our ties with and differences from chimpanzees, Jane Goodall, *The Chimpanzees of Gombe: Patterns of Behavior* (Cambridge, MA, 1986), and Frans De Waal, *Chimpanzee Politics: Power and Sex Among the Apes* (New York, 1982), are classics. On the domestication of fire, Johan Goudsblom, *Fire and Civilization* (London, 1992), and Stephen J. Pyne, *World Fire: The Culture of Fire on Earth* (New York, 1995), seem sure to become classics too.

Two fine efforts at synthesis about how humans spread around the world are Brian M. Fagan, *People of the Earth: An Introduction to World Prehistory*, 9th ed. (New York, 1997), and I. G. Simmons, *Changing the Face of the Earth: Culture, Environment and History* (Oxford, 1989). For more personal points of view on the same themes, see Clive Gamble, *Timewalkers: The Prehistory of Global Colonization* (Phoenix Mill, UK, 1993); Ian Tattersall, *The Fossil Trail: How We Know What We Think We Know About Human Evolution* (Oxford, 1996); and Rich Potts, *Humanity's Descent: The Consequences of Ecological Instability* (New York, 1996). For an authoritative account of both sides of the extinction controversy, see Paul S. Martin and Richard G. Klein, eds., *Quaternary Extinctions: A Prehistoric Revolution* (Tucson, AZ, 1984).

On dance as a form of social communication and consolidation, William H. McNeill, *Keeping Together in Time: Dance and Drill in Human History* (Cambridge, MA, 1996), stands forlornly by itself; but three books from the enormous learned literature on language struck us as especially enlightening: Barbara King, *The Information Continuum: Evolution of Social Information Transfer in Monkeys, Apes and Hominids* (Sante Fe, NM, 1994); Derek Bickerton, *Language and Species* (Chicago, 1981); and Robin Dunbar, *Grooming, Gossip and the Evolution of Language* (London, 1996). In addition, the advent of language and much else is discussed in innumerable edited symposia that try to keep up with new ideas about prehistory. Among them we recommend: Paul Mellars and Chris Stringer, eds., *The Human Revolution: Behavioral and Biological Perspectives on the Origin of Modern Humans* (Princeton, 1989); Kathleen R. Gibson and Tim Ingold, eds., *Tools, Language and Cognition in Human Evolution* (Cambridge, 1993); and Glendon Schubert and Roger D. Martin, eds., *Primate Politics* (Carbondale,

IL, 1991), as well as numerous articles in the periodicals *Current Anthropology* and *Journal of Human Evolution.*

For more on the three examples of the intensified exploitation of seasonal food supplies in the late Paleolithic, see T. Douglas Price and James A. Brown, eds., *Prehistoric Hunter Gathererers: The Emergence of Cultural Complexity* (Orlando, FL, 1965); Phillip Drucker, *Cultures of the North Pacific Coast* (San Francisco, 1965); Kenneth M. Ames and Herbert D. G. Maschner, *Peoples of the Northwest Coast: Their Archaeology and Prehistory* (London, 1999); Hans Georg Bandi, *Eskimo Prehistory* (College, Alaska, 1969); and Donald O. Henry, *From Foraging, to Agriculture: The Levant at the End of the Ice Age* (Philadelphia, 1989).

II

Bruce D. Smith, *The Emergence of Agriculture* (New York, 1995), offers a persuasive global survey of the changed relationships that set in between humans and domesticated plants and animals. He led in the discovery of the earliest forms of agriculture in the North American woodlands, and this book surveys the rest of the world using that pattern of domestication as a template. David Rindos, *The Origins of Agriculture: An Evolutionary Perspective* (Orlando, FL, 1984), approaches the question from a botanist's angle of vision, emphasizing processes and downplaying purposes in explaining what happened between humans and their domesticates. Jack R. Harlan, *Crops and Man*, 2nd ed. (Madison, WI, 1992), and Juliet Clutton-Brock, *A Natural History of Domesticated Animals* (Cambridge, 1999), summarize the views of two pioneers of the contemporary understanding of domestication. Jared Diamond, *Guns, Germs, and Steel: The Fates of Human Societies* (New York, 1997), and Stephen Oppenheimer, *Eden in the East: The Drowned Continent of Southeast Asia* (London, 1998), are delightfully provocative and well-informed books that challenge older views and emphasize the importance of Southeast Asia. Peter Bogucki, *The Origins of Human Society* (Malden, MA, 1999), carefully summarizes new evidence and theories for every part of the world.

Charles Keith Maisels, *The Emergence of Civilization: From Hunting and Gathering to Agriculture, Cities and the State in the Near East* (London, 1990), brings a very sophisticated mind to bear on that pioneer region, while his *Early Civilizations of the Old World: The Formative Histories of Egypt, the Levant, Mesopotamia, India, and China* (London, 1999) does the same for Eurasia as a whole. Andrew Sherratt, *Economy and Society in Prehistoric Europe: Changing Perspectives* (Edinburgh, 1997), explores the European outlier of the Southwest Asian style of cultivation. Sherratt was the first to recognize the expanded exploitation of domesticated animals which gave that style of agriculture its remarkable flexibility.

No incisive account of the beginning of agriculture in India seems to exist, but Bridget and Raymond Allchin, *The Rise of Civilization in India and Pakistan* (Cambridge, 1982), and Jane R. McIntosh, *A Peaceful Realm: The Rise and Fall of the Indus Civilization* (New York, 2002), describe the rather scanty archeological finds from that part of the world. For China, Kwang-shih Chang, *The Archaeology of Ancient China*, 4th ed. (New Haven, 1986), provides an overview of recent discoveries, updating older accounts such as Ping-ti Ho, *The Cradle of the East* (Hong Kong, 1975). On the early cultivation of rice, and its effect on Chinese and other Asian societies, Francesca Bray, *The Rice Economies: Technology and Development in Asian Societies* (Oxford, 1986), is still the reigning authority.

For early Southeast Asian and Australasian society and agriculture, Timothy F. Flannery, *The Future Eaters: An Ecological History of the Australasian Lands and Peoples* (Chatswood, NSW, 1994), is a useful complement to Stephen Oppenheimer's book cited above. For the Americas,

Richard E. W. Adams, *Ancient Civilizations of the New World* (Boulder, CO, 1997), is brief, recent, and very well informed, and Richard S. MacNeish, *Early Man in America* (San Francisco, 1973), highlights his pioneering studies of how Mexican agriculture started.

On population growth, Massimo Livi-Bacci, *A Concise History of World Population* (Cambridge, MA, 1992), offers a set of speculative figures for prehistoric populations; another useful overview is in Joel Cohen, *How Many People Can the Earth Support?* (New York, 1995). On early warfare, see Lawrence H. Keeley, *War Before Civilization* (New York, 1996), and Jonathan Haas, ed., *The Anthropology of War* (Cambridge, 1990).

III

Though much of her archeological data and historical reconstruction are contested, Jane Jacobs, *The Economy of Cities* (New York, 1969), offers a convincing, imaginative analysis of how cities changed social relationships in Southwest Asia. For a brief but stimulating overview of urbanism, see Paul Bairoch, *Cities and Economic Development from the Dawn of History to the Present* (Chicago, 1988). G. Algaze, *The Uruk World System: The Dynamics of Expansion of Early Mesopotamian Civilization* (Chicago, 1993), presents an archeologically up-to-date and far more cautious account of urban origins; while A. Leo Oppenheim, *Ancient Mesopotamia* (Chicago, 1964), distills a lifetime of reading cuneiform documents into a careful book. Cf. also C. K. Maisels, *The Emergence of Civilization* (London, 1990), mentioned for chapter 2.

Yigael Yadin, *The Art of Warfare in Biblical Lands in the Light of Archaeology* (New York, 1963), is the best guide to changes in military equipment and organization from 3000 B.C.E. onward. For Near Eastern religion, William Foxwell Albright, *From the Stone Age to Christianity, Monotheism and the Historical Process*, 2nd ed. (Baltimore, 1967), offers a learned synthesis, while Hershel Shanks, ed., *Ancient Israel: A Short History from Abraham to the Roman Destruction of the Temple* (Englewood Cliffs, NJ, 1988), explains the way Judaism came into existence.

For steppe pastoralists and their impacts, the best general overview is Rene Grousset, *The Empire of the Steppes* (New Brunswick, NJ, 1970). Vladimir N. Basilov, ed., *Nomads of Eurasia* (Seattle, 1989), concentrates on steppe life and culture, while Thomas Barfield, *The Perilous Frontier* (Cambridge, MA, 1989), focuses on politics and war along the frontier with China.

On India, A. L. Basham, *The Wonder That Was India*, 3rd rev. ed. (London, 1985), is a fine general survey; for an excellent up-to-date textbook, see Stanley Wolpert, *A New History of India* (New York, 1997). Walter A. Fairservis, *The Roots of Ancient India* (Chicago, 1975), uses anthropological concepts to explain the social diversity of ancient India; on caste, J. H. Hutton, *Caste in India: Its Nature, Function and Origins* (Cambridge, 1945), remains helpful.

For China, Kwang-chih Chang, *Art, Myth, and Ritual: The Path to Political Authority in Ancient China* (Cambridge, MA, 1983), puts the case for the central role of family rituals in early Chinese society and politics. For Confucianism, it is best to start with the words of the sage himself as translated by D. C. Lau, *Confucius: The Analects* (New York, 1988). On the general intellectual setting, see Benjamin I. Schwartz, *The World of Thought in Ancient China* (Cambridge, MA, 1985).

For ancient Greece, A. Andrewes, *Greek Society*, 4th ed. (Lexington, MA, 1992), is a good place to begin. W. G. Forrest, *The Emergence of Greek Democracy, 800–400 B.C.* (New York, 1979), describes what it meant to be a citizen. Victor Davis Hanson, *The Western Way of War: Infantry Battle in Classical Greece* (New York, 1989), explains phalanx fighting, though some of his views are controversial. For Greek literature as a whole, Edith Hamilton, *The Greek Way* (New York, 1983), is a good introduction for those too busy to take on Homer, Herodotus, Thucydides, Aeschylus, Sophocles, Euripides, Plato, Aristotle, and other classic writers in any of the numerous translations available.

On Rome, M. Cary and H. H. Scullard, *History of Rome Down to the Reign of Constantine* (New York, 1975), is a standard introduction. See also Jacques Heurgon, *The Rise of Rome to 164 B.C.* (Berkeley, 1973), and Colin Webb, *The Roman Empire* (London, 1992). For the transformation of the Roman army into a professional force, see Lawrence Keppie, *The Making of the Roman Army: From Republic to Empire* (Totowa, NJ, 1984). On the emergence of Christianity, Robin Lane Fox, *Pagans and Christians* (San Francisco, 1988), and Ramsay MacMullen, *Christianizing the Roman Empire A.D. 100–400* (New Haven, 1986), may be recommended; but there is no substitute for reading the New Testament itself.

On disease history, see William H. McNeill, *Plagues and Peoples,* new ed. (New York, 1998). For ecological impacts, Thorkild Jacobsen, *Salinization and Irrigation Agriculture in Antiquity* (Malibu, CA, 1962), and Russell Meiggs, *Trees and Timber in the Ancient Mediterranean World* (Oxford, 1982), are worth consulting, together with J. D. Hughes, *Pan's Travail* (Baltimore, 1994), and Robert M. Adams, *Heartland of Cities: Surveys of Ancient Settlement and Land Use on the Central Floodplain of the Euphrates* (Chicago, 1981).

IV

Among books that look across civilizational boundaries, Jerry H. Bentley, *Old World Encounters: Cross-Cultural Contacts and Exchanges in Pre-Modern Times* (New York, 1993), Philip D. Curtin, *Cross-Cultural Trade in World History* (Cambridge, 1984), and Vaclav Smil, *Energy in World History* (Boulder, CO, 1994), are brief and instructive.

For the role of Iranians and Turks between 200 and 1000, Rene Grousset, *The Empire of the Steppes* (New Brunswick, NJ, 1970), offers a clear and masterly overview. Robert Canfield, ed., *Turko-Persia in Historical Perspective* (Cambridge, 1991), and Anatoli M. Khazanov, *Nomads and the Outside World* (Cambridge, 1984), are more technical; and S. A. M. Adshead, *Central Asia in World History* (London, 1993), is provocatively idiosyncratic.

On India, K. N. Chaudhuri, *Trade and Civilization in the Indian Ocean: An Economic History from the Rise of Islam to 1750* (Cambridge, 1985), and a successor volume, *Asia Before Europe: Economy and Civilization of the Indian Ocean from the Rise of Islam to 1750* (Cambridge, 1990), deal squarely with themes emphasized in this chapter. So do Hsin-ju Liu, *Ancient India and Ancient China: Trade, Religion and Exchange. A.D. 1–600* (Delhi, 1988), and J. Innes Miller, *The Spice Trade of the Roman Empire, 29 B.C. to A.D. 641* (Oxford, 1969).

For Islam, W. Montgomery Watt, *Muhammad, Prophet and Statesman* (London, 1961), is a standard scholarly introduction to the life of a person who changed world history more dramatically than anyone before or after, and Karen Armstrong, *Muhammad: A Biography of the Prophet* (San Francisco, 1992), is a good popular one. For a brief summation of Islamic achievements, try Annemarie Schimmel, *Islam: An Introduction* (Albany, NY, 1992), or Karen Armstrong, *Islam: A Short History* (New York, 2000). Marshall G. S. Hodgson, *The Venture of Islam. Vol. 1: The Classical Age of Islam* (Chicago, 1974), is harder to read but uniquely perspicacious. For topics emphasized here, Richard W. Bulliet, *The Camel and the Wheel* (Cambridge, 1975), Andrew Watson, *Agricultural Innovations in the Early Islamic World* (Cambridge, 1983), and an old classic, George F. Hourani, *Arab Seafaring in the Indian Ocean in Ancient and Early Medieval Times*, new ed. by John Carswell (Princeton, 1995), fill out details admirably.

For China, Mark Elvin, *The Pattern of the Chinese Past* (Stanford, 1973), offers a provocative overview. For Chinese encounters with the outside world, Thomas Barfield, *The Perilous Frontier* (Cambridge, MA, 1989), Wolfram Eberhard, *Conquerors and Rulers: Social Forces in Medieval China* (Leiden, 1965), and Edward Schafer, *The Golden Peaches of Samarkand: A Study of T'ang Exotica* (Berkeley, 1963), are particularly interesting. Pan Yihong, *Son of Heaven and Heavenly Qaghong: Sui-Tang China and Its Neighbors* (Bellingham, WA, 1997), is helpful on Chinese foreign relations. Frank A. Kierman Jr. and John K. Fairbank, eds., *Chinese Way of Warfare* (Cambridge, MA, 1974), explores a formerly underestimated aspect of Chinese imperial history. On Buddhism, Arthur F. Wright, *Buddhism in Chinese History* (Stanford, 1959), is a concise, graceful introduction. See also David McMullen, *State and Scholars in T'ang China* (Cambridge, 1988). A vastly learned and provocative essay by S. A. M. Adshead, *China in World History* (New York, 1988), is very much worth reading, though some of what he has to say has not won general acceptance.

For Japan, Korea, and Southeast Asia: Conrad Totman, *A History of Japan* (Malden, MA, 2000); John Whitney Hall, *Japan: From Prehistory to Modern Times* (Ann Arbor, 1970); Roger Tennant, *A History of Korea* (London, 1996). Southeast Asia is well served by D. G. E. Hall, *A History of South East Asia*, 4th ed. (New York, 1981), and Kenneth R. Hall, *Maritime Trade and State Development in Early Southeast Asia* (Honolulu, 1985). Other noteworthy books, each with charms of its own, include: G. B. Sansom, *Japan: A Short Cultural History* (London, 1987); William W. Farris, *Heavenly Warriors: The Evolution of Japan's Military, 500–1300* (Cambridge, MA, 1992); Paul Wheatley, *The Golden Chersonese: Studies in the Historical Geography of the Malay Peninsula Before* A.D. *1500* (Kuala Lumpur, 1961); and George Coedes, *The Indianized States of Southeast Asia* (Honolulu, 1968).

For African history, John Reader, *Africa: A Biography of the Continent* (New York, 1998), as well as John Iliffe, *Africans: The History of a Continent* (Cambridge, 1995), offer up-to-date and perspicacious overviews. More detailed is Christopher Ehret, *An African Classical Age: Eastern and Southern Africa in World History, 1000 B.C. to A.D. 400* (Charlottesville, VA, 1998). Always useful is James Newman, *The Peopling of Africa: A Geographical Interpretation* (New Haven, 1995).

Early medieval European history can be approached nicely through a sadly neglected textbook, Robert S. Lopez, *The Birth of Europe* (New York, 1967), and Averil Cameron, *The Mediterranean World in Late Antiquity,* A.D. *395–600* (London, 1993). At a more advanced level, see Judith Herrin, *The Formation of Christendom* (Princeton, 1987); Warren Treadgold, *A History of the Byzantine State and Society* (Stanford, 1997); Robert Browning, *The Byzantine Empire*, rev. ed. (Washington, DC, 1992); Dimitri Obolensky, *The Byzantine Commonwealth: Eastern Europe 500–1453* (Crestwood, NY, 1982); and Peter Brown, *Power and Persuasion in Late Antiquity: Towards a Christian Europe* (Madison, WI, 1992). Four classics are also exceptionally interesting: B. H. Slicher van Bath, *The Agrarian History of Western Europe.* A.D. *500–1850* (London, 1966); Lynn White, *Medieval Technology and Social Change* (Oxford, 1962); and a pair of books by Archibald R. Lewis, *Naval Power and Trade in the Mediterranean. 500–1100* (Princeton, 1951) and *Shipping and Commerce in Northern Europe. A.D. 300–1100* (Princeton, 1958).

For America, Richard E. W. Adams, *Ancient Civilizations of the New World* (Boulder, CO, 1997), is a brief, up-to-date overview. Lynda Shaffer, *Native Americans Before 1492: The Moundbuilding Centers of the Eastern Woodlands* (Armonk, NY, 1992), makes sense of

Amerindian history in what is now the United States. Two other fine avenues of approach to the Amerindian past are Michael D. Coe, Dean Snow, and Elizabeth Benson, *Atlas of Ancient America* (New York, 1986), and Stuart J. Fiedel, *Prehistory of the Americas*, 2nd ed. (New York, 1992). For the altiplano, Alan Kolata, *The Tiwanaku: Portrait of an Andean Civilization* (Cambridge, MA, 1993). For possible trans-Pacific contacts with America, see Joseph Needham and Lu Gwei-djen, *Trans-Pacific Echoes and Resonances: Listening Once Again* (Singapore, 1984).

V

Many of the books listed for chapter 4 also deal with the period treated here. Books that deal with the intensification of trade and technological exchanges within the Old World Web include Janet Abu-Lughod, *Before European Hegemony: The World System A.D. 1250–1350* (New York, 1989); and Philip D. Curtin, *Cross-Cultural Trade in World History* (Cambridge, 1984). Thomas C. Carter, *The Invention of Printing in China and Its Spread Westward*, 2nd ed. (New York, 1955), and Joseph Needham, *Science and Civilization in China.* Vol. 7: *The Gunpowder Epic* (Cambridge, 1987), deal with the development and diffusion of the two most important innovations of the age.

Travelers' reports in English from these centuries include Marco Polo, *The Travels of Marco Polo,* ed. Ronald Latham (New York, 1982); Ross Dunn, *The Adventures of Ibn Battuta: A Muslim Traveller of the Fourteenth Century* (Berkeley, 1986); Christopher Dawson, ed., *Mission to Asia: Narratives and Letters of the Franciscan Missionaries in Mongolia and China in the Thirteenth and Fourteenth Centuries* (reprinted Toronto, 1980); Jeanette Mirsky, ed., *The Great Chinese Travelers: An Anthology* (New York, 1964); and Morris Rossabi, *Voyager from Xanadu: Rabban Sauma and the First Journey from China to the West* (Tokyo, 1992).

The first stop for Chinese history in this period is Frederick Mote, *Imperial China, 900–1800* (Cambridge, MA, 1999). For the transformation of Chinese society under the Song, Yoshinoba Shiba, *Commerce and Society in Sung China* (Ann Arbor, 1970), is an eye-opener. On Chinese iron production, Robert Hartwell, "A Cycle of Economic Change in Imperial China: Coal and Iron in Northeast China, 750–1350," *Journal of Economic and Social History of the Orient,* 10 (1967), and Joseph Needham, *The Development of Iron and Steel Technology in China* (London, 1980), are authoritative. For Chinese shipbuilding and navigation, Joseph Needham, *Science and Civilization in China,* Vol. 3, Part 3 (Cambridge, 1971), supersedes earlier accounts; and Louise Levathes, *When China Ruled the Seas* (New York, 1994), offers a summary account of Ming voyages into the Indian Ocean. For the Mongols, David Morgan, *The Mongols* (Oxford, 1986), is brief and authoritative, as is Thomas Allsen, *Culture and Conquest in Mongol Eurasia* (New York, 2001).

For the transformation of Islam, Richard Bulliet, *Islam: The View from the Edge* (New York, 1993), Annemarie Schimmel, *The Mystical Dimension of Islam* (Chapel Hill, 1975), J. Spencer Trimingham, *The Influence of Islam Upon Africa*, 2nd ed. (New York, 1980), and Michael Dols, *The Black Death in the Middle East* (Princeton, 1977), are all instructive. Marshall Hodgson, *The Venture of Islam.* Vol. 2: *The Expansion of Islam in the Middle Period* (Chicago, 1974), provides an incisive overview.

For the Ottoman frontier, Paul Wittek, *The Rise of the Ottoman Empire,* rev. ed. (New York, 1971), Rudi Paul Lindner, *Nomads and Ottomans in Medieval Anatolia* (Bloomington, 1983), and Cemal Kafadar, *Between Two Worlds: The Construction of the Ottoman State* (Berkeley, 1995), offer varying interpretations of the basis of Ottoman success. On Islam in India and Southeast Asia, see Jos Gommans, "The Silent Frontier of South Asia, c. 1100–1800," *Journal of World History* 9 (1998), 1–24; Andre Wink, *Al-Hind: The Making of the Indo-Islamic World.*

Vol. 2: *The Slave Kings and the Islamic Conquest. 11th–13th Centuries* (Leiden, 1997); and Richard Maxwell Eaton, "Approaches to the Study of Conversion to Islam in India," in Richard C. Martin, ed., *Approaches to Islam in Religious Studies* (Tucson, AZ, 1985).

For medieval Europe, Robert Bartlett, *The Making of Europe: Conquest, Colonization and Cultural Change. 950–1350* (Princeton, 1993), is admirably comprehensive. The disasters of the fourteenth century are treated in William C. Jordan, *The Great Famine: Northern Europe in the Early Fourteenth Century* (Princeton, 1996); Philip Ziegler, *The Black Death* (Harmondsworth, UK, 1982); and William H. McNeill, *Plagues and Peoples* (New York, 1976). For the economic rebound, see Robert S. Lopez, *Commercial Revolution of the Middle Ages, 900–1350* (Cambridge, 1976), and Harry Miskimin, *The Economy of Early Renaissance Europe 1300–1460* (Cambridge, 1965). Charles Homer Haskins, *The Rise of Universities* (reprinted Ithaca, NY, 1979), is a classic. Alfred W. Crosby, *The Measure of Reality: Quantification and Western Society, 1250–1600* (New York, 1997), provides the basis for our remarks about "creeping digitalization" in the fourteenth century; and George Ifrah, *From One to Zero: A Universal History of Numbers* (New York, 1985), puts arithmetic innovation into its global context. For Europe's unique response to printing, see Elizabeth Eisenstein, *The Printing Revolution of Early Modern Europe* (Cambridge, 1983). On commercialization of organized violence, see Michael E. Mallett, *Mercenaries and Their Masters: Warfare in Renaissance Italy* (London, 1974), and William H. McNeill, *The Pursuit of Power: Technology, Armed Force, and Society Since A.D. 1000* (Chicago, 1982). On initial European ventures overseas, Pierre Chaunu, *European Expansion in the Later Middle Ages* (Amsterdam, 1979), is a classic.

On Africa, George E. Brooks, *Landowners and Strangers: Ecology, Society and Trade in Western Africa, 1000–1600* (Boulder, CO, 1993), offers a view informed by climate history. On East Africa, a compact treatment is Derek Nurse and Thomas Spear, *The Swahili: Reconstructing the Language and History of an East African Society, 800–1500* (Philadelphia, 1985). Useful for all of early African history is James Newman, *The Peopling of Africa: A Geographical Intepretation* (New Haven, 1995).

On the rise of Muscovy, Robert Crummey, *The Formation of Muscovy, 1304–1613* (London, 1987), Janet Martin, *Treasure of the Land of Darkness: The Fur Trade and Its Significance for Medieval Russia* (Cambridge, 1986), and Robert E. F. Smith, *Peasant Farming in Muscovy* (Cambridge, 1977), are all helpful.

On changes in the Americas, Inga Clendinnen, *Aztecs: An Interpretation* (Cambridge, 1991), Ross Hassig, *Aztec Warfare: Imperial Expansion and Political Control* (Norman, OK, 1988), Geoffrey W. Conrad and Arthur A. Demarest, *Religion and Empire. The Dynamics of Aztec and Inca Expansionism* (Cambridge, 1984), and John V. Murra, *The Economic Organization of the Inca State* (Greenwich, CT, 1979), are variously provocative. Recent views are summarized in *The Cambridge History of the Native Peoples of the Americas* (Cambridge, 1999–), a multivolume compendium with numerous editors.

VI

On West and Central Africa, we recommend Roderick McIntosh, *The Peoples of the Middle Niger* (Oxford, 1998); Robin Law, *The Horse in West African History* (Oxford, 1980); and John Thornton, *The Kingdom of the Kongo* (Madison, WI, 1983). On the Pacific, a reliable survey is Patrick V. Kirch, *The Evolution of the Polynesian Chiefdoms* (New York, 1984). On Central Asia after the Mongols, a starting point is Beatrice Forbes Manz, *The Rise and Rule of Tamerlane* (Cambridge, 1989). Frank Salomon and Stuart Schwartz, eds., *The Cambridge History of the*

Native Peoples of the Americas. Vol. III: *South America* (New York, 1999), is an authoritative compendium with much on pre-Columbian Amerindian history. Alvin M. Josephy, ed., *America in 1492* (New York, 1992), contains several useful essays; technical essays on roads and communications in pre-Columbian America are available in Charles D. Trombold, ed., *Ancient Road Networks and Settlement Hierarchies in the New World* (New York, 1991).

On ships and shipbuilding in Europe, Richard Unger, *The Ship in the Medieval Economy, 600–1600* (London, 1980), and Ian Friel, *The Good Ship: Ships, Shipbuilding and Technology in England, 1200–1520* (Baltimore, 1995), are excellent. On Chinese shipbuilding and navigation, Joseph Needham, *Science and Civilization in China.* Vol. IV, Part 3: *Civil Engineering and Nautics* (Cambridge, n.d.), is unsurpassed, but see also the long chapter "Communications and Commerce" by Timothy Brook in Denis Twitchett and Frederick Mote, eds., *The Cambridge History of China.* Vol. 8: *The Ming Dynasty, 1368–1644,* Part 2 (Cambridge, 1998), 579–707. Indian Ocean maritime developments are surveyed in K. N. Chaudhuri, *Trade and Civilization in the Indian Ocean* (New York, 1985), ch. 7.

On Siberia, James Forsyth, *A History of the Peoples of Siberia* (New York, 1992), and Yuri Slezkine, *Arctic Mirror: Russia and the Small Peoples of the North* (Ithaca, NY, 1994), are very useful, as is the earlier Raymond Fisher, *The Russian Fur Trade, 1550–1700* (Berkeley, 1943).

On Southern and East Africa in the sixteenth to eighteenth centuries, in addition to works cited earlier, we recommend Richard Elphick and Hermann Giliomee, eds., *The Shaping of South African Society, 1652–1840* (Middletown, CT, 1989); Joseph Miller, *The Way of Death* (Madison, WI, 1988); and J. Middleton, *The World of the Swahili: An African Mercantile Civilization* (New Haven, 1992).

Lively new books on these centuries in Pacific, New Zealand, and Australian history include James Belich, *Making Peoples: A History of the New Zealanders from Polynesian Settlement to the End of the Nineteenth Century* (Auckland, 1996); Timothy Flannery, *The Future Eaters* (Chatswood, NSW, 1994); Robert Hughes, *The Fatal Shore: A History of the Transportation of Convicts to Australia, 1787–1868* (New York, 1987). Less lively, but authoritative are D. J. Mulvaney and J. Peter White, eds., *Australians to 1788* (Broadway, NSW, 1987), and Ian Campbell, *A History of the Pacific Islands* (Berkeley, 1989).

On intellectual currents, see Toby Huff, *The Rise of Early Modern Science: Islam, China, and the West* (New York, 1993); Alfred Crosby, *The Measure of Reality: Quantification and Western Society, 1250–1600* (New York, 1997); Irfan Habib, ed., *Akbar and His India* (Delhi, 1997); and Frederick Kilgour, *The Evolution of the Book* (Oxford, 1998), on printing.

On political, social, and economic history, we recommend Richard Foltz, *Mughal India and Central Asia* (Delhi, 1998); Roger Savory, *Iran Under the Safavids* (Cambridge, 1980); Svat Soucek, *A History of Inner Asia* (Princeton, 2000); Stephen P. Rosen, *India and Its Armies* (Delhi, 1996); Rhoads Murphey, *Ottoman Warfare, 1500–1700* (New Brunswick, NJ, 1999); Halil Inalcik, *An Economic and Social History of the Ottoman Empire.* Vol. I: *1300–1600* (New York, 1994); Conrad Totman, *Early Modern Japan* (Berkeley, 1993); Geoffrey Parker, *The Military Revolution: Military Innovation and the Rise of the West, 1500–1800* (Cambridge, 1988); John K. Thornton, *Warfare in Atlantic Africa, 1500–1800* (London, 1999); Thomas Barfield, *The Perilous Frontier: Nomadic Empires and China* (Cambridge, MA, 1989); Clifford J. Rogers, ed., *The Military Revolution Debate* (Boulder, CO, 1995); John F. Richards, *The Mughal Empire* (Cambridge, 1993); James A. Millward, *Beyond the Pass: Economy, Ethnicity, and Empire in Qing Central Asia, 1759–1864* (Stanford, 1998); Sanjay Subrahmanyam, *The Portuguese Empire in Asia, 1500–1700* (New York, 1995); Jeremy Black, *War and the World* (New Haven, 1998); Anthony Reid, *Southeast Asia in the Age of Commerce,* 2 vols. (New Haven, 1988), and his

Charting the Shape of Early Modern Southeast Asia (Bangkok, 1999); and Rene Barendse, *The Arabian Seas, 1640–1700* (Leiden, 1998).

VII

On communications and technology, see Peter Hugill, *Global Communications Since 1844* (Baltimore, 1999); David Vincent, *The Rise of Mass Literacy* (Cambridge, 2000); Daniel Headrick, *The Tentacles of Progress: Technology Transfer in the Age of Imperialism, 1850–1940* (New York, 1988); Rick Szostak, *The Role of Transportation in the Industrial Revolution* (Montreal, 1991); and Peter Stearns, *The Industrial Revolution in World History* (Boulder, CO, 1998). Joel Mokyr, ed., *The British Industrial Revolution* (Boulder, CO, 1998), is strong on the technical aspects of industrialization, as is Tessa Morris-Suzuki, *The Technological Transformation of Japan* (Cambridge, 1994). Kenneth Pomeranz, *The Great Divergence* (Princeton, 2000), is provocative on why industrialization happened first in England and not China.

On health and disease, see James C. Riley, *Rising Life Expectancy: A Global History* (Cambridge, 2001); Roy Porter, *The Greatest Benefit to Mankind: A Medical History of Humanity from Antiquity to the Present* (London, 1997), a vast compendium of information on (mainly) European medicine; and Sheldon Watts, *Epidemics and History: Disease, Power, and Imperialism* (New Haven, 1998). On population and the demographic transition, see the books cited earlier by Joel Cohen and Massimo Livi-Bacci, and Ts'ui-jung Liu et al., eds., *Asian Population History* (Oxford, 2001).

For European political changes and the rise of nationalism, see James B. Collins, *The State in Early Modern France* (Cambridge, 1995); Wim Blockmans, *A History of Power in Europe: People, Markets, States* (Antwerp, 1997); Robert Wiebe, *Who We Are: A History of Popular Nationalism* (Princeton, 2002); and an old classic, E. J. Hobsbawm, *The Age of Revolution* (Cleveland, 1962).

On China in the nineteenth century, we recommend Jonathan Spence, *God's Chinese Son: The Taiping Heavenly Kingdom of Hong Xiuquan* (New York, 1996), and Philip Richardson, *Economic Change in China, c. 1800–1950* (Cambridge, 1999). Ecological changes in China are the theme of Mark Elvin and Ts'ui-jung Liu, eds., *The Sediments of Time: Environment and Society in Chinese History* (Cambridge, 1998). For Japan, the relevant portions of Conrad Totman's *A History of Japan*, cited earlier, is the place to begin. Other approaches to nineteenth-century Asian history are Nicholas Tarling, ed., *The Cambridge History of Southeast Asia*, vol. 2 (Cambridge, 1992); C. A. Bayly, *Empire and Information: Intelligence Gathering and Social Communication in India, 1780–1870* (Cambridge, 1996); and Resat Kasaba, *The Ottoman Empire and the World Economy: The Nineteenth Century* (Albany, NY, 1988).

Interesting takes on African history for this period include Paul Lovejoy, *Transformations in Slavery: A History of Slavery in Africa* (Cambridge, 2000); Mervyn Hiskett, *The Sword of Truth: The Life and Times of the Shehu Usuman dan Fodio* (Evanston, IL, 1994); James McCann, *Green Land, Brown Land, Black Land: An Environmental History of Africa, 1800–1990* (Portsmouth, NH, 1999). A convenient introduction to Latin America for this period is the latter parts of Peter Bakewell, *A History of Latin America: Empires and Sequels, 1450–1930* (Malden, MA, 1997). On North America, a good starting point is D. W. Meinig, *The Shaping of America. Vol 2: Continental America, 1800–1867* (New Haven, 1993).

Philip Curtin, *The World and the West* (New York, 2000), is helpful on imperialism; David Ralston, *Importing the European Army* (Chicago, 1990), covers military reforms in self-strengthening efforts. On the abolition of slavery and serfdom, we found helpful: Terence Emmons, *The Russian Landed Gentry and the Emancipation of 1861* (Cambridge, 1968); Hakan Erdem, *Slavery in the Ottoman Empire and Its Demise, 1800–1909* (New York, 1996); and Suzanne Miers and Richard Roberts, eds., *The End of Slavery in Africa* (Madison, WI, 1988). David Northrup, *Indentured Labor in the Age of Imperialism, 1834–1922* (New York, 1995), is useful on labor migrations, together with P. C. Emmer and M. Mörner, eds., *European Expansion and Migration* (New York, 1992). Most of our figures on the world economy come from Angus Maddison, *The World Economy: A Millennial Perspective* (Paris, 2001), but see also David Held et al., *Global Transformations* (Stanford, 1999).

VIII

Two useful general surveys of the twentieth century are Michael Howard and William Roger Louis, eds., *The Oxford History of the Twentieth Century* (Oxford, 1998), and Eric Hobsbawm, *The Age of Extremes, 1914–1991* (New York, 1994). An idiosyncratic but interesting perspective is Theodore Von Laue, *The World Revolution of Westernization* (New York, 1987). For post–World War II, see David Reynolds, *One World Divisible: A Global History Since 1945* (New York, 2000). An older survey remains insightful, Geoffrey Barraclough, *An Introduction to Contemporary History* (London, 1967).

On population and urbanization, see Joel Cohen, *How Many People Can the Earth Support?* (New York, 1995), and James Lee and Wang Feng, *One Quarter of Humanity: Malthusian Mythology and Chinese Realities* (Cambridge, MA, 1999). On religion, Fred Spier, *Religious Regimes in Peru* (Amsterdam, 1994), is full of interesting ideas. On late-twentieth-century religion, see Gilles Kepel, *The Revenge of God* (University Park, PA, 1994). The technology and politics of communication is handled by Peter Burke and Asa Briggs, *A Social History of the Media* (Cambridge, 2002). On science and technology, Vernon Ruttan, *Technology, Growth and Development* (Oxford, 2001), and Arnulf Grübler, *Technology and Global Change* (Cambridge, 1998), are useful. On energy and environment, see J. R. McNeill, *Something New Under the Sun: An Environmental History of the Twentieth-Century World* (New York, 2000). On the international economy, Harold James, *The End of Globalization: Lessons from the Great Depression* (Cambridge, MA, 2001), is illuminating. Also helpful are the data and analysis in Angus Maddison, *The World Economy: A Millennial Perspective* (Paris, 2001), and Sidney Pollard, *The International Economy Since 1945* (London, 1997).

On World War I, a lively narrative is Martin Gilbert, *The First World War* (New York, 1994), and trenchant analysis appears in Roger Chickering and Stig Förster, eds., *Great War, Total War: Combat and Mobilization on the Western Front* (Washington, DC, 2000). Among the great war memoirs is Robert Graves, *Good-bye to All That* (New York, 1998 [1927]). For a sense of the battles of the western front, there is an excellent chapter on the Somme in John Keegan, *The Face of Battle* (New York, 1976). A recent survey of the Russian Revolution is Orlando Figes, *A People's Tragedy* (New York, 1996); a much shorter and very penetrating account is Theodore Von Laue, *Why Lenin? Why Stalin?* (New York, 1971). On World War II, Richard Overy, *Why the Allies Won* (New York, 1995), provides a compelling analysis; Gerhard Weinberg, *A World At Arms* (Cambridge, 1995), is an excellent general treatment. A brief and insightful treatment of the Cold War is David Painter's *The Cold War: An International History* (London, 1999). On the collapse of the USSR, see Stephen Kotkin, *Armageddon Averted* (Oxford, 2001). On modern India, Sugata Bose and Ayesha Jalal, *Modern South Asia: History, Culture, Political Economy* (Delhi, 1997), is a good introduction. For recent Chinese history, Jonathan Spence, *The Search for Modern China* (New York, 1990), is thorough and readable.

INDEX

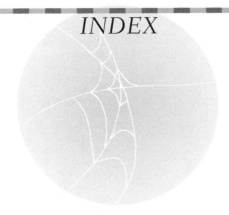

Page numbers in *italics* refer to tables and maps.

Mozambique, 186, 308
Mughal Empire, *159*, 180, 182, 185, 190, 192,
    194, 196, 197, 199, 224, 240
Muhammad, 89–90, *91*, 93, 181
mules, 31
multinational corporations, 311–12
mumps, 80
Murasaki Shikibu, 149
Muscovy, 152
music, 13, 14, 271
musical notation, 145
muskets, 193, 196
Muslim Brotherhood, 274
Mussolini, Benito, 290, 292
Mycenae, 68–69
myrrh, 97

Nakayama Miki, 251
Nanak, 182
Napoleon I, emperor of France, 226, 227
Nasser, Gamal Abdel, 270, 308
nationalism, 227–28, 229, 238, 294, 306–7
Natufian sites, 23
natural selection, 276
navigation, 34, 94, 163–64, 165, 202
Neanderthals, 12
Nebuchadnezzar II, king of Babylon, 60, 61
Neo-Confucianism, 121
Netherlands, *see* Holland
Newfoundland, 94, 165
New Guinea, 33–34, 38, 150, 156, 263
newspapers, 180, 270
New Testament, 78, 78*n*
New Zealand, 15, 94, 150, 158, 160, 177, 215–16,
    229, 261, 295
Nigeria, 171, 258, 269, 272, 313
Niger River, 98, 99, 136, 151
Nile River, 43, 52, 128
nomadism, 101
Norway, 260
Novgorod, 152
Nubia, 53, 98
nuclear weapons, 298, 301, 304

Oda Nobunaga, 195
Ohio River, 112
oil, 285, 293, 303
Old Kingdom, 53
Old World Web, 5, 41–42, 59, 68, 75, 82,
    153–54, 156–57
  African expansion of, 167–72
  and American web, 172–74
  Australian and Pacific expansion of, 176–78
  expanding of, 94–103, 214–16
  globalization of, 155–212
  impact of, 1500–1800, 178–211
  instability of, 154
  maritime links in, 157–58
  Pacific flank of, 147–50

Siberian expansion of, 174–76
southern and northern flanks of, 150–52
wealth and power shifts in, 82–94
olives, 29
Olmecs, 44, 110
Olmen, Ferdinand von, 165
Oman, 192, 200
Omoto sect, 251
Opium War, First, 242, 246
oracle bones, 55
Order of Assassins, 131
Ottoman Empire, 135, 137, *159*, 161, 174, 180,
    182, 183, 190, 191, 192, 194, 195, 196, 197,
    198, 199, 202, 207, 224, 228, 237, 247,
    256, 257, 305, 306
  under Mahmud, II, 245
  in World War I, 289
oxen, 32

paddy fields, 32–33, 96, 102, 111, 148, 150
paganism, 106
Pakistan, 272, 313, 314
Palestinians, 313, 314–15
Pampas, 208
paper currency, 121
parasites, 19
Paris, University of, 146
Parsees, 61, 92
Parthians, 84, 85
pastoralism, 31, 49, 50, 58, 59, 101, 132, 134, 195
peasants, 42, 106, 117, 128–29, 138
peat, 230
Perón, Eva, 270
Perón, Juan, 270
Persian Gulf, 45*n*, 166
Persians, 56, *57*, 72–73, 74, 103, 130, 133–34
Peru, 82, 108, 153, 169, 172, 185, 260, 272
  see also Incas
Peter III, tsar of Russia, 256
phalanx warfare, 69, 72
Philip II, king of Macedonia, 74
Philippines, 150, 186, 203, 260, 314
philosophy, 73–74
Phoenicians, 60, 70, 72, 73
photosynthesis, 324
physics, 276–77, 278, 279
pidgin languages, 263–64
pigs, 209
pikemen, 143
piracy, 148, 190
Pizarro, Francisco, 172, 205
place value numeration, 117–18
plantation economies, 128, 145, 168, 170, 204,
    208
plastics, 278
Plataea, Battle of, 73
Plato, 74
plows, 28, 32, 48, 101, 102
plow teams, 141–42